Logos and Muthos

SUNY series in Ancient Greek Philosophy
_____
Anthony Preus, editor

Logos and Muthos

Philosophical Essays in Greek Literature

Edited by

WILLIAM WIANS

Published by State University of New York Press, Albany

© 2009 State University of New York

Printed in the United States of America

Cover art: The Andokides Painter. The Lysippides Painter. *Two-handled jar (amphora) with Achilles and Ajax* (detail). Greek, Archaic Period, about 525–520 BC. Place of Manufacture: Greece, Attica, Athens. Ceramic, Black Figure and Red Figure (Bilingual). Height: 55.5 cm (21$^7/_8$ in.); diameter: 34 cm (13$^3/_8$ in.). Museum of Fine Arts, Boston. Henry Lillie Pierce Fund, 01.8037.

For information, contact State University of New York Press, Albany, NY
www.sunypress.edu

Production by Cathleen Collins
Marketing by Anne M. Valentine

Library of Congress Cataloging-in-Publication Data

Logos and muthos : philosophical essays in Greek literature / edited by William Wians.
    p. cm. — (SUNY series in ancient Greek philosophy)
  Includes bibliographical references and index.
  ISBN 978-1-4384-2735-5 (hardcover : alk. paper)
  ISBN 978-1-4384-2736-2 (pbk : alk. paper)
  1. Philosophy, Ancient. 2. Literature—Philosophy. 3. Greek literature—History and criticism. 4. Mythology, Greek. I. Wians, William Robert.

B178.L64 2009
180—dc22   2008050541

10 9 8 7 6 5 4 3 2 1

Contents

Acknowledgments

An edited collection depends on the combined work of many parties, and it is my pleasure to acknowledge the good will, sustained effort, and advice of so many. My first thanks must go to the contributors, whose enthusiasm and cooperation were exemplary. It was a pleasure to work with every one of them. Next, I want to thank several individuals who gave generous advice on how to make the volume better: Rose Cherubin, Michael Davis, Robert Hahn, George Heffernan, Mitchell Miller, and Gerard Naddaf. A special thanks goes to Erin Stackle for the hard work of putting endnotes and bibliographic entries into proper form. Summer research grants from Merrimack College and the generous support of Dan and Linda Ciejek for research in the liberal arts helped me to complete both my chapter for the volume and editorial work in preparation for final submission. I wish also to thank the Department of Philosophy at Boston College for giving me the opportunity to teach two graduate seminars on topics pertaining to the collection. Finally, I thank Tony Preus of Binghamton University and Michael Rinella, my editor at SUNY Press, for their support and patience, and Cathleen Collins and the entire SUNY Press staff for their work on producing the final product.

About the Cover

The image of the warriors Ajax and Achilles seemingly at their ease playing dice was a popular subject for vase painters. But as Emily Vermeule suggests in her classic study, *Aspects of Death in Early Greek Art and Poetry* (Berkeley and Los Angeles: University of California Press, 1979), 80–82, the simple game of chance is a metaphor for the risks of mortal life. In fact, neither warrior would return from the war at Troy. Nevertheless, a measure of immortality is won for the heroes through the *kleos* preserved by the work of the artist. The vase is a powerful reminder to the modern viewer of both the persistence of *muthoi* in Greek culture and the subtlety with which they can convey their lesson.

Introduction

From *Muthos* to . . .

WILLIAM WIANS

Logos and Muthos: Philosophical Essays in Greek Literature consists of twelve essays, each of which has been written for this volume. The title conveys the collection's two main intentions. First, not from *muthos* to *logos*, but *logos* **and** *muthos*, implying a whole range of interactions, reactions, tensions, and ambiguities arising between different forms of discourse. Scholarship in recent years has moved decisively beyond old assumptions of a simple progression from myth to reason, and the collection takes full advantage of that work. But the special emphasis of *Logos and Muthos* becomes apparent in the subtitle. All of the volume's chapters explore philosophical dimensions of literary authors—Homer, Hesiod and the archaic poets, the tragic playwrights—rather than concentrating on standard philosophical figures, even those like Plato who make extensive use of mythic or literary elements. This is not to say that individual contributors devote no attention to philosophers like Plato or Parmenides. But the main analysis of each chapter focuses on figures and works not usually central to histories of ancient philosophy.

The purpose of the collection is not, then, to mount another challenge to the old opposition, or to search for the "beginnings of philosophy," or to seek anything like a comprehensive definition of myth (though several chapters address these issues along the way). Rather, it intends to consider philosophical issues and ideas as they arise from or can be applied to literary, usually poetic, texts—to *muthoi*, in one sense of that Protean term.[1] What concerns do literary authors share with their philosophical contemporaries? How do questions of ethics and epistemology, of language and reality figure in their texts? To what extent must these works be read differently from their philosophical shelf-mates if shared concerns are to be properly appreciated? How might asking such questions shed light on the goals and character of ancient philosophizing and the ancient intellectual enterprise more generally?[2]

1

If the chapters in *Logos and Muthos* challenge any single assumption, it is that literary texts are somehow lacking when measured against standards of philosophical reasoning and argument. Typically, the works discussed reveal sophisticated intellectual outlooks, sometimes drawing on contemporary philosophical positions, sometimes critical of them, but never simply deficient in comparison to them. In general, the essays presented here demonstrate that the poets and playwrights of ancient Greece exhibit a high degree of critical self-awareness and reflection on issues more typically associated with ancient philosophers, and that the work to identify their concerns amply rewards scholarly effort.

It must be admitted that the twelve essays of the collection deal with only a small part of ancient Greek literary output, mainly poetic works from the eighth to the fifth centuries BCE. They constitute a choice part, to be sure, and the part many nonspecialists will first think of when they think of Greek literature. But of necessity, much is left out. A quick survey will determine that there are only scant mentions of Aristophanes and Herodotus, for instance, and only relatively brief discussions of the sophists and Thucydides, despite their significance for ancient literary criticism. What's more, there is almost no attention paid to Hellenistic or later authors, whether literary or philosophical. While such omissions may be regretted (even while limitations of space have made them necessary), the result is a high degree of mutual reinforcement in the problems addressed and the previous scholarship that is responded to. I hope, therefore, that the concentration on a relatively few authors from a relatively restricted period may in fact be seen as a strength.

The Myth of "From *Muthos* to *Logos*"

The story of how scholarship moved beyond the old opposition between *muthos* and *logos* is well documented.[3] There has been a long-enduring attitude among scholars of ancient thought, traceable to the still influential study by W. Nestle (1940), that between roughly the sixth and fourth centuries BCE an intellectual revolution took place. A childlike faith in tales of the creation of the world and its order, in which various gods with distinct personalities played a major role, gradually gave way to nonanthropomorphic, naturalistic explanations in terms of materials and forces (even if these retained some characteristics of the divine personages they were meant to displace).[4] Mythological accounts were to be found especially in the poems of Homer and Hesiod; these came to be supplanted by rational accounts advanced by the first historians, medical writers, and the pre-Socratic philosophers.

The heroic, positivistic, and even nationalistic versions of this story have justifiably been challenged.[5] For many reasons, scholars have come to recognize that attempting to mark a clear separation of the two terms of the opposition is fraught with difficulties. What definitively counts as myth or mythic as opposed to reason or rational? Already in Hesiod, one finds reason applied critically, as the poet reshapes traditional elements in his account of the generation of the gods and fills in gaps by rational means.[6] And even Nestle had to admit that rational elements appear in Homer's depictions of the gods.[7] Moving beyond Homer and Hesiod, much recent scholarship has underlined what is at best the incomplete nature of the revolution. Many Greeks remained happy to accept the old stories, and *muthoi* in various relevant senses remained vital throughout the ancient period, retaining at least a partial hold on new patterns of thought and expression.[8] There was, as Buxton nicely puts it, "a constant to-ing and fro-ing between the mythical and the rational."[9] We now also realize that the combative insistence on the purity of the new *logoi* often contained more than a small element of bluff and bluster, so that a degree of disingenuousness marked many of the ancient rejections of myth.[10] More fundamentally, the entire historiographical enterprise that identified and celebrated the intellectual revolution has been found guilty of a lack of self-examination regarding the assumptions it itself employed. Historians of ancient thought essentially perpetuated the rhetorical self-fashioning of early philosophers in which *muthos* became a term of derision for anyone with whom an author contended. "From *muthos* to *logos*" has itself been revealed to be a myth.[11]

Clearly, talk of progress from myth to philosophy—or any simple movement from the credulous to the critical—is no longer tenable. But to deny one version of the story is not to deny that a shift—or shifts[12]—did take place in ancient Greece (at least in the attitudes of certain elite subsets of Greek society and at various levels of generality). Over the course of several centuries, a wide range of thinkers who were engaged in various activities and inquiries displayed in various ways increasingly critical reflections on and reactions to mythic material. Changes, however complex and qualified, did occur.

Much recent scholarship has been concerned with questions of how those changes should be characterized. Perhaps the most common way of doing so is to say that faith in a certain kind of authoritative utterance shifted to rival kinds. Poetic *muthoi* had been regarded as authoritative utterances. That authority came to be challenged by rival claimants including philosophers, historians, physicians, and sophists, who presented themselves as advancing more "rational" accounts expressed in the language of proof and demonstration.[13]

Putting it this way is certainly correct as far as it goes.[14] However, it risks overlooking a group as much influenced by new patterns of thought as any other—I mean the poets themselves. The rational response to myth—where *myth* is understood as a stage in a culture characterized by a naïve, unreflective faith in traditional stories of gods and mortals—played out over a wide field of activities, including the philosophical, historical, and scientific, but also the literary and poetic. Once one discards a positivist notion of progress, one can see that poets, just as often as philosophers and many other participants in Greek intellectual life, took an active part in the intellectual revolution. Significantly, like many of their philosophical contemporaries, they gave sustained attention to the complexities and ambiguities of language and persuasion that seemed calculated to draw attention to language's limits.[15]

Certainly by the time of the tragic playwrights (and leaving open the question of how long before), any rivalry between the authority of *muthoi* and *logoi* had ceased to be between a simple-minded poetic piety and the cool rationality of philosophers. Both parties reflected self-consciously on the use of *muthoi*—the fictionalized shortcomings of a literally minded Euthyphro cannot be imputed to the authors of the Oedipus plays or the *Oresteia*. The continued deployment of myth by the poets was a decision arrived at rationally, not an unreflective perpetuation of a primitive mentality. It reflected in a profound way a playwright's considered attitude toward the world and the best means to communicate essential lessons about it.

If those who continued to employ myth and mythic elements did so for determinable rational purposes, what does the distinction between *logos* and *muthos* come down to in the end? To put it in terms of slogans, "from myth to reason" is not equivalent to "from myth (or poetry) to philosophy." Reason is applied as rigorously in Sophocles as in Socrates, in Aeschylus as in Aristotle. The challenge is for philosophers, formed as we are by our own modes of professional discourse, to learn to recognize the way poets may do so.

Logoi and Muthoi

Aristotle famously complains in the *Metaphysics* that an audience tends to demand the type of presentation with which it is familiar. The complaint might be applied to some modern philosophical readers of ancient literature. Just as an ancient audience reared on *muthoi* had to learn how to understand philosophical and other new forms of thinking (and often resisted doing so), so philosophers trained in logical analysis may need to be shown how to approach ancient literature. If the meaning of a literary *muthos* depends essentially on narrative elements that a philosophical *logos* lacks, then approaching an epic or tragic poem with expectations usually brought to a philosophical text will almost inevitably make the literary work seem deficient. One must proceed quite differently if one is to discern the philosophical significance of a Homer or Aeschylus rather than a Plato or Aristotle. Perhaps it is this that has led to the relative neglect of Greek literature by historians of ancient philosophy, especially of works coming after Homer and Hesiod, and to the limited scope of the questions asked when these scholars do turn to literary works.

The twelve chapters of *Logos and Muthos* are presented in two groups. The first six essays take Homer as their starting point. The poems of Homer laid the foundations of Greek culture. In many ways, Homer was a monument, in other ways, a challenge, in still others an enigma. His influence—in the many senses of that term—was everywhere.

One topic that has drawn philosophical interest to Homer has been texts bearing on the question of human knowledge. James Lesher's far-ranging essay reexamines the general character of the early Greek view of knowledge. Lesher shows that there are three basic features of the Homeric view. Knowledge can be derived from direct observation, from reliable secondhand testimony, and most interestingly, from epistemically instructive trials or tests (all apparent in the process by which Odysseus comes to be recognized by his household). He then develops several themes regarding human knowledge that run through early Greek poetry. Most importantly, he argues that humans were held to face insuperable difficulties in achieving any understanding of what Lesher terms the larger scheme of things. The narrowness of human understanding is practically a defining characteristic of human beings. This distinctly religious perspective creates a role for the inspired poet, who is empowered by the gods to speak a truth others cannot possess. Homer, Hesiod, Theognis, Pindar, and even Parmenides are shown to recognize an obligation to share such special knowledge with others.

Where Lesher's essay identifies the persistence of the Homeric view of knowledge, Fred Miller treats Homer as a source of enduring philosophical *aporiai*. He concentrates on three areas in which Homer's poems posed a challenge to philosophical psychology that could not be ignored. First, Homer's characters clearly express a sense of self. But where does that self reside, and what is the nature of self-identity? Similar *aporiai* involve the Homeric concept of fate and responsibility. Even though characters deliberate, the outcome often seems predetermined by fate and the gods, strongly suggesting a fatalistic view of human action. Yet Homer's gods, particularly in the *Odyssey*, regularly blame the moral failings of human beings. Miller then turns to the question of the *psuchē*, which is often the animating life force, akin to breath, and sometimes is the seat of awareness. But it seems distinct from the self, and is sometimes joined with *thumos* and sometimes contrasted with it. Miller concludes that interpreters are left with are rich, complex, and sometimes puzzling descriptions—but not explanations—of human thought and action.

Another aspect of Homer's challenge to early philosophy is at the heart of Rose Cherubin's chapter. Rejecting the notion that poetic elements in Parmenides function merely as window dressing, Cherubin argues that his central contributions to philosophy—the role of deductive argument and the exploration of *to eon*—arise directly from his engagement with poetry. She traces the connection to the poet's traditional duty to apprehend and promulgate *alētheia*. To be able to tell the truth requires relating all that is relevant to the context of one's subject, without omission, embellishment, or concealment, while recognizing the limits of one's own knowledge. Cherubin documents the poetic roots of this morally tinged notion of *alētheia* in texts from Homer, Hesiod, Bacchylides, and Pindar. In turning to Parmenides, she finds a thinker reflecting critically on his poetic inheritance, who repeatedly emphasizes the need for one's own inquiry in place of a reliance on divine inspiration. In other words, Parmenides develops his treatment of *to eon* out of the requirements and implications of poetic *alētheia*.

The remaining three chapters in part 1 treat further aspects of the philosophical challenges Homer posed for later thinkers. Ramona Naddaff explores the depiction of Helen and the question of her responsibility for the Trojan War. Starting from the provocative claim that there is not one Helen but many, Naddaff shows how the *Iliad* became the "master text" from which a series of meditations on human agency derive. The argument over Helen's responsibility begins in the *Iliad* itself, where through her self-condemnation, Helen reveals an interiority that seeks to define her self against the will of the gods and thus to assume ethical responsibility for her own actions. Naddaff then traces how this interiority is subjected to a series of post-Homeric revisions that limit Helen's power of choice. In Gorgias's defense of Helen, she becomes an unthinking symbol for rhetoric's own power, able to manipulate commonsense thinking, but not to be blamed for this power. Euripides, by contrast, defends Helen through an absurd logic of fiction—the Trojan War was fought for a phantom. Only Sappho preserves Helen's disruptive force, depicting her as a lover of love, an activity both within and beyond one's control.

Later phases of the Homeric *muthos* become even more complex. Gerard Naddaf traces the origins and development of allegoresis, the attempt to save the "truth" of the poems of Homer and Hesiod by approaching them allegorically. He argues that thinkers such as Theagenes of Rhegium who were unwilling to give up the privileged status afforded to Homer and Hesiod as educators of Greece fought back with *mutho-logia*, a *logos* about myth. This strategy proved so effective that philosophical successors to Xenophanes and Heraclitus were convinced that Homer and Hesiod maintained the same doctrines as the philosophers themselves. This is a story that has gone largely untold, and Naddaf's essay gains considerable interest by documenting the broad extent of allegorical approaches among ancient thinkers. What makes the chapter particularly suited to the present volume is that Naddaf does not resort to a simple opposition between philosophers and the allegorists. Instead, he shows how *philosophia* and *mythologia* can be so intimately connected that distinguishing between them becomes difficult and ultimately a barrier to understanding.

The effort to find defensible philosophical content in the impugned old poems did not, of course, stop with the ancients. Just as Plato's Socrates allowed for poetry to be readmitted into the just city if it were provided with a valid defense, philosophers from the ancient world to the present have attempted to defend Homer. Catherine Collobert provides an illuminating survey of three stages of this interpretive history extending from the ancient to the contemporary, identifying the hermeneutical principles on which each is based, and what could count as a "relevant" philosophical reading of Homer. She then sets out principles for her own reading, an approach that insists on the essential poetic (as opposed to philosophical) identity of Homer, while recognizing the host of genuine *aporiai* that have fruitfully engaged both philosophers and readers generally for centuries. The implication of her essay, it seems to me, is that the impulse to defend poetry is perhaps as much a part of the Western philosophical tradition as is the Platonic tendency to resist its allure.

The volume's second group of six chapters is devoted mainly to Greek tragedy. If the mythic mentality is taken to mean something primitive and unreflective, then there is nothing mythic about Greek tragedy. Every tragedy is the product of a well-established literary culture, and crucially of a literate culture (though, as a few contributors observe, the effects of literacy cannot be assumed to be simple or unambiguous). One sign of the sophistication of the tragic playwrights—a sign explored in one way or another by every chapter in the section—is how the *muthoi* of the playwrights assume a renewed urgency and vitality in the face of challenges to traditional poetic authority.

Part 2 begins with three chapters devoted to plays of Aeschylus. Sara Brill examines the playwright's ambivalent use of *muthoi* in his obscure and puzzling *Suppliants*. Building on the insight that classical suppliant dramas exploit the ambiguity between the familiar and the foreign, and strength and vulnerability, Brill shows how Aeschylus inquires into the foundations of power and authority. At the heart of this exploration are the protagonists of the tragedy, the fifty daughters of Danaos, who claim a hatred of violence but display a disturbing propensity toward it, threatening to direct it even at themselves. These contradictory impulses are represented in their employment of the *muthos* of their ancestor Io. Brill gives particular attention to the role of Zeus in the myth, in which he is both violator of the mortal Io and her savior by means of his healing touch. Brill concludes by asking how the characters' use of myth reflects the reworking of myth in the hands of the playwright himself.

In the editor's contribution to the volume, William Wians argues that the *Agamemnon* is a sustained meditation on the limits of human knowledge, extending the pessimism of the archaic poets well into fifth-century Athens. In fact, Aeschylus displays an attitude that in crucial respects is even more pessimistic than that of the archaic poets. Even when based on direct experience, human claims to know are surrounded by pervasive doubts and irremediable uncertainties that tend toward a virtual skepticism. Yet at the same time, *muthoi* provided by the playwright trace patterns and purposes of what was previously experienced without full comprehension and so supplement the limited vision of ordinary human beings who inevitably are immersed in the immediate. By making the limits of human knowledge one of the play's central themes, Aeschylus both exhibits and justifies the poet's status as moral instructor of the city, allowing himself to assume the position of successor to his poetic forebears.

Christopher Smith offers perhaps the most radical challenge to the primacy of *logos* over *muthos*. Taking as his starting point Heidegger's *destruktion* of metaphysical abstractions, Smith engages in a searching analysis of one extended passage from the *Agamemnon*, the exchange or *amoibaion* between Cassandra and the chorus. Smith seeks to recover the original character of lived persuasive speech, a pre-philosophical orality conceived acoustically and embodied in the singing and dancing of words we have only as a written text. Through the acoustical conjuring of inarticulate cries and unheard-of metaphors punctuated by deep silence, Cassandra calls into being and makes present for the audience something that did not exist before. Even in Cassandra's wildest utterances, Aeschylus lets us hear how pre-philosophical "reasoning" might have sounded. In this way, he counteracts a cartographic *theoria*-from-above of stabilized, intelligible realities and a *logos* of argument and demonstration.

David Reeve also shows how later poets retain the Homeric role of providing moral instruction to an audience in need of compensation for its own lack of memory and judgment. Taking his start from Nussbaum's work on philosophy and tragedy, Reeve asks to what extent Pindar, Aeschylus, and Sophocles regard virtue to be vulnerable to luck? For Pindar, an agent's virtue may in a sense be invulnerable, but due to contingent circumstances, it may go unrecognized. To ensure that virtue is recognized, the divinely inspired poet preserves the memory of genuinely virtuous individuals that otherwise would be lost. In the case of Aeschylus's Agamemnon and Creon in Sophocles' *Antigone*, both rulers would be regarded as happy by conventional measures. But the playwrights reveal profound flaws in their moral judgment, making their status unsustainable, and so throwing conventional standards of happiness in doubt. In neither case is the audience asked to sympathize with a virtuous man undone by bad luck.

The surviving plays of Sophocles are the subject of a synoptic essay by Paul Woodruff. According to Woodruff, Sophocles is the first writer in the European tradition to make human action as distinct from the divine his central subject. Every action Sophocles stages can be shown to have a human cause. Nevertheless, Woodruff contrasts Sophocles' humanism with what he labels the godless humanism of the sophists and other new thinkers (Thucydides is his main example). Such thinkers simply leave the gods out altogether. Sophocles' *muthoi* are meant to counter the *logoi* of these thinkers. Though the gods do not appear on the Sophoclean stage, their influence is felt everywhere, especially when human beings go wrong by forgetting their status as limited mortal creatures. Sophocles expresses a reverent humanism, one that places responsibility for action in the hands of human agents, but which is aware of a moral order that transcends the human. Regarding particulars of the latter, Sophocles displays an appropriate silence.

Logos and Muthos concludes with another powerful challenge to the primacy of *logos*. The *Helen* of Euripides has long puzzled critics. Its willful reworking of familiar myths skirts between the tragic and the comic, veering sometimes toward melodrama and sometimes toward farce. In a close reading of the play, Michael Davis finds the key to the whole in the question of identity. Questions of identity surround almost every character in the play, starting with the "real" Helen, who was spirited away to Egypt at the start of the Trojan War while a phantom made of air and cloud took her place in the besieged city. Through these and other confusions, Euripides throws in doubt the possibility of knowing others or ourselves at all. The timeless fixity such knowledge would require cannot, Euripides seems to say, be achieved by living, changing human beings.

Davis's chapter nicely rounds out the themes of the volume. In part, it returns to Homer (and to material discretely hidden in Homer) and to the problem of human knowledge. More fundamentally, it shows how the authority of both *muthos* and *logos* can be challenged by a *muthos* formed from rational reflection on *muthoi*. Reason undercuts myth but in the process undercuts itself, leaving a question mark where knowledge was thought to have been. *Muthos* to *logos* gives way—perhaps inevitably—to *muthos* once more.

Notes

1. Because poetry was the traditional medium of myth, poetic works and their authors were typically the targets of early philosophers and other rationalizing thinkers who attacked the authority of myth. On the problem of speaking of *literature*, see the next note.

2. The term *literature* has come to be understood as having ideological overtones, privileging certain kinds of texts over others. For theoretical issues surrounding the identification of Greek literature, see T. Whitmarsh, *Ancient Greek Literature* (Malden, Mass.: Polity Press, 2004), chap. 1; also pp. 107–08. Simply at a pragmatic level, the collection distinguishes between texts that might and those that might not be covered in a typical college course on Greek philosophy.

3. Recent surveys of the literature on the question of *logos* vs. *muthos* can be found in the introduction to R. Buxton, ed., *From Myth to Reason?* (Oxford: Oxford University Press, 1999) and K. Morgan, *Myth and Philosophy from the Presocratics to Plato* (Cambridge: Cambridge University Press, 2000), chap. 1. For a detailed look at how different ancient thinkers presented themselves as alternatives to myth, see G. E. R. Lloyd, *The Revolutions of Wisdom* (Berkeley and Los Angeles: University of California Press, 1987), chap. 1. An extended critique of Lloyd's approach forms the main part of the survey of literature in the first chapter of R. Hahn, *Anaximander and the Architects* (Albany: State University of New York Press, 2001).

4. Gradualism is a key part—or concession—of virtually every version of the story honest enough to admit that mythic holdovers persist in the attitudes and practices of those cast as the heroes of rationalism.

5. See especially G. Most, "From Logos to Mythos," in Buxton 1999, 25–47.

6. Hesiod's *Theogony* often serves as a kind of no-man's-land between *muthos* and *logos*, usually being placed just short of the boundary where rationalizing myth gives way to philosophy.

7. W. Nestle, *Vom Mythos zum Logos* (Stuttgart: Alfred Kröner, 1940), 24–48.

8. L. Brisson, "Myth and Knowledge," in J. Brunschwig and G. E. R. Lloyd, eds., *Greek Thought: A Guide to Classical Knowledge* (Cambridge: Harvard University Press, 2000).

9. Buxton 1999, 5.

10. The studies by Lloyd are central here.

11. See, among many others, Most 1999.

12. "It is not . . . that there is *one* boundary, in Greece, between *muthos* and *logos*, but rather a coruscating variety of them in different writers, indeed sometimes within the same writer, and in different texts." G. E. R. Lloyd, "Mythology: Reflections from a Chinese Perspective," in Buxton 1999, 156.

13. M. Detienne, *The Masters of Truth in Archaic Greece* (New York: Zone Books, 1996; orig. 1967); Lloyd 1987; Morgan 2000, 16–24; Whitmarsh 2004, 106–16.

14. Of course, the new thinkers also often saw one another as rivals as well. One need only recall the Hippocratic criticism of Empedocles near the end of *On Ancient Medicine* and the opening invective of *The Nature of Man.*

15. Excellent analysis of the tragic playwrights' concern with language can be found in two books by Simon Goldhill: *Language, Sexuality, Narrative: The* Oresteia (Cambridge: Cambridge University Press, 1984), and *Reading Greek Tragedy* (Cambridge: Cambridge University Press, 1986). This can be compared with a statement by Morgan, meant to distinguish early philosophers from their poetic predecessors: "What distinguishes them is that their use of myth is self-conscious and designed to raise second–order questions about the use of language (both their own and that of the poets)"; Morgan 2000, 35. Though not referring to tragic playwrights, Morgan's statement serves to establish a criterion that justifies taking later poets seriously as philosophically relevant thinkers.

Part I

Homer and the Philosophers

1

Archaic Knowledge

J. H. LESHER

In some ways it may seem anachronistic to speak of *knowledge* in the context of archaic Greek poetry.[1] The Greek expressions we routinely translate into English as "knowledge" or "wisdom"—*epistēmē, gnōsis, sophia,* and *nous*—were either unattested in this earlier period or else had a more specialized meaning. When *epistēmē* makes its first appearance, in a fifth-century poem by Bacchylides, it is placed in apposition to the arts of poetry, divination, and archery.[2] The noun *gnōsis* appears for the first time in a fragment of Heraclitus (composed at some point near the outset of the fifth century) with the apparent meaning of "awareness" or "recognition."[3] In its one appearance in the Homeric poems (*Iliad* 15.412) *sophia* designated the skills possessed by an expert carpenter;[4] only gradually will it come to connote mastery of a particular field of study or a generally intelligent approach to living.[5] And even when the poets speak of individuals who either have or lack knowledge, they do so in verbal rather than nominative ways. Homer speaks of the seer Kalchas as one who "knew (*ēdē*) the things that were, that were to be, and that had been before" (*Il.* 1.69–70), of the Muses who "know all things" (*iste te panta*; 2.485), of the experienced counselor Nestor who "well knows (*eu eidōs*) the battles of old" (4.310), and of the wily Odysseus who "knows many things" (*eidota polla*; *Od.* 9.281). The nouns *noos* and *mētis* figure prominently in both epics but designate a quality of "intelligence" or "cunning" (as exemplified by Odysseus and Penelope) rather than a body of knowledge of facts or truths. The noun *histōr* (meaning "observer" or "judge") appears twice in the *Iliad* (18.501, and 23.486) but *historia*, meaning "inquiry" or "the knowledge obtained through inquiry," is unknown before Herodotus's *History* and the Hippocratic treatise *On Ancient Medicine*. In light of all this, why should we suppose that anything like knowledge was a matter of interest or importance for the poets of archaic Greece?

It would be a mistake to infer from the fact that the speakers of the language in a particular period lacked the noun form "X," that they could have had

13

no concept of X or no appreciation of what is involved in being an X. Homer's
Greek lacked a noun corresponding to our English *will* but no one would want
to say that neither Homer nor his audiences had any sense of the nature of willful conduct.[6] In this case, as elsewhere, the lack of a nominative expression can
be offset by the use of various related verbs, adjectives, and adverbs. So if we
find evidence that early Greek poets spoke of human beings engaged in an effort
to grasp the significance of the events taking place around them we might fairly
speak of an "early Greek concept of knowledge" even in the absence of any noun
equivalent in meaning with our English "knowledge."

As we shall see, early Greek poets spoke often and in different ways of
individuals who discover, notice, realize, and come to know about various matters
and, perhaps more often, of those who fail to do so. From time to time they also
speak of one or more of the impediments to human knowledge as well as the
degree to which they as divinely inspired singers were able to overcome them. As
a result, when more philosophically minded individuals such as Xenophanes and
Heraclitus began to articulate and explore epistemological questions, they could
draw upon a set of shared assumptions about the sources and methods appropriate
to knowing as well as a set of its acknowledged paragons.

Homeric Ways of Knowing

Until rather recently there was something approaching a consensus view of the
general character of "the early Greek view of knowledge." According to Bruno Snell,
Kurt von Fritz, and Hermann Fränkel, among others, during this early period the
various Greek expressions for knowing—*eidenai, gignōskein, noein, manthanein,* and
sunienai—were closely associated with sense perception. One datum often cited in
this connection was that the Greek verb *oida* (typically translated as "I know") was
actually a second perfect tense form of *eidō* ("I see") and meant "I have seen."[7]
Thus, as Snell put it, in the Homeric poems "knowing" was essentially a matter
of "having seen"; only gradually did the Greek expressions for knowledge acquire
a more "intellectual" orientation.[8] One important corollary of the early outlook
was that where there was no prospect of direct experience, neither there was any
prospect of knowledge. When combined with some awareness of the obvious
spatial and temporal restraints under which human beings must live and operate,
the identification of knowledge with what can be directly experienced gave rise to
a decidedly pessimistic view of the prospects for human knowledge. The classic
expression of this outlook is the famous "second invocation of the Muses" in *Iliad* 2:
"for you are goddesses, you are present at and know all things, whereas we mortals
hear only a report and know nothing" (*Il.* 2.485–86). According to some versions
of what we might term the "developmentalist" view, the close connection between

knowing and seeing continued to be felt by various pre-Socratic thinkers (e.g., in Heraclitus's conception of *nous* as a capacity for direct intuition of the nature of things) and only with Parmenides' identification of "reasoned discourse" (*logos*) as an alternative way of inquiry did early Greek thought begin to move away from a virtual identification of knowledge with accumulated sense experience.[9] According to other versions, a "higher" or "more intellectual" way of knowing emerged when the poet Archilochus urged his *thumos* (his "mind" or "spirit") to "know what rhythm holds man in its sway" (fr. 67a Diehl), and Solon spoke of "the hardest part of judgment (*gnōmosunē*)" as "grasping the unseen measure that alone holds the limits of all things" (fr. 16 Diehl).[10]

Recent scholarship, however, has challenged the developmentalist view on a number of fronts.[11] It has been pointed out that even Homer allowed for knowledge gained from a source other than direct visual observation (e.g., in *Iliad* 20 when Aeneas claims that he and Achilles know [*idmen*] their lineage strictly on the basis of what they have been told by others).[12] In addition, whatever degree of pessimism may have been expressed in the invocation to the Muses in *Iliad* 2 did not prevent the singer from claiming to have ascertained the names of "all those who came beneath Ilios."[13] And while there is good reason to think that the pre-Socratics came increasingly to focus on the importance of grasping the intelligible structure that lies beneath or beyond appearances, there is no reason to suppose that every advance in philosophical thinking was immediately reflected in ordinary language.

Nevertheless, it is possible to identify some basic features of "Homeric knowledge." First, as Snell and others noted, Homer commonly credits both gods and mortals with discovering the truth by means of direct observation of events. Menelaus affirms the connection between the two when he says to Antilochus:

Since you have observed it for yourself (*auton eisoroōnta*), I think you
Already know (*gignōskein*) that a god has rolled destruction on the
    Danaans
And given victory to the Trojans. (*Il.* 17.687–88)[14]

Elsewhere, as just mentioned, other sense faculties are involved. As Aeneas explains to Achilles:

We know (*idmen*) each other's lineage and each other's parents,
Having heard words of mortal men of olden times (*epea prokluta*),
But not by sight (*opsei*) have you seen my parents, nor I yours.
    (*Il.* 20.203–05)[15]

We also find references to knowledge in the form of physical skills or expertise achieved through extensive experience or practice:

But well I know (*eu oida*) the battles and slayings of men.
I know (*oida*) how to wield to the right and left a shield of seasoned
      hide . . .
I know (*oida*) also how to charge into the battles of swift mares,
And I know (*oida*) how to do the dance of Ares one-on-one. (*Il.* 7.237–41)

Similarly, we hear of warriors who are *epistamenoi polemidzein*—"skilled in fighting" (*Il.* 2.611) and *toxōn eu eidōs*—"well skilled in archery" (*Il.* 2.718), and of
healers who are *ēpia pharmaka eidōs*—"skilled in soothing drugs" (*Il.* 4.218). In
the *Odyssey* there are fewer references to skill in the arts of war or medicine and
more references to individuals such as Odysseus who are "skilled in all manner of
devices and tricks" (*eidotes . . . kerdea, Od.* 13.296–97).[16]
      In addition, both mortals and gods can achieve knowledge through the use
of an especially instructive trial or testing procedure. When Zeus threatens to hurl
into Tartarus any god he catches giving aid to either side of the conflict at Troy,
he boasts that such an act will confirm the magnitude of his powers:

Then you shall know (*gnōsete*) just how mighty among the gods I am.
But come, gods, make trial (*peirēsasthe*) so you will all know (*eidete*).
      (*Il.* 8.18)

In the *Iliad*, the relevant form of testing is often a "trial by arms" in order to
determine which is the superior warrior:

But come, make trial (*peirēsai*), so that these too may know (*gnōōsi*)
Straightway your dark blood will flow around my spear. (*Il.* 1.302–03)[17]

While in the *Odyssey*, the testing can also take the form of athletic competition:

Of the rest, if any man's heart and spirit bid him,
Let him come here and be put to a trial (*peirēthētō*) . . .
But of the others I will refuse none and make light of none,
But I wish to know (*idmen*) and try them (*peirēthēmenai*) face to face.
      (*Od.* 8.204–05, 212–13)

The frequency with which we hear of various "tests" or "trials" reflects the high
level of concern felt by Homer's heroes to prove themselves "to be the best and
excel all others" and to avoid the "disgrace or shame" (*to elenchos*) that comes
from failing the test.
      Each of these "ways of knowing"—direct observation, relying on the testimony
of others, and the staging of a test or trial—figures in the discovery of Odysseus's
identity by the members of his household. Telemachus learns the truth when Odys-

seus tells it to him outright (*Od.* 6.188); the old hound Argos knows his master the moment he spots him (*hōs enoēsen*, 17.301); while Eurycleia and the shepherds recognize Odysseus by first touching (19.468) and then seeing (21.217–25) the identifying scar on his leg. Penelope, however, discovers the stranger's identity neither from any visual indicators nor on the basis of any verbal assurances, but rather by putting the stranger to a trial or test (cf. *peirōmenē* at 23.81). When her seemingly casual request to relocate the marital bed sparks a flash of anger from Odysseus (23.181–204), she gets the unmistakable indicator (*sēma*) she had been waiting for. Thus while Homer and generations of singers before him invoked the aid of divine powers as they set out to perform their songs, the stories they told often portrayed individuals engaged in the process of acquiring knowledge through a variety of means. A person might appropriately assert *autos oida*—"I know for myself"[18]—on the basis of what he or she had directly observed; another might claim to have learned the truth from a reliable source; while a third might make a claim to knowledge on the basis of a trial or testing process.[19]

The Archaic View of Knowledge: Three Themes

Three broad themes relating to human knowledge run through much of early Greek poetry. The first, especially important for the unfolding drama of the *Odyssey*, relates to the frequency with which human beings fail to grasp the full significance of the events taking place around them. While others fail to see Odysseus weeping, for example, Alcinous notices him (*enoēsen*, *Od.* 8.533). When Odysseus appears in disguise among the Trojans, only Helen recognizes who he really is (cf. *anegnōn*, *Od.* 4.250). And although there are many signs of impending disaster, only the seer Theoclymenus is able to "take note of" (*noeō*) the evil about to befall the suitors (*Od.* 20.351). The ability to manipulate as well as "see through" appearances is a hallmark of Homeric *noos*, with Odysseus and Penelope its twin exemplars. So frequent and central to the story of Odysseus's return are moments of discovery—or failures in discovery—that Aristotle identified "recognition" (*anagnōrisis*) as the poem's main theme (*Poetics* 1459b15).

A second theme, developed in both the *Iliad* and *Odyssey*, highlights the importance and difficulty of achieving a broad understanding of what might be termed "the larger scheme of things"—or as Homer expresses the idea—"knowing how to think of what lies before and after" (*eidenai noēsai prossō kai opissō*).

The phrase *prossō kai opissō* has commonly been understood to imply that the ancient Greeks conceived of the past and future as lying "before and behind," so that what has already occurred lay directly before them, while future events were approaching them from behind.[20] It now seems clear, however, that this understanding is at odds with a considerable body of linguistic evidence. G. E. Dunkel has shown that the association of past events with what lies "in front" and future events with what lies "behind" was not peculiarly Greek but is attested to in Vedic and Hittite, and in all probability reflected a feature of Indo-European. In a number of Vedic texts, for example, past and future events are said to lie "before and after," *relative not to the observer but to each other*—that is, past events lie ahead of present and future events in the order of succession.[21] In this connection Dunkel quotes a portion of the Vedic hymn to Dawn:

> Among the days <=along time>, of these earlier sisters, the back/later one approaches the front/earlier one from behind. Let these newer ones now, just as of old, shine richly for us, dawns who bring good days. (1.124.9)

So if we are to think of events in accordance with epic Greek ways of speaking, we must think of them as occurring in much the same way in which cars exit from a tunnel, or bullets are shot from the barrel of a gun. The event that happens first (and is now past) was the first one "out of the chute"; the event just behind that one was the next event to occur, and so forth. So the poet's claim that mortal beings lack the capacity to look "before and after" means that they are incapable of broadening their viewpoint to comprehend two series of events, one that stretches into the past as well as the other that extends into the future.

The headstrong Achilles faults the headstrong Agamemnon in just these terms:

> Nor does he know how to think of before and after (*prossō kai opissō*)
> So the Achaeans might safely wage war beside their ships. (*Il.* 1.343–44)

Similarly, the failure of Penelope's suitors to sense the disaster that awaits them marks them as *nēpioi*—"fools who did not realize (*ouk enoēsan*) that over them one and all the cords of destruction had been made fast" (*Od.* 22.31–32). In his speech to the suitor Amphinomous Odysseus identifies the inability to direct one's thoughts toward future events as a defining characteristic of the race:

> Nothing feebler does earth nurture than man,
> Of all the things that move and breath on the earth.
> For he thinks that he will never suffer evil in the time to come (*opissō*),
> So long as the gods give him prosperity and his knees are quick;
> But when again the gods decree him sorrow;
> This too he bears with a steadfast heart.
> For such is the mind (*noos*) of man upon the earth,
> Like the day the father of gods and men brings to him. (*Od.* 18.130–37)

On occasion, those who are able to "see *prossō kai opissō*" are said to "know this best themselves"; that is, those who can take up the broader view must expect that their knowledge and advice will go unheeded by all the others who lack such a capacity.[22] As the seer Poulydamus explains the problem to Hector:

> To one man god has given works or war,
> To another, dance, and to another lyre and song,
> And in the breast of another, Zeus, whose voice is borne afar,
> Puts a valuable mind (*noon . . . esthlon*)
> From which many men get profit, and many he saves,
> But he knows this best himself. (*malista de kautos anegnō, Il.* 13.730–35)[23]

The restricted temporal range of mortal *noos* provides one of the major themes in early Greek poetry, as in the *Homeric Hymn to Demeter* (256–57):

> Unknowing (*nēides*) are humans and foolish
> Not foreseeing the good or evil that comes upon them.

Similarly, Archilochus, fr. 70:

> Of such a sort, Glaucus, is the mind (*thumos*) of mortal man,
> Whatever Zeus may bring him for the day,
> For he thinks such things as he meets with.

Semonides, fr. 1:

> There is no mind (*noos*) in men,
> But we live each day like grazing cattle,
> Not knowing how god shall end it.

Theognis, 141–42:

> Mortals think vain things, knowing nothing,
> While the gods accomplish all to their intentions.

Simonides, fr. 22:

> You who are a human being,
> Never say what tomorrow will bring,
> Nor when you see someone prosper, how long this will last.
> For change is swifter than the changing course of the wide-winged fly.

Solon, fr. 13:

> We mortal men, good and bad, think in this way:
> Each holds his opinion before something happens to him, and then he
>   grieves,
> But before that we rejoice open-mouthed in vain expectations.

Solon, fr. 1:

> All that we do is fraught with danger;
> No one can ever know where a thing may end, when it has once
>   begun . . .
> For us no visible limit of wealth is appointed;
> Those blessed beyond others with wealth hunger for double the sum.

Pindar, *Nemean* 6.6–7:

> We know not where, according to what the day or night brings to us,
>   fate has
> Appointed as the end toward which we hasten.

Pindar, *Nemean* 11.43–47:

> What comes from Zeus is not accompanied by any sure sign (*saphes
>   tekmar*).
> We embark on bold endeavors, yearning after many exploits,
> For our limbs are fettered by importunate hope.
> But streams of foreknowledge (*promatheias*) lie far from us.

Since mortals can think of events only in terms of what they themselves have experienced or "met with," they inevitably fail to detect the larger patterns in human affairs—how long health and prosperity will last, whether victory or defeat lies ahead, and what end awaits each individual. "Wisdom" for such creatures resides in seeking the kind of truth that accords with their nature, and "not aiming too high."

The archaic view of knowledge, therefore, is entirely consistent with what William Arrowsmith once termed the Greek view of "the great gamut of being":

> At the very top is god, sheer power, intense being, the quality possessed by
> what is wonderful and unique, the special radiance of the exceptional and
> the prodigious. . . . Every power a being possesses is pertinent to his place
> along this great gamut of being running from the omnipotence of Zeus to the

undifferentiated powers of the great feudal barons of Olympus, down to the modest particularisms of the nymphs, and lesser powers, to the god-aspiring *arēte* [excellence] of the hero, to the routine world of ordinary mortals, to weak women, helpless children, and chattel slaves. Each order suffers the cumulative *anankē* [necessity] of the orders above it in an ascending curve of freedom and power.[24]

The Olympian gods and goddesses are exemplars of knowledge insofar as they live forever and can observe the wide world from their superior vantage points.[25] And when Homer speaks of the *noos* that Zeus "puts into the breast of a man" he implies that all human knowledge or understanding is ultimately a divine dispensation, a gift of the gods.[26] Particular areas of expertise are also spoken of as divine gifts—as in the case of the carpenter who is "well skilled in all manner of craft (*sophiēs*) by the promptings of Athene" (*Il.* 15.411–12); Kalchas "who had guided the ships of the Achaeans to Troy by the soothsaying Phoebus Apollo had bestowed upon him" (*Il.* 1.69–72); and the Sirens who promise Odysseus that he will "know more" since they themselves "know all things that come to pass" (*Od.* 12.188). The poets of archaic Greece surveyed the powers and limitations of human intelligence from a distinctly religious perspective, and thereby articulated a view of the limits of what any mortal being may hope to know.[27]

A third, related theme was the conception of the poet as one whose association with divine powers both empowers and authorizes him to speak on a wide range of questions. At the outset of the Catalogue of the Ships in *Iliad* 2 the singer explains how the Muses empower him to perform such "superhuman" feats as reciting the names of all the leaders who came to fight at Troy:

> But the vast number [of leaders] I could neither tell nor name,
> Not if I had ten tongues, and ten mouths,
> An untiring voice, and a heart of bronze within me,
> Did not the Muses of Olympus, daughters of Zeus who bears the aegis,
> Call to my mind (*mnēsaiath*) all those who came beneath Troy. (487–92)

Hesiod also speaks of his role as poet in the context of widespread human ignorance: "Yet the will of Zeus who holds the aegis [i.e., the order of events as they unfold] is different at different times, and it is hard for mortal men to grasp it" (*Works and Days*, 483–84). At least part of his task is to impart his knowledge of the various recognizable signs that mark important turning points so that Perses and indirectly those in the poet's audience will know how best to conduct their affairs. And as he undertakes to relate "the mind of Zeus"—as seen in the cycles of winds and weather—he claims that because he is a servant of the Muses he can tell the truth concerning matters with which he has little or no direct experience:

I will show you the measures of the loud-resounding sea,
Although I am skilled (*sesophismenos*) in neither ships nor seafaring;
For never yet have I sailed by ship over a broad sea . . .
So much is my experience (*pepeirēmai*) of many-pegged ships.
Nevertheless, I will tell you the mind of Zeus who holds the aegis,
For the Muses have taught me to sing in marvelous song. (648–50,
    660–62)[28]

Similarly, at the outset of the *Theogony*, Hesiod asserts his claim to epistemic superiority by describing the scope of his art in the same terms Homer used to character the knowledge possessed by the seer Kalchas—*ta t'eonta ta t'essomena pro t'eonta* (38).[29] Theognis also speaks of the poet as obligated to share his superior knowledge:

A servant and messenger of the Muses, if preeminent in knowledge (*perisson eideiē*), should not be begrudging of his expertise (*sophia*), but should seek out these, point out those, invent other things, for to whom is he useful if he alone is knowledgeable (*epistamenos*)? (769–72)

Pindar similarly assigns to the poet a greater than human level of understanding:

concerning these things the gods are able to prompt wise poets, though it is impossible for mortal men to find it out. But since you maiden Muses know all things, you are permitted this, along with Memory and the cloud-wrapped father, so listen now, for my tongue loves to pour forth the choicest and sweetest bloom of song. (*Paean* 6.51–58)

The singers who appear in the Homeric poems speak of the aim of their craft as affording pleasure to others, but the stories they tell are rich in moral exemplars—of individuals who strive always to be the best, gain honor and fame through their actions while avoiding the disgrace of defeat, demand recognition in proportion to their merit, give aid and protection to their family and friends, offer and receive good advice, and show respect to gods, parents, suppliants, and strangers.[30] In *Works and Days* Hesiod offers advice on sound business and agricultural practices, but he speaks also of the value and importance of hard work, personal hygiene, a good marriage, and remaining on friendly terms with the neighbors. The criticisms of Homer and Hesiod leveled by Xenophanes and Heraclitus confirm their standing as acknowledged authorities on a wide range of practical questions: "since from the beginning all have learned according to Homer" runs fragment B10 of Xenophanes, where the verb for learning (*manthanō*) carries a connotation of learned behavior.[31] Heraclitus similarly criticizes those who follow the poets and take the singers as their guides to conduct:

What understanding (*noos*) or intelligence (*phrēn*) do they possess? They place their trust in the popular singers (*dēmōn aoidoisi*) and take the throng for their teacher, not realizing that the many are bad and the few are good. (B104)

And when the goddess of Parmenides' poem declares to the youth who has come to her house for instruction that it is "both right and just" (*themis te dikē te*) that he should learn all things (B1.28), it seems clear that the old stricture against "aiming too high" is being set aside.

Knowledge, Experience, and Divine Inspiration

One might wonder how, in the context of an assumed association of knowledge with direct experience, Greek poets could have credibly presented themselves to their audiences as paragons of wisdom on a wide range of factual and moral questions. Or to divide this complex question into its component parts, one might ask: How could the poets have imagined that in creating and performing their works as they did they were displaying a body of factual and moral *knowledge*? And, second, how could they have imagined that the knowledge they claimed to possess had been obtained from some *divine* source?

Part of the answer to the first question relates to the way in which early Greek poets and their audiences understood the nature of the poetic art. Democritus and Plato will later characterize the process of poetic creation as a matter of "divine madness" or "possession" in which the mind (or *thumos*) of the poet is taken over and manipulated by powers external to him. Recent accounts, however, have called attention to the frequency with which early Greek poets spoke of their poetic ability as a teachable and learnable craft.[32] In a remark to the suitor Antinous the swineherd Eumaeus groups the "divine minstrel" (*thespin aoidon*) together with prophets, physicians, and builders as one of the "public workers" (*dēmioergoi*) who are welcomed in whatever city they may visit (*Od.* 17.383–86), thus suggesting the view of the poet as a practitioner of a kind of expertise. And while Homer speaks in terms of a god "breathing" or "implanting" a song in the *thumos* or *noos* of the poet, he speaks also of what the poet has been "taught."[33] Singers are praised when they perform their works "in due order"[34] and references to the "skill" or "expertise" of the poet appear throughout early Greek poetry.[35] In the act of performance the bard achieves access to the past, the names of persons and places of ancient places and times live on in his creations, and his prodigious powers of recall are obvious for all to see.[36] In the absence of competing written accounts, the singer's version of events would naturally be accepted as an invaluable link with the events of yesteryear.[37]

In answering the second question, it is worth remembering that the poets were not the only individuals who believed that mortals could come into contact with powers or agents that in some sense existed "outside" or "above" them. Evidence that the idea of divinely inspired knowledge was widely accepted can be found in the enormous popularity of the ancient oracles at Delphi, Dodona, and elsewhere. And no account of ancient political and military decision-making would be complete that did not include an acknowledgment of the important role played by diviners who practiced *mantikē* of one sort or another.[38] In an age in which the occurrence of any unusual event readily provoked suspicion of a divine intervention, it would have been natural for a gifted poet to conclude that his ability to perform extremely complicated works over great periods of time betokened some degree of divine assistance. As E. R. Dodds has explained:

> The recognition, the insight, the memory, the brilliant or perverse idea, have this in common, that they come suddenly, as we say "into a man's head." Often he is conscious of no observation or reasoning which has led up to them. But in that case, how can he call them "his"? A moment ago they were not in his mind; now they are there. Something has put them there, and that something is other than himself.[39]

Modern poets still speak of the creative process as an experience that brings them into contact with powers that lie in some sense "outside" or "beyond" them. Performers of various kinds still speak of their successful performances as exceeding their own expectations and understanding, of being "in the zone" or having "a golden touch." So it is not difficult to understand how, in spite of the traditional association of knowledge with direct experience, the poets of archaic Greece could think of themselves, and be regarded by others, as purveyors of a wisdom imparted to them by greater than human powers.

Notes

Portions of this chapter appear in section 2 of "The Secularizing of Knowledge," in P. Curd and D. Graham, eds., *The Oxford Handbook of Presocratic Philosophy* (Oxford: Oxford University Press, 2008). I am grateful to William Wians and Alex Purves for their helpful criticisms of an earlier version of this essay.

1. The dimensions of the archaic period have been variously defined. Here it is understood to extend from approximately 800 to 450 BCE. Among the poets active during this period were Homer (eighth to seventh centuries); Hesiod and Archilochus (seventh century); Solon (c. 640–588); Ibycus, Sappho, Semonides, and Theognis (sixth century); and Simonides (c. 556–468). I include Pindar (522–443) in the discussion since his work reflects the older poetic traditions rather than the thinking of his philosophical and scientific contemporaries. All translations are my own.

2. Bacchylides, fr. 9 (Edmunds): "Various are the paths men seek that will lead them to conspicuous fame, / And ten thousand are the *epistamai* [Doric for *epistēmai*] of

man. / For one thrives in golden hope because he has expertise (*sophos*) / Or is honored by the Graces, or skilled (*eidōs*) in divination, / And another because he can pull the dappled bow against all."

3. Fr. B 56: "People are deceived in their *gnōsis* of what is obvious."

4. "But as the carpenter's line makes straight a ship's timber in the hands of a carpenter skilled in all manner of craft (*pasēs . . . sophiēs*)." Similarly, in *Works and Days* (649) Hesiod speaks of himself as "unskilled in seamanship" (*oute ti nautiliēs sesophismenos*); and in fr. 306 (Clement, *Strom.* I, p. 121) Hesiod describes the singer Linus as "learned in every skill" (*pantioēs sophiēs dedaēkota*).

5. The course of development is summarized in W. K. C. Guthrie, *A History of Greek Philosophy* (Cambridge: Cambridge University Press, 1965), Vol. 2, 27–34.

6. As pointed out by Bernard Williams in his *Shame and Necessity* (Berkeley and Los Angeles: University of California Press, 1993). Of course it would also be an error to conclude that no such term existed in the language simply because it does not appear in any surviving text.

7. See the pioneering study by Bruno Snell, *Die Ausdrücke für den Begriff des Wissens in der vorplatonischen Philosophie*, Philologische Untersuchungen 29 (Berlin: Weidmann, 1924), and his *Discovery of the Mind: The Greek Origins of European Thought* (New York and Evanston: Harper and Row, 1960), an English translation by T. G. Rosenmeyer of the second edition of *Die Entdeckung des Geistes* (Hamburg: Classen and Goverts, 1948), with a chapter added on "Human Knowledge and Divine Knowledge"; and "Wie die Griechen lernten was geistige Tätigkeit ist," in *The Journal of Hellenic Studies* 93 (1973), 172–84; reprinted in *Der Weg zum Denken und zur Wahrheit*, Hypomnemata 57 (Göttingen: Vandenhoeck and Ruprecht, 1978); Kurt von Fritz, "*Noeō, Noein*, and Their Derivatives in Pre-Socratic Philosophy (Excluding Anaxagoras)," *Classical Philology* 40 (1945), 223–42 and 41 (1946), 12–34, reprinted in A. P. D. Mourelatos, ed., *The Pre-Socratics: A Collection of Critical Essays* (Garden City, N.Y.: Anchor Doubleday, 1974); and Hermann Fränkel, *Dichtung und Philosophie des frühen Griechentums*, trans. M. Hadas (Munich: C. H. Beck, 1962), and J. Willis, *Early Greek Poetry and Philosophy* (New York and London: Harcourt Brace Jovanovich, 1973); and "Xenophanesstudien," *Hermes* 60 (1925), 174–92; reprinted in his *Wege und Formen frügriechischen Denkens* (Munich: C. H. Beck, 1960); a portion of this study was translated by Cosgrove and Mourelatos and included in the latter's *Pre-Socratics* as "Xenophanes' Empiricism and His Critique of Knowledge," 118–31.

8. Snell 1960, 137.

9. Von Fritz 1946, 40–41.

10. Snell 1978, 20–21.

11. I present these objections here only in summary form; for a more extended discussion see Lesher, "The Emergence of Philosophical Interest in Cognition," *Oxford Studies in Ancient Philosophy* 12 (1994), 1–34. While it seems clear that there were some significant developments in the early Greek view of knowledge (perhaps most notably, in the disparaging remarks made about "the testimony of eye and ear" by Heraclitus and Parmenides), it is implausible to see these developments as marking a change in the commonly understood meaning of the various Greek verbs for *knowing*.

12. As noted by E. Hussey, "The Beginnings of Epistemology: From Homer to Philolaus," in S. Everson, ed., *Companions to Ancient Thought I: Epistemology* (Cambridge:

Cambridge University Press, 1990), 11–38; E. Heitsch, "Das Wissen des Xenophanes," *Rheinisches Museum* 109 (1966), 193–235; and Lesher 1994, 6n.

13. The skeptical reading has recently been challenged by H. M. Zellner, "Scepticism in Homer?" *Classical Quarterly* 44 (1994), 308–15, on the grounds that the invocation of the Muses in *Iliad* 2, and similar passages elsewhere in the Homeric poems reflect not so much a "folk epistemology" or "pre-philosophical theory of knowledge" but rather the religious conviction that mortal capacities pale by comparison with those of the gods. In what follows here, however, I attempt to identify three themes that collectively merit being identified as a "pre-philosophical" view of the sources, limits, and nature of human knowledge.

14. Cf. *Od.* 16.470: "And I know (*oida*) at least one other thing, for I saw it with my own eyes (*idon ophthalmoisin*)"; similarly *Il.* 11.741; 14.153–54; 17.84–86, 115–16; *Od.* 5.77–78, 215; 8.560; 15.532; 16.470–71, among many others.

15. Among many other instances: Aegisthus learns his fate when the gods "spoke to him, sending keen-sighted Hermes" (*Od.* 1.38); Echenor the Corinthian learns his from the expert seer Polyidus (*Il.* 13.666); and Odysseus learns what the future holds for him from the words of the ghost of the seer Teiresias (*Od.* 11.100ff.). W. Wians has pointed out to me that this exchange between Achilles and Aeneas presents the poet as a paragon of knowledge insofar as his stories transmit knowledge of ancient persons and their exploits to later generations.

16. As has often been noted, Homer also speaks of "knowing" where we might speak of experiencing certain feelings and desires, or of harboring certain dispositions. Menelaus says of Patroclus that *pasin gar epistato meilichos einai*, "for he knew gentleness to all," while Nestor and Menelaus are described as sailing home from Troy *phila eidotes allēloisin*, "knowing friendly things to one another" (*Od.* 3.277). For a detailed discussion of this aspect of early Greek thought, and its relationship to classical accounts of thought and action, see M. J. O'Brien, *The Socratic Paradoxes and the Greek Mind* (Chapel Hill: University of North Carolina Press, 1967) and J. R. Warden, "The Mind of Zeus," *Journal of the History of Ideas* 32 (1971), 3–14.

17. For other examples, cf. *Il.* 13.448–49, 457; 16.243; 18.69–70; and 21.226.

18. For this use of *autos* meaning "of one's own accord" or "by oneself," see Smyth, *Greek Grammar* (Cambridge: Harvard University Press, 1984), Sec. 1209a and *Od.* 16.470; *Od.* 5.215: "I know for myself (*oida kai autos*) that in appearance and stature wise Penelope fails to compete with you"; *Od.* 1.216: "For never yet did any man know for himself (*autos anegnō*) his own parentage"; cf. also *Il.* 13.729; 17.686–88; *Od.* 6.188.

19. Cf. also the common expression "tell me so that I/we may know" (as in *Il.* 1.363, and elsewhere). So natural is the idea of learning from the words of others that the verb *peuthomai/punthanomai* commonly means "to learn about some matter from another person." Similarly, *akouō*, "hear," can mean "learn of or come to know about by hearing," as at *Il.* 24.543: *to prin akouomen olbion einai*—"we hear/know that earlier you had been prosperous." The same attitude is reflected in the odd remark at *Od.* 6.185, that when two like-minded people become husband and wife "they become a great sorrow for their enemies and a joy to their friends, but they *hear* this best themselves"—*malista de t' ekluon autoi.*

20. Cf. LSJ s.v. *opisō* II; and Bernard Knox, *Backing into the Future: The Classical Tradition and Its Renewal* (New York: Norton, 1994), 11–12.

21. For an analysis of this feature of ancient Greek and other Indo-European languages, see the discussion by G. E. Dunkel, "Prossō kai Opissō," *Zeitschrift für Vergleichende Sprachforschung* 96 (1982–83), 67–87.

22. As is evident from the responses to the advice given by the seers Poulydamus and Halitherses at *Il.* 18.250, and *Od.* 24.452.

23. Hesiod similarly praises the man who "taking thought thinks of all things himself, both the things to happen next (*epeita*), and how it will be better at the end. Good also is one who can learn from others wiser than himself, but useless is he who can neither think for himself nor take the good advice of others" (*Works and Days*, 293–97).

24. William Arrowsmith, *Euripides' Alcestis* (New York and London: Oxford University Press, 1974), 7.

25. Cf. *Il.* 8.51–52: "And [Zeus] himself sat on the mountain peaks exulting in his glory, looking down upon both the city of the Trojans and the ships of the Achaeans"; Hesiod, *Works and Days* 267: "the eye of Zeus, seeing all things and taking note of all things," among similar remarks.

26. Cf. Luc Brisson: "Going back as far as we can in ancient Greece, we find that human knowledge, both practical and theoretical, originated with the gods. All the efforts made over the centuries to ground knowledge in observation and to confirm it by experimentation never severed that link; indeed, by the end of antiquity it had grown stronger"; from "Myth and Knowledge," in J. Brunschwig and G. E. R. Lloyd, eds., *Greek Thought* (Cambridge: Harvard University Press, 2000), 39.

27. In general terms, this conclusion is consonant with Snell's view of the emergence of a more optimistic outlook among the philosophers, against a broad background of "poetic pessimism." My reservations about Snell's account (or accounts, since he returned to this topic on numerous occasions) relate to his view of the meaning of the Homeric knowledge verbs, when the more optimistic view may be said to have emerged, and how that novel development is best understood. For additional details, see the discussion in Lesher 1994.

28. Similar testimonials to the powers of the Muses appear in Ibycus, 3.23; Solon, 1.49; Bacchylides, 19.1, 5.31, 9.3; Pindar, *Paean* 7.b5ff.

29. Cf. Detienne: "The prehistory of the philosophical *Alētheia* leads us to the system of thought of the diviner, the poet, and the king of justice, three figures for whom a certain type of speech is defined by *Alētheia*"; M. Detienne, *The Masters of Truth in Archaic Greece* (New York: Zone Books, 1996); translated by Janet Lloyd from *Les Maîtres de vérité dans la grèce archaïque* [Paris: Maspero, 1967]. 37). Similarly Chadwick: "The fundamental elements of the prophetic function seem to have everywhere been the same. Everywhere the gift of poetry is inseparable from divine inspiration. Everywhere this inspiration carries with it knowledge—whether of the past, in the form of history and genealogy; of the hidden present, in the form commonly of scientific information; or of the future, in the form of prophetic utterance in the narrower sense. . . . The lofty claims of the poet and seer are universally admitted, and he himself holds a high status wherever he is found"; N. K. Chadwick, *Poetry and Prophecy* (Cambridge: Cambridge University Press, 1942), 14. And Dodds: "By that [divine] grace poet and seer alike enjoyed a knowledge denied to other men. In Homer the two professions are quite distinct; but we have good reason to believe that they had once been united, and the analogy between them was still felt"; E. R. Dodds, *The Greeks and the Irrational* (Berkeley and Los Angeles: University of California Press, 1963), 81.

30. I owe to Jessica Wissmann the point that while Homer was universally regarded as the didactic poet par excellence, Homer himself consistently praised the poet's art on the basis of the pleasure it afforded to those in his audience.

31. "Since from the beginning all have learned according to Homer" (*ex archēs kath' Homēron epei memathēkasi pantes*, from Herodian, *On Doubtful Syllables*, 296.6). For

the behavioral connotation of *manthanō*, cf. *Il.* 6.444–45: "learning (*manthanein*) to be valiant always" and Xenophanes B3: "having learned (*mathontes*) useless luxuries from the Lydians."

32. For Democritus see B18 (Clement, *Stromateis*, 6.168): *poiētēs de hassa men an graphēi met' enthousiasmou kai hieroou pneumatos, kala karta estin.* For Plato's view of the poet as possessed by a divine mania, see the *Ion*, esp. 533dff. The difficulties in Plato's views as applied to early Greek poetry are discussed in Dodds 1963, 80–82; E. N. Tigerstedt, "*Furor Poeticus*: Poetic Inspiration in Greek Literature before Democritus and Plato," *Journal of the History of Ideas* 31 (1970), 163–78; and Penelope Murray, "Poetic Inspiration in Early Greece," *Journal of Hellenic Studies* 101 (1981), 87–100.

33. Cf. *edidaxe* at *Od.* 8.488; *dedaōs* at *Od.* 17.519; and *autodidaktos* at *Od.* 22.347; similarly *edidaxan* in Hesiod, *Theogony*, 22.

34. Cf. *kata kosmon . . . eideis* at *Od.* 8.489; and *kata moiran katalexēis* at 496.

35. Cf. Homer, *Od.* 11.368 (*aoidos epistamenos*); Theognis, 771 (*sophia*), Archilochus, 1 (*epistamenos*); Xenophanes B2 (*sophiē*); Solon, fr. 13.52 (*epistamenos*); Sappho, 56 (*sophian*); Pindar, *Ol.* 1.116 (*sophia*); *Ol.* 14.7; *Pyth.* 1.41; and fr. 52h 18–20 (*sophos*). For *eidenai*: "For I sing graceful songs and know how to speak graceful words" (*charienta d'oida lexai*, Anacreon 374); "The truly expert poet (*sophos*) is one who knows/has skill in (*eidōs*) many things by nature" (Pindar, *Ol.* 2.86); and so forth.

36. Studies of modern oral poetry describe performances that extend over days and weeks. See the discussion of the work of Mathias Murko in Fränkel 1962, 19–21.

37. If it seems implausible to suppose that what was in many respects an artfully crafted tale could be taken seriously as a historically reliable version of events, one need only note the number of moviegoers who accepted Oliver Stone's version of the Kennedy assassination. Of course we moderns have access to alternative written accounts, but when individuals know nothing of those accounts, or choose to ignore them, they are in essentially the same position as the members of an oral society.

38. For an account of the various techniques of seers and oracles, and their impact of public life see Walter Burkert, *Greek Religion* (Cambridge: Harvard University Press, 1985), 109ff.

39. Dodds 1963, 11.

2

Homer's Challenge to Philosophical Psychology

Fred D. Miller Jr.

The Poet Who Taught Greece

"Everyone at first learned from Homer," observed the philosopher Xenophanes of Colophon.[1] What he taught, however, included impious legends about the gods:

Homer and Hesiod attributed to the gods everything
which among men is shameful and blameworthy—
theft and adultery and mutual deception.[2]

Similarly, in Plato's *Republic*, Homer receives mixed praise as "the poet who taught Greece" (*Rep.* 10.606e–607a). Although Socrates himself has loved and respected the bard since childhood, Homer's poems must be banned from the ideal city because they contain false and morally subversive claims about the gods and heroes, and "no one is to be honored more than the truth" (*Rep.* 10.595b–c; cf. 3.388c–392c). Rather than dismissing Homer as a mere poet, Xenophanes and Plato singled him out as an educator who had overpowering authority, but whose teachings were often paradoxical and even inconsistent.

 Werner Jaeger, in agreement with many other scholars, remarks, "It seemed to [Xenophanes] self-evident that the poet is the only real educator of the people, and his work the only genuinely responsible authority of *paideia* [i.e., education]." Yet Homer was also the mainstay of serious doctrinal errors. Xenophanes therefore began the work of refuting Homer and "of deliberately transfusing the new philosophical ideas into the intellectual blood-stream of Greece."[3] A primary objective was to substitute a new philosophical theology for Homer's anthropomorphism. Although Homer taught that the world was governed by intelligent and purposeful gods under a supreme ruler, he also represented them as subject to human limitations and desires and consequently as divided among themselves and perpetrating immoral acts. Against this, Xenophanes famously asserted, there is

> One god, greatest among gods and humans,
> similar to mortals in neither shape nor thought.[4]

No less challenging was Homer's portrayal of mortal beings. His dramatic and detailed descriptions offer valuable insights; yet, when taken literally, they often sound paradoxical and even inconsistent. In this essay I shall argue that a careful study of Homer helps set the stage for philosophical inquiry regarding three general topics: personal identity; responsibility and fate; and life and afterlife. I will follow the method of Aristotle, who often begins a philosophical investigation by setting out the phenomena (*tithentas ta phainomena*) and then going through the puzzles (*diaporēsantes*).[5] In an analogous manner, the following sections will set out the "phenomena" drawing from representative Homeric texts and discuss the *aporiai* (puzzles) they present. In the concluding section, I argue that the "aporetic" character of Homer's texts shows how they would have served as a stimulus for early philosophers speculating about the soul; and it may also help to shed light on recent scholarly controversies over Homeric psychology.

Personal Identity

That Homer has a concept of self is apparent from the fact that he uses the word *autos* (and related grammatical forms) in much the same way that modern speakers use "self" and equivalent terms to identify the speaker (or other individuals referred to by the speaker) and distinguish him or her from other individuals. The word *autos* serves to indicate that an action or thought involves, affects, or regards the agent in some way or that it has a bearing on the agent's well-being. This term plays a prominent role in some scenes that illustrate the Homeric code of warrior values. For example, when Menelaus upbraids his comrades for cowering before Hector:

> Ah me! You brave in words, you women, not men, of Achaea!
> This will be a defilement upon us, shame upon shame piled,
> if no one of the Danaans goes out to face Hector.
> No, may all of you turn to water and earth, all of you
> who sit there spiritless (*akērioi*) each of you, utterly dishonored.
> I myself (*egōn autos*) will arm against this man. While above us
> the threads of victory are held in the hands of the immortals. (*Il.* 7.96–
> 102)[6]

Here Menelaus uses the term *autos* to set himself apart and emphasize that he alone has the courage to confront Hector. The word *autos* thus underscores his superiority to the other Achaeans. Likewise, within the walls of Troy, Hector explains to his wife Andromache why he must go out to fight these same Achaeans:

> . . . I would feel deep shame
> before the Trojans, and the Trojan women with trailing garments,
> if like a coward I were to shrink aside from the fighting;
> and the *thumos* will not let me, since I have learned to be valiant
> and to fight always among the foremost ranks of the Trojans,
> winning for my father great fame, and for my own self (*autou*). (*Il.*
> 6.441–46)[7]

The hero thus distinguishes himself from others by his courage and thereby achieves fame for himself as well as for his kinsmen and city.

Selfhood is also expressed by means of the proper name. A dramatic illustration is Odysseus's tale of how he concealed his identity from Polyphemus:

> Cyclops, you ask me for my famous name. I will tell you
> then, but you must give me a guest gift as you have promised.
> "Nobody" (*Outis*) is my name. My father and mother call me
> Nobody, as do all the others who are my companions. (*Od.* 9.364–67)

After Odysseus and his surviving comrades manage to blind Polyphemus with a sharpened stake, the giant calls out to the other Cyclopes: "Good friends, Nobody is killing me by force or treachery" (*Od.* 9.408). Although his friends try to restrain him, Odysseus reveals his name:

> Cyclops, if any mortal man ever asks you who it was
> that inflicted upon your eye this shameful blinding,
> tell him that you were blinded by Odysseus, sacker of cities,
> Laertes is his father, and he makes his home in Ithaca. (*Od.* 9.502–05)

The joke backfires when Polyphemus prays to Poseidon to place a curse on the perpetrator, who is condemned to several years of additional wandering and suffering. Odysseus is thus tripped up by his desire for fame.[8]

Although this episode graphically illustrates the hero's ill-advised self-indulgence, it also explains why Odysseus disregards his comrades' pleas not to provoke the Cyclops as they make their escape: "So they spoke, but could not persuade my great-hearted *thumos* in me, / but once again with an enraged *thumos* I cried to him. . . ." (*Od.* 9.500–01).

What is this thing that Odysseus calls his *thumos*? In Homer it is often associated with courage, resoluteness, or endurance, as when Hector says to Achilles, "But now the *thumos* in turn has driven me / to stand and face you" (*Il.* 22.252–53). The *thumos* is involved with a wide range of emotions: fear, hope, love, joy, reproach, sorrow, and so forth.[9] Odysseus makes the aforementioned reference to his "great-hearted *thumos.*" *Thumos* is often linked with the heart (*ētor, kēr, kardiē,* or *kradiē*), which is also implicated in emotions such as anger, happiness, and grief. For example, like angry wasps, "the Myrmidons possessing heart (*kradiē*) and *thumos* poured forth from their ships" (*Il.* 16.266). The heart by itself also exhibits emotions: for example, the heart (*ētor*) is mourning or happy (*Il.* 22.169, 23.647–48).

The *thumos* is also spoken of as located within the *phrenes.* As Hector says to Achilles, "I know that I could not / persuade you, since indeed in your *phrenes* is a *thumos* of iron" (*Il.* 22.356–57). *Phrenes* (plural form of *phrēn*) refers to an organ located in the chest. Patroclus's spear strikes Sarpedon, "where the *phrenes* encloses the dense heart" (*Il.* 16.481; cf. 242). Later Patroclus "pulled the spear out of his flesh, and the *phrenes* followed it too" (*Il.* 16.504).[10]

It has been noted already that a person's *thumos* may resist others' attempts at persuasion. Even more striking, however, are instances in which individuals speak to their own *thumos.* Thus, Hector, before the battle with Achilles, "deeply troubled, spoke to his own great-hearted *thumos*" (*Il.* 22.98). After killing Hector, Achilles wonders how the Trojans will react: "Yet still, why does my dear *thumos* debate on these things?" (*Il.* 22.385).[11] Homer's heroes frequently engage in these dialogues with their own *thumos.* Two passages, both involving Odysseus, are noteworthy. In the first, Odysseus stands in a battlefield watching the other Argives flee from the Trojans:

> And troubled, [Odysseus] spoke then to his great-hearted *thumos*:
> "Ah me, what will become of me? It will be a great evil
> if I run, fearing their multitude, yet more dreadful if I am caught alone;
> and Cronus's son drove to flight the rest of the Danaans.
> Yet still, why does my dear *thumos* debate on these things?[12]
> Since I know that it is the bad ones who walk out of the fighting,
> but if one is to be the best in battle, he must by all means
> stand his ground strongly, whether he be struck or strike down another."
> While he was pondering these things in his *phrēn* and *thumos*
> the ranks of the armored Trojans came on against him . . . (*Il.* 11.403–12)

Odysseus confronts a dilemma, and his *thumos* ponders the alternatives. But Odysseus interjects with what "I know" (*oida*) to be the case: if I flee I will be a coward, but if I stay and fight I will be the best of warriors. It is as if Odysseus himself must remind his *thumos* about what is most important: his own honor.

Although we are familiar with the situation Homer describes, Odysseus's distinction between "I" and "my dear *thumos*" is puzzling, as if the *thumos* were another person who needed to be reminded.

A passage from the *Odyssey* describes the phenomenon in somewhat different terms. Odysseus, on returning to Ithaca, enters his home in disguise only to be abused by the suitors. After plotting his revenge, he goes outside and beds down in the forecourt:

> There, thinking evil things in [his] *thumos* for the suitors,
> Odysseus lay awake; and out of the palace issued
> those women who in the past had been going to bed with the suitors,
> full of merriment and greeting each one with laughter.
> But the *thumos* in the dear chest was stirred by this,
> and he deliberated (*mermērize*) many things in his *phrēn* and *thumos*,
> whether to spring on them and kill each one, or rather
> to let them lie this one more time with the insolent suitors
> for the last and latest time; but the heart (*kradiē*) was howling within
>   him . . .
> He struck himself on the chest and scolded his heart (*kradiē*) with a
>   speech:
> "Bear up, heart (*kradiē*). You have had worse to endure before this." (*Od.*
>   20.5–21)

As in the previous passage Odysseus deliberates in his *thumos* and *phrēn*, but here the act of thinking (*phroneōn*) occurs within the *thumos* itself.[13]

This passage raises even more questions than the first. What is the relation of Odysseus "himself" to the heart (*kradiē*) that he addresses in this passage? And what is the relation of the heart to the *thumos* and *phrenes* that are mentioned earlier in the passage? The *thumos* and *phrenes* are engaged in deliberation while the heart displays raw emotion (although the heart possesses enough awareness to "listen" to a speech).[14] But how, for that matter, are each of these items related to Odysseus "himself"? Although Odysseus manifestly has a concept of self, as seen previously, his self seems to disintegrate before our eyes, if we take Homer's description literally. Homer's narrative presents many *aporiai* concerning self-identity.[15]

Responsibility and Fate

Although Homer's heroes deliberate about what action to perform, there are frequent indications that the outcome was already predestined. The *Iliad* recounts how "the will of Zeus was accomplished" in the conflict between Agamemnon and Achilles (*Il.* 1.3–5). Many events result from the intervention of gods who provoke, deceive, and manipulate mortals into action. Moreover, humans are subject to the fates (*moirai*) that direct the course of their lives from the time of birth. In discussing the future of Odysseus, Alcinous compares fate to spinners generating the thread of one's life from birth to death:

> ... there in the future
> he shall endure all that his destiny (*assa*) and the heavy Spinners (Clōthes)
> spun for him with the thread at his birth, when his mother bore him. (*Od.*
> 7.196; cf. *Il.* 20.127)

Another famous simile involves the scales of Zeus:

> ... then the father balanced his golden scales, and in them
> he set two fateful portions of death, which lays men prostrate,
> one for Achilles, and one for Hector, breaker of horses,
> and balanced it by the middle; and Hector's fatal day sank down
> and went downward toward Hades ... (*Il.* 22.209–13; cf. 8.69–72, 16.657,
> 19.223)

Soon after, Hector recognizes his destiny:

> Hector knew in his *phrenes* and spoke aloud,
> "No use. Here at last the gods have summoned me deathward ... "
> (*Il.* 22.296–97)

Earlier Hector had warned Andromache that this might be his fate (*moira* or *aisa*):

> No man is going to hurl me to Hades, beyond destiny (*huper aisan*),
> but as for fate (*moira*), I think no man yet has escaped it
> neither brave man nor coward, once it has taken its first form. (*Il.* 6.487–
> 89)

Sometimes, however, a hero such as Aeneas has a good destiny:

> It is fated (*morimon*) that he shall be the survivor,
> that the generation of Dardanus shall not die, without seed
> obliterated, since Dardanus was dearest to Cronus's son
> of all his sons that have been born to him from mortal women.
> (*Il.* 20.302–03)

These passages, taken together, suggest a fatalistic view: that human beings do not have ultimate control over their own decisions and actions, and that what ultimately becomes of them—good or ill—hinges on fate and the gods.

The gods directly influence the motivations of human beings, for example, when Athena breathes strength into Diomedes (*Il.* 10.11–12; cf. 24.250) or when she puts courage into the *phrenes* of Nausicaa and takes fear from her limbs (*Od.* 6.140–41). If we are motivated to perform some action by the gods, it seems, our actions are not brought about solely by ourselves.

An apparent implication of this is that human beings cannot claim credit for their own deeds when they are ultimately caused by the gods. This view is expressed by Patroclus with his dying words. After Apollo struck Patroclus and "confusion (*atē*) seized his *phrenes*" (16.805), the dazed hero was hit by a spear cast by Euphorbus. Arriving on the scene to finish him off, Hector begins to gloat, but the dying Patroclus replies:

> Now is your time for a great boast, Hector. Yours is the victory
> given by Cronus's son, Zeus, and Apollo, who have subdued me
> easily, since they themselves stripped the arms from my shoulders.
> Even though twenty such as you had come in against me,
> they would all have been broken beneath my spear, and have perished.
> No, deadly fate (*moira*), with the son of Leto, has killed me,
> and of men it was Euphorbus; you are only my third slayer. (*Il.* 16.844–
> 50)

It is unclear what Patroclus means by calling Hector the "third" slayer. Euphorbus is evidently the second. Is the primary cause of death Apollo (in the Aristotelian sense of "proximate cause"), or is he lumping all of the divine agents (Zeus and fate along with Apollo) together? Again, is personified fate (here almost equivalent to death) supposed to have a distinct causal role? In any case, the point is that Hector deserves little credit.

Another apparent implication of divine influence is that human agents are not to blame (*aitioi*) for what they do because they are merely carrying out the will of the gods. For example, when the Trojans criticize Helen for the woes she has brought to their city, King Priam offers her this excuse: "You are not to blame (*aitiē*) to me; to me the gods are to blame (*aitioi*) / who drove upon me this sorrowful war against the Achaeans" (*Il.* 3.164–65). This line of defense is developed more fully in the apology of Agamemnon, who explains why he started the disastrous quarrel with Achilles:

> This is the word the Achaeans have spoken often against me
> and found fault with me in it, yet I am not to blame (*aitios*)
> but Zeus is, and Fate (Moira) and mist-walking Fury (Erinys)
> who in assembly caught my *phrenes* in savage confusion (*atē*)
> On that day I myself stripped from him the prize of Achilles.
> Yet what could I do? It is the god who accomplishes all things.
> (*Il.* 19.85–90)

Here Agamemnon refuses to accept blame for his actions, on the grounds that he was himself a victim, deceived and deluded by the gods and fate. Does this mean that Agamemnon is not responsible for what he did? Yet, when he realizes that he acted as he did *because* he was confused, he agrees to make restitution to Achilles:

> But since I was beguiled and Zeus took my *phrenes* away from me,
> I am willing to make all good and give back gifts in abundance. (*Il.*
>   19.137–38)

Agamemnon's reasoning is perplexing. The reason why he is not to blame (*aitios*) is the very reason why he accepts responsibility. Is he confused? Or is he, perhaps, being disingenuous? Or does Agamemnon have a different concept of responsibility from our own?[16]

At the end of the same book (*Iliad* 19) there is a bizarre echo to Agamemnon's apology, when Xanthus the horse addresses Achilles:

> We shall still keep you safe for this time, O hard Achilles.
> And yet the day of your death is near, but it is not we
> who are to blame (*aitioi*), but a great god and powerful fate (*moira*). . . .
>   (*Il.* 19.408–10)

What is the point of this curious episode? Does the horse Xanthus purport to be blameless in the same sense as Agamemnon? How seriously should we take Xanthus's disavowal? Should this scene prompt us to reconsider Agamemnon's earlier disclaimer?

In any case it is debatable whether the foregoing speeches represent Homer's "official" view on fate and responsibility. The speaker in each case has cause for special pleading: Patroclus to diminish Hector's victory, Priam to excuse Helen, and Agamemnon to exculpate himself. These speeches in the *Iliad* may be intended to shift credit or blame from the speaker or someone else to the gods. In the *Odyssey*, however, Zeus contemptuously rejects this line of defense:

> Oh for shame, how the mortals place the blame on us (*aitioōntai*)
> gods, for they say evils come from us, but it is they, rather,
> who by their own recklessness win sorrow beyond fate (*huper moron*) . . .
> as now lately, beyond fate, Aegisthus married
> the wife of Atreus's son and murdered him on his homecoming,
> though he knew it was sheer destruction, for we ourselves had told him,
> sending Hermes, the mighty watcher, Argeïphontes,
> not to kill the man, nor court his lady for marriage;
> for vengeance would come on him from Orestes, son of Atreides,
> whenever he came of age and longed for his country.

So Hermes told him, but for all his good intention (*phroneōn*) he could
not
persuade the *phrenes* of Aegisthus. And now he has paid for everything.
    (*Od.* 1.32–43)

Zeus implies that Aegisthus had only himself to blame, because the gods with good
will warned him as to the consequences of the actions that he intended.[17]
    It is only in the *Odyssey* that Zeus explicitly disavows blame for human mis-
steps.[18] The *Iliad* lays ample ground for such a disavowal, however, when humans
defy fate and ignore the warnings of the gods. For example, Patroclus ignores the
warning of Apollo to stop attacking the Trojans (*Il.* 16.707–09) and thus helps
bring about his own destruction.
    Mortals may also simply fail to understand omens and prophecies from the
gods. For example, Polyphemus the Cyclops realizes his error as soon as Odysseus
reveals his name:

Ah now, a prophecy spoken of old is come to completion . . .

how I must lose the sight of my eye at the hands of Odysseus.
But always I was on the lookout for a man handsome
and tall, with great endowment of strength on him, to come here;
but now the end of it is that a little man, niddering, feeble,
has taken away the sight of my eye, first making me helpless
with wine. (*Od.* 9.507, 512–17)

By misinterpreting the prophecy Polyphemus contributes to its fulfillment.
    Zeus's defense of the gods relies on a crucial presupposition: Human beings
face alternatives and are able to follow different courses of action. This may be
suggested by Zeus's allegation that Aegisthus acted "beyond fate"—or in defiance
of his destiny—when it was revealed to him. Similarly Patroclus voluntarily defied
the warning of Apollo when he continued to attack the Trojans.
    This presupposition may be justified if human beings can act on their own
initiative even when they are influenced by the gods. This is implied when Phoenix
futilely urges Achilles to suppress his anger and accept Agamemnon's gifts: "But do
not think (*noei*) these things in your *phrenes*, and may no / *daimōn* turn you that
way, dear friend" (*Il.* 9.600–01). The word *daimōn* refers to a divine agent who
might lead Achilles astray.[19] A puzzle arises, however, from Phoenix's subsequent
observations that Achilles has made his own *thumos* savage (628–29) and that the
gods "made the *thumos* in [Achilles'] chest implacable and bad for the sake of a
girl" (636–38). How can it be up to Achilles whether his *thumos* is savage if a
divine agent is really in control? Phoenix seems to see no problem, because he tries
to persuade Achilles to settle his dispute with Agamemnon. Elsewhere, however,

Homer suggests a tension between human agency and divine causation. As to why Telemachus mysteriously departed, Medon says to Penelope,

> I do not know whether some god moved him, or whether his own *thumos*
> had the impulse to go to Pylos, in order to find out
> about his father's homecoming, or what fate he had met with. (*Od.*
> 4.712–13)

Here self-direction and divine motivation seem to be incompatible explanations.

Achilles offers a possible explanation how individual self-direction might be reconciled with fate:

> For my mother Thetis the goddess of the silver feet tells me
> I carry two sorts of destiny (*kēr*) toward my end in death. Either,
> if I stay here and fight beside the city of the Trojans,
> my return home is gone, but my fame shall be everlasting;
> but if I return home to the beloved land of my fathers,
> the excellence of my glory is gone, but there will be a long life
> left for me, and my end in death will not come to me quickly. (*Il.* 9.410–
> 16)

Achilles, like his comrades, has, in effect, a disjunctive destiny. Fate offers them a choice, and each alternative has predictable consequences. Although everyone is fated to die eventually, when and how is up to each person. Human beings, it would seem, are to that extent the masters of their fates.[20]

We should, however, again be wary of taking Achilles as Homer's official spokesman about fate. Achilles' assumption that he controls his destiny will soon be called into question. What he says is partly true. The decision whether or not to fight is up to him. But his refusal to fight sets in motion a series of untoward events: the deaths of many comrades including Patroclus, whom he allowed to die. Although, as his mother reminds him, Zeus has accomplished what he prayed for (*Il.* 18.74–77), Achilles has lost Patroclus and hence his desire to live: "I must die soon, then; since I was not to stand by my comrade / when he was killed" (*Il.* 18.98–99). After exacting his revenge from Hector, Achilles says,

> I will accept my own destiny (*kēr*) at whatever
> time Zeus wishes to bring it about and the other immortals.
> For not even the strength of Heracles escaped destiny,
> although he was dearest of all to lord Zeus, son of Cronus,
> but his fate (*moira*) beat him under, and the wearisome anger of Hera.
> So I likewise, if such is the fate which has been wrought for me

shall lie still, when I am dead. But now I shall win excellent fame. (*Il.* 18.115–21)

Achilles now accepts his fate and impending death. But his attitude is active rather than passive fatalism as he returns to the field of battle.

In the closing scene of the *Iliad* Achilles recognizes the parallel between Priam and his own father Peleus, who is also soon to mourn a son slain in battle. With the famous image of the two urns of Zeus, the one of evils, the other of blessings, Achilles realizes that all human beings are in the grip of fate, suffering violent reversals of fortune beyond their control. So he puts aside his wrath and permits Priam to take Hector's body for proper burial (*Il.* 24.525–30).

Homer's purpose was of course not to present a theory of agency and responsibility, but to tell a story in the course of which many characters—mortal and divine—seek to justify their actions or excuse themselves, attempt to change the course of fate, and reconcile themselves to unexpected misfortunes. Still, Homer's references to fate and divine intervention raise difficult questions: Are human actions due to external forces (the gods) as well as to human agents themselves? If so, are these actions causally "overdetermined"? To the extent that our actions are predestined and not really up to us, how can we be responsible for them? Do we deserve credit or blame for what we do, or should we be excused when the outcome is due to forces beyond our control? Even if our lives are governed by fate, is the course of these lives determined in important ways by our own choices? Do our own free choices have a role in the unfolding of fate? Is it possible for us to defy our own destiny, or are all such efforts doomed to fail? If we think that we cannot overcome fate, is the appropriate response passive acquiescence or active engagement? These perplexing questions are part of Homer's legacy to philosophical psychology.

Life and Afterlife

Homer's term *psuchē* is notoriously difficult to translate. It does not correspond to "soul" as used in modern English.[21] Sometimes it seems to refer to the force that animates a living creature. In this sense it is closely related to the verb *psuchō*, "breathe." For example, when Achilles pursues Hector around the walls of Troy and "they ran for the *psuchē* of Hector," *psuchē* seems to be equivalent to "life" (*Il.* 22.159–61; cf. 9.322, *Od.* 9.423, 22.245). When the *psuchē* is lost, only a body (*sōma*) or corpse (*nekros*) remains (see *Il.* 22.257–59): after Patroclus kills Sarpedon, he pulls his spear out of the body, "and the *phrenes* came away with it / so that he drew out with spearhead the *psuchē* of Sarpedon" (*Il.* 16.504–05). Here the *psuchē* exits the wound like a final breath. But the *psuchē* also continues to exist after death:

[Patroclus] spoke, and as he spoke the end of death closed in upon him,
and the *psuchē* fluttering out of the limbs went down into Hades' house
mourning her destiny (*potmos*), leaving youth and manhood behind.
     (*Il.* 16.855–57; cf. 22.361–63)

Patroclus's *psuchē* here is spoken of as fluttering like a bird; but when it appears to
Achilles in a dream, it is described as an image (*eidōlon*) of the living man:

And there came to him the *psuchē* of unhappy Patroclus
all in his likeness for stature, and the lovely eyes, and voice,
and wore such clothing as Patroclus had worn on his body;
and it stood over his head and spoke a word to him:
"You sleep, Achilles; you have forgotten me; but you were not
careless of me when I lived, but only in death. Bury me
as quickly as may be, let me pass through the gates of Hades.
The *psuchai*, the images (*eidōla*) of dead men, hold me at a distance,
and will not let me cross the river and mingle among them,
but I wander as I am by Hades' house of the wide gates . . . "
. . . with his own arms [Achilles] reached for him, but could not
take him, but the *psuchē* went underground, like smoke,
With a thin cry . . .
. . . Achilles uttered sorrowful words:
"Oh wonder! Even in the house of Hades there is something left,
a *psuchē* and an image (*eidōlon*), but there is no *phrenes* in it at all."
     (*Il.* 23.65–74, 99–101, 102–04)

Here, because the *psuchē* lacks vital organs, it sounds like a disembodied ghost.[22]
     This account raises several questions. The powers of awareness and of com-
munication are explicitly attributed to the *psuchē* (or *eidōlon*) after death but not
to the *psuchē* (or life force) before death. Does *psuchē* then denote two distinct
and unrelated entities? Or did the *psuchē* possess these powers all along but we are
unaware of this during life? There is no indication of such an unconscious soul in
the Homeric texts.[23] It is thus left unexplained how these different powers—the
life force and awareness—are connected.
     Another difficulty involves the relation of the *psuchē* to the deceased person.
To call the *psuchē* of Patroclus an image of him implies that it is something different from him. This distinction is also implied by the opening lines of the *Iliad*
quoted earlier:

. . . the wrath of Peleus's son Achilles
and its devastation, which put pains countless upon the Achaeans
and hurled to Hades many strong *psuchai*

Of heroes, but gave them (*autous*) to be the feasting of dogs
and of all birds . . . (*Il.* 1.1–5)

Here the hero is distinguished from his *psuchē*: *he* is fed to dogs and birds, while
his *psuchē* goes to the underworld. If the hero continues to exist after death in
any form, it is as his body (*sōma*) or corpse (*nekros*). The posthumous existence of
the *psuchē* does not indicate what we would understand as *personal* survival after
death. For as Achilles remarks, the *psuchē* lacks the vital organs (*phrenes*) necessary
for thought, feeling, and intention. A more complicated view of the deceased,
however, is expressed by Andromache, who speaks to her dead husband, Hector:
"Now you go down to the house of Hades in the secret places / of the earth,
and left me here behind in the sorrow of mourning . . . " (*Il.* 22.482–83). The
"you" (*su*) addressed by Andromache here seems to be the *psuchē* that has vacated
Hector's body and gone to Hades' house. Later in this soliloquy, Andromache
addresses Hector again:

> But now on you, beside the curving ships, far away from your parents,
> the writhing worms will feed, when the dogs have had enough,
> [you who are] naked, though in your house there is clothing laid up . . .
> But all of these I will burn up in the fire's blazing,
> no use to you, since you will not be laid away in them . . . (*Il.* 22.508–10,
>   512–13)

Here Andromache uses "you" to refer to Hector's corpse. How can Andromache
identify Hector with both his corpse and with his *psuchē*? We would expect identity
claims to satisfy the requirement of transitivity. If A is the same as B and B is the
same as C, then we would expect A to be the same as C.

Another, possibly related, difficulty involves the relation between *psuchē*
and *thumos*. In contrast to the *thumos*, which is involved in thoughts, feelings,
and intentions, the *psuchē* on Homer's account has no such involvement in the
conscious lives of human beings. Does this mean that the *psuchē* and the *thumos*
are different things?[24] However, both the *psuchē* and the *thumos* are lost at death,
as Odysseus hears from his mother's *psuchē* in the underworld:

> . . . it is the way of mortals, whenever they die,
> The sinews no longer hold the flesh and the bones together,
> and once the *thumos* has left the white bones, all the rest
> is made subject to the fire's strong fury,
> but the *psuchē* flitters out like a dream and flies away. (*Od.* 11.218–22)

Perhaps the *psuchē* and *thumos* have different fates after death. The *psuchē* (the
"breath-soul" or animating principle) survives after death and flies to the underworld

(*Il.* 16.856, 22.362). The *thumos* (the "sentient soul," the principle of conscious awareness) leaves the limbs at death (*Il.* 22.68) but ceases to exist. The surviving *psuchē* without *thumos* is incapable of a genuine conscious life. This neat solution unfortunately faces serious textual difficulties. Nestor tells the Achaeans how Peleus, father of Achilles, would die if he heard of their cowardice:

> Now if he were to hear how all cringe away from Hector,
> many a time he would lift up his very hands to the immortals,
> and the *thumos* from his limbs would go down to the house of Hades. (*Il.*
> 7.129–31)

Homer also indicates that the deceased person still has a *thumos*: for example, when Deïphobos avenges his friend Asius, he boasts,

> Now Asius lies not all unavenged. I think rather,
> as he goes down to Hades of the Gates, the strong one,
> he will be cheerful in *thumos*, since I have sent him an escort. (*Il.* 13.414–
> 16)

These passages suggest that Homer is inconsistent in his use of terms. He sometimes distinguishes *thumos* and *psuchē* and sometimes treats them as if they were equivalent, for example, in a passage describing Andromache's reaction when she sees her dead husband Hector's body being dragged behind Achilles' chariot:

> She fell backward, and gasped the *psuchē* from her, and far off
> threw from her head the shining gear that ordered her headdress . . .
> And about her stood thronging her husband's sisters and the wives of his
> brothers
> and these, in her despair for death, held her up among them.
> But when she breathed and the *thumos* was gathered into her *phrenes* . . .
> (*Il.* 22.467–75)

When she faints the *psuchē* leaves her body—fainting is a "near death" experience. But when she recovers, it is the *thumos* rather than the *psuchē* that is gathered into her *phrenes* (cf. *Od.* 5.458, 24.349).

  Is Homer in fact using these terms loosely, or are there subtle distinctions that we do not detect? If he does use them imprecisely, does this reflect an inexactness endemic to ordinary language? Or is he perhaps guided in his choice of words by poetic considerations? Homer leaves us then with puzzles: What is the relation of *psuchē* to the *thumos*? And what is the relation between the *psuchē* in life and the *psuchē* after death?[25] If something of a human being remains after death, what does it take with it—any of the life, thoughts, feelings, and intentions—of the living person? If anything does survive, is it in some way the same as the person who was formerly alive?[26]

Homeric *Aporiai* and the Origins of Philosophical Psychology

The previous sections show that a careful reading of Homer reveals serious *aporiai* (puzzles): For example, are we unified selves or compounds of conflicting elements? Are we responsible for our actions or merely instruments of fate or the gods? Do we survive our deaths and, if so, in what form? Different and antithetical answers to these questions are implied by different passages of Homer. The many speeches represent widely varying and opposing perspectives, of gods and mortals, men and women, heroes and ordinary people, brave men and cowards. Homer himself may not have been aware of these problems. Many of us hold problematic or even inconsistent beliefs without realizing it. But the difficulties lying just beneath the surface can be unearthed by a skillful interrogator or through critical self-examination. It is not surprising that the careful listeners (and later readers) of Homer found themselves in perplexity.[27]

Such *aporiai* gave rise to philosophy, as Aristotle remarks:

It is because they wonder that human beings both philosophize now and began at first to philosophize; originally they wondered at the obvious absurdities, then little by little they progressed and went through the puzzles about greater matters, for example, what happens concerning the moon, sun, and stars and the genesis of the whole universe. A man who is puzzled and wonders thinks himself ignorant (that is why the lover of myth is in a way a philosopher, for myth is composed of wonderful things). (*Metaphysics* A.2.982b12–19)

In addition to the cosmological wonders mentioned here by Aristotle, Homer's epics also contain many psychological wonders that served to fuel philosophical speculation. This "aporetic" approach to Homer was anticipated by W. C. Greene, who argued that "On the whole Homer recognizes no essential conflict, as did certain later poets and philosophers, between the power of Fate and the will of Zeus (and other gods), between the remote power and the immediate agency." According to Greene, "to ask whether Homer believes in fate or in freedom of the will is to ask an idle question; like most men he believes in both—in the power of external forces (*Moira*, given expression by Zeus), and in man's own choices."[28]

The aporetic approach also provides a useful perspective on recent Homer scholarship. The contending interpretive schools may be viewed as attempts to resolve the *aporiai* within a coherent reconstruction of Homeric "folk psychology." Over the past century many scholars have joined either of two opposed schools of interpretation. According to one school, Homer represents a "primitive" folk psychology prevalent in his era that later gave way to the more sophisticated philosophical psychology of classical Greece. The influential Bruno Snell argued that Homer had no term for the whole of a human's mental faculty, corresponding to the "mind" or "soul" in the modern sense.[29] In fact, Snell contended, Homer did not even conceive of the body as a unity. "Of course the Homeric man had a body exactly like the later Greeks, but he did not know it *qua* body, but merely as the sum total of his limbs." For example, Homer's term *sōma* refers only to the corpse. Likewise, Snell argued, Homer had no concept of the mind as a unity. "What we interpret as the soul, Homeric man splits up into three components each of which he defines by the analogy of physical organs." These three components are *psuchē*, *thumos*, and *noos*. Of these, *psuchē*, "the force which keeps the human being alive," has no connection with "the thinking and feeling soul." *Thumos* is "the generator of motion or agitation" corresponding roughly to the power of emotion and to individual impulses to act. Unlike *psuchē*, which survives in the house of Hades, *thumos* is inextricably tied to the *phrenes*, so it ceases to exist after death. *Noos*, as "the cause of ideas and images," involves both the power of intelligence and individual thoughts or images. Because Homer has no concept of mind, he has no concept of "mental conflict"; what we understand as such, Homer describes as "the contention between a man and one of his organs." Moreover, there is no concept of a human being as a responsible agent. There are no "genuine personal decisions; even where a hero is shown pondering two alternatives the intervention of the gods plays the key role. . . . Mental and spiritual acts are due to the impact of external factors, and man is the open target of a great many forces which impinge on him, and penetrate his very core." Because the gods greatly surpass humans in power and intelligence and often control human actions, they are capable of responsible action in a way that humans are not. Snell and his allies argued that it was anachronistic to ascribe to Homer modern "rationalist" conceptions of consciousness, personal identity, and autonomy.[30]

This once dominant interpretation has come under fierce attack in more recent years. Hugh Lloyd-Jones objected that Snell and Dodds had gone too far in emphasizing the irrational features of Greek thinking, "believing that or acting as if Homer's world were itself primitive and depriving his human characters of all power of decision and mental independence."[31] Bernard Knox also noted passages that suggest a Homeric conception of the unified individual personality: "There is above all the hero's name, the name he proudly bears and proclaims on all occasions, whether exulting over a fallen enemy or claiming his share of glory, that name Odysseus conceals in the Cyclops' cave and later proudly—and, as it turns out, rashly—announces to his blinded enemy."[32] The proper name designates "the heroic self." Further, Bernard Williams argued that Homer's characters are manifestly "unities" to which thoughts and experiences belong. Homer's characters have desires, beliefs, and purposes, and hence reasons for action, and they deliberate on the basis of these reasons and act as a result of their deliberations. Although Homer's words differ from ours, beneath them "lies a complex net of concepts in terms of which particular actions are explained, and this net was the same for Homer as it is for us. Indeed, if it were not how could we understand Homer as presenting us with human actions at all?"[33] Richard Gaskin, finally, contended that "Homeric decision-making stands up as a fully self-conscious, autonomous activity."[34]

From the aporetic standpoint defended in this essay, these opposed interpretations are different ways of trying to resolve the manifest difficulties in Homer's text within the context of Homeric folk psychology. However, a reconstruction of Homeric folk psychology presupposes answers to controversial questions about what Homer "really meant." When Homer uses a term such as *psuchē* in different contexts, does he intend to refer to the same thing or to different things?[35] Whenever Homer uses two different words, for example *psuchē* and *thumos*, does he always intend to refer to different things?[36] If Homer does not have a word for something, for example, "mind," does this show that he lacks the corresponding concept?[37] When Homer describes a psychological process, for example, a person speaking to his own *thumos* or heart, should this be understood literally or treated as a *façon de parler*?[38] What background assumptions is it reasonable to make in interpreting a given event as described by Homer? Is the fact that Agamemnon finally makes amends to Achilles (*Il.* 19.137; cf. 9.115–19) evidence of his "undiminished responsibility" as we would understand it? Would it matter to Homer whether or not Agamemnon was in "control" of himself when he insulted Achilles?[39]

The aporetic approach proposed here does not require definitive solutions to these difficult issues, because it is concerned instead with how Homer's works were received by later Greek thinkers. The approach is consistent with the hypothesis that Homer may have used poetical language to express ideas that were not fully developed and that he may have expressed claims without recognizing that they were puzzling or paradoxical. The analysis of concepts and the resolution of *aporiai* were not, after all, in Homer's job description.

The Greek philosophers grasped that Homer was not one of them. Heraclitus criticized Homer, "the wisest of all the Greeks," for what he failed to see: "For some children who were killing lice deceived him by saying, 'What we saw and caught we leave behind, what we neither saw nor caught we take with us.' "[40] Homer failed to see the paradoxical character of the phenomena as he described them. Aristotle contrasted Homer with a philosophical poet: "Homer and Empedocles have nothing in common but the meter. That is why it is right to call the one a poet, and to call the other a natural scientist rather than a poet" (*Poetics* 1.1447b17). Aristotle's main point was that Empedocles should not be called a poet, but he could well have added that Homer should be called a poet *rather than a natural scientist*. For Homer was not concerned to present a theoretical explanation of thought and action, and it is sometimes uncertain whether his selection of a particular term is due to poetic rather than semantic considerations. For all that, Homer's robust

portrayals of thought and action abound with *aporiai* and marvels that have been
an enduring source of wonder and speculation.

Notes

The author acknowledges Thomas Banchich for helpful suggestions and Pamela Phil-
lips for many valuable comments on several drafts of this essay. I am also very grateful to
William Wians for editorial guidance.

1. DK 21B10, from Aelius Herodian, *Peri dichronōn* 16.17–22.

2. DK 21B11, from Sextus Empiricus, *Adversus mathematicos* 9.193; cf. 1.289
(trans. Jonathan Barnes).

3. Werner Jaeger, *The Theology of the Early Greek Philosophers* (Oxford: Clarendon
Press, 1947), 42.

4. DK21B23, from Clement of Alexandria, *Stromata* 5.14.109.

5. *Nicomachean Ethics* 7.3.1145b3–4. Aristotle's method is to resolve the puzzles
by confirming all of the "reputable opinions" (*endoxa*) about the subject matter or, failing
this, the majority of them and the most authoritative.

6. "*Akērioi*" means literally "without a heart" (*kēr*), a term discussed further on.
Translations from Homer are based on Richmond Lattimore, *The Iliad of Homer* (Chicago: University of Chicago Press, 1951) and *The Odyssey of Homer* (Chicago: University
of Chicago Press, 1965), although changes are made wherever necessary for the sake of
consistency, including the spelling of proper names and the translation or transliteration
of psychological terms.

7. The word *thumos* along with other key psychological terms in Homer—including
psuchē, phrenes, and *noos*—will remain transliterated throughout this essay. These words have
no precise English equivalents, and translations such as "soul," "spirit," and "mind" often have
misleading implications. The meanings of each of these difficult terms will be discussed.

8. Bernard Knox, *The Oldest Dead White European Males and Other Reflections on
the Classics* (New York: Norton, 1993), 43, views this passage as evidence for "a Homeric
conception of the unified individual personality." Later Alcinous asks a stranger for his
name: "No one among all the peoples, neither base man / nor noble, is altogether name-
less, once he has been born, / but always his parents as soon as they bring him forth put
upon him / a name" (*Od.* 8.550–55). The stranger replies: "I am Odysseus son of Laertes,
known before all men / for craftiness, and my fame goes up to the heavens" (9.19–20). A
hero's name may even be the source of immortal fame, as the suitors in the underworld
tell Achilles: "Even now you have died, you have not lost your name, but always / in the
sight of mankind your fame shall be great, Achilles" (*Od.* 24.93–94).

9. *Thumos* is associated with anger (4.494, 13.660, 21.456), awe (6.167), care
(23.62), expectation or hope (10.355, 13.8), fear (8.138, 9.8, 13.163, 17.625), joy (1.256,
7.189), love (1.196, 9.343), reproach (3.438), shame (15.561), sorrow (2.171), and vengeance
(7.254). This is a small sample; there are also many examples in the *Odyssey*.

10. Although *phrenes* is commonly translated "midriff" or "diaphragm," it may instead
refer to the lungs. Robert B. Onians argues that the *phrenes* (identified with lungs) surround
the *kēr* (i.e., heart) and hold the *thumos* (i.e., breath), in *The Origins of European Thought*

about the Body, the Mind, the Soul, the World, Time, and Fate (Cambridge: Cambridge University Press, 1951), 23–43. This interpretation is defended by Richard Janko, *The Iliad: A Commentary, Vol. 4, Books 15–16* (Cambridge: Cambridge University Press, 1992), 379–80. In contrast, Michael Clarke argues that "since Homer does not think in terms of X-rays and neat textbook diagrams, the organs will naturally be less sharply defined for him than for us, so that the distinctions between different organs and processes will necessarily seem blurred," in *Flesh and Spirit in the Songs of Homer: A Study of Words and Myths* (Oxford: Clarendon Press, 1999), 79.

11. The epithet "dear" (*philos*) is often used for one's own parts, e.g., *philon kēr*, "dear heart," at *Iliad* 1.491.

12. The same refrain is uttered by Achilles at *Iliad* 22.385, cited previously. See also 17.97, 21.562, 22.122.

13. The verb *phroneō*—often meaning to think, consider, meditate, have a mind to, etc.—is connected with the noun *phrēn*. Sometimes this verb is closely linked to motivation: "They were thinking ahead and eager to fight" (*Il.* 13.134; cf. 12.124 and *Od.* 5.89 and 7.75). Again, "If she thinks friendly things in her *thumos*, there is hope that you will see your loved ones and return to your home" (*Od.* 6.313–14, 7.75–76).

14. Similarly Achilles suggests that what he says in his *thumos* is opposed by the anger in his heart (*Il.* 9.645–46).

15. Plato was fascinated by the episode at *Odyssey* 20.5–21. Indeed he quotes from it three times: once in the *Phaedo* (94d) and twice in the *Republic* (3.390d, 4.441b). Although he uses the example very differently in these two dialogues, he derives the same fundamental lesson: the apparent simplicity of the human self conceals a deeper complexity. Later on, Heraclitus the Grammarian (ca. 100 AD) accused Plato of stealing his tripartite psychology from Homer (*Homeric Problems* 17–18).

16. For contrasting treatments of this passage see E. R. Dodds, *The Greeks and the Irrational* (Berkeley and Los Angeles: University of California Press, 1951), chap. 1, and Richard Gaskin, "Do Homeric Heroes Make Real Decisions?" in Douglas L. Cairns, ed., *Oxford Readings in Homer's Iliad* (Oxford: Oxford University Press, 2001 [orig. 1990]), 147–69. On the relation between Homer's term *aitios* and later Greek concepts of responsibility, see Mario Vegetti, "Culpability, Responsibility, Cause: Philosophy, Historiography, and Medicine in the Fifth Century," in A. A. Long, ed., *The Cambridge Companion to Early Greek Philosophy* (Cambridge: Cambridge University Press, 1999), 271–89.

17. The failure of humans to heed warnings of their own fate is an important theme of the *Odyssey* (beginning with 1.7). Penelope's suitors disregard prophecies of their eventual death at the hands of Odysseus. For example, Eurymachus dismisses the prediction of Halitherses (*Od.* 2.155–88) and later that of Theoclymenus (20.350–62). Ironically, soon after Zeus rejects the blame for the fate of Aegisthus, Telemachus remarks that "Zeus is somehow to blame (*aitios*), who gives to each man the way he wills it" (*Od.* 1.348–49; cf. 6.187–88, 11.558–60).

18. Some scholars maintain that the *Odyssey* places greater emphasis than the *Iliad* on individual responsibility of human beings. See, for example, Herman Fränkel, *Early Greek Poetry and Philosophy*, trans. Moses Hadas and James Willis (Oxford: Oxford University Press, 1975); Albin Lesky, "Divine and Human Causation in Homeric Epic," trans. Leofranc Holford-Strevens, in Douglas L. Cairns, ed., *Oxford Readings in Homer's Iliad* (Oxford: Oxford University Press, 2001 [orig. 1961]), 170–202; and Janko 1992, 3–4.

This involves thorny problems about how, when, and by whom the Homeric epics were composed, concerning which a recent overview is Robert Fowler, "The Homeric Question," in Robert Fowler, ed., *The Cambridge Companion to Homer* (Cambridge: Cambridge University Press, 2004), 220–32.

19. Lattimore's translation misleadingly locates the *daimōn* within Achilles: "Listen then; do not have such a thought in your mind; let not / the spirit within you turn you that way, / dear friend." Lattimore's "within you" corresponds to nothing in the Greek. Hence, Lesky 2001, 178, comments, "The modern translator finds the dual causality unfamiliar and attempts to eliminate it by making the *daimōn* another power operating inside the human being. That is of course un-Homeric, for the *daimōn* operates from outside the human being's *phrenes*, from the divine world." Lattimore does assume an external agent elsewhere, for example, at *Iliad* 11.480: "some spirit (*daimōn*) leads that way a dangerous lion."

20. Similarly, the seer Polyidos told his son Euchenor that he must die at home of a painful illness or go to Troy and be killed, so that Euchenor "knew well his destiny (*kēr*)" when he boarded the ship for Troy (*Il.* 13.665–68).

21. Clarke 1999, 39, emphasizes the hazards of translating terms such as *psuchē*: "Words like 'soul,' 'mind,' and 'self' lack concrete or verifiable referents, so they have an especially insidious power over the categories of our thought." A cardinal thesis of his book is that translating *psuchē* as "soul" implies a body-soul dualism that is alien to Homer's thought.

22. Limitations of space prevent fuller treatment of Homer's descriptions of postmortem existence, which involve further complications and apparent inconsistencies. I plan to discuss these issues in a future essay.

23. Pindar (fr. 131) makes reference to such an "image of life" (*aiōnos eidōlon*) that survives death and that sleeps while the human being is awake. Erwin Rohde argued that this expresses what Homer meant by the *psuchē* "far more explicitly than Homer"; see *Psyche: The Cult of Souls and Belief in Immortality among the Ancient Greeks*, trans. W. B. Hillis (Chicago: Ares, 1987, repr. eighth ed. [orig. 1893]), 7. Otto criticized this interpretation as anachronistic and without basis in Homer, and was forced to view Homer's usage as equivocal; W. F. Otto, *Die Manen oder Von den Urformen des Totenglaubens* (Darmstadt: Wissenschaftliche Buchgesellschaft, 1983 [orig. 1923]), 4–10; cf. Jaeger 1947, 75–76.

24. This is argued by Onians 1951 and Bruno Snell, *The Discovery of the Mind*, trans. T. G. Rosenmeyer (Cambridge: Harvard University Press, 1953 [orig. 1948]). See section 6.

25. Martha Nussbaum argues that Heraclitus's treatment of *psuchē* as a central life faculty is a radical departure from and implicit criticism of Homer, in "*Psuchē* in Heraclitus," *Phronesis* 17 (1972), 1–16 and 153–70. Nussbaum relies heavily on Snell's interpretation (on which the last section in this chapter).

26. Related to questions about the *psuchē* is the issue of *noos* and human knowledge. The problems that this raises are complex and require separate treatment, which I hope to pursue on another occasion. For important and often diverging treatments of these issues, see: K. von Fritz, "*Nous* and *Noein* in the Homeric Poems," *Classical Philology* 38 (1943), 79–93, and "*Nous, Noein,* and Their Derivatives in Pre-Socratic Philosophy (excluding Anaxagoras)," *Classical Philolology* 40 (1945), 223–42; Snell 1953; H. Fränkel, "Xenophanes' Empiricism and His Critique of Knowledge," trans. Matthew R. Cosgrove, in Alexander P. D. Mourelatos, ed., *The Pre-Socratics: A Collection of Critical Essays* (New York: Anchor, 1974 [orig. 1925]), 124 n. 20, and, *Wege und Formen frühgriechischen Denkens: Literarische*

und philosophiegeschichtliche Studien, ed. Franz Tietze (Munich: C. H. Beck, 1968, third ed.); E. Heitsch, "Das Wissen des Xenophanes," *Rheinisches Museum* 109 (1966), 193–235; E. Hussey, "The Beginnings of Epistemology: From Homer to Philolaus," in Stephen Everson, ed., *Companions to Ancient Thought vol. 1: Epistemology* (Cambridge: Cambridge University Press, 1990), 11–38; J. H. Lesher, "The Emergence of Philosophical Interest in Cognition," *Oxford Studies in Ancient Philosophy* 12 (1994), 1–34; and "Early Interest in Knowledge," in A. A. Long, ed., *The Cambridge Companion to Early Greek Philosophy* (Cambridge: Cambridge University Press, 1999), 225–49.

27. Marcel Detienne, *The Creation of Mythology*, trans. Margaret Cook (Chicago: University of Chicago Press, 1986 [orig. 1981]), 68–70, argues that the introduction of writing facilitated an intellectual distance between traditional texts and their later readers and thus permitted interpretation and criticism of the sort offered by Xenophanes and Heraclitus.

28. William Chase Greene, *Moira: Fate, Good, and Evil in Greek Thought* (New York: Harper & Row, 1963 [orig. 1944]), 14, 22.

29. Snell acknowledged as an important source the dissertation by Joachim Böhme, *Die Seele und das Ich im homerischen Epos* (Leipzig and Berlin: Teubner, 1929).

30. Snell 1953, 8–9, 12–15, 19–20. This primitivist approach was also embraced by E. R. Dodds 1951, 15, who reiterated that "Homeric man has no unified concept of what we call 'soul' or 'personality,'" Along similar lines, Robert Onians 1951, 2, cautioned that "the perfection of [Homer's] art and the rationalism of his race must not blind us to the strangeness of his world." This approach has been defended more recently by Christian Voigt, *Überlegung und Entscheidung: Studien zur Selbstauffassung des Menschen bei Homer*, Beiträge zur klassischen Philologie, Heft 48 (Meisenheim am Glan: Anton Hain, 1972) and H. Erbse, "Nachlese zur homerischen Psychologie," *Hermes* 118 (1990), 1–17.

31. Hugh Lloyd-Jones, *The Justice of Zeus* (Berkeley and Los Angeles: University of California Press, 1971), 10.

32. Knox 1993, 43–44.

33. Bernard Williams, *Shame and Necessity* (Berkeley and Los Angeles: University of California Press, 1993), 21–38.

34. Gaskin 2001, 167.

35. The difficulty of providing a satisfactory interpretation of Homeric *psuchē* is illustrated by two recent books: David B. Claus, *Toward the Soul: An Inquiry into the Meaning of* Psuchē *before Plato* (New Haven, Conn.: Yale University Press, 1981) and Jan Bremmer, *The Early Greek Concept of the Soul* (Princeton: Princeton University Press, 1983). Claus argues that *psuchē* is essentially a "life-force," whereas for Bremmer it above all represents "the individuality of the person," so that it is able to preserve the identity of the self, in distinction from the mortal body. In a review of both works, Leonard Woodbury argues that each suffers from a certain one-sidedness: "Neither view can, I believe, be accepted, but each may nevertheless serve as a complement and corrective to the other. For we should not doubt that *psuchē* is some kind of life-principle, while affirming that it contributes also, in some sense, to the identity of the man"; L. Woodbury, "Two New Works on the Early Greek View of the Soul," *Ancient Philosophy* 3 (1983), 200–10.

36. A difficulty for Snell's thesis that Homer sharply distinguishes *thumos*, the "organ" of emotion, from *psuchē*, which departs the limbs at death, is that Homer describes *thumos* as leaving the body for Hades, and he ascribes *thumos* to the deceased in the underworld

(see *Iliad* 7.131, quoted earlier in this chapter). Conceding that "the concepts of *thumos* and *psuchē* are easily confused," Snell 1953, 11, conjectures that the substitution of *thumos* for *psuchē* is due to a "contaminated" verse, probably due to "a rhapsode who confused several sections of verses in his memory, a common enough occurrence in oral delivery." G. S. Kirk describes *Iliad* 7.131 as "casual, not to say careless, since it is the *psuchē* not the *thumos* that normally descends to Hades," in *The Iliad: A Commentary*, Vol. 2, *Books 5–8* (Cambridge: Cambridge University Press, 1990), 252.

37. A thing does not become "an object of thought . . . until it is seen and known and designated by a word" (Snell 1953, 8). This "lexical principle" also seems open to obvious counterexamples. Knox 1993, 41–42, remarks that English lacks an exact equivalent to *Schadenfreude*, yet English speakers understand very well what it means to enjoy the misfortunes of others. See also Gaskin 2001, 151–54, for criticisms of Snell's lexical principle.

38. T. Jahn argues that terms such as *thumos, phrenes, kradiē,* and *kēr* are chosen on poetical grounds; *Zum Wortfeld 'Seele-Geist' in der Sprache Homers, Zetemata*, 83 (Munich: C. H. Beck, 1987).

39. See Dodds 1951, 3, and Gaskin 2001, 155, for very different interpretations of this passage.

40. DK 22 B56, in Hippolytus, *Refutation of All Heresies* 9.9 (trans. Jonathan Barnes).

3

Alētheia from Poetry into Philosophy

Homer to Parmenides

Rose Cherubin

Parmenides was the first Greek philosopher to speak thematically about *to eon* (what is, being, that which is). He also furnished the earliest extant examples of deductive inference in Greek philosophy and gave them a central place. In large part because of these contributions, the histories of philosophy find in his work the origins or first steps or foundations of crucial features of philosophy as we know it today.

Parmenides' groundbreaking philosophical work was a poem. It has frequently been suggested, at least since Plato, that there is a quarrel or conflict, or at minimum a strict division, between philosophy and poetry.[1] Ancient Greek poetry routinely conveyed uninvestigable tales and praised gods and humans on unexamined conventional grounds. The more that philosophy draws on and develops Parmenides' innovations—the more that it pursues systematic inquiry and investigation into the nature of what is, and the more that it uses and explores deductive reasoning—the more we today might expect it to diverge from poetry.

In so far as the projects, practices, and exigencies of philosophy differ in many aspects from those of any kind of poetry, it is appropriate to raise the question of how and why philosophy and poetry might function together in a single work, and specifically in Parmenides' poem. For example, what ends could they combine to pursue, and how could they do so? We have no warrant to assume at the outset that Parmenides' use of poetic elements and form was merely a formal literary device or a kind of window dressing (i.e., superficial to his meaning), or that it represents a lapse in his pursuit of philosophical goals, or a failure to take philosophical procedures and exigencies seriously.[2]

Against a "window-dressing" interpretation we may note first that Parmenides' fragments make extensive and integral use of phrases, images, and terminology

51

borrowed from earlier poetry. His use of verse was not simply a matter of having chosen a metered structure over an unmetered one. Secondly—and this begins to address the other unwarranted assumptions as well—the fragments do not rehearse unreflectively a divinely inspired account, nor do they pay uncritical allegiance to conventional mores.[3] Parmenides' poem, then, did not simply echo or reaffirm earlier notions, but rather developed them in radically transformative ways. Parmenides' philosophical work, I will argue here, depends both on poetic features and on their transformation through a kind of critical analysis.

The very features I have cited as Parmenides' best-known and most consequential contributions to philosophy—the central role of deductive argument and the thematic exploration of *to eon*—grow from his engagement with poetry. Specifically, they are intimately connected to his view of *alētheia* as the orientation of a road of inquiry. Poets in and before Parmenides' time saw the apprehension and promulgation of *alētheia* as a central duty of poetry. Parmenides, I will show, significantly extended and developed the notion of *alētheia*. It is precisely this development that issues in his thematic exploration of *to eon* and in his use (and, conceivably, introduction) of explicit deductive inference.

Let us begin by opening the questions of the meaning and the role of *alētheia* in the fragments of Parmenides. Asking these questions is crucial not only for our understanding of Parmenides, but also for our understanding of those ways of thinking today that claim him as a predecessor, and for our understanding of the possibilities of philosophy itself. In his references to *alētheia*, might Parmenides have intended something in addition to, or instead of, what has been attributed to him so far? If so, as I will argue here, then Parmenides will have shown us a road of inquiry to which we have been oblivious.

Alētheia in Poetry from Homer to the Fifth Century

Over the past century philosophers and philologists have developed two main lines along which to read *alētheia* in Parmenides. The first takes *alētheia* to mean "truth," "*Wahrheit*," "*vérité*," "*verdad*," and so forth. The second, drawing on the etymology of the word as alpha privative plus *lēthē*, takes it to mean "unconcealment," "unhiddenness," "*Unverborgenheit*," "*dévoilement*," "*noncrypture*,"[4] and the like.[5] I propose to show here why neither of these is adequate. I do not assert that either is wholly inaccurate. Rather, I will show first of all that both *truth* and *unconcealment* fail to capture important features of known usage of *alētheia* in and before the early fifth century BCE.[6] Secondly, I will show, neither *truth* nor *unconcealment* requires (or ensures) that *eon* will have the characteristics that Parmenides' goddess attributes to it in B8.

To begin to understand the role of *alētheia* in Parmenides, let us investigate first its meaning and use in and before his time.[7] It is now generally accepted that the root of *alētheia* (*alatheia* in Doric dialect) is *lath-* / *lēth-*, a root signify-ing forgetting, oblivion, escaping notice, lack of awareness. In and before the fifth century, *lanthanō* or *lēthē* means "I escape notice," "I am unnoticed." *Lēthomai* or *lanthanomai* means "I forget," "I let [something] escape me." *Lēthē* means "for-getting," "forgetfulness," and is the name of a place of oblivion. *Alētheia* adds an alpha privative to this root, and so should connote something opposed to these. But opposed in what way?

Some contemporary thinkers would assimilate all *alētheia* to unconcealment or disclosure, all *lēthē* to concealment or closing off. Heidegger, for example, says that *lanthanō* means "I am concealed" ("*Lanthanō* heißt: 'ich bin verborgen' ").[8] The illustrations he provides do not in fact establish this. He cites first (on page 34) *Odyssey* 8.93, where Odysseus, shedding tears, is not noticed (*elanthane*) by anyone but Alcinous. Odysseus is not noticed because he has covered his head with his cloak (verses 83–85). Thus he is unnoticed *because* he has concealed his face; this does not suggest that *elanthane* itself *means* that he (or his weeping) was concealed. Heidegger's second illustration (35) is *Iliad* 22.277, where Athena retrieves Achilles' spear and returns it to him, and is unnoticed by Hector (*lathe d' Hektora*) in doing so. Heidegger holds that "Thought in a Greek way, however, it means (heißt es): Athena was concealed to Hector in her giving back of the spear." Yet it is not at all clear why the expression should *mean* that; Homer gives no indication as to why Hector did not notice Athena.

J.-P. Levet differs from Heidegger in that he finds *alētheia* to refer to trans-missions of information more than to the reality about which information is transmitted. Still, Levet understands *alētheia* in terms of what he calls the "non-voilé-dévoilant," the not-veiled-unveiling. He portrays *alētheia* as the dissipation of "l'ignorance qui obscurcit [la] conscience," the ignorance or lack of awareness that obscures or clouds consciousness.[9] Thus his gloss of *alētheia* derives from his reliance on the metaphor of obscuring, darkening, covering, clouding. Levet does not consider whether any circumstance other than concealment could be responsible for the failure to notice something.

To understand what *alētheia* might mean and to what it might refer, then, we must make another study of its usage. Homer uses *alētheia* exclusively or almost exclusively to characterize expressions, reports, or transmissions of information; specifically, he uses it of communications that are supposed to be true, compre-hensive of all relevant details, undistorted, free of falsehoods, and complete.[10] As I will argue presently, examples of usage from Homer to the fifth century show that *alētheia* is not the same as unhiddenness, unconcealment, *Unverborgenheit*, *dévoilement*. It is quite possible to fail to notice something that is not concealed. Anyone who has ever searched a house for keys that he or she was holding in hand during the search, or who has ever looked for the eyeglasses he or she was wearing while looking, can attest to that. Nor do forgetting or ignoring necessarily entail concealment. As Krischer has noted, "in 'verborgen sein [to be concealed]' the possibility of observation is denied, however in *lanthanein* the occurrence of it [sc. is denied]," and *lēthē* makes even direct observation full of gaps.[11] For instance, in observing one thing we may overlook another that was in fact available to sense. *Alētheia* invokes the notion of not going unnoticed. It does this without reference to any specific reason or means (e.g., concealment, obtuseness of the observer) for why something fails to be noticed or for why someone fails to notice.

Some representative Homeric examples: At *Odyssey* 11.507, Odysseus recounts his response to a request by Achilles' shade for information about Peleus and Neoptolemus. Odysseus says that he has heard nothing of Peleus, but that he will tell all the *alētheia* (*pasan alētheiēn muthēsomai*) concerning Neoptolemus.[12] Odysseus draws his fairly detailed account of Neoptolemus's exploits from what he himself has witnessed, and ends where the two parted ways. Odysseus's ability to give the *alētheia* thus extends as far as he has information that is reliable (he has witnessed the events himself and is considered a competent judge of what he has witnessed) and complete in all the relevant details. Nothing suggests that Odysseus is concealing anything. Nothing suggests that anything about Neoptolemus's deeds or character during the time they were together has been concealed from him. The fact that Odysseus contrasts his ignorance of Peleus's situation with his firsthand knowledge of Neoptolemus's suggests that his ability to transmit *alētheia* depends also on his awareness that he has not missed anything relevant.

At *Odyssey* 17.108, Telemachus tells Penelope that he will detail to her the *alētheia* (*alētheiēn katalexa*) concerning his journey to find out about Odysseus.[13] He recounts exactly the pertinent details of what Nestor and Menelaus told him. He even mentions that part of Menelaus's report in which Menelaus vowed not to digress from the story, deceive, or hide or conceal anything (*parex epoimi paraklidon oud' apatēsō . . . ouden . . . krupsō oud' epikeusō*, 139 and 141; cf. 4.348 and 350). Thus the presentation of *alētheia* implies awareness of pertinent detail, either directly or from a reliable (e.g., sworn and trustworthy) source, complete conveying of that detail, and avoidance of embellishment, digression, deception, and concealment (i.e., these are not to be included even in addition to the true and accurate details).

At *Odyssey* 21.212, Odysseus promises to reward the herdsmen for their loyalty and assistance if he should succeed in vanquishing the suitors: *hōs esetai per, alētheiē katalexō*, "I will tell you the *alētheia*, just as it will be." Depending on what one takes to be the subject of *esetai*, the *alētheia* may characterize either the content of Odysseus's speech or the object, the reference of his speech. Constantineau reads in the latter way, so that in this speech *alētheia* refers to *what* will be, to *what* is to come.[14] To say "how it is" is the same thing as to say "that which is," argues Constantineau ("dire 'comment c'est,' c'est la même chose que dire 'ce qui est,' " 223), so that *alētheia* is "comment cela a été, est, ou sera" (225).

The association between *alētheia* and addressing the whole of a situation accurately is reinforced by the final example that I will present from Homer, *Iliad*

23.359–61. There Achilles stations Phoenix at the turning post of the chariot racecourse, *hōs memneoito dromou kai alētheiēn apoeipoi*, "so that he might mark the running and report the *alētheia*."[15] Phoenix is being charged with the task of taking careful note of what happens in the race and then conveying this to the others accurately and completely. Certainly we may infer that he is not to conceal things, but to focus on that issue misses the point that he is being placed at the turning post so that he might notice things that others could not (and not necessarily because those things were concealed).

In this example we see *alētheia* linked with *mimnēskō*, "I mark," "I notice," "I remember." This is entirely in keeping with an opposition to *lanthanō*, "I escape notice," and *lanthanomai*, "I forget."[16] Later poets such as Parmenides' contemporaries Pindar and Bacchylides emphasize the connections between *alētheia* and *mimnēskō/mnēmē* (remembrance, memory, keeping in mind), and between *alētheia* and *noein*. They also consider *alētheia* in opposition to the opposites of these: forgetting and oblivion.

Indeed, in their odes Bacchylides and Pindar often describe the poet's task as assuring the continued awareness, the persistence of memory, of the athletes' great deeds, and thus assuring the immortality of the deeds themselves. In *Ode* 9, Bacchylides says that his song will make Automedes' victory at Nemea "manifest to generations yet to come," that Automedes' "noble deed, as it wins hymns of praise, will be placed above with the gods," and that "with [the aid of] the *alatheia* of mortals, a most beautiful plaything of the Muses [viz., the poem] is left when one dies" (9.81–87).[17] The first word of the ode is *doxan*, "fame" or "repute"; Bacchylides calls upon the Muses to grant the repute that convinces mortals (*peisimbroton*, 9.2). In verses 20–21 of *Ode* 8, he declares that with *alatheia* it is appropriate that all [things] shine forth (or, all must shine forth, *sun alatheiai de pan lampei chreos*). *Ode* 3.90–98 asserts that it is not silence that brings adornment to the man of accomplishment, but rather the *alatheiai* of his achievements as sung by the poet. Here as well, Bacchylides marks a contrast between silence or oblivion on the one hand and *alatheia* on the other. He implies that only a Muse-inspired poet such as he can furnish the *alatheia* (*areta[s]* . . . *ou minuthei brotōn hama s[ōm]ati phengos, alla Mousa nin tr[ephei]*, 90–92).

In *Ode* 13, Bacchylides elaborates on the importance of his work. Verses 199–209 ask that the wise man be praised *sun dikai*, with justice or as is just. For mortals, the poet says, blame (*mōmos*) is in every deed (that is, mortals find something blameworthy in every deed), but *alatheia* loves to win out, and time always increases (makes grow) that which is nobly done, while the speech of enemies wanes. Detienne argues that *mōmos* is closely associated with silence or oblivion.[18] Bacchylides' *Ode* 13 certainly invites such a reading. The poet states that he is doing what is just in hymning great deeds and wisdom, that his poem will demonstrate this (*alatheia* will be victorious), and time will bear him out. The poem is crucial to the victory of *alatheia* and to the fulfillment of justice.

Without it, time might not have the opportunity to preserve and emphasize the noble deed, and an injustice would be done.

In *Olympian* 10, Pindar imprecates a Muse and the personified Alatheia, daughter of Zeus, to help him pay with interest the debt of song he owes Hagēsidamos (10.4–9).[19] Failure to pay this would result in blame or reproach (*epimomphan*, etymologically related to *mōmos*, 10.8). Consonant with Detienne's thesis, Pindar later declares that with this poem, Hagēsidamos's beautiful victory will win fame instead of silence (10.91–96). At 10.52–59, the middle of the poem, we find what may be a further guarantor of the appropriate fame of poet and athlete: The founding of the Olympic Games, Pindar says, was attended by the Moirai and Chronos *ho t' exelenchōn monos alatheian etētumon*, "the only assayer/prover of what truly is." As *etētumos* often refers to what will turn out to be, or to be true, the meaning may be that Chronos (Time) is the only one who can assess what will really and wholly turn out to be.[20]

Similarly, in *Olympian* 2, proclaiming under oath (*enorkian*) the *alatheia* aims for the great fame (*eukleas*) of Thērōn. In this ode, Pindar holds that what is in his mind or awareness (i.e., not just his words) bears *alatheia*; he will speak *alathei nooi*, "with the *alathēs* in mind."

With access to *alētheia* comes responsibility for its promulgation and use. *Olympian* 10 spoke of the poet's responsibility to convey it in the case of a victory. At *Nemean* 5.14–18, Pindar says that he will not tell of a deed that was not done in justice, for "not every exact *alatheia* is more profitable for showing its face and silence is many times the wiser for a person to conceive" (*ou toi hapasa kerdiōn phainoisa prosōpon alathei' atrekēs kai to sigan pollakis esti sophōtaton anthrōpōi noēsai*). The deed not done in justice was associated with the early days of a founding (mythological) family of the athletic victor's city, so the wisdom of keeping silent about it would suggest that the deed deserves no fame, and that the greatness of the city and its citizens would be sullied or vitiated by a retelling of that fundamental base act. The poet has evidently judged that the victor and his family do not deserve such an indignity.

Nemean 7 considers a further implication of the poet's access to *alētheia*. Mnēmosunē, goddess of memory and mother of the Muses, enables inspired poets to provide a reward or recompense for the toils that result in beautiful deeds (7.14–16). Pindar warns, though, that some poets do not convey the *alatheia*; he finds Homer to have failed in this regard. Most people, Pindar says, have a blind heart (*tuphlon ētor*), failing to see (*idemen*) the *alatheia* for themselves (7.20–25). It is therefore the responsibility of the inspired poet to correct the false information imparted by others, for the good of the listeners.

Two additional features of *alētheia* will be noteworthy for the interpretation of Parmenides. First, let us note that for Pindar and Bacchylides, the beings who convey *alētheia* are divinities and, with their aid, some kings and inspired poets. For these poets, as Pindar and Bacchylides both declare and illustrate, presenting *alētheia* about a victory calls for an account of the past exploits of the victor, his family's high station, the great deeds of his forebears, the founding and history of his city, and the establishment of the games at which he distinguished himself.[21] If, as its etymology suggests, *alētheia* means something like non-oblivion; or if, as earlier poets have implied, presenting *alētheia* means not letting relevant facts go unnoticed and not consigning important things to oblivion; then what Pindar and Bacchylides do in their odes is just what the task of conveying *alētheia* would demand. They are acknowledging the history, the context, and the origins of the praiseworthy deeds and people. They are trying to bestow on their subjects and to convey to their listeners a full measure of glory.

More than that, Pindar and Bacchylides are working to *show* that this praise is what is due.[22] They do this by displaying the wider context of the victory and the place that the victor occupies in the larger scheme of the life and history of the Greeks. For Pindar and Bacchylides, this work involves tracing the victor (and his greatness) back to his origins, understood genealogically.[23] Pindar makes this explicit in *Olympian* 7.13–23: in praising Diagoras of Rhodes, Pindar is also praising Diagoras's father Damagētos, who pleases Dikē (Justice). The poet declares further that in presenting this account he will set forth their story from its *archē* (source). This source is the establishment of the cities of Rhodes and the deeds of its founder, Diagoras's ancestor Tlapolemos. In Parmenides, this requirement that *alētheia* reach the origins of its subject will be reflected in the connection between *alētheia* and the inquiry into what is in its completeness; the origins sought will not be only genealogical. While Parmenides' goddess calls her account of a road in DK B8 a *muthos*, that account does not take us to that remote "mythological" past (such as the founding of Rhodes) to which only Muses and gods have direct access, and which they sometimes reveal to inspired poets. Instead, as we will see in the following section, Parmenides' goddess bids us examine roads of inquiry, of human seeking.

The last important feature of *alētheia* that I will mention is the connection between *alētheia* on the one hand, and *themis* and *dikē* on the other. Bacchylides sometimes associates *alētheia* with *dikē* or with what is due: 13.202, discussed previously; 5.187–97; compare Pindar *Olympian* 10.1–25, and *Nemean* 5.14–18, also discussed previously.[24] In Parmenides, of course, Dikē and Themis guide the young man to the goddess who announces that he is to learn the heart of *alētheia* (B1.29), and both show up again in her discussion of the characteristics of *to eon* in B8.[25] Parmenides mentions *anankē* (necessity) and *moira* (portion) in the same context, and I will consider their relationships to *alētheia* presently.

Let us summarize, then, our findings concerning the sense and reference of *alētheia* from Homer to the early fifth century. *Alētheia* is not equivalent to truth or to unconcealment, though it incorporates truth and it can involve unconcealment. To present *alētheia* is to do more than to say something true, or to state the truth. Whereas the opposite of truth is falsity or falsehood, *alētheia* is opposed not only to *pseudos* (lie, falsehood) but also to *lēthē* (oblivion, forgetting) and its relatives. We might start to characterize *alētheia* by saying that it is something like the truth, the whole truth, and nothing but the truth. We would then need to add the further specifications that *alētheia katalegein* cannot include lies, mistakes, errors, misapprehensions, gaps, or other inaccuracies; and cannot (wittingly or unwittingly) distort, conceal, omit, or ignore anything pertinent to the topic at hand. To be able to tell *alētheia* requires an awareness of the whole of what is relevant, and awareness of the context of one's subject. This suggests another contrast with truth: we can say that someone has "guessed the truth," or that he or she has "stated the truth" in making an accurate surmise from less than complete evidence. I have found no comparable uses of *alētheia* in and before the early fifth century, and I suggest cautiously that there can be none.[26] As Odysseus's careful specification of the limits of his awareness of the fates of Peleus and Neoptolemus shows, the ability to state *alētheia* depends on being aware of the limits of one's knowledge. (Ultimately, in Xenophanes and Parmenides, the ability to say how what is, is will require an awareness of the whole of what is, *as* whole.) In Pindar and in Hesiod's account of the Muses, awareness of the origins of things (of the cosmos, of a city, of a family) is a requisite for presenting current events properly in one's poem. Awareness of these origins is necessary in order to be able to give each thing and person its due and to present each in its proper place (according to *dikē*) in the world. There is then something explanatory in *alētheia*, and that aspect will figure prominently in Parmenides' fragments.

Alētheia in the Fragments of Parmenides

The word *alētheia* appears in Parmenides in three places: At DK B1.29–30, the goddess announces that her visitor, the *kouros* in the chariot, is to learn both the heart of *alētheia* and the opinions of mortals. At B2.3–4, discussing roads of inquiry, she identifies the road *hopōs estin te kai hōs ouk esti mē einai*—roughly, how it is and how it is not not to be—as the road of Peithō and Alētheia. This seems to be the road that she discusses from B8.1–49, after which (8.50–51) she abruptly announces a stop to her "trustworthy speech and *noēma amphis alētheiēs*"—all around *alētheia*.

Since Parmenides wrote of roads of inquiry and a journey of learning, we must ask a further question: How was *alētheia* supposed to be learned or gained? The verbs that fifth-century and earlier poets used to name the awareness that allows one to present *alētheia* were *mimnēskō*, *noeō*, and their relatives. How did one come by these? Homer's Odysseus, Menelaus, Phoenix, and Nestor are supposed to be able to state *alētheia* or the *alēthēs* on the basis of personal observation and trustworthy promises. Telemachus and Menelaus can do so on the basis of having heard reports from people who have shown themselves to be trustworthy.

Hesiod, Pindar, and Bacchylides get their *alētheia* from the Muses (daughters of Mnēmosunē). None of these writers mention any form of seeking *alētheia* besides imprecating Muses and asking questions of eyewitnesses.

In common with the other poets, Parmenides invokes *noein* often in the goddess's account of the road associated with *alētheia*.[27] Strikingly, though, in the fragments of Parmenides there are no words related to *mnēmē* (memory) or *mimnēskō* (I remember, I mark).[28] Instead, the road associated with *alētheia* in Parmenides is a road of inquiry (*hodos dizēsios*, B2.2, B6.3, B6.4; by implication B7.3, B8.1, 8.18). The other poets did not connect *dizēsis* with *alētheia*, much less did they invoke *elenchos* (B7.5).

More than striking, then, Parmenides' account is revolutionary. In associating a road of inquiry with *alētheia*, he is suggesting that *alētheia* might be accessible by inquiry or seeking. Or at very least, he is suggesting that inquiry can be oriented or guided by *alētheia*.[29] He is suggesting that sometimes even where we cannot witness something ourselves, where we may have overlooked or forgotten something about a situation, where we cannot find a reliable witness, and where the gods or their agents have not chosen to reveal things to us; even when these traditional means are not available, we may still have access to a road whose orientation is governed by *alētheia*, and that road is a road of inquiry.

Alētheia, Inquiry, and the Binding of *To Eon*

But how, when, and why would inquiry be up to the task of attaining *alētheia*? One would think that such an unusual suggestion would call for some justification, and we are fortunate to have material in the fragments of Parmenides that offers just that. The characteristics of *to eon* on the road of B8.1–49 provide the key. I propose to show that if *alētheia* is to be accessible through or even compatible with inquiry, then *to eon* must have these characteristics. If we say and conceive (B6.1, B8.8) that *to eon* has these characteristics, inquiry will be possible and will be compatible with *alētheia*.

We may begin by noting that the characteristics that the goddess says belong to *to eon* on the road of inquiry that she discusses from B8.1–49 are more than what is needed to support truth in an everyday sense. For example, what would characteristics of what *is* such as freedom from coming to be and destruction (8.3, 8.13–14, 8.21), continuousness (8.6, 8.25), and leaving nothing unfulfilled (8.32, and 8.4 reading *ēde teleston* with Cordero and Tarán) have to do with what is true *now*?[30] It is hard to see what these characteristics have to do even with eternal truths such as those of mathematics: is it necessary that all of what is be free from coming to be and destruction in order for there to be eternal truths about numbers?[31]

While Parmenides does not use a word equivalent to *knowledge* in the discussion of roads of inquiry, he does carry on the traditional association of *noein* (to conceive, to have in mind, to intend) with *alētheia*.[32] However, he delineates that association in a new and more precise way. *Noein* addresses precisely that which is, but it can be mistaken.[33] Parmenides investigates the question of exactly when we can justifiably trust that *noein* will not be mistaken, the question of when and how *alētheia* and *noein* go together.

Let us now consider the relationship between *alētheia* and the specific characteristics that the goddess says *to eon* must have on the road of inquiry in B8.1–49. The goddess says that *to eon* is bound to have these characteristics by Dikē, Anankē, and Moira. At B8.6–21, Dikē binds *to eon* so that it neither comes to be nor is destroyed. *Dikē* was traditionally associated with enforcing patterns, regularities, order, and the "appropriate way" of a thing or kind of thing.[34] According-ing to Parmenides' goddess, as we will see, coming to be and destruction introduce discontinuity and so are inimical to the presence of any overall order, pattern, or way of things. Now, the possibility of inquiry or seeking relies on the presence of regularities and order. We could not inquire about anything if it followed no consistent order, or if it could come to be from any random thing, or from nothing (so that there was no assurance that anything persists through the metamorphosis). The very possibility of using a language or any other symbol system for seeking would be undermined, for a system of symbols has rules and patterns.

What has Dikē's binding of *to eon* to do with *alētheia*? We have seen that giving *alētheia* often involves indicating the origins of a thing or situation in order to show what makes it what it is. If what is, or any being, could come to be or be destroyed, there would be no reliable way to identify the origins or the basis of anything.[35] If, as the goddess argues, what is cannot come to be or perish, then in principle a basis is available. For at least some kinds of things this will produce a fundamental tension, since after all one kind of origin is supposed to be a beginning in time, or else the coming-into-being of something. Also, iden-tifying exactly what something is seemingly includes identifying where and when it begins and ends.

If on our road of inquiry we give up the notion that what is can come to be and perish, what if any advantage do we gain? If giving *alētheia* means being able to explain what a thing or situation really is, and situating it in its appropri-ate context, then it would be reasonable to hold that giving the *alētheia* involves accounting for the thing or situation in terms of some sort of origins. After all, that should give insight into the nature of the subject, and explain what brought it to be as it is. The goddess argues that one should not and cannot say or conceive that what is came to be from what is not (8.7–8, 8.12–13) or from nothing (8.10).[36] Now, to be assured that what came before did in fact bring a thing or situation to be as it is, one needs to understand why these conditions *must* have had the result one is claiming for them (namely, the way the thing under study is now). And this simply cannot be done, the goddess argues, if we insist on a temporal beginning (8.9–15). It cannot be done if we insist on a temporal beginning for the whole of what is, and it cannot be done if we insist on a temporal beginning for any individual *eon* among a purported multitude.

If we specify a temporal beginning in order to account for a thing through its origin, we must say how and why that is the beginning. We must ask what that which began came from, and how it came to be. If it came to be, it did so either from nothing or from something other than itself. If something could come to be from nothing, however, all possibility of explanation would be lost; our whole project of accounting would be in vain. For *nothing* could not be a cause or a reason for anything (B8.9–10). If we took "nothing" to be a reason or cause, then we would have to say that anything could be as it is for any reason or for no reason, and anything could follow from anything else. There would be no explanation. If *alētheia* involves grasping the whole of something, or grasping something through its origins, then to conceive that what is could come to be from nothing will be incompatible with *alētheia*.

Would *alētheia* allow that something could come to be from something else, or that one situation could arise out of another? (This idea might arise if we read *esti* and *eon* predicationally, and so allow that there could be more than one *eon*.)[37] But if something came to be out of something that was not it, then any account of the origin of the new thing must explain the fate of and provide a reckoning for those aspects of the old one that are not aspects of the new one and vice versa. For example, if a thing B came to be physically from another thing A, what happened to the shape, color, and constituents of A? How can we trace the appearance of the shape, color, and constituents of B? We have seen that we cannot say that the old features vanished into nothing and the new came to be from nothing, and still hope for *alētheia*. The only way to preserve the possibility of *alētheia* would be if we could conceive (with consistency) of the old thing or condition and the new as continuous with one another, in such a way that the aspects of one can be traced and shown to be the necessary cause or effect of the aspects of the other. In that case, there would be no gap or division between the old and the new; they would be one. The purported change from old to new would be continuous, so one might well ask how distinct states and things could be determined at all, without contradiction. That problem will await Aristotle. For Parmenides' goddess, the result is simply that coming to be and perishing are ruled out on the road of inquiry in question, at B8.20–21.

So much for the work of Dikē. How does Anankē's binding of *to eon* on the road of inquiry of B8.1–49 square with the exigencies of *alētheia*? Traditionally, *anankē* was associated with constraint and with the necessary ensuing of consequences.[38] Understood in this way, *anankē* is a requisite for the drawing of conclusions, for if it is not in place, we cannot reason about consequences, causes, or effects. If *anankē* is not in place, anything (or nothing) could follow from anything. The process of elimination is unimaginable without something like *anankē*. Therefore *anankē* is a requisite for *dizēsis*, inquiry or seeking. The roads of which

Parmenides' goddess speaks are precisely roads of *dizēsis*. In Parmenides B8.31–33, Anankē binds *to eon* such that it is not incomplete (*ateleutēton*) or lacking (*epidees*). Without *anankē* as just described, *to eon* could indeed be incomplete or lacking: necessary implications and consequences might not be fulfilled, and nothing would be a necessary or a sufficient condition for anything.

Fulfillment and completion were also traditionally associated with statements of *alētheia*, as Detienne has shown.[39] We might say that *to eon* is complete if we find in it all causes, ramifications, implications, and results that must appertain to it in order for it to be what it is. We might then say that *to eon* would be incomplete if it did not include some undeniable consequence, aspect, cause, or association of what it is. We have seen that *alētheia* requires awareness of all relevant details, or grasp of the whole of a situation, which means it also requires that all relevant details be available to grasp. Surely that is not possible if *to eon* is incomplete, or if our conception of it implies that it is incomplete.

For example, if Odysseus had failed to take into account some circumstances that would prevent him even in victory from fulfilling his promise to the herdsmen, he would not have been telling them *alētheia*. Pindar warns us in *Nemean* 5.16–18 that he is going to leave out some inglorious details instead of letting show *alathei' atrekēs* (precise or accurate *alētheia*) when it is better to observe (*noēsai*) silence. Clearly, then, *alētheia* requires that what is be complete, without gaps or lacks; and it requires that we conceive and speak of it as complete. To be able to present *alētheia*, one must be aware of what is *as* complete.

The binding of *to eon* by Moira supplies another of the requisites for inquiry and for *alētheia*, namely, that what is must be whole, unmoving, and unaccompanied (B8.36–38). As fate, lot, or proper portion, *moira* traditionally assured that proper or due consequences ensued, that each thing and person had a proper place and certain range of characteristics proper to it: a proper or due share of what is.[40] That inquiry relies on this is evident; we could not tell what to look for or what we were looking at if each thing did not have characteristics proper to it and a certain place or set of relationships with respect to others. From this we can see what Moira would have to do with *to eon*'s being whole, unmoving, and unaccompanied. While *whole* (*oulon*) sometimes means "complete," which sense we have treated in discussing *anankē*, it can also mean "without internal divisions," "all of a piece," "not composed of discrete parts." This sense of *whole* connotes continuity (B8.6 and 22). If the sum of things and relations was not continuous, if it had gaps, then causal and explanatory linkages could not be ascertained, and we could not identify a proper place or range for each thing. Then we could not identify things with any assurance. Similarly, if the complex of things and relations were unstable (not *akinēton*, 8.38), we could not determine what was proper to each. If something else, that is, something discontinuous with *to eon*, were to be alongside of it (*allo parex tou eontos*, 8.37), then we could not account for anything that is without accounting for that which is outside of *to eon*. But outside of *to eon* could not be what is not, according to Parmenides' goddess, so the case returns to that of the internally divided *to eon*. We have seen that that case precludes inquiry.

If there are gaps or discontinuities in what is, or if there is fundamental instability, then *alētheia* will not be possible. We have seen that *alētheia* leaves nothing out, renders everything in its proper condition and relations, and is incompatible with gaps in knowledge or in awareness of the topic at hand. But if *alētheia* requires that there be no gaps in one's knowledge or awareness, it requires that there be no gaps, no unexplainable breaks, in what that knowledge or awareness addresses.

With this we see how *alētheia* requires that *to eon* be as Parmenides' goddess describes it in B8.1–49. We can also see why one might set such requirements for *to eon*: they make inquiry and coherence possible as well, and so suggest that the human endeavor of inquiry could at least in principle lead to the discovery and articulation of *alētheia*. More precisely, inquiry may lead to the discovery and articulation of *alētheia* if their requisites are not contradictory or paradoxical.

Parmenides has presented to us the conditions for the possibility of inquiry and of *alētheia*, given the ways of speaking and conceiving that make the poem intelligible. Let us note that the goddess's account of the roads of inquiry and the opinions of mortals is reached through a journey that invokes the social and cosmic landscapes that contribute to the everyday experience of a fifth-century Greek. As we have seen, the ways of speaking and conceiving that make the poem intelligible, and the familiar social and cosmic landscapes mentioned in the proem (and of course in other poetry), are in fact at odds with some of the requisites of inquiry and *alētheia*, even as they provide others. In other words, at least when the journey begins from the framework Parmenides presents, the requisites of inquiry and *alētheia* do seem to be in some conflict. Whether, then, those conditions of the possibility of inquiry and *alētheia* can be fulfilled is another question. It is a question that calls for reflection on the implications of the terms through which those conditions are brought to light (as exemplified in the tale of the journey and in the goddess's use of negatives and plurals in her speech). Only with this reflection will the full force and potential of *alētheia* be available.

Alētheia, Truth, and Unconcealment

What of truth and unconcealment? I have argued that the characteristics that the goddess lays out in B8.1–49 for the road associated with *alētheia* go far beyond what is required to support truth, unconcealment, or both together. I will now provide three examples to illustrate this point. All have to do with the issue of the completeness of *to eon*.

(1) Suppose that we assert that there are at least some discrete spatial things. Through measuring, counting, and calculation we can come up with statements that

we say are true concerning these spatial things. These include statements about the dimensions of the things, the distances between them, and so on. These statements will be true in the sense that they conform to the operative axioms and theories, can be checked, and have predictive success.

In accounting for these spatial things so as to explain and to try to verify their properties and their relationships to one another, we might say that they have definite sizes. If they did not have definite dimensions, or if we could not tell, we would not have grounds for saying they were discrete. We might then add that these sizes can be determined by measuring with sufficiently small units. The most exact measurement, the one that we need in order to show the precise borders and thus the distinctions between things, would use the smallest units. These smallest units could not have zero magnitude, for then aggregations of them would not constitute a positive magnitude. But if each such unit has a positive magnitude, then *its* precise extent needs to be determined, which would require the use of even smaller units, and so on. Pinpointing—and thus verifying—the boundaries of any spatial object calls for an infinite series of measurements, and thus fails to pinpoint anything.[41]

This is not to imply that there are no discrete spatial things. It merely shows that the conceptions through which we try to account for discrete spatial things are inadequate to that task. If we use these conceptions, then our overall notion of what is, is incomplete. It fails to include all that it shows to be needed in order to for what is to be as it is.

(2) Suppose that we assert that questions of the nature of what is are to be answered through scientific pursuits and that questions of purpose, goal, direction, value, good, and meaning are completely distinct from what the sciences study (and hence perhaps to be pursued only through religious faith, mythology, ethics, or the arts). Suppose that we assert further that each of these sets of questions has no bearing on the other, and that indeed their subject matters are essentially independent of one another.[42] In other words, suppose that we assert that we can account for the nature of what is without considering or invoking direction, purpose, good, or value; and that we can explore direction, purpose, good, and value without investigating our basic conception of the nature of what is. We might then call statements "true" when they identify valid implications, when they conform to operative theories and axioms, when they have predictive success (in whatever way that is understood), and so on.

If we make these assertions, we invite questions as to the grounds or warrant for our assertions. If we invoke scientific accounts to justify the separation, our original assertions become either self-contradictory or circular. They become self-contradictory if we have to use scientific accounts to explain the nature of purpose, direction, good, and so on, so as to show why they are incompatible with scientific accounts. They also become self-contradictory if we try to use scientific accounts to show why the two areas *should* be treated separately. Our initial assertions become circular if we are simply assuming that the scientific standpoint is appropriate for making the assertions about how the various kinds of questions are to be treated.[43]

We might then look for a third standpoint that could account for both sides, and so explain their fundamental independence. This third standpoint would have to be able to comprehend both descriptive scientific investigations of the nature of what is, and investigations of purpose, good, and so forth. But the availability of a third standpoint would invalidate the original assertions, because it would imply that the original two sides are compatible and connected, that there is one discourse that can express and analyze both of them and show the relationships between them. If the two sides are connected, they are not entirely independent. Therefore, the idea that there must be distinct and independent spheres for investigating what is misses something that follows from its own description of what is. It posits but cannot account for a separation, and so presents what is as incomplete.

(3) If we assert that what is, is matter and energy, and that nothing that is not matter and/or energy affects what is, then we cannot prove this assertion by using any conception that takes our assertion as axiomatic. Any conception of what is that takes the assertion as axiomatic presents *to eon* as incomplete. Modern natural sciences, then, are not oriented toward *alētheia*, even as they pursue truth. Whether the latter pursuit is in any way hindered by its divergence from the road associated with *alētheia* is not a question for Parmenides, but it is for Aristotle, and it could well be one for us—since we have not answered it.

In all of these cases (1–3), one who made *to eon* out to be incomplete could make true statements. We might say that these statements were conditionally true, true if their assumptions are correct, and/or logically true. One who made *to eon* out to be incomplete but who revealed his or her assumptions as fully as possible would not be concealing anything. Still, one who made the assertions I have mentioned would *not* be presenting *alētheia*, for he or she would not have accounted for the assertions or acknowledged all of what is, all that affects what the assertions address. He or she would have consigned something to oblivion, to *lēthē*. A road whose destination is truth is not oriented by *alētheia*.

Neither does directing one's efforts toward unconcealment orient one entirely toward *alētheia*. As we have seen, there are many ways in which we might fail to be aware of things that are not concealed, many ways other than concealment in which things might escape our notice, and *alētheia* would require gaining awareness of these things too. Further, suppose that the features of what is that were disclosed to us, or our account of them, were to include or invoke arbitrary actions by divinities, or a beginning in time, or a beginning of time, or any other discontinuities. Then our account would be incompatible with *alētheia* as Parmenides has portrayed it, as he has argued that inquiry requires it to be. Therefore, most of the accounts in early Greek poetry, as well as some scientific accounts, will diverge from the pursuit of *alētheia*.

Alētheia, Poetry, and Philosophy in Parmenides

As we have seen, *alētheia* in and before Parmenides' time was supposed to involve being aware of just how things are, or how what is, is: the nature of things, what came before, the sources of things or what made them be as they are, the way things stand now, and what will be. This awareness was supposed to be attainable only through certain kinds of firsthand experience or else through a report from a reliable and reputable source, often necessarily a divine one. Therefore it was not easily available, and there were no systematic or sure ways of seeking it. Firsthand experience might be impossible or inadequate (some things might be beyond one's capacity to notice), and Muses and other divinities might refuse one's requests or willfully deceive.[44] *Alētheia* was prized, and poets strove to imprecate the Muses to convey it, on account of its importance to the best life. *Alētheia* mattered because to see how things really are, to see the real order of the universe, was understood to allow one to know what to do and whom (and how) to praise; and so it was understood as allowing one to live the best life possible, in the sense of following the order and promoting the values that the gods favored and according to which the cosmos worked.

Parmenides demonstrated that the pursuit of *alētheia* required something beyond revelation and observation. Moreover, he showed that there is more to being aware of what is than the earlier poets seemed to suggest. In fact, he revealed that the understanding of the requisites of *alētheia* implicit in that poetry was incomplete and in crucial respects inadequate. The earlier poets had not noted that in order for *alētheia* to be what they described, one who would have or acknowledge it would have to conceive of what is in a certain way. That way was in many respects at odds with what the poets and their listeners took for granted about the world. For Parmenides' goddess argued that to acknowledge that *alētheia* was as described, one must say and conceive that what is, is as the goddess says it is on the road of inquiry she discusses in Parmenides B8.1–49, namely, one, continuous, complete, ungenerated, indestructible, undivided, unchanging, unmoving, and so on. This condition is incompatible and incommensurable with the world of multiple things that we customarily say are, and of which the poets sing. Further, in order to acknowledge *alētheia* as described, one must accept a principle of non-contradiction with respect to *to eon* (see the section on *alētheia* in Parmenides' fragments earlier in this essay, and cf. B6.1–2 and B8.15–18), so that one cannot attempt to resolve the incompatibility by saying that the singular what is both had a beginning and did not, or that the eternal and unchanging *eon* at some point began to generate familiar things. Thus Parmenides' treatment of *to eon* and his use of deductive argument appear through his exploration of the requisites and implications of the poetic goal of *alētheia*. We can therefore see his groundbreaking philosophical contributions as a response to earlier poetry.

Parmenides' development of the implications of *alētheia* reveals it as more than unconcealing and more than truth, and as something beyond what is available through observation, divine revelation, or reports thereon. His expanded vision of *alētheia* challenged his contemporaries and successors, and challenges us, to reconsider and to investigate basic assumptions about what is, and about whether it could be as it is said to be, and indeed about the meaning and validity of speaking and conceiving in terms of being (or coming to be, perishing, change, and so on) at all.

This presents a puzzle, as we have noted. The poets sought to present *alētheia* concerning the nature and condition of the things traditionally said to be, namely, the familiar denizens and furniture of the cosmos: gods, humans, other animals, plants, mountains, and so forth. *Alētheia* was supposed to present what was, what is, and what will be, just as it was, is, or will be. Parmenides' goddess holds that on the road of inquiry she associates with *alētheia*, we must say and conceive that what is, is fundamentally incommensurable and incompatible with the traditional conception, even to the point of precluding a "was" and a "will be" (B8.5). We cannot ignore the conflict, nor can we assume that Parmenides did, first of all because Parmenides frames and introduces the goddess's speech with the tale of the journey by the *kouros* through the familiar environment. The proem if anything emphasizes motion and plurality. Second, and perhaps more importantly, the goddess warns that, on the road of inquiry she associates with *alētheia*, what is (*eon*) is bound by Dikē, Anankē, and Moira. These make inquiry possible, for Parmenides, but they are defined on and in terms of the world of things traditionally said to be. For example, *dikē* was supposed to ensure the regularity of seasonal cycles and the proper characteristics of kinds of things.[45]

This discovery of conflict is not, I suggest, a blow to Parmenides' conception of *alētheia*. Instead, we may look on the discovery of conflict as a further development or implication of *alētheia*. If the project of seeking *alētheia* is to bring all that is, or all that we can conceive to be, to non-oblivion, then it should include the exposition of fundamental difficulties within our conception of what is. In this way we find that Parmenides brought together philosophy's commitment to inquiry (*historia, dizēsis*) and the conception of *alētheia* articulated in poetry, to the transformation, deepening, and development of both.

Notes

Earlier versions of this essay were presented at the 2003 meeting of the Society for Ancient Greek Philosophy, and at the 2004 meeting of the Ancient Philosophy Society. I would like to thank J. Kelsey Wood for his very acute and enlightening response to the essay; William McNeill for his helpful critical questions; and William Wians for his excellent comments and suggestions, as well as for his patience.

This essay is dedicated to the memory of H. S. Thayer, from whose teaching I first learned about Parmenides, and about inquiry.

1. *Republic* 607b. We should note, however, that philosophical work in poetry was not out of the ordinary in Parmenides' time, the fifth century BCE. While most of

the pre-Platonic philosophers whose work survives wrote in prose, Xenophanes before and Empedocles after Parmenides wrote in verse.

2. For an examination of a variety of ways of interpreting poetic elements in Parmenides, see Rose Cherubin, "Parmenides's Poetic Frame," *International Studies in Philosophy* 36 (2004), 7–38.

3. The discussion of *to eon* and roads of inquiry, and all of the deductive inferences, appear within a speech made by a goddess character. It would be mistaken, however, to conclude from this that Parmenides was simply presenting an argument from authority. First of all, the goddess argues for her points about *to eon*, rather than simply stating them. Second, she is discussing what *to eon* must be like (and what it cannot be like) on or for a road of *dizēsis*, inquiry or seeking. Third, she commands her listener in fragment DK B7.5–6 *krinai de logōi poludērin elenchon ex emethen rhēthenta*, "judge/distinguish for yourself by means of reason/an account a much contesting challenge out of what I have said." She exhorts her listener to reason, judge, and understand for himself, not to absorb what she has said without examination. Cf. Patricia Curd, *The Legacy of Parmenides* (Princeton: Princeton University Press, 1998), 20, 62 n107, and 63 n109. (Except where indicated, all translations are my own.)

4. Alexandre Lowit's gloss of *Unverborgenheit* in "Le 'principe' de la lecture heideggerienne de Parménide (*Parmenides*, GA, 54)," *Revue de Philosophie Ancienne* 4 (1986), 163–210, pages 169–72.

5. Exponents of the first line of interpretation include Jonathan Barnes, *The Presocratic Philosophers*, second ed. (London: Routledge and Kegan Paul, 1982), chaps. 9–11 and 14; Montgomery Furth, "Elements of Eleatic Ontology," *Journal of the History of Philosophy* 6 (1971), 111–32; and W. K. C. Guthrie, *A History of Greek Philosophy*, vol. 2 (Cambridge: Cambridge University Press, 1965), part I.A. Exponents of the second include Martin Heidegger, *Vom Wesen der Wahrheit*, in Gesamtausgabe Band 34 (Frankfurt: Klostermann, 1988) and *Parmenides*, in Gesamtausgabe Band 9 (Frankfurt: Klostermann, 1976); and Jean-Pierre Levet, *Le Vrai et le faux dans la pensée grecque archaïque* (Paris: Editions les Belles Lettres, 1976). The two lines need not be mutually exclusive: Ernst Heitsch, *Parmenides*, third ed., Tusculum series (Zurich: Artemis and Winkler, 1995), 92–98, explores the role of proof or evidence in Parmenides, while taking *alētheia* to embrace both *Wahrheit* and *Unverborgenheit*.

6. Cf. Marcel Detienne, *Les Maîtres de vérité dans la grèce archaïque*, rev. ed. (Paris: Editions La Découverte, 1990), 48 and n107.

7. Parmenides' extensive use of images and phrases that refer back to Homer and Hesiod is generally acknowledged and has been illuminated by several important studies; see, e.g., A. H. Coxon, *The Fragments of Parmenides* (Assen/Maastricht, the Netherlands, and Wolfeboro, N.H.: Van Gorcum, 1986); Hermann Diels, *Parmenides Lehrgedicht* (Berlin: Reimer, 1897); Alexander P. D. Mourelatos, *The Route of Parmenides* (New Haven: Yale University Press, 1970); Maja E. Pellikaan-Engel, *Hesiod and Parmenides* (Amsterdam: Hakkert, 1974); Horand Pfeiffer, *Die Stellung des parmenideischen Lehrgedichtes in der epischen Tradition* (Bonn: Habelt, 1975). I will argue in this chapter that lyric poetry of Parmenides' own time offers further clues to his meaning and usage. I do not claim that Parmenides did not innovate, or that meaning and usage were not evolving. The study of earlier and contemporaneous uses gives us a starting point and a point of comparison for our examination of Parmenides.

8. Heidegger 1982, 33.

9. Levet 1976, 96–97.

10. My survey of instances of the term in Homer largely bears out Thomas Cole's description: "*alētheia* is that which is involved in, or results from, a transmission of information that excludes *lēthē*, whether in the form of forgetfulness, failure to notice, or ignoring." See "Archaic Truth," *Quaderni Urbinati di Cultura Classica* 42 (1983), 7–28; his description is on page 8. For Cole, *alētheia* in Homer characterizes speeches rather than objects or states of affairs (8–22).

11. "Dieser Unterschied besteht darin, daß in 'verborgen sein' die Möglichkeit der Wahrnehmung negiert wird, in *lanthanein* aber das Stattfinden derselben." Tilman Krischer, "ETYMOS und ALETHES," *Philologus* 109 (1965), 161–74; pages 162–63.

12. Homer, *The Odyssey*, trans. A. T. Murray, 2 vols., The Loeb Classical Library (Cambridge: Harvard University Press, 1919–1995; vol. I repr. 1984; vol. II second ed. revised by George Dimock, 1995).

13. Here as often in Homer (e.g., at *Od.* 21.212 and *Il.* 24.406), the verb used of the transmission is *katalegō*, "recount at length," "in order," "enumerate," "tell in detail."

14. Philippe Constantineau, "La Question de la vérité chez Parménide," *Phoenix* 41 (1987), 217–40, page 223. Constantineau takes *alētheia* generally to characterize states of affairs and not communications; as Cole (see n10 in this chapter) has shown, this is at odds with other Homeric usage. I think Constantineau is justified, however, in associating *alētheia* with accounts that touch on the whole of a situation and the nature of the situation with accuracy (compare the opening of Pindar *Nemean* 5). Also, Parmenides' range of usage may diverge somewhat from Homer's, as Cole notes (Cole 1983, 24–26).

15. Homer, *The Iliad*, trans. A. T. Murray, 2 vols., The Loeb Classical Library (Cambridge: Harvard University Press, 1924–1925; vol. I repr. 1988; vol. II repr. 1993).

16. See also Egbert Bakker, "Remembering the God's Arrival," *Arethusa* 35 (2002), 63–81; page 70.

17. David Campbell, ed. and trans., *Greek Lyric IV: Bacchylides, Corinna, and Others*, The Loeb Classical Library (Cambridge: Harvard University Press, 1992).

18. Detienne 1990, 21–25. Detienne seems to me to go too far, however, in saying that *mōmos* can be defined, in certain aspects, as a lack of praise (22).

19. Pindar, *Pindar*, ed. and trans. William H. Race, 2 vols., The Loeb Classical Library (Cambridge: Harvard University Press, 1997). On the importance of the notion of fulfillment of promises and oaths in Parmenides, see Rose Cherubin, "Light, Night, and the Opinions of Mortals," *Ancient Philosophy* 25 (2005), 1–23.

20. For a valuable discussion of Homeric examples see Krischer 1965, 166–67.

21. See, e.g., Pindar *Ol.* 2.5–15, 41–52, and 90–95; *Ol.* 10.24–59; *P.* 4.1–67; Bacchylides 13.77ff. Cf. Detienne 1990, 20–21 and 27.

22. The notion that the poem is the victor's due is especially clear in the opening of *Ol.* 10. Pindar owes the poem to Hagēsidamos because he has promised it and the athlete is the poet's guest-friend; but lines 24 and 25 assert that the ordinances (*themites*) of Zeus called forth (*ōrsan*) the song in the first place. *Dikē*, justice, was frequently associated with the rendering of what is due; on the relationship between *dikē* and *alētheia*, see the section on *alētheia* in the fragments of Parmenides later in this essay.

23. Detienne, following Vernant, finds a parallel case in Homer and Hesiod: the ability of those Muses, inspired poets, and seers who can present the *alēthea* (the *alēthēs*

things) to state what is, what will be, and what was (*Theogony* 32 and 38; cf. *Iliad* 1.70 without the word *alēthēs*). See Detienne 1990, 18; and Jean-Pierre Vernant, *Mythe et pensée chez les Grecs*, second ed. (Paris: Editions La Découverte, 1996), part 2, esp. 109–16. See also Constantineau 1987, 223. I present this parallel with the caution that the relationship between *alētheia* and the *alēthēs* is neither simple nor obvious.

24. Respecting the caveat of the previous note, we may compare this with *Theogony* 233–36, where Nereus the *apseudēs* (unlying) and *alēthēs* does not forget (*oude . . . lēthetai*) *themistes* and knows just counsels (*dikaia . . . dēnea oiden*). At *Theogony* 80–90, the daughters of Mnēmosunē, the very Muses who can say *alēthēs* things, confer on some kings the ability to *diakrinonta themistas / itheiēisi dikēisin* (to decide cases with straight judgments; 85–86). The text of Hesiod used here is *Hesiodi Theogonia; Opera et Dies; Scutum; Fragmenta Selecta*, third ed., ed. F. Solmsen, R. Merkelbach, and M. L. West, Oxford Classical Texts (Oxford: Oxford University Press, 1990).

25. For the numbering of the fragments of Parmenides' poem, and for the numbering and text of the fragments of other pre-Platonic philosophers cited here, I follow Hermann Diels and Walther Kranz, *Die Fragmente der Vorsokratiker*, sixth ed. (Berlin: Weidmann, 1951). The text of Parmenides' fragments that I have used, except where otherwise noted, is David Sider and Henry W. Johnstone, Jr., *The Fragments of Parmenides*, Bryn Mawr Greek Commentaries (Bryn Mawr, Penn.: Bryn Mawr Commentaries, 1986).

26. Something close to the notion of guessing the *alēthēs* appears in the next century at *Meno* 97b. There Plato's Socrates refers to *doxa alēthēs*, true opinion (which may be the result of hearsay or guessing), and uses the phrase essentially interchangeably with *orthē doxa*, right opinion. But Plato may well have intended this usage to be problematic. He has Socrates goes on to argue that such opinions are fleeting and need to be bound by means of reasoning about cause (98a). As we have seen, stability and an accounting for sources were features of *alētheia*.

27. The road is that of B2.4, the "road of Peithō." Whether Alētheia follows on Peithō or the reverse depends on whether one accepts the emendation Alētheiēi for Alētheiē. I will not enter into this controversy here. Clearly, though, the goddess is saying that Alētheia and Peithō go together, so that Alētheia is associated with the road of Peithō. When the goddess concludes her account of this road at B8.50–51, she says that this account has been *amphis alētheiēs*, "all around *alētheia*," reinforcing the association between the road and *alētheia* in particular. While the manuscripts of Parmenides' fragments do not have capitalization, some references in the fragments to Alētheia, Peithō, Dikē, Anankē, Moira, and Themis appear to invoke personifications (deities); and these I have identified in this essay with initial capitals and roman type. When discussing the unpersonified features or forces of the same names and powers (*alētheia, dikē*, and so on), I have used lowercase letters and italic type.

28. There is one word that connotes or implies memory, namely *komisai*, "carry away," "preserve," "convey," "take care of," at B2.1. The word is unrelated to *mnēmē*, and the differences are significant. *Komizō* is often used of the preservation or carrying away of material things (as, e.g., at *Works and Days* 393 and 600; Pindar *Pythian* 3.56 and *Olympian* 2.14), whereas *mimnēskē* is not. *Mimnēskō* refers to an activity of soul, but *komizō* need not. *Komizō* emphasizes the aspects of preservation and conveyance, and is indifferent to the provenance of what is to be preserved or conveyed, whereas *mimnēskō* emphasizes the aspect of noticing or being aware.

29. This ambiguity arises because it is not clear what "of Peithō" (Peithous) in B2.4 means: Does the road lead to Peithō and Alētheia? Do these goddesses possess or rule the road, so that any movement along it must accord with what they require?

30. Nestor-Luis Cordero, *Les Deux chemins de Parménide*, second ed. (Paris: Vrin and Brussels: Ousia, 1997), 26 and 188 n31; Leonardo Tarán, *Parmenides* (Princeton: Princeton University Press, 1965), 82 and 94.

31. Hussey, for example, finds it intriguing that Parmenides might have connected the absence of coming to be and perishing, on the one hand, and the possibility of "knowledge" and "truth" on the other; see Edward Hussey, *The Presocratics* (London: Duckworth, 1972; reprint, Indianapolis: Hackett, 1995), 89–90. Cf. Aristotle, *de Caelo* 298b22f. I will explore this point further later in the chapter and in n35.

32. Cf. Pindar *Ol.* 2.92, *N.* 5.16–18.

33. See Rose Cherubin, "LEGEIN, NOEIN, and TO EON in Parmenides," *Ancient Philosophy* 21 (2001), 277–303; especially 287–88); on *noein* and mistakes, consider Parmenides B6.6 and 7.2. For an account of why *noein* should not be considered equivalent to knowledge or to thinking, see Kurt von Fritz, "*NOOS* and *NOEIN* in the Homeric Poems," *Classical Philology* 37 (1943), 79–93; and "*NOYS, NOEIN*, and Their Derivatives in Pre-Socratic Philosophy (Excluding Anaxagoras)," *Classical Philology* 40 (1945), 223–42; James H. Lesher, "Perceiving and Knowing in the *Iliad* and *Odyssey*," *Phronesis* 26 (1981), 2–24; and Gregory Nagy, "*Sema* and *Noesis*: Some Illustrations," *Arethusa* 16 (1983), 35–55.

34. Passages in which Dikē or *dikē* is responsible for regulation and balance either cosmically, sociopolitically, or both include *Iliad* 16.384–93, *Odyssey* 14.84, *Works and Days* 220–24 and 275–85, the Anaximander fragment, Solon fr. 4 West, and Heraclitus DK B80 and B94. At *Od.* 11.218, 19.43, and 19.168, the *dikē* of a person or of a kind of thing is the way or the appropriate way of that person or thing. Dikē is one of the Hōrai, Seasons, and a daughter of Themis, at *Theogony* 901–02.

35. The notion that the possibility of knowledge depends on the presence of something eternal (and, generally, unchanging) is taken up by Plato and Aristotle. Examples in Plato include *Phaedo* 66e and 78b–80c, *Republic* 479a–b and 484b, and *Philebus* 58a–59d. At *De caelo* 298b15ff. (the passage Hussey discusses; see n31), Aristotle notes that for the followers of Parmenides and Melissus, nothing can come to be or perish. While he disagrees with this view in many respects, Aristotle argues that these predecessors were right to realize that unchanging things are necessary if there are to be *phronēsis* and *gnōsis*. Cf. *Post. An.* 74b5, on *epistēmē*: *ho gar epistatai, ou dunaton allōs echein* (a thing known cannot be otherwise than it is); also 73a20, 71b10. On the relationship between *alētheia* and the presence of what does not change, see the discussion to follow on Moira.

36. B8.13–14, 21, and 27–28 imply that *to eon* is also not to be said or conceived to perish into nothing or into not-being.

37. For a comprehensive statement of such a position, see Curd 1998, chaps. 3 and 4.

38. Ananke or *ananke* refers to constraint or necessity at *Iliad* 6.458, *Odyssey* 7.215–19 and 10.434, Aeschylus's *Persians* 293 and *Prometheus Bound* 105–08 and 514–20, and Simonides 5.29–30 Bergk (=542.29–30 Page). *Ananke* is responsible for the necessity of consequences and implications at *Prometheus Bound* 507ff.

39. Detienne 1990, 53–60.

40. Moira or *moira* is lot or share or portion, especially the share or portion that is supposed to be appropriate to one, at *Iliad* 15.117 and 187–95, *Odyssey* 4.97 and 20.171, *Theogony* 413, and *Prometheus Bound* 294. It refers to one's lot or share in life or death, that is, one's destiny or fate, at *Il.* 16.433–38. *En moirēi* means "rightly, duly, in the appropriate manner" at *Il.* 19.186.

41. Cf. Zeno DK 29B1, B2, B3.

42. Descartes asserts just this in *Discourse on Method* Part 3, AT 28: once he has accepted and put aside the maxims of his provisional moral code and the principles of faith, he avows, he can call into doubt all of his other beliefs (viz., about the nature of the universe). *Discours de la méthode*, ed. Laurence Renault (Paris: Flammarion, 2000).

43. The same inadequate alternatives result if we assume that religious or ethical or artistic principles can explain why investigations of what is are independent of investigations of purpose, direction, and so forth.

44. Cf. *Theogony* 26–28; and Detienne 1990, 13–14 and 26–28.

45. The question may arise as to whether and how one could know whether the requisites of inquiry are in effect; certainly to ask about them would be to assume that they are in place. One might also ask how one could know what they were. Parmenides does not claim to know the requisites unconditionally, nor to know unconditionally that they are in effect. Rather, the effect of the structure of the poem (the goddess's speech framed by the tale of the journey through the familiar world) is to make the inferences within the goddess's speech conditional on the acceptance of the framework assumptions needed to make the tale of the journey coherent. That is, given the fundamental assumptions about the nature of the universe reflected in the proem, certain conditions will have to obtain in order for inquiry to be possible; those conditions are expressed by the binding functions of Dikē, Anankē, and Moira (also Themis). At no point does Parmenides or the goddess assert that the basic assumptions are adequate or accurate (in fact, the goddess's arguments suggest that they undermine themselves), or that what is, is as we say it is, or that inquiry is possible (or not). To follow a road of inquiry means accepting, at least provisionally, a certain conceptual vocabulary through which to frame questions. By the same token, neither Parmenides nor the goddess argues that we can have unconditional knowledge of the nature or requisites of *alētheia*.

4

No Second Troy

Imagining Helen in Greek Antiquity

RAMONA NADDAFF

In memoriam Isabelle Fouchard, a true friend

There are many women, but there is only one Helen—a woman so beautiful and desired that the very image of her face "launched a thousand ships," exciting Achaeans and Trojans to war for an epic-length ten years. Is this truly the case, however? Was there only one Helen, as described in Homer's *Iliad*, the "daughter descended of Zeus," "lovely-haired," "of the white arms," "shining among women"? Only one who caused "Trojans and strong-greaved Achaians / To suffer long anguish for a woman like that."[1] As will become apparent, the answer to this question is "no." For each man (Homer, Gorgias, and Euripides) and for at least one woman (Sappho), there is another Helen, if not two. So, then, if there is more than one Helen, one might ask: What is unique about any of these Helens? If it is true, as many have argued, that Helen is the name of a woman "universally desired" and "perfect," could it be that her essential perfection lies in that fact that she is Everywoman, easily interchanged and exchanged, metamorphic and multiple, never the same as herself? If this is the case, what might be remarkable about Helen—even perfect—is that no matter how much she is *not* herself, she is always the subject of desire.

Nicole Loraux has already brilliantly analyzed how Greek texts on Helen explore the dilemma of desire as a complex and conflict-ridden experience of loss and *pothos*.[2] At the same time—and intimately connected—one can also claim, as Barbara Cassin does—that Helen's representations relate perpetually back to *the* one and only subject of Greek history, "the Trojan War and its narrative." Indeed, Cassin turns the subject of Helen into a starker revelation about the nature of causes

73

in the narrow sense of that which is an effect: "Helen is the name of the cause (of the thing insofar as it produces an effect)."[3] Quite literally, then, what Helen causes, within a series of Homeric and post-Homeric accounts, is a rethinking of the causes of the Trojan War. Is she to blame or not for this debacle? Moreover, the subject of Helen causes—and this is the specific focus of this essay—a series of reflections and quandaries about the very nature of human responsibility in a world inevitably inhabited by omnipotent, strategically wily, divinities. As if positing an individual's agency and autonomy were not already problematic enough in ancient Greece, the issues become even more complicated when Helen is represented. It is this debate around Helen, the various arguments and strategies authors use to resolve the dilemmas of the scope, limits, and dangers of Helen's agency, especially insofar as she is imagined as being either a responsible or nonresponsible *casus belli*, that concern me here.

Homer's Iliadic Helen

It is probable that Homer's *Iliad* is the first story told about Helen, the "master text" from which Greek variations on this theme derive.[4] From the start, two essential features are notable. First, Helen's actual appearance in the epics is minimal. To use the most obvious marker: in both epics, she speaks in only five of the forty-eight books. References to her, usually short and formulaic, amount to a mere twenty-four. In the *Iliad*, the most likely place for Helen to take center stage, Helen speaks only seven times and is spoken of only fourteen times. When Helen or others do speak of her role in the Trojan War, it is as an inevitable, albeit lamentable, fact of life as they know it. Helen's power is mostly represented in these contexts as limiting: she has contributed to restricting the choices of Trojans and Achaeans alike. Because of her, the full range of their experiences has withered; the war, like Helen, is above all a *pēma*, a grief and a burden. Even if Helen is granted a privileged status as a metaphor of poetic speech because she, like Penelope, engages in the art of weaving, the subject of her weaving is not a metaphorical account but a factual one. Like epic, but without words, she chronicles the events of the war: "[Iris] came on Helen in the chamber; she was weaving a great web / a red folding robe, and working into it the numerous struggles / of Trojans, breakers of horses, and bronze-armoured Achaians / struggles that they endured for her sake at the hands of the war god" (*Il.* 3.121–28).[5]

The fact that Helen's speech acts are few in Homer's epics immediately establishes the first paradox about Helen's character: the less she says and the less is said about her, the more there is to say about her identity and actions. Helen's own words matter little to her audience. She is not heard; she is first and foremost, seen. What matters most—even above and beyond her resemblance to divinities—is that she be seen and heard of no more. Exile is necessary; contact to be avoided at all costs: "Terrible is the likeness of her face to immortal goddesses. / Still, though she be such, let her go away in the ships, lest / she be left behind, a grief [*pēma*] to us and our children" (*Il.* 3.158–60). It is not that Helen is born from a god, that she resembles a goddess, or even that she is worshipped as a goddess. Rather, she does not possess the powers, like divine beings, to disguise her beauty, reserve and diminish the dazzling glory she emanates. As Jean-Pierre Vernant explains, divinities take cautionary measures when they enter onto the human perceptual field: "only the tiniest bit of the splendor of the god's size, stature, beauty and radiance can be allowed to filter through, and this is already enough to strike the spectator with *thambos*, stupefaction, to plunge him into a state of reverential fear."[6] Helen is powerless to protect her human spectators from the harms of her dazzling body. Stupefied, her spectators do not worship in "reverential fear." Her magnificence does not inspire, upon first sight, an overflowing of words, praising her body, poetically assuring her *kleos*. Her *kleos* is rather that no more be said of her because no more shall she be seen and spoken of: "Let her be left behind." This, of course, is the impossible dream: Helen cannot be left behind. Once seen, she is heard about repeatedly, no matter how little she speaks.

Furthermore, in Homer's *Iliad*, a type of *dissoi logoi* emerges that argues both for and against Helen's human responsibility. On the one hand, since Helen herself chose to follow Paris to Troy, she must assume responsibility and accept shame for her willingness to have acted thus. On the other, since both Zeus and Aphrodite deliberately determined Helen's destiny as a dishonorable adulteress, she remains without blame, fated to terrible action through no fault of her own. Recognition of this double-sided narrative dovetails nicely with more recent arguments, especially those of Bernard Williams in *Shame and Necessity*, that counter the omnipresence of an omnipotent divine will whose imposition in Homeric epic renders individual agency a fallacious non sequitur. Indeed, proponents of an irreducible and unambiguous divine destiny have succeeded to flatten the dilemmatic and multiple experiences and reactions of Homer's characters, ones that are relentlessly exposed from a variety of perspectives.[7] Rare are those humans, even when heroes, who surrender to the decisions of their divine makers without resistance, questioning, argument, shame, even rage and loathing. The question to be asked, then, is *not* whether Homeric characters' decisions are morally relevant or not. It is rather: *How* do Homeric characters react to the gods' actions? These characters may not decide deliberately who they are and what actions they intend to pursue as ethical human agents. Instead, they respond to internal and external conditions; they speak to and against the gods and themselves; they potently articulate their emotions and desires. In their very responsiveness, they emerge as active and reactive, if not ethical, beings. In short, they are literary characters that fabricate stories *after the fact of the gods' actions* about their individual identities, actions, dispositions, and predilections. The deliberations and musings that precede or follow actions—or their lack thereof—allow, as Williams writes, "Homeric poems [to] contain people who make decisions and act on them . . . Homer's characters are constantly wondering what to do, coming to some conclusion, and acting. . . . Moreover, they seem able to regret what they have done, wish they had done something else, and much else of the same kind."[8]

In other words, human actions, even when caused by gods, become an object of self-conscious reflection. There may not be consciousness of responsibility—as emerges in tragic drama—but there is a conscious delineation of both the possible and actual effects their all too human actions have caused, both to themselves and to others.[9] For example, at *Il.* 6.318–68, Helen encounters the saddened Hector, fully aware of the suffering she has caused and the blame she deserves. (I will discuss this more fully shortly). Helen attempts, ultimately unsuccessfully, to persuade Hector that a reward exists for war and suffering. From strife and battle, warrior endurance and steadfastness, will come poetic song—song that both creates and preserves for future generations heroic *kleos*. Present rest and future songs will provide comfort to a Hector whose heart is heavy with fighting and sorrow: "But come now, come in and rest on this chair, my brother, / since it is on your heart beyond all that the hard work has fallen for the sake of dishonoured me and the blind act of Alexandros, / us two, *on whom Zeus set a vile destiny, so that hereafter we shall be made into things of song for the men of the future*" (6.354–56, my emphasis). Against the "vile destiny" to which Helen was passively subjected, another destiny awaits, fabricated for humans about humans. Helen consciously imagines this future, not perhaps as penance for her crimes but as relief to others for the suffering she has caused. As Maria Pantelia has argued, Helen is differentiated from other Homeric characters by her consciousness of how poetic discourse shapes heroic *kleos*: "Helen understands the predestined futility of Hector's struggle. In *Iliad* 6, she speaks about a different kind of glory, one that does not depend upon the survival of a man or a city, but upon the continuity of mankind. . . . At the end of the poem, Helen is not only a mourner but also a composer, a real contributor to the creation of epic poetry."[10]

If the Helen of the *Iliad* is continually associated with poetry, especially lament reserved as the sole form of public speech available to women, she also reserves the poetic right to lament self-consciously about the consequences of her fate, weaving an alternative tale about how she herself would have created an irreversible identity.[11] When Iris explains to Helen that the public war between Trojans and Achaeans is to become a private contest between Menelaus and Paris, and that Helen herself shall become the victor's "possession" and "beloved wife," Helen's heart becomes full with "sweet longing for her former lord and her city and parents" (*Il.* 3.139–40). This longing brings forth a "light tear," the first tangible sign of her own grief as opposed to the grief she has brought and brings to others. Expressions of grief and longing, regret and loss, follow Helen whenever she appears in this epic poem. Such grief in turn is intermingled with the harshest words uttered against this queen: Helen's own self-debasement and judgment—"slut that I am" (*kunōpidos*) or "nasty bitch evil-intriguing" (*Il.* 3.180 and 6.344, respectively). Between her longing and self-slandering, Helen announces her desire for death as the only way possible to stop her present tears and reverse her "vile destiny":

> I wish bitter death had been what I wanted, when I came hither
> following your son, forsaking my chamber, my kinsman,
> my grown child, and the loveliness of girls my own age.
> It did not happen that way: and now I am worn with weeping. (3.173–76)

> ... how I wish that on that day when my mother first bore me
> the foul whirlwind of the storm had caught me away and swept me
> to the mountain, or into the wash of the sea deep-thundering
> where the waves would have swept me away before all these things had happened. (6.345–49)

> ... my husband is Alexandros, like an immortal, who brought me
> here to Troy: and I should have died before I came with him. (24.763–64)

Although Helen recognizes, even mourns, her "ill luck" and more than once invokes the impossibility of resisting or changing the gods' choice of her destiny, she nonetheless conjures up another image of how a different set of desires and wishes could have determined actions other than those willed for her by the gods: "I wish bitter death had been what I wanted" (*Il.* 3.173), or "how I wish that on that day when my mother first bore me / the foul whirlwind of the storm had caught me away and swept me / to the mountain ... before all these things had happened" (*Il.* 6.345–49). Only in the realm of death, where she would be other than she is by ceasing to have been altogether, can Helen imagine herself free of blame, acting outside and independently of divine powers.[12]

Given the impossibility of realizing this wish, however, Helen is left, despite her knowledge of the gods' ultimate responsibility for her destiny, to blame herself for following Paris. Torn between her knowledge of divine power (*daimon*) and self-knowledge of her character (*ethos*) and desires, Helen locates the origin of her action within herself. Blaming herself for what she has done, she appears to herself as *aitiōs*, the cause affecting her own actions. This perhaps delusional sense of autonomy also manifests itself when Helen attempts in 3.410–12 to defy Aphrodite's order for her to go to Paris's chamber after his loss to Menelaus: "Not I. I am not going to him. It would be too shameful. I will not serve his bed, since the Trojan women hereafter / will laugh at me, all, and my heart even now is confused with sorrows." Despite her own desires, Helen, frightened by Aphrodite, follows, yet again, Paris whom now she wishes dead: "Oh, how I wish you had died there /

beaten down by the stronger man who was once my husband." The death wish becomes here, as in the other episodes I have mentioned, the only way Helen can counteract divine will, once she has—inevitably—failed on her own.[13]

In my reading of Homer's Helen thus far, I have interpreted her moments of self-slandering and blame, longing and regret, as hints of a heightened consciousness of and self-reflection on the causes and effects of her behavior. Helen—it must be remembered—possessed another viable alternative. Blaming the gods, she could herself have escaped from blame, becoming one of the many unwitting victims and vehicles of divine will and fate that animate Homeric verse. To have protected herself from a trial borne of self-accusations and, to have, in turn, safeguarded her *kleos*, her reputation, Helen would only have had to turn herself and her fate over to the gods—just as most Homeric characters from Achilles to Priam to Agamemnon do.[14] Priam, in fact, desires Helen to know that being human entails accepting a lack of moral responsibility and subservience to divine *atē*: "I am not blaming you: to me the gods are blameworthy who drove upon me this sorrowful war against Achaians" (3.164–65). The burden of proof, as it were, could then have fallen on the side of the gods and not on herself. Turning her thoughts inward, approaching the interior realm of her desires and wishes as if they were her own private kingdom and not the gods' property, Helen, however, attaches herself to harsh self-judgment. Why does she resist being freed from blame? Why this desire for self-incrimination?

Two possible responses explain Helen's propensity for self-blame and self-slander. Each response, in turn, indicates Helen's attempt to fashion her identity in reaction to, even as a violation of, predetermined roles and expectations. First, Helen's willingness to shroud herself in the language of blame might be a strategic ploy worthy of the most seductive and dangerous of all women. (Hector alone seems capable of resisting her persuasive charms and beauty.)[15] What better way to have men forgive and forget than to conjure up the image of a weak woman lost and forsaken, unable to save herself from her own worst enemy, her vulnerable, desiring self? Moreover, this is the Helen whom we learn in *Odyssey* 4.266–89 is an accomplished mistress of imitation. Mimicking wives' voices, she provokes "waves of longing" in the Achaeans enclosed in the "hollow horse" until they are silenced and restrained by the "great hands" of Odysseus, himself the other great wily master of mimesis. Although Menelaus himself would prefer to consider Helen's mimetic powers as the effect of "some superhuman power that planned an exploit for the Trojans," her performance of the repentant adulteress results perhaps from the awesome theatrical artistry of Helen, the demigoddess. Possessing the skills to imitate the voice of an embarrassed, misunderstood woman, Helen's mimed self-incriminations displace and diminish the power of the actual judgments of peers and superiors. Imitating and incorporating their severe reprimands, Helen composes a different identity for herself, one whose legacy will never, unfortunately, rival the necessary fortunes of her name described thus by Aeschylus in *Agamemnon*: "Who is he that named you so fatally in every way? . . . Appropriately death of ships (*helenas*), death of men (*helandros*), death of the city (*helepolis*)" (*Aga.* 681–89).

Second, Helen's self-incriminations reflect the ethical dictates of the shame culture she inhabits.[16] Indeed, we saw previously that, when attempting to disobey Aphrodite's commands, a failed exercise in self-rule, Helen fears less the goddess's anger than the shame caused by Trojan women's laughter (3.410–13). Knowing that her honor is tainted "hereafter," Helen proceeds to voice the slanderous assaults her disrepute will of necessity demand. In reciting these defamations as her own, Helen uses them to both shield herself from and enact the community's incrimination. Her *kleos* as an honored woman compromised, she recognizes that she will never be surrounded by silence, the mark of praise due to an obedient, morally correct wife. Helen speaks for herself what others might justifiably say of her: "slut," "nasty bitch evil-intriguing." The embarrassed Helen does not just desire to hide herself; she desires death, the most radical form of disappearance. She wishes and desires, in her own voice, the desires of kin and community: a "bitter death" if not at the moment after she was born, then at the moment forging her illicit companionship. In this way, Helen strives to fabricate her own slanderous reputation, choosing to join in with the choir of voices defaming her. Being the *aitiōs* of war, Helen cultivates a form of *aidōs* that simultaneously binds her to and separates her from the community.

As significantly, this self-inflicted blame becomes the means by which Helen aims to "save face." To regain her position in the society of women whose respect she yearns for, she composes a narrative that speaks of the havoc wreaked on her being and desires by a "vile destiny" she so little desired. She becomes for herself and through her own subjective experiences and desires what she was to the old men who witnessed her terrible magnificence: a "grief" that must be "left behind." Assuming this burden as her own, exposing the shame of her continued survival, Helen defines her particular identity as an incontinent, grieving woman, one who is "worn with weeping" (3.176). Furthermore, as I have already suggested, Helen's self-blame emanates from an interiority that defines its desires and inclinations over and against those of the gods. Behind her self-deprecation and incrimination lurks the powerful illusion of being an equal to the gods, deciding by and for herself to commit the crime of passion and to self-inflict punishment for her arrogant actions. Identifying with the gods, she also attempts to limit their powers of divine intervention inasmuch as it concerns how her identity is formed through her predestined transgression. To the external physical beauty they endowed her with, she counters the ugly interior subjectivity of a "nasty bitch evil-intriguing." The strategy of self-blame allows Helen to embrace her fate as her own, assuming ethical responsibility for what she has done and who she has become as a result.

Helen Reimagined: Post-Homeric Revisions

By the time of the Greek lyric poets, the image of a self-denouncing Helen bur-
dened with the history of her own shame disappears and is replaced by the image
of a shameless, morally sanitized Helen.[17] The image that begins to emerge with
Sappho but most definitely with Stesichorus is of a woman blamelessly driven to
comply with forces beyond her control. Gone is the image of Helen as a malevolent
seductress who victimizes Achaeans and Trojans. In its place appears the vision of
a woman victimized—to the point of becoming a scapegoat, if not martyr—not
only by the gods, but by *eros*, by the persuasive powers of the rhetorical *logos*,
and by the values of an aristocratic warrior culture as well as militarist impulses
of Athenian imperialists. Although each of the authors from Sappho, Gorgias,
Stesichorus, to Euripides uses Helen as a site to innovate new epistemological,
ontological, even political conceptions, I want rather to concentrate on the persistent
interest displayed in limiting the domain of Helen's power and longing she evoked
in Homer to envision herself as a powerful actor in, even agent of, the Trojan
War.[18] Insisting on Helen's *lack* of choice in making the fatal move to follow Paris
and to betray Menelaus, a tradition of post-Homeric tales arises, offering various
narratives—with varying motivations and functions—for why Helen should *not*
be blamed for the Trojan War.

Robbed of her role as the war's prime mover—though Priam had already
suggested just this—Helen's moral and erotic destiny is reshaped such that her
dunamis, perhaps as a woman, to influence human desires is severely curtailed. Even
when she is believed to be the cause, for example, of the desire for war, there is
always something other, someone else, displacing and overriding her. In the words
of Norman Austin, Helen is a "shameless phantom."[19] Morally inculpable, Helen is
blameless. Blameless, she is deprived of those inchoate potentialities that marked her
subjecthood, at least in Homeric accounts, as a being desiring, deliberating, even
willing unto death to appropriate as well as question the divine destiny allotted to
her. For all the post-Homeric authors here discussed—except perhaps Sappho—Helen
becomes but a woman to defend—against her own desires, against the dangerous
effects her desiring body incites. The virtually uncontainable force that was the
Iliad's Helen now transforms into a morally wounded, vulnerable woman living out
a mistaken identity and destiny. The Helen of Euripides' *Helen* explains: "I have
done nothing wrong and yet my reputation / is bad, and worse than a true evil is
it to bear / the burden of faults that are not truly yours" (269–71). Furthermore,
in rescuing Helen from her notorious adulterous passion, post-Homeric accounts
partially recreate Helen into that which "any woman" should be: blameless, honorable, chaste, and loyal. Once a dangerous woman whose story perhaps served as a
cautionary tale of sorts, Helen now serves as a model, even an exemplum, of the
morally incorruptible woman safeguarded by well-shielded, self-enclosed illusions.
Sappho alone seeks to preserve Helen's disruptive power and force by imagining

her, above all, as a lover of love, an activity and destiny paradoxically both within and beyond one's control. Sappho's Helen, as I will explain momentarily, makes a choice without choosing.

A. R. Burn envisions Sappho, the lesbian lyric poet, as sincere in her intense erotic passions. This honesty translates into an "absence of shame" about whom and how she loves and the lyric writing she produces.[20] The lyric poem may well be the genre par excellence for the expression of "shamelessness." Be that as it may, in fragment 16, Sappho uses this form to identify the many forms of shameless lovers and to prove, syllogistically and analogically, why love itself is shameless. At the center of this fragment Helen, like Sappho, emerges as a shameless lover whose ethics of desire allow not only for "illicit" attachments but also necessarily entail the acceptance of loss. As such, Sappho's Helen neither laments nor regrets her loves and losses. She just loves whom she loves, invulnerable to the dilemmas such shameless love creates for others and for herself. If indeed, as Page Dubois has argued, Sappho announces a new and "modern" subjectivity, it is also true that Sappho's Helen exists only as an individual subject in relation to others, in particular, to the individual with whom she happens to discover the experience of love.[21] Her identity, in other words, is a somewhat hapless effect of her intersubjective relations as well as of the relations that are excluded from attaching herself to *one* and not to *another* individual. The destiny of her identity, as it were, has now shifted from the gods' desires for her to her own desires for herself. Her own desires, however, are never truly her own. They are always shaped through erotic encounters where she both loses and gains an identity for herself. If, in fragment 16, Sappho identifies with Helen the lover, an important difference persists.[22] On the one hand, Sappho's beloved Anaktoria is, as we shall see, "absent." Her identity as a lover and as a poet results from this distance and the possibility of differentiation, even individuation, it allows. Helen, on the other hand, is face to face with her lover. No mediation exists and she becomes who she is only because of the immediate and urgent bond *eros* affects, an *eros* that, like Helen herself, is shameless, surpassing "in beauty . . . all humanity."[23]

In fragment 16, Sappho portrays Helen as the supreme example of the logic of beauty and desire. As Matthew Gumpert writes: "In a poem about beauty and desire, Helen is by definition the most beautiful and the most desired. Helen functions as a foil here because she is a universal cap or climax."[24] Equally, Helen is the "universal exemplum" of that which is most "beautiful and desired" when it comes to love: to be a lucid decision-maker who chooses, despite all odds, to follow the imperative commands of love. In Helen's particular case, this means: to choose to depart to Troy, "abandoning her husband." I quote in full the fragmentary stanzas that remain of this poem:

Some assert that a troop of horsemen, some of foot-soldiers, some
a fleet of ships is the most beautiful thing on the dark earth; but I

assert that it is whatever anyone loves. It is quite simple to make
this intelligible to all, for she who was far and away preeminent in
beauty of all humanity [she that far surpassed all mortals in beauty], Helen,
   abandoning her husband
. . .
      went
sailing to Troy and took no thought for child or dear parents, but
beguiled . . . herself [(love) beguiled her] . . . , for . . . lightly . . . reminds me
now of
Anaktoria
absent: whose lovely step and shining glance of face I would
prefer to see than Lydians' chariots and fighting men in arms.[25]

   An unspoken question precedes the poem: "What is most beautiful (*kallis-tos*)?" Sappho's answer to this proto-platonic question is radical: "*ego dē kēn hottō tis eratai*," translated as "but I assert that it is whatever anyone loves," and also as "but I say, it is what you love."[26] Before discussing the meanings and context of this response, let me first note, as other have before me, that Sappho's response criticizes and competes with the value system of the aristocratic warrior code of epic poetry as much as it incorporates, even "grafts," the epic to the lyric genre.[27] Sappho's question does not concern particular individuals; in fact, it does not relate to individuals at all. She does not wonder about "who" is most beautiful. Rather, she addresses directly the question of the beautiful in relation to a thing, "whatever," "what" [*hottō*], that is more an object than an individual subject. As the poem will tell, this "object" of love—whatever the beloved may turn out to be—tends to be a person or persons ("horsemen," "foot soldiers," "Paris," "Anaktoria") rather than a thing. ("Ships" are actually the only objects that human beings love in this poem, artifacts that become quite functional for Helen as they enable her to set "sailing to Troy" and satisfy her desire for the "most beautiful.")
   It may well be that the emphasis should not be placed on the direct object, "whatever," but on the verb "to love." Such accenting changes the directive of the response: it is not *what* one loves but *that* one loves.[28] And yet, Sappho's sensa-tionalist erotics also seems to demand that in loving, one must love the "whatness" of a thing or person, that is, the very particular materiality of the beloved that moves one to fight (warriors), to abduct and abandon (Helen), and to remember (the "I" of the poem). "On this dark earth," only the love and beauty of particular beings brings value to our bodily, ephemeral existence. Soldiers and Helen of Troy risk their lives and reputation for such love. The narrator of the poem, however, remains invulnerable as far as we can tell from this fragment. She chooses her values and affirms her preferences. As Jack Winkler writes, "against the panoply of men's opinions on beauty . . . Sappho sets herself—'but I'—and a very abstract proposition about desire."[29] And yet to desire and to love safely and abstractly,

from a distance, within the empty frame of reason, is but a comforting illusion. To desire is to not have; it is to lose something, someone.

This is the other side of the poem's coin. If the poem asks "What is most beautiful," it also presents a chilling counterfactual: "What would happen if human beings did not seek the most beautiful?" The poem answers: there would be no war; there would be no motherless children and childless parents; there would be no longing for an absent beloved. In short, if human beings ceased to desire, they would no longer live and suffer losses. When it comes to Helen of Troy, both Homer's *Iliad* and Sappho's poem make this inevitable economy of loss evident. Homer's warriors were driven to war not only because of their love of war but also their desire to possess goods, to possess the particular good of Helen.[30] Whatever, whomever they capture to satisfy their desire for glory, possessions, honor, or revenge, they still lose. Helen of Troy, in both the *Iliad* and Sappho's poem, whether she follows her own desire or not, also forsakes attachments. The difference between the epic and lyric Helen is that the latter, even though "she took no thought," is conscious of the choice she is making, the losses she will gather. She self-consciously assumes the responsibility for her desire. Sappho represents Helen as wanting life, not death, of sacrificing complete plenitude for the chance to desire as an incomplete, human being. And this is the paradox of desire that Sappho embodies in her Helen. Helen, who is "far and away pre-eminent in beauty of all humanity"—the most beautiful of all—still desires that which is beautiful.[31] Perhaps Helen desired a beauty that differs from her own—an "intellectual," "spiritual," or "aesthetic" beauty rather than a physical one—or that the judgment about Helen's beauty erred and the war, among other things, was the result of a flawed and faulty system of evaluation. Or perhaps, on this "dark earth," the most beautiful still seeks the universal form of Beauty. Restated less platonically: even the most completely beautiful human being still desires to desire, to experience love and loss, forever completely incomplete.

From the perspective of *eros*, then, Helen's love for Menelaus, like men's love of war, is above all a thing of beauty, an aesthetic experience that transforms not only an individual's values and perceptions, but also their actions and behavior. Most surely they suffer from this desire, but the cause of their suffering is not Helen but their own desire. Further, according to Sappho, the desire for someone or something is an effect of individual tastes and preferences; one could almost say it is a choice, albeit of the type "rather this than that." Just as Sappho herself "prefers" to see Anaktoria's "lovely step and shining glance of face," rather than the "Lydians' chariots and fighting men in arms," the "some" men of this poem value and long for the occasions of military displays more than they desire the beautiful Helen. This desire causes both Sappho and men to do strange things—strange, that is, from each other's perspective. The logic and motivation of their actions become "intelligible to all," however, once Helen's story is recalled and revised. "Sappho's Helen," writes Winkler, "is held up as proof that it is right to desire one thing above all others, and to follow the beauty perceived no matter where it leads."[32]

Sappho's retelling of Helen's tale concerns precisely the question of Helen's own desire. Sappho uses Helen to prove the irrefutable logic of her subjective claim: "but I assert that it is whatever anyone loves." The Helen Sappho imagines is neither the self-effacing prisoner of her own longings and "if only," nor is she the victim or plaything of the gods' irreversible decisions about an individual's *atē*. Sappho's Helen is presented with a choice: she can either "abandon her husband" and "sail to Troy" to be near her beloved or she can remain in her homeland with her husband, caring for "child" and "dear parents." Either way, as I have already explained, she will suffer a loss. It is not the price she has to pay, however, but her desire to be in Troy that takes precedence during this imagined process of decision-making. A beauty herself, she chooses to experience the "most beautiful thing on the dark earth." It is perhaps because she is "preeminent in beauty of all humanity" that she possesses the force to withstand her own desire and act according to its dictates, imperatives that are every bit as challenging as those of the gods.[33] And Sappho, distant from her Anaktoria, knows this as well as she knows that desire experienced from within is a power that comes from without, leaving one "beguiled," without any choice but to choose desire madly. This decision itself is an act of madness. Once desire strikes, one is no longer able to see things, except those of beauty, clearly. Sappho's Helen is beyond blame, madly acting out the wild drama of a desire that strikes from both within and without. Anne Carson provides an incomparable description of this very process: "Desire is a moment with no way out. . . . *Eros* comes out of nowhere . . . lights on you from somewhere outside yourself and, as soon as he does, you are taken over, changed radically. You cannot resist the change or control it or come to terms with it."[34]

If Sappho attempts to displace the question of Helen's blame and shame by concentrating on the preferences and choices generated by eros, the fifth-century orator and sophist Gorgias of Leontini, a foreigner who brings the formidable *technē* of rhetoric to Athens, places the question of blame at the center of his discourse. Foreign magician of bewitching and beguiling speech, Gorgias could find no better rhetorical occasion to display his awesome skills to Athenians than to mount a campaign that revises not only Helen's history as a *casus belli* but also, by implication, the very history of the Trojan War. Performed as if in competition to win the prize for the most persuasive orator, operating as if a rhetorical exercise in the construction of the best speech, the *Encomium* testifies to the reconfiguration by epideictic speech of Helen's identity as a virtually powerless agent, especially insofar as she herself is a sentient, embodied being incapable of "thinking" and "reasoning" about such things as love and moral choices. She is, as I will discuss, a strategic excuse for displaying the pragmatically flexible wares of the rhetorical craft. If there is power for and in Helen's body and desires, it is a power only attributed to her through association and identification with the rhetorical art.[35]

Indeed, Gorgias takes the superficially simple, even naïve, question of whether Helen was to blame for war as the ultimate pretext to exploit and explore the multiple possibilities of rhetorical manipulation and reversal of commonsense thinking. If the nonrhetorical taletellers and audiences believe Helen is to blame, Gorgias will overturn their belief systems through sheer verbal and affective force. His speech will reverse poetic tradition through the secular powers of argument, displacing divine destiny onto the human determinacy of the linguistic signifying field. The challenge is doubled, as is the skill required: the most dangerous feminine body of desire will neither be demonized nor incriminated. She will be defended. Gorgias's *Encomium* is a *defense* of Helen, a persuasive, seductive series of rhetorical arguments that aim to convince listeners that Helen is a shameless victim through no choice of her own.

First, in his *Encomium of Helen*, Gorgias contends that it is logically impossible to conceive of Helen as an agent who actively made choices about her desires and actions. To defend Helen, it is necessary to prove just the opposite: that Helen herself neither chose to do one thing or another nor was she presented with a situation in which there were any choices to be made. She cannot even be granted the illusion of imagining herself, or of being imagined, as one who chose sovereignly between two options. In other words, Helen's situation and desire are neither dilemmatic nor paradoxical. Only a set of necessary and logically inextricable objective and subjective realities motivated her departure to Troy. Second, Helen must not only be defended, she must also be proven innocent. Gorgias's fictive legal proof strives to demonstrate, beyond a reasonable doubt, one thing: Helen is without effect. She causes nothing; she is *anaitiōs*. Even if Helen was predisposed by internal or external forces to commit the "crime" of sailing to Troy, she cannot be held responsible for her actions. They were beyond her control and, for precisely this reason, she should not be blamed for causing the Trojan War.

Gorgias presents his defense of Helen in the form of an "encomium," a literary genre that in its very structure exonerates Helen from blame: "A man, a woman, a speech, a deed, a city, and an action, if deserving praise, one should honour with praise, but to the undeserving one should attach blame."[36] Gorgias's *éloge* begins with the claim that those who blame Helen do so out of "error and ignorance" (*hamartia kai amathia*). In not speaking *orthōs* (correctly) about her (that is, praising her), they not only misrepresent her *kosmos* (grace), but they turn speech from truth telling to lying. The *Encomium*'s task follows logically upon these failures of *logoi*, and Gorgias proposes to "say what ought to be said" about Helen and thus to accomplish four goals: "to free the slandered woman from the accusation and to demonstrate that those who blame her are lying and both to show what is true and to put a stop to their ignorance." By "adding some reasoning to speech"—and it is difficult not to believe that "reasoning" is the supplement to the *logoi* of Helen's previous authors, Homer and Sappho—Gorgias constructs four arguments to disprove or correct former conceptions about this woman who, "pre-eminent among pre-eminent men and women, by birth and descent, is not obscure to even a few" (l. 3). The arguments are as follows: 1. If Helen went to Troy, it was because she was compelled to do so by divine necessity (*Argument from divine force*; line 6). 2. If Helen went to Troy, it was because she was compelled to do so by Paris's physical strength (*Argument from physical force*; 7). 3. If Helen went to Troy, it was because she was compelled by the *dunamis*, the power, of speech. Given that persuasive speech causes "deviations of mind and deceptions of belief," Helen lost possession of her senses and was forced to believe in false speech, to "obey what was said and to approve what was done" (*Argument from linguistic force*; 8–14). 4. Finally, if Helen went to Troy, it was because, incited and pleased by the vision of Paris, she was compelled to do so from the human disease of *eros* (*Argument from emotional force*; 15–9). It follows therefore that these forces conspired and Helen went to Troy through no fault of her own. If any charges are to be brought, they are against those who falsely blame Helen by assuming that she either acted willingly or willed her own actions. As victim of a multiplicity of forces, Helen's passivity is the very ground on which Gorgias restores her honor. Although Gorgias is engaged in "free, imaginative creation," what he finally describes as his "plaything" (*emon de pagnion*; 21), the object of his discourse is deadly serious. Gorgias uses Helen as the occasion, if not the pretext, to praise and define the art of persuasive and poetic speech, and especially its power to change almost magically accepted realities and beliefs.[37]

"Under the name of play," Gorgias reverses Helen's fortune; he persuades his audience "to take everything back" about what they ever believed about Helen. Her dangerous power is overshadowed, if not eclipsed, by an equally dangerous and extraordinary experience, that of rhetorically persuasive sophistic and poetic speech, which is used here not to describe but to defend Helen in the argument from linguistic force: "Speech is a powerful ruler. Its substance is minute and invisible, but its achievements are superhuman; for it is able to stop fear and to remove sorrow and to create joy and to augment pity" (8). In particular, "false speech," like the image remaining of the past and falsely maligned Homeric Helen, captures the mind "by violence . . . expelling sense" so that it is "bewitched with an evil persuasion" (14).[38] A shift of focus occurs—a dangerous effect still surrounds Helen but she is subjected to, not the subject of, it. For Gorgias, then, Helen's overdetermined response to external forces shields her, on the one hand, from blame, but confines her to the realm of passive victimization and subjugation.

This passivity, which still grants Helen the virtue of having done something rather than nothing at all, appears as the only way that Gorgias can logically guarantee Helen's innocence. Even if this encomium is but a solipsistic amusement, Gorgias's game is nonetheless strictly governed by the rules of an inflexible logic that aims not only to make Helen's behavior comprehensible to the audience but also to legitimize the ethical authority of sophistic oratory. This contrasts with the dramatist Euripides' encounter with Helen in his play *Helen*. To defend her, Euripides enters into the realm of the absurd, asking his audience to suspend everything they know about the workings of divine and human reality (not to mention the reality of their mythic past), and to adopt the truly contorted logic of the fictive, the make-believe world of phantom and shadowy beings.

Euripides, as Nietzsche wrote in the *Birth of Tragedy*, "watched the performances of his predecessors' plays and tried to rediscover in them those fine lineaments which age . . . had darkened and almost obliterated. . . . There was . . . much in the language of older tragedy that he took exception to, or to say the least, found puzzling. . . . Euripides sat in the theater pondering, a troubled spectator. In the end he had to admit to himself that he did not understand his great predecessors."[39] Euripides, in Nietzsche's well-known argument, is the tragedian most responsible for the death of tragedy, the evacuation of the primitive Dionysian spirit in favor of the Apollonian rationalist method and ultimately an "inartistic naturalism." In the aforementioned quote, Nietzsche concentrates on how Euripides—the spectator and the thinker—took Aeschylus's and Sophocles' plays as perplexing objects of critical thought, problems to be solved through a rational and conscious diminishing of tragic moral ambiguity. Rethinking "every aspect of drama," Euripides rewrote and revised the tragic form and function so that it would, Nietzsche claimed, "fit his [own] specification."[40] I allude to Nietzsche's powerful commentary on Euripides to forefront Euripides' self-conscious dialectical relationship with his predecessors, the tragedians. An antagonistic relation, it was also the creative source of Euripides' formulation of his own signature style, at least according to Nietzsche. However, when discussing Euripides' 412 BCE "tragedy," *Helen*, one must also consider another source, the epic poet Homer.

It goes without saying that behind every successful Greek dramatist stands Homer and the reinterpretation of his legends. In the case of Helen, Euripides seems to go one step further. In his retelling of the mythic life of Helen, Euripides chooses Hesiod, Herodotus, and Stesichorus *over* Homer. All three versions, in different ways, fashion a tale of the Trojan War that differs from the Homeric etiology and therefore are, in principle, viable alternatives for forming a coherent narrative of the war's legendary beginnings. Stesichorus, for example, once believed in Homer's account until he was struck blind. Seeing no way out, he had the insight to recant and apologize, revising history and rectifying the Homeric *muthos* accordingly. He begins the story of the war anew, this time speaking true *logoi*. His famous palinode, a literary invention of his own, reads thus: "I spoke nonsense and I begin again. / That story is not true. / You never went away in the benched ships. / You never reached the citadel of Troy."[41] As is the case with Hesiod and Herodotus (and as we shall soon see with Euripides), Stesichorus embraces a tale as improbable, even nonsensical, as that of Homer's: the Trojan War was fought for a phantom image, a "body double" of Helen. Helen never arrived in Troy. In fact, Stesichorus seems to imply that her whereabouts are unknown. She may have never gone anywhere. In Herodotus's version, however, the geographical and biographical facts are more precise: the real, flesh and blood Helen, was safely exiled in Egyptian lands, her honor preserved and protected by a foreign king, Proteus, while a war was fought over an empty, unreal—albeit beautiful—image. Euripides appropriates both these tales and apparently dismisses Homer, as well as Helen, to the sidelines of history and mythmaking.

And yet, it is not entirely correct to state that Euripides only realigns himself with these two authors and distances himself from Homer. His work on the myth is more synthetic and complicated. On the one hand, a certain sarcastic skepticism and pessimism insinuates its way into the play, suggesting that ultimately no narrative—rational or irrational—is ideologically forceful enough to account for why, in war, "a thousand toils were toiled in vain" (603).[42] Just as Euripides in *Helen* insists over and again on how empirical information-gathering necessarily deceives, so too does he insinuate the impotency of any narrative—Homer's, Herodotus's, Stesichorus's, even his own—to make sense of the political supremacy of war as a resolution to conflict.[43] On the other hand, Euripides opts out of making serious, tragic art about war. He chooses instead to create the comforting optimistic illusions of romantic comedy, even a screwball remarriage comedy.[44] The real tragedy—if there is one—is that it took Menelaus and Helen so long to reunite and recognize the enduring beauty of conjugal love. In a happy ending, Menelaus repossesses Helen as his rightful wife. Fortune and fate and a "hateful" sister have ethically betrayed Theoclymenus, the new, intended husband of Helen:

Theoclymenus: Who has right over what is mine [Helen]?
Servant: The man her father gave her to.
Theoclymenus: Fortune gave her then to me.
Servant: And fate took her away again. (*Helen*, 1635–36)

Euripides' version of the Helen myth is so fabulous and unbelievable that it is repeated at least eight times throughout the play, in different versions and words by almost every character, as if its constant retelling would make the scenario not only more credible and realistic but also less traumatic and nonsensical.[45] Hera, angered by Paris's judgment, devises a plan to outwit and punish mortals and immortals. From the beautiful body of Helen, she creates a "breathing image out of the sky's air" in its perfect likeness. This image is not Helen, but nonetheless has the name. As we already know from Stesichorus, the Helen who is the original source of the phantom reproduction does not go to Troy. Exiled and protected in foreign Egyptian land, Helen is left there to observe and lament from a distance the suffering her namesake and double has caused Trojans and Achaeans, strangers and kin: "Because of me, beside the waters of Scamander, / lives were lost in numbers; and the ever-patient I / am cursed by all and thought to have betrayed my lord / and for the Hellenes lit the flame of a great war. / Why do I go on living, then?" (52–56). In this barbarian kingdom, Helen's honor has been protected, her happiness and reputation ultimately guaranteed by the return and renewed trust of Menelaus, and her voyage home secured by the Chorus's coaxing and Theonoë's final decision to privilege her commitment to justice over familial duty to her brother, Theoclymenus. Helen spends much of the play convincing the men and women around her that she herself did nothing, that she and they are monstrous victims of her "ill-starred beauty," and that illusions are as real as reality, and reality as illusory as illusions, especially when one relies on optical vision for their perception. As Charles Segal writes, emphasizing especially Euripides' ironic metaphysical vision: "The central irony of the *Helen* lies in its antithesis of appearance and reality. What is the real nature of the world? What is 'word' (*onoma*) and what 'fact' or 'deed' (*pragma*)? . . . The ultimate irony in Euripides' treatment of these basic antitheses lies in the fact that the play never completely resolves the question of which aspect of reality is the true one."[46] Although the differentiation of reality from illusion remains an open-ended query throughout the play, this confusion does not ultimately affect the reconstitution of Helen's reputation. Her "name" is made good—even a land shall bear her name (1673–75)—and her honor no longer depends on what she has or has not done or suffered in the past. Her strategic reaction to the immediate presence of her beloved husband transforms her into an exemplary wife, "great and noble." Theoclymenus has the final words on the noble character of this most beautiful, divine creature: "Know that you [Dioscuri] are born of the same blood from which was born / the best and the most faithful sister in the world. / Go then rejoicing for the great and noble heart / in her. There are not many women such as she" (1682–85).

To Sappho's question, then, "What is most beautiful?" Euripides provides a conventional and traditional answer: a devoted wife who will do anything and everything—even deceive and strategize—to remain faithful to the husband she loves. In revisioning Helen's character as staunchly honorable, Euripides is still haunted by Homer's melody, and he uses it to sing the praises of a Helen who secures the reestablishment of a divinely disrupted domestic harmony. Indeed, in the play, Helen uses all her cunning skills to devise a plan in order to outwit her future relations, to escape from marriage, and to return from a wandering exile with her one and only husband. Only deceit allows her to regain her lost dream of marital bliss. The mimetic powers of the *Odyssey*'s Helen are reenacted and we find a feminine beauty as strategically resourceful as the epic's hero Odysseus. Helen's path to success is paved by her active manipulation of Theoclymenus and Theonoë. The newly committed-unto-death exiled wife transparently announces to her disbelieving husband Menelaus: "What we need now is strategy. . . . There is a single hope for escape, a single way" (814–15). In this way, Euripides' Helen becomes an unexpected mirror image and double of the *Odyssey*'s Penelope. At the same time, although an image of Penelope, Helen is merely an artistic simulacrum, an image of an image, of Odysseus's wife. In Euripides' "reversal of the myth of Helen," Helen is, as Froma Zeitlin explains, "not Penelope, but in the normative tradition, her exact opposite, the woman who ran off with another man, the woman whose beauty caused the Trojan war. Helen, in fact, is the 'baddest' of women, who through the poet's art, is recreated as the best of them."[47] It takes a twisted artistic tale to transform Helen thus as well as the advent of a new adulterous ontological split between "that which is" and "that which appears to be"—both in the phenomenal world and in the realm of dramatic art.

Helen can only appear as the "best" of all women, indeed as a feminine agent who actively and strategically releases *herself* from an unjust imprisonment threatening her honor and shame precisely because she imitates, is the imitation of, the "good" wife. In other words, she performs, in exaggerated fashion and under exceptional circumstances, the role of the exemplary wife, not only doggedly loyal, fierce and protective of her hearth, but also supremely beautiful and artful in her connivances and maneuvers. She reenacts a fantasy wherein the feminine female resembles both the active and passive *aner* without threatening the masculine male. Menelaus, at first, fears that his own honor as a masculine man will be threatened by Helen's eager desire to master the situation: "I would rather die in action than die passively" (814). But, as we already know, he submits to Helen's plan, making sure to introduce a strategy he believes to be of his own making but is as much the effect of Helen's "gentle" manipulation:

> *Menelaus*: To do what? What is the hope you lead me gently to?
> *Helen*: That she [Theonoë] will *not* tell her brother you are in the land.
> *Menelaus*: If we won her over, could we get ourselves out of here?
> *Helen*: With her help, easily. Without her knowledge, no.
> *Menelaus*: Best for woman to approach woman. *You do this.* (my emphasis; 825–830)

Only in the comic mode can Helen be a blameless, shameless, active responsible agent, the "best" of all wives. Only in the comic mode can Helen, as "every woman" and "any woman," impersonate, even parody, the myth of the essentially feminine female that "normative tradition" exemplified by Penelope.

If *Helen* were purely and simply a comedy, and Euripides' Helen merely a comic character, it would then be possible to claim that, through the subversive reversals and ethical upheavals of the genre, Helen has won herself respectable moral agency for the first time in her literary history: she did not cause the Trojan War; she did not commit adultery. She *did* do everything within her powers to remain loyal and return home morally unscathed by what she names "this destiny on which I am fastened[.] Was I born a monster among mankind?" (255). Comedy makes Helen "human"—as humanly responsible as is possible when gods still own destinies and men still possess women as subordinate subjects. Morally responsible, domesticated, tamed—through her own desire, willingness and preferences—Euripides' Helen only dangerously disrupts for the sake of personal good and individual happiness. She is "depoliticized"—moved away from war and the polis into the confines of the real and imaginary private *oikos*. But Euripides *Helen* is not only comedy; it is part tragedy, even if only a parody of its hyperbolic language of undue suffering and high-pitched lament. From the "tragic" perspective, Helen's situation is so pitiful and senseless, her destiny so utterly beyond her control and arbitrarily willed by the gods, that she remains throughout most of the play a suppliant at Proteus's tomb. She mourns relentlessly her own bad luck and the curse of her beauty, lacking even the force to sing the sorrows she has suffered through no fault or action of her own: "Here, with a song of deep wretchedness for the depth of my sorrows, / what shall be the strain of my threnody, what singing spirit / supplicate in tears, in mourning, in sorrow? Ah me . . . " (164–66).

Her only exit strategy, prior to her reunion with Menelaus, is suicide. This, as Nicole Loraux has written, is "morally disapproved in the normal run of everyday life. But, most important, it was a woman's solution and not, as has sometimes been claimed, a heroic act."[48] Almost imitating the suicide of her mother by hanging, Helen chooses to imagine a more noble and beautiful death: "When one hangs by the neck, it is ugly / and it is thought a bad sight for the slaves to look upon. / Death by the knife is noble and has dignity / and the body's change from life to death is a short time" (298–300). Even when finding "liberty in death," to recall Loraux's words, Helen must maintain appearances, be conscious of her effect on others as well as the preservation of her exceptional status as the woman "whose very beauty . . . has ruined me."[49]

Helen does not kill herself; she is ultimately and fantastically redeemed. However, this matters little in the tragic mode: the event of the war, its memory, the very real death and suffering it provoked remains. This can never be erased—even in art, if only because it begins in art—by knowledge of the real Helen's nonresponsibility. Nowhere is the inefficacy, even futility, of this knowledge better displayed than in the exchange between the Messenger and Menelaus (who also initially refused to believe Helen's story, "trust[ing] my memory of great hardships more than you"):

Messenger: Is she not mistress of sorrows for the men in Troy?
Menelaus: She is not. We were swindled by the gods. We had our hands upon an idol of the clouds.
Messenger: You mean it was for a cloud, for nothing, we did all that work? (703–07).

Helen herself, as we have seen in the speech previously cited, is not oblivious to the irreversible damage and unproductive strife caused by her double. In proper Iliadic fashion, she lapses into moments of self-blame, this time accusing herself not for what she did or did not do but for what she is: "my beauty is to blame. I wish that like a picture I had been rubbed out and done again, made plain, without this loveliness, for so the Greeks would never have been aware of all those misfortunes that now are mine" (261–65). As the beautiful original from which the equally beautiful and thus perfect-copy Helen was made, Helen suffers from being the passive cause of suffering. Without the original, no image. Without the image, no Helen powerful and dangerous enough to deceive men into trusting their senses and acting by desire instead of through reason.

Already, however, I have moved beyond the image of Euripides' Helen to the image of Helen in Plato's dialogues. Plato does not make apologies for Helen; he does not offer either tragic or comic relief and redemption. He only philosophically uses her literary body to warn against the dangers of beliefs founded in sensual perception and of actions motivated by ethical misjudgments. Plato provides strong reasons why Helen's image poses the most real and powerful of all dangers: she is the embodiment of bodily pleasures and desires. For Euripides, the collapse between illusion and reality—like Helen's own dilemma—has a comic effect whose ironic and paradoxical dimensions can be resolved by congenial, romantic solutions rather than by an ideal, eternal reality and truth that constructs destructive deviations from this highest form and way of life. It takes a specifically rationalist and antiphenomenal philosophy like that of Plato to expose systematically the necessary separation of and distinction between illusion and reality, and rational thought from bodily desires, and to explicate, not with humor but with ridicule, why their all-too-frequent collapse is not "an ethereal dance above the abyss" (to echo Zuntz) but a tragic descent into "barbaric slough" (*borborō barbarkō*; *Rep.* l.533d1). This, however, is another story—the story, as it were, of how Platonic "philosophy" transforms Helen into "Everywoman," a dangerous, desiring being who appears anywhere, in any place, at any time.

Notes

An earlier version of this essay was published in *Greekworks.com*, January 15, February 3, and February 17, 2003. I gratefully acknowledge the useful comments of Peter Pappas and William Wians and an anonymous reader. Elizabeth Wadell assisted me greatly in the final preparation of this chapter.

1. *The Iliad of Homer*, trans. Richmond Lattimore (Chicago: University of Chicago Press, 1951), 3.199, 329, 121, 156–57, respectively. Unless otherwise stated, all quotations of the *Iliad* are taken from this translation.

2. Nicole Loraux, *Les expériences de Tirésias: Le féminin et l'homme grec* (Paris: Editions Gallimard, 1989), 232–52.

3. Barbara Cassin, *Voir Hélène en toute femme* (Paris: Institut d'édition Sanofi-Synthélabo, 2000), 14.

4. See Cassin 2000, 11, for a clear rendering of Helen's genealogical tree. In this essay, due to a lack of space, I will not treat the question of the representation of "Helen" in Homer's *Odyssey*. In short, I have argued elsewhere that this "Helen" is always the "evil twin" and "double" of someone other than herself (for example, Briseis, Achilles, and most

obviously Penelope). Most importantly, she is transformed in this epic into the opposite of how she appears in the *Iliad*. This domesticated "Helen" no longer causes grief. Rather she brings and causes "good news" (see *Odyssey* 15.223–25).

5. Helen's weaving has often been compared to the activity of poetic composition. See for example, Ann Bergren, "Helen's Web: Time and Tableau in the *Iliad*," *Helios*, 7 (1979), 19–34. To date, I find Nancy Worman's "The Body as Argument: Helen in Four Greek Texts," *Classical Antiquity* 16.1 (April 1997), 151–203, the most compelling argument about the association of Helen's body with the operative of persuasive, textual argument and narrative.

6. Jean-Pierre Vernant, "Dim Body, Dazzling Body," in Michel Feher, Ramona Naddaff, and Nadia Tazi, eds., *Fragments for a History of the Human Body*, vol. 1 (New York: Zone Books, 1989), 39.

7. Bernard Williams, *Shame and Necessity* (Berkeley and Los Angeles: University of California Press, 1993).

8. Williams 1993, 21–22.

9. On the "tragic consciousness of responsibility" and the separation of divine and human action and power, see Jean-Pierre Vernant, "The Historical Moment of Tragedy in Greece," in Jean-Pierre Vernant and Pierre Vidal-Naquet, *Myth and Tragedy*, trans. Janet Lloyd (New York: Zone Books, 1988), 27.

10. Maria C. Pantelia, "Helen and the Last Song of Hector," *Transactions of the American Philological Association* 132 (2002), 26.

11. See Linda Clader, *Helen: The Evolutions from Divine to Heroic in Greek Epic Tradition* (Leiden: Brill Academic Publishers, 1976).

12. It is important to note that Helen poses an alternative to her own death—that of Paris. If his death is impossible, another infeasible transformation is required—that he become a better man: "Oh, how I wish you had died there / beaten down by the stronger man who was once my husband" (3.428–29); "I wish I had been the wife of a better man than this is, / one who knew modesty and all things of shame that men say" (6.350–51).

13. This assumption of a freedom that defies divine intervention and necessity stands, for example, in sharp contrast to Priam's judgment of Helen: "I am not blaming you: to me the gods are blameworthy / who drove upon me this sorrowful war against Achaians" (3.164–65).

14. See *Odyssey* 19.329–34: "If a man is harsh himself and thinks harsh thoughts, all men pray that pains should befall him hereafter while he is alive. And when he is dead, all men . . . ridicule him. But if a man is blameless himself and thinks blameless thoughts, the guest-strangers he has entertained carry his *kleos* far and wide to all mankind, and many are they who call him . . . worthy." Translation from Gregory Nagy, *The Best of the Achaeans: Concepts of the Hero in Archaic Greek Poetry* (Baltimore: Johns Hopkins University Press, 1979), 257. I am grateful to an anonymous reader for pointing out that Homeric heroes blame the gods for their strife even if this implies a diminishing of human dignity.

15. See *Iliad* 6.359–62: "Do not, Helen, make me sit with you, though you love me. You will not persuade me. / Already my heart within is hastening to defend / the Trojans, who when I am away long greatly to have me."

16. Williams 1993, 78, makes the following salient comments on this culture: "The basic experience connected with shame is that of being seen, inappropriately, by the wrong people, in the wrong condition. It is straightforwardly connected with nakedness, particularly in sexual connections. The reaction is to cover oneself or to hide." Citing Gabriele Taylor he

also notes that with this "emotion of self-protection": "one's whole being seems diminished or lessened. In my experience of shame, the other sees all of me and all through me, even if the occasion of shame is on the surface . . . and the expression of shame, in general as well as in the particular form of it that is embarrassment, is not just the desire to hide, or to hide my face, but the desire to not be there" (89).

17. There are three notable exceptions to this claim wherein Helen is envisioned as a morally dubitable character: Hesiod's *Works and Days*, Aeschylus's *Agamemnon*, and Euripides' *The Trojan Women*. These exceptions are beyond the scope of the present essay but deserve further study.

18. As Matthew Gumpert argues in *Grafting Helen: The Abduction of the Classical Past* (Madison: University of Wisconsin Press, 2001), 84: "(Helen is always a reference to the Trojan War) so that putting her into a poem makes it both a 'private' and a 'public' or 'intertextual' dialogue." While Gumpert's interpretations of the figure of Helen make clear the "intertextual" dialogue with Homeric epic, he does not have as much to say about how the "references" to the Trojan War work and operate in the multiple discourses on Helen. One might argue that Norman Austin in *Helen of Troy and Her Shameless Phantom* (Ithaca: Cornell University Press, 1994) overestimates the value of the references to the Trojan War by seemingly accepting that the Greeks really believed in Helen's myth as the *causus belli*. In her reading of Sappho's "Helen," Page Dubois, *Sappho Is Burning* (Chicago: University of Chicago Press, 1995), brings the question of the Trojan War very much to the fore by offering a thoroughgoing analysis of the mechanism of money and war and Helen's symbolic interconnection.

19. The title of Austin's comprehensive study of Helen is *Helen of Troy and Her Shameless Phantom*. See also note 27 in this chapter.

20. A. R. Burn, *The Lyric Age of Greece* (London: Edward Arnold, 1960), 231, cited in Gumpert 2001, 87.

21. See Dubois 1995, 106.

22. For a coherent analysis of Sappho's identification with Helen, see Gumpert 2001, 93–94. Gumpert also makes the two following important points about identification in the poem. First, he remarks that "Helen's crime is a crime of passion but so is Sappho's writing of the poem" (92). And second, that Helen, like Paris, like Sappho, asks the same question, "What is most beautiful, most valuable, best?"

23. Dubois 1995, 67–68, has been most persistent in her analysis of Helen as a mediating term functioning analogically to the mechanism of money.

24. Gumpert 2001, 67.

25. Translation by Jack Winkler, "Gardens of Nymphs: Public and Private in Sappho's Lyrics," in *Reflections of Women in Antiquity* (New York: Gordon and Breach Science Publishers, 1981), 71. As I have indicated in brackets, an alternate translation of line 5 is "far surpassed all mortals in beauty" and for line 8 where to make "love" or "Aphrodite" is the subject of the verb "beguiled" (*paragag*).

26. The first translation is by Winkler 1981, 71; the second is by Denys Page, *Sappho and Alcaeus: An Introduction to the Study of Ancient Lesbian Poetry* (Oxford: Oxford University Press, 1955), 52–53. I follow Dubois 1995, 105, in her reading of this poem as a "pre-philosophical text . . . Sappho is . . . suggesting that there is such a thing as an abstract notion of eros . . . [she] attempt[s] to universalize her insight." I believe it is important to phrase the question Sappho the poet asks more abstractly than Dubois does: "What is the

most beautiful (thing) on the dark earth?" Although this is the specific question of the warriors, of Helen, and of the "I" represented in the poem—who may or may not be the real Sappho—the author Sappho is not only interested in what is best to love "here below," "on the dark earth." She is also intent on asking a more global, abstract question about love that is situated anywhere, anytime, and for anyone, any particular situation.

27. Winkler 1981, 71 remarks: "it is easy to read this [poem] as a comment on the system of heroic poetry." Gumpert 2001, 92, "positions the poem "in an intertextual economy: in other words, to show how it grafts epic and lyric genres, as it grafts its reader and speaker into its structure."

28. William Wians has suggested just such an interpretation.

29. Winkler 1981, 71.

30. Sappho corrects the Homeric representation of the cause of the Trojan War. Whereas it might appear that men suffered through war because of and for Helen, they were moved by a force greater than her, their love of "horsemen," "foot soldiers," and "a fleet of ships." Helen then did not cause the war. Rather, she is the cause of men's desire for war, which they love and find most beautiful, *kallistos*, in life.

31. On this paradox, see especially, Dubois 1995, 100–01.

32. Winkler 1981, 72.

33. R. Bespaloff in *On the Iliad* (New York: Pantheon Books, 1947) suggests that the Iliadic Helen's beauty weakens her capacity to respond as an active agent.

34. Anne Carson, *Eros the Bittersweet* (Princeton: Princeton University Press, 1986), 148.

35. Worman 1997, 171–80, has presented a completely compelling argument about the inextricable relation of Helen's body and the body of rhetorical speech, or as she puts it "the dangerous mobility and attraction of Helen's body and that of sophistic speech" (172). She concentrates especially on the sensationalist nature of sophistical epistemology—especially as concerns touch, sight, and hearing. I refer readers to her close reading of the *Encomium*. Worman's interpretation grants the figure of Helen more agency than I am inclined to accept. She writes, for example, that "[Gorgias's] treatment of Helen, initiated by the *Iliad* and distilled by Sappho, regards her as a possible agent in the viewing process and the arousal of desire" (171) or "Gorgias represents Helen as a fulcrum for desire, emphasizing the persuasive power of her body and isolating it as a centripetal force for others of equal brilliance" (173). Gumpert, 2001, 72–73, focusing on the identification as foreigners of Helen of Troy, Gorgias, and of "rhetoric" reads the *Encomium* as a reenactment—not only of Helen's exile but also of the "dislocation" of metaphor. "Poetry for Gorgias," he writes, "performs a figurative *abduction* upon the listener, it 'enraptures and translates the soul' " (76). Helen, like Gorgias's poetry, activates the same type of enrapture and abandon. For a reading of Gorgias's *Encomium* that situates the text within the historical conditions of women in fifth-century BCE and offers a reading explicitly addressing the question of gender, see "Gorgias's Encomium of Helen: Violent Rhetoric or Radical Feminism?" *Rhetoric Review* 13.1 (Autumn 1994), 71–90.

36. Gorgias, *Gorgias's Encomium of Helen*, translated by D. M. MacDowell (Glasgow: Bristol Classical Press, 1982), l. 1.

37. Jacqueline de Romilly is especially interested in the magical dimension of Gorgias's conception of language in "Gorgias et le pouvoir de la poésie," *Journal of Hellenic Studies* 93 (1973), esp. pp. 159–62. For other discussions of Gorgias's preoccupation in the *Enco-*

mium with the linguistic effect, see Giovanni Casertano, "L'amour entre Logos et Pathos: Quelques Considerations sur L'Hélène de Gorgias," in Barbara Cassin, ed., *Positions de la Sophistique* (Paris: Librarie Philosophique J. Vrin, 1986); Barbara Cassin, "Encore Hélène: une sophistique de la jouissance," *Littoral* 15 /16 (1985); Charles Segal, "Gorgias and the Psychology of Logos," *Harvard Studies in Classical Philology* 66 (1962); Froma Zeitlin, "Travesties of Gender and Genre in Aristophanes' *Thesmophoriazousae*," in Helene Foley, ed., *Reflections of Women in Antiquity* (New York: Gordon and Breach Science Publishers, 1981), esp. pp. 207–11. Segal 1962, 109 remarks: "the speech itself, in fact, is as much an encomium on the power of the logos as on Helen herself; and thus the *Helen* expresses a view of literature and oratory which touches closely Gorgias' own practice and probably his own beliefs. Hence the speech may even have served as a kind of formal profession of the aims and methods of his art, a kind of advertisement." Zeitlin 1981, 210, in turn explains why Gorgias chose Helen in the first place: "Helen, as the paradigm of the feminine, is the ideal subject/object of the discourse; first, in sexual terms, as the passive partner to be mastered by masculine rhetorical persuasion, and second, in aesthetic terms. Helen, as the mistress of mimesis and the object of mimesis, is a fitting participant in the world of make-believe, the anti-world which reverses the terms in mimetic display and reserves the right under the name of play to take everything back."

38. Gorgias does indeed claim that he will revise existent beliefs about Helen through the use of "true" speech, but at the same time he indicates that one cannot know whether or not his own speech, though ordered by "reason," corresponds to the true nature of things and thereby moves beyond a "slippery" and "unreliable" *doxa* (see l. 11). Being only under the influence of Gorgias's linguistic reality, what can prevent his audience from becoming like Helen, victims of the various intellectual and emotional powers of speech? What defense does Gorgias offer to protect his own speech from functioning, in the words of Charles Segal, through an "emotional *bia* or *ananke*" or through "the persuasive force of reason"? Or, for Gorgias, is such a defense even necessary if by the end of his speech he has succeeded to alter previous perceptions of reality and ethical judgments in order to include praise of Helen?

39. Friedrich Nietzsche, *The Birth of Tragedy*, trans. Francis Golffing (New York: Doubleday Anchor Press, 1956), 74–75.

40. Nietzsche 1956, 79.

41. See Plato, *Phaedrus*, 243A, 3–9: "and for those who have sinned in matters of mythology there is an ancient purification, unknown to Homer, but known to Stesichorus. For when he was stricken with blindness for speaking ill of Helen, he was not, like Homer, ignorant of the reason, but since he was educated, he knew it and straightway he writes the poem . . . and when he had written all the poem, which is called the recantation, he saw again at once." C. W. Bowra in "The Two Palinodes of Stesichorus," *The Classical Review* 13.3 (Dec. 1963), 245–52, provides a striking hypothesis to answer the question of "To whom is this palinode addressed?" Bowra surmises it is the Muse: "it is tempting to think he has a special reason for doing so—because it is she who must now put right what he has said before and help him to produce a more respectful version of the doings of Helen" (247). Bowra also suggests that the third and fourth lines of the palinode may be addressed directly to Helen. As with Stesichorus so with Euripides: "Helen" will hear a very different song. Both versions, as I discuss here, are rectifications and repudiations of the Homeric myth and aim to restore a more "respectable"—if not absurd—position to Helen.

42. Euripides, *Helen*, trans. Richmond Lattimore (Chicago: University of Chicago Press, 1969). It must be put on the record here again that *Helen* was written during the winter following the defeat of Athens in the Sicilian expedition.

43. The most forceful lines about both the unreliability and reliability of the senses are found in lines 575–80, upon Helen and Menelaus's first encounter: *Menelaus*: "Am I in my right senses? Are my eyes at fault?" *Helen*: "When you look at me, do you not think you see your wife?" *Menelaus*: "Your body is like her. Certainty fails me." *Helen*: "Look and see. What more do you want? And who knows me better than you?" *Menelaus*: "In very truth you are like her. That I will not deny." *Helen*: "What better teacher shall you have than your own eyes?"

44. For readings of the genre of *Helen*—whether romance, tragedy, comedy, comedy of ideas, see, for example, J. G. Griffith, "Some Thoughts on the 'Helena' of Euripides," *Journal of Hellenic Studies* 73 (1953), 36–41; A. N. Pippin, "Euripides' *Helen*: A Comedy of Ideas," *Classical Philology* 55 (1960), 151–63; Anthony J. Podlecki, "The Basic Seriousness of Euripides' *Helen*," *Transactions and Proceedings of the American Philological Association* 101 (1970), 401–18; Charles Segal, "The Two Worlds of Euripides' *Helen*," in *Interpreting Greek Tragedy: Myth, Poetry, Text* (Ithaca: Cornell University Press, 1986), 222–67; and the chapter by Michael Davis in this volume.

45. See, for example, ll. 16ff., 235ff., 362ff., 603ff., 648ff., 870ff., 1115ff., 1650ff.

46. Segal 1986, 224–25.

47. Zeitlin 1981, 189. Zetilin also remarks in this same passage: "When women asked the kinsmen earlier why Euripides had never put any Penelopes upon the stage, he replied that Penelopes were nowhere to be found any more."

48. Nicole Loraux, *Tragic Ways of Killing a Woman*, translated by Anthony Forster (Cambridge: Harvard University Press, 1987), 9.

49. On Helen's imagined suicide, see Loraux 1987, 16. For a discussion of the figure of Helen in Euripides *Troades*, see especially Worman, 1997, 180–98. Worman argues that "Helen's speech in the *Troades* formulates a world in which issues of human responsibility have no place. It is a world invigorated by arguments mapped onto the body—most particularly Helen's own—that reproduce the force of desire that drove her actions" (198).

Min utem deliqui eugue min ut essit lore tion velesti nciduis num del ea feummod ex eniatum irilisl ute cor si blam, quat, consequis nim dit, sectet ad tem deliquisit ad tetum quat utat lamet lamcore ercilit ipsuscincin henisit pratie tionullam, se commy nonse tat velis alit wiscidu iscinis iscilit ad eu facidunt luptat illa autem incil illan ute velisit atie modolum in velenisl ipsustrud doloborem vullutat wis alisl in velis am dolobortie feu feu faci blaore magna facidunt do elis augait aciniamcore modoloborem dolore conum irit ver suscilit wisi.

Loborer ostrud ea facilla mcommy nibh er ip ea consequam, quam do core vullan ut ad te venis dolestie modolore commolore ea faccumsan vel irilit accumsandit, volorpe riustrud mod tatem vel in henim il ut lore faciliscil illandio eniate do dit at ipit lametum amet la consequat praesto enisim iriuscipit utpat. Ure doloborper suscidunt utpat. Giamcon umsandigna corpero et nim irit lut praestrud delestie min utat. Os aliqui tat wisi blaortin utat.

Dionsed tio eugue conummy nulla commolo borperci eu feugait ulput volorper sisi.

5

Allegory and the Origins of Philosophy

GERARD NADDAF

The birth of philosophy is generally identified with the rejection of *mythopoiesis* and the adoption of rational explanations in terms of causality (e.g., Cornford, Guthrie, Vernant, Burkert, West, Curd, Laks, Long), whence the popular expression from *muthos* to *logos* or from myth to reason. Much has been written on this famous transition, which many once considered a "miracle."[1] However, there is little on how the proponents of myth responded. They fought back with *mutho-logia*, that is, with a *logos* about myth. This "rational" approach invoked the same *logos* that is generally associated with *philosophia*. In fact, *philosophia* and *mythologia* are at times so intimately connected that, until the Enlightenment period, it is often difficult to distinguish between them.[2] This is due to the "spell" of myth, particularly Greek/Homeric myth, or to be more precise, because of the allegorical interpretation of Homeric myth.

In this essay, I examine the origins and development of this rather unremarked—albeit remarkable—"story." I want to show to what degree the pre-Platonic project of philosophy was at times overshadowed by the allegorical approach to myth. Given the importance of allegoresis, that is, allegorizing as an interpretative mode, it is most surprising that histories of ancient philosophy rarely mention the notion in the development of early Greek philosophy.[3]

The history of allegoresis is complex. It features many actors with widely different positions and roles. The initial protagonists are, of course, Homer and Hesiod. Their works constitute the original and primary object of allegoresis. It is difficult to understand the origin of allegoresis without some background into how and why the two great poets were canonized as the "educators of Greece." This point is almost invariably passed over in silence, at least in the present context. Then there are the Milesians. They are the real heroes in this affair—although never acknowledged as such by contemporary scholars. Indeed, within a generation or two of their articulation, their naturalistic theories—with which we associate the origins of philosophy—appeared so convincing to the intellectual milieu that there is a sense in which they were uncontested. If Homer and Hesiod were to maintain their unparalleled prestige as the guarantors of the cultural past, their poems had to be seen as conveying the same ideas as those of the Milesians, at least by a large portion of the intelligentsia. This is already clear in the scholium to the late sixth-century BC grammarian Theagenes of Rhegium.

We also have Xenophanes and Heraclitus, who were the first to challenge publicly the idea that Homer and Hesiod had any claim to "truthful knowledge." Until their very public scolding of the two great poets, there was nothing to indicate that Homer and Hesiod were understood otherwise than literally. It was only when Xenophanes and Heraclitus drew attention to the consequences of a literal interpretation that allegoresis, a radical new way of interpreting Homer and Hesiod (and later Orpheus) was introduced. Xenophanes and Heraclitus thus appear to have paved the road for the aforementioned Theagenes of Rhegium, a younger Italian (or western Greek) contemporary, who is the first person credited with writing an allegorical exegesis of Homer as a reply to the poet's detractors. It is unclear if Theagenes initiated allegoresis (there are, as we will see, many positions), but I will argue that his counterattack against the detractors of Homer and Hesiod was so effective and convincing that the traditional philosophical successors to Xenophanes and Heraclitus thought that Homer and Hesiod had access to the doctrines they themselves espoused. Indeed, there is evidence that in some instances they thought that their respective doctrines were defensible because they were "somehow" endorsed by Homer and Hesiod. There is thus a complex reciprocal relation between philosophy and poetry—the author of the Derveni Papyrus shows just how complex this history really is—that has never been fully appreciated, in which poetry acts as a catalyst in the post-Heraclitean development of philosophy. As I hope to show, all the pre-Socratic philosophers, including Parmenides, Anaxagoras, Empedocles, Democritus, and even the sophists, employ allegory and/or allegoresis to various degrees and, no doubt, for various reasons. I will also examine a number of other players in this *historia* including the author of the Derveni Papyrus and several minor but relevant pre-Socratics and contemporaries of Plato. However, I will also endeavor to examine the contemporary debate/controversy concerning how allegoresis originated.

Given the complexities of the history of allegoresis, it should be no surprise that allegory itself is, as Anthony Long notes in his seminal article "Stoic Readings of Homer" (1992), "a very complex notion."[4] By way of clarification, Long distinguishes between calling a text allegorical in a *strong* or in a *weak* sense: "A text will be allegorical in a *strong* sense if its author composes with the intention of being interpreted allegorically," while "a text will be allegorical in a *weak* sense if, irrespective of what its author intended, it invites interpretation in ways that go beyond its surface or so-called literal meaning" (43). We could also characterize the *strong* and *weak* senses as intentional and nonintentional or deliberative and nondeliberative respectively. Long's aim was to clarify how the Stoics read Homer. I am more interested in the pre-Stoic attitude toward Homer (albeit not just Homer) and allegory. I will have more to say on the notion of allegory as we progress.

With these historical and semantic complexities in mind, let us begin with the relation between *muthos* and *logos*.

Muthos and *Logos*

The word *myth* is difficult to define, and no one definition has gained universal acceptance.[5] The word is a transliteration of the ancient Greek word *muthos*, the basic meaning of which seems to have been "something one says." Thus the word appears in Homer in the sense of "story"—for example, "Listen to the story (*muthon akousas*) of the wanderings" at *Odyssey* 4.324—but never with the modern, pejorative connotation that the story is a fiction. This is also the case with Hesiod. In fact, both Homer and Hesiod—the primary sources of traditional Greek tales of gods and heroes—seem to employ *muthos* and *logos* interchangeably.[6] This lack of differentiation is not restricted to the two great poets, as it is also the case with the pre-Socratic philosophers, whom we consider the initiators of *logos* in the sense of a rational and argumentative account. Xenophanes (c. 570–470), who is the first to vigorously denounce the old traditional theology—that is, the mythology—of Homer and Hesiod and to replace it with a new "rational" theology, employs the plurals *muthoi* and *logoi* almost synonymously in the same phrase (DK 21B1.13–14). Even Parmenides (c. 515–450), the father of deductive logic, characterizes his ultimate account of truth as both a *muthos* and a *logos* (DK 28B8.1–2; B8.51–51).

We should not infer from this that *logos* referred to anything other than a "rational" discourse. That it carried this meaning is clearly the case with Heraclitus (c. 540–480), in whose writings there are *no* occurrences of *muthos*, while *logos* is omnipresent. The primary reason why *logos* carried this meaning is found in its root, **leg-*, the fundamental meaning of which is "gathering," "picking up," "choosing." The verb *legein* (as opposed to *mutheomai*) was thus not originally a saying verb but a word that described a physical activity and by extension an activity of the mind.[7] When *legein* later became a saying verb—thanks to its figurative meaning of "recounting, telling over, reckoning up"—the noun *logos* retained in Attic Greek the rational values of the root **leg-* and applied them to speech. This explains why despite the numerous meanings that the word *logos* was to take, one can reduce them to two: speech and reason. Subject the first to the second, and *logos* takes on the sense of a "rational discourse," that is, a discourse that is argumentative and open to criticism, a discourse that can be logically and/or empirically verified.

In the final analysis, the famous *muthos/logos* dichotomy is not clearly attested prior to Plato, although the germs may be discerned in some authors.[8] It is with Plato that the opposition we generally associate with these words begins.[9]

Meanwhile, what Plato understands by myth (*muthos*) is much more than simply a "traditional tale" or fiction, which is "unbelievable." As Brisson (1998) has
shown, a contextual analysis of Plato's use of the term *muthos* reveals that what
Plato understands by myth is synonymous with what an ethnologist would call
"oral literature." For an ethnologist, myth is a message or set of messages that a
social group thinks it has received from its ancestors and that it transmits orally
from generation to generation.[10]

In the Greek oral tradition, myths took the form of poetry. Plato considers the
poet not only as a myth-teller but also as a mythmaker, indeed, the mythmaker par
excellence. In the ancient Greek tradition, as it is abundantly evidenced by Plato,
it is the great poets, Homer and Hesiod, who are seen as the primary "creators"
of "oral tradition" and, by extension, of "myth." This is also Herodotus's position
(2.53) when he states that "Homer and Hesiod are the poets who composed our
theogonies and described the gods for us, giving them all their appropriate titles,
offices, and powers." The gods (*theoi*) were so named, Herodotus notes, because "they
disposed all things in order" (*hoti kosmoi thentes ta panta pragmata*; 2.52.1)—that
is, established the physical and moral/social order of the universe.[11]

The relation of Homer and Hesiod to myth is, in fact, complex and not
always fully appreciated. In a world in which myths are always and hence "naturally" conveyed in oral accounts, writing "denaturalizes" myth. With the advent of
writing, Greek myths were open to interpretation, since they could be recorded in
a literary form.[12] This brings us to the notion of mythology.

Mythology

The word *mythology*, from the Greek *muthologia*, is a compound of two elements:
muthos and *logia*. The term *logia* explains why the word *mythology* can have several
different meanings. Indeed, mythology can mean: the set of myths proper to a
civilization; the act of gathering or collecting myths; simply telling myths; making
myths; or the study and/or critical evaluation of myths. The fact that Plato was
the first to employ the word *mythologia*—in ways that include *all* of the above
meanings (contra Kirk)[13]—does not mean that these meanings did not exist prior
to him. Although we use the expressions "from myth to philosophy" or "from myth
to logos," these expressions were not employed by the philosophers with whom we
associate this intellectual revolution. Homer and Hesiod called themselves *aoidoi*,
bards or singers, rather than *poiētai*, poets (that is, "creators of myth"), and they
did not employ the word *muthos* to characterize their respective accounts of the
gods and heroes. Homer and Hesiod themselves nonetheless practiced *mythologia* in
several different ways. First, they "gathered" or "collected" myths (and thus chose
what to include and what not to include); they told myths; they made myths (from
preexisting material, it is true); and the result was the creation of a set of myths.

They did not themselves, to our knowledge, "study" or "critically examine" myths, although when Hesiod states that the Muses can speak both truth and falsehood (*Theogony* 24–28) or when Homer contends that there are deliberate acts of deception (*Od.* 19.203), one could argue that he is making a "critical evaluation" of what to include as truth and what to exclude—an eventual incitement to allegorical interpretations.[14] All of this suggests, I think, that Homer and Hesiod were literate composers, but given that they were at the very dawn of literacy in ancient Greece, they would have been composing for a listening rather than a reading audience, since it is clear that written poetry was meant to be performed.

What did Homer and Hesiod see themselves as doing? There can be little doubt, I believe, that Homer and Hesiod saw themselves as disseminators of a historico-genealogical tradition. In the case of the Homeric epics, the Greeks of the subsequent generations never doubted the authenticity of the Trojan War and the heroes who participated in it. And while it is true, as Thucydides notes, that "people are inclined to accept all stories of ancient times in an uncritical way" (1.20), in particular those of poets like Homer (1.10, 21), he is nonetheless well aware that he is dependent on Homer's account of the Trojan War in his reconstruction of the early history of Greece.[15]

Homer's account of the Trojan War is, of course, a perfect example of oral tradition as defined here. It was how the personalized gods openly intervened in human affairs and how they behaved toward one another that was later to raise eyebrows. Indeed, while there is quite obviously a strict code of behavior based on the sacred tradition, what stands out in the Homeric epics is the devious and perverse behavior of the gods, behavior that is not only seen as mirroring human action but as providing its primary motivation: "Zeus [or any divinity] made me do it."

There are a number of contradictions here. On the one hand, Zeus is the protector of social order, and to ignore this is to invite an Achillean type of divine wrath. On the other, he appears to endorse, indeed actively participate in, extreme asocial behavior. The gods sanction devious and antisocial actions, including murder, rape, and theft, as long as these actions take place outside the spheres of their individual concerns. In this respect, as Burkert notes, "the very model of behavior" that the myths of the gods offer is one in which one must not do X if there is a danger of offending, but if there is no danger of offending, X is permitted.[16] In fact, it is quite stunning to what degree the order of events in the Trojan War is actually dictated by Aphrodite's sphere of activity, and this is also the case in Hesiod's *Theogony*. Aphrodite seduces Paris, who in turn seduces Helen. Sex and intrigue, seduction and carnal pleasure, go hand in hand throughout the epic. Hera is well aware that sex, if anything, will take Zeus's eyes off the Trojan War (*Il.* 14.160ff.; 215ff.). And the various homecomings of the heroes are no less haunted by the same phenomena: adultery, incest, and murder.

Hesiod's *Theogony* shows that this amoral or asocial behavior was, to some degree, at the foundation of the present world order. The *Theogony* describes the

origin of the world and of the gods and the events that led to the establishment
of the present order. It explains how Zeus, after a series of sociopolitical power
struggles, defeated his enemies and distributed, as the new ruler, the portions of
honors among the Immortals (see *Theogony* 391ff.). As such, it explains the origin
of the organizational structure and code of values of the gods (and by extension
the heroes and humans) that we see in action in Homer's *Iliad* and *Odyssey*. From
this perspective, Hesiod's *Theogony* is perhaps more of a basic textbook (following
Herodotus 2.53) of Greek religion and mythology than are Homer's epics.

Did Homer and Hesiod themselves believe in these oral, traditional accounts?
Given that the Greeks of subsequent generations did not doubt the authenticity
of the Trojan War (to which one could add the Lelantine War and other more
historical events alluded to by Hesiod in his *Works and Days*), there is little doubt,
I believe, that this was also the case for Homer and Hesiod as well as their poetic
predecessors. But did they believe that the gods and goddesses actually intervened
in human events in the ways described? Did they believe that the heroes were in
part of divine origin, albeit "mortal"? Did they believe that the gods actually were
anthropomorphic and, once born, behaved toward one another in reprehensible
ways? It was in fact these "nonhistorical" embellishments that were later to be
associated first and foremost with *muthoi*, that is, "myths."

There is no good reason to believe that Homer and Hesiod did not also have
a "literal" belief in the "nonhistorical" component of their traditional accounts.
Indeed, there is good evidence that this view was widely accepted for generations
by the proponents of traditional religion and morality (the nonintellectual class
and thus, it seems, the majority: or what Heraclitus would call the *hoi polloi* or
"ignorant masses" in DK 22B104). As David Furley has shown,[17] Euthyphro is a
perfect example of this. He is a religious interpreter and representative of traditional
religious (and moral) beliefs who takes a literal or orthodox interpretation (analogous
to contemporary fundamentalists) of the bloody and cruel battles among the gods
as they are portrayed in Hesiod's *Theogony* (*Euthyphro*, 5d–6d).[18] A similar popular
view is echoed in Aristophanes' *The Clouds* (c. 423) by Strepsiades, an uneducated
farmer, who represents traditional morality and the old education. It seems inconceiv-
able to Strepsiades that anything but Zeus is behind the meteorological phenomena
(*Clouds* 365–75). Nor was this restricted to the "uneducated class." It has become
a cliché, in light of Plato's observations in the *Republic*, that Homer (and Hesiod
to a lesser degree) was considered "the educator of Hellas" (*Republic* 606e), that
is, the founder of traditional education (*Republic* 10.598d–e). What Plato means
is that most Greeks believed that Homer and his cohorts knew "all the arts and
all things pertaining to virtue and vice, and all things divine" (10.598e; reiterated
in the *Ion*; see also further on in this chapter). For Plato, this is nonsense and
the source of the "old quarrel" (*palaia diaphora*) between philosophy and poetry
(*Republic* 10.607b). It is unclear when Plato sees the quarrel as having originated.
This brings us back to the origin of philosophy.[19]

The Origin of Philosophy

As I have noted, the origin of philosophy is generally identified with the rejection of *mythopoiesis* and the adoption of rational/natural explanations. There is a sense in which the first philosophers, or *phusiologoi* as Aristotle characterized them, discovered "nature," that is, nature as an objectivity. As Vlastos correctly observes, the first philosophers were "united in the assumption that the order which makes our world a cosmos is natural, that is to say, that it is immanent in nature."[20] The world order derives from the essential characteristics of the components themselves; consequently, there is no need for the intervention of the supernatural entities we see in "mythical" accounts. There is indeed a consensus that the first philosophers were all engaged with what the Greeks called *historia peri phuseōs*, that is, an "investigation into nature" and that the primary preoccupation of this investigation was to give an account of *all* things based on rational argumentation.[21]

The first philosopher to have written a book reflecting this new vision of nature was Anaximander of Miletus (c. 610–546). Anaximander's book, *Peri phuseōs*, was one of the first known examples of prose in Greek and the first philosophical prose treatise. His choice to write in prose rather than in verse may have been an attempt to free the language of philosophy (or what was to become philosophy) from the undesirable preconceptions of poetry. However, the picture is complicated.

Anaximander's new concept of nature is evidenced in a number of ancient sources. One of particular importance describes how Anaximander conceived the formation of the universe (DK 12A10 = Pseudo-Plutarch *Miscellanies* 2). The central idea is that the cosmos grows, like a living being, from a seed or germ.[22] According to the doxography, the cause of all natural change is the reciprocal action of the opposites—that is, hot, cold, wet, and dry—which are the basic components or principles of all things. Once the separation of the mutually hostile opposites commences, the cosmogonic process perpetuates itself in a cyclical process through the natural operation of the reciprocal power of the opposites. This is corroborated in Anaximander's sole surviving fragment, which explains how the present order of things is maintained: "things [natural things] perish into those things from which they have/derive their being [= the opposites], according to necessity; for these things [the primary opposites] pay penalty and retribution to one another for their injustice according to the assessment of time." The order of nature is based on an equilibrium of rights and obligations, an equilibrium that results when the constituent powers or primary opposites act as equals. In sum, the natural order of things is the result of a constant interchange between the primary powers or opposites, the same powers or opposites that were behind the initial formation of the universe: hot and cold; wet and dry. The interchange between the primary opposites is behind all natural phenomena: night and day; the changing of the seasons; meteorological phenomena;[23] the birth and death of living things,[24] and so forth, with Time as the guarantee that a stalemate will result indefinitely.

It is from the combination and interaction of the hot and cold, and wet and dry that originate, on the one hand, the four regions of the visible universe: Fire (that is, the upper atmosphere considered as such), Sea, Air, and Earth, and, on the other, the four elemental bodies associated with these: earth, air, fire, and water. Thus dry is associated with earth, cold with air, hot with fire, and wet with water (DK 12A16 = Aristotle, *Physics* 204b22–29).[25]

Anaximenes (c. 584–528), Anaximander's younger contemporary and fellow citizen, introduced the contrasting processes of rarefaction and condensation (associated again with hot and cold) to account for all natural change. These processes explain how the four great masses of the universe, the four "basic" elements, and the various meteorological phenomena all originate from air, Anaximenes' primordial principle. The first thing to form was the earth due to the condensation of air (DK 13A6). The earth is a flat disk (which accounts for its stability) that not only formed from air but also rests on a cushion of air (DK 13A6, 7, 20). The other heavenly bodies result from exhalations of moisture from the earth. Also flat, they float on air and are carried around by its movement (DK 13A7). When air is rarefied it becomes fire, when it is condensed it becomes wind, then cloud, then water, then earth, and then stones (DK 13A5, 7). The transformations air undergoes also account for various meteorological phenomena, including clouds, rain, snow, hail, thunder, lightning, rainbows, and earthquakes (DK 13A7, 17, 18, 21).

For both Anaximander and Anaximenes there is no role for the traditional gods; indeed, as far as we know they do not enter into the picture. This brings us back to the ancient quarrel between philosophy and poetry.

The Ancient Quarrel

We are all familiar with Xenophanes' (c. 570–470) scathing remarks with regard to Homer and Hesiod's portrayal of the traditional gods: "Homer and Hesiod have attributed to the gods every kind of behavior that among men is the object of reproach: stealing, adultery, and cheating each other" (DK 21B11).[26] This remark was the first known salvo in what Plato later called "the ancient quarrel between philosophy and poetry" (*palaia diaphora philosophai te kai poiētikai*; *Republic* 607b5). The criticism Xenophanes directed against the two Greek icons and their crass anthropomorphism[27] centers on the idea that if the gods do indeed behave this way, then there is no reason to worship them. Indeed, their portrayal of the gods is socially irresponsible, for it fosters social disharmony and civil strife.[28] In DK 21B1.21–22, Xenophanes disparagingly characterizes the compositions of the poets—with a particular reference to the battle of the giants—as *plasmata tōn proterōn*, that is, "fabrications of old" for precisely the same reasons: they encourage civil strife.

Xenophanes was well aware that Homer had the reputation of being the "educator of the Greeks." Indeed, he was the first to mention Homer by name in this context: "From the beginning [of one's life] all have learned according to Homer" (DK 21B10).[29] Heraclitus of Ephesus (540–480), a younger contemporary of Xenophanes, concurs with him when he states: "Hesiod is the teacher of most men" (DK 22B57), or again when he characterizes Homer as "the wisest of all the Greeks" (DK 22B56). And yet Heraclitus's criticism is even more bitter than that of Xenophanes: "Homer deserved to be expelled from the [rhapsodic] competition and beaten with a staff (*rhapizesthai*)" (DK 22B42).[30] Hesiod fares no better, for after stating that "Hesiod is the teacher of most men," Heraclitus derides him with the contention that he didn't even recognize that "day and night are one and the same thing" (DK 22B57; see also DK 22B106). Heraclitus is both appalled and frustrated that the ignorant crowd or *hoi polloi* believes that what the *aoidoi* or poets say is true (DK 22B104). Xenophanes and Heraclitus object first and foremost to Homer and Hesiod as a source of wisdom. The Muses cannot be used as a source of *alētheia*, or even *doxa*, for that matter, when it comes to truth claims. The gods simply do not reveal "truth" about the universe to humans, including poets; humans must search for themselves, using their minds and the senses, that is, rational argument and observation, to arrive at valid conclusions about the nature of the universe and our place in it. In sum, the two great poets are denied any claim to "truthful knowledge" (Most 1999, 338; Morgan 2000, 58).[31]

It seems clear that both Xenophanes and Heraclitus are not only familiar with the poetry of Homer and Hesiod through oral recitations but that they have also read and reflected on the poetic texts.[32] Despite their hostility toward Homer and Hesiod, it seems also clear that both Xenophanes and Heraclitus presume that the texts of Homer and Hesiod are transparent and their meaning unambiguous. They appear to make no distinction between what Homer and Hesiod intended and what their texts literally said. This suggests that what Homer and Hesiod were saying was not a concern for those toward whom their criticism was addressed and it seems that their criticism was directed toward a wider public.[33]

This is where the plot thickens. As Glenn Most notes, by denying Homer and Hesiod any claim to "truthful knowledge," Xenophanes and Heraclitus not only initiated one of the most tenacious polemical traditions in Western poetics, but they also laid the foundation for the most influential way of safeguarding the poets from such attacks, namely allegorical interpretation. The most stunning and ironical surprise in this recuperative measure, given the stakes in the polemic, is that "the allegorist believes that the only true doctrine is in fact the one the philosopher possesses" (Most 1999, 339). The allegorist does not claim that the obvious reading of the poet's text is incompatible with the philosopher's doctrine but in fact asserts that, "though the poet may seem to be saying one thing that contradicts the [philosophers'] truth, in fact he means another that is entirely compatible with it" (339). There are, as we will see, a number of variations on this claim. Indeed, Most's claim seems to accommodate "allegorists" who are not themselves "philosophers." But, as we will see, many of the early philosophers appear to have been smitten with the allegorical bug themselves, and when they did dabble in allegoresis, they seem to have had a more positive interpretation of the poets. So when and with whom did this originate?

The Advent of Allegorical Interpretation

The first person credited with having written an allegorical exegesis of Homer was Theagenes of Rhegium.[34] A scholium to Venetus B manuscript, attributed to the Neoplatonist philosopher and philologist Porphyry (AD 234–c. 305), provides an example of Theagenes' method.[35] The passage refers to *Iliad* 20.67ff. (= DK 8.2), in which the gods, with Zeus's permission, descend to the plain and battle each other for the fate of Troy. The gods line up in opposition to one another—Poseidon against Apollo, Ares against Athena, Hera against Artemis, Leto against Hermes, and Hephaestus against Scamander—and the scholiast/Porphyry notes the following:

> Homer's doctrine on the gods usually tends to be useless and improper, for the myths he relates about the gods are offensive. In order to counter this sort of accusation, some people invoke the mode of expression (*tēs lexeōs*); they feel that all was said in an allegorical mode (*allēgoria*) and has to do with the nature of the elements, as in the case of the passage where the gods confront one another. Thus according to them, the dry clashes with the wet, the hot clashes with the cold, and the light with the heavy. In addition, water extinguishes fire, while fire evaporates water; in a similar way, there is an opposition between all the elements making up the universe; they may suffer destruction in part, but they endure eternally as a whole. In arranging these battles, Homer provides fire with the name of Apollo, Helios, or Hephaestus, he calls water Poseidon or Scamander, the moon Artemis, air Hera, and so on. In the same way, he sometimes gives names of gods to dispositions, the name Athena is given to wisdom/intelligence,[36] Ares to folly, Aphrodite to desire, Hermes to speech, all according to what is associated with each. This kind of defense is very ancient and goes back to Theagenes of Rhegium, who was the first to write about Homer.[37]

Porphyry provides us with no information other than this reference with regard to Theagenes, but according to the second-century AD Greek-speaking Christian philosopher Tatian (*Greek Discourses* 31 = DK 8.1), Theagenes was a contemporary of the Persian King Cambyses (530–522), which means that he would have been living during the same period as Homer's detractors. Moreover, Tatian places Theagenes at the head of list of those who first studied "Homer's poetry, life, and time" (DK 8.1; this also found in the *Suidas* DK 8.3). Theagenes is also cited for variant readings of *Iliad* 1.381 (DK 8.4) and characterized as a *grammatikos* or grammarian who initiated the proper use of the Greek language (*hellēnismos*, DK 8.1a). There is to be sure a fair amount of controversy regarding this now famous figure, albeit almost exclusively in the domain of literary criticism. However, the relevance, indeed importance, of Theagenes of Rhegium for the history of the origin and development of Greek philosophy is rarely mentioned in this context.

The most common interpretation of this reference from Porphyry is that Theagenes sought to "defend" Homer against his detractors. This may well be the case, but it is unclear why.[38] Indeed, it is unclear just what "profession" Theagenes practiced. It is often suggested that he was a rhapsode.[39] Rhapsodes were professional reciters of Homer who also interpreted him (as we see in Plato's *Ion* 530c–d and Xenophon's *Symposium* 3.6). The testimonia cited here suggests that Theagenes was a genuine Homerphile. But if Theagenes were a rhapsode, he was clearly not one of the much-scorned type that are often evoked (e.g., Xenophon's *Symposium* 3.6, following Niceratus's boast). Given his knowledge of the new Milesian *historia*, he must have been a member of the intelligentsia and thus a member of the aristocratic community and/or the nouveaux riche. Andrew Ford recently conjectured that Theagenes (and his Homeric successors) transformed the "panhellenic epic into esoteric text" (2002, 76). Ford argues that the reason was primarily political.[40] Theagenes, according to Ford, was a member of the aristocracy of Rhegium (the famous "1,000").[41] And the ever-popular epics now became "a riddle (*ainos*) to be deciphered by the wise," that is, the aristocracy (2002, 78). It was another way for the elite or a certain elite (if we consider the pretensions of the Pythagoreans in the same area and at the same time) to affirm their "cultural leadership." I find this hypothesis very persuasive. But on this reading it is unclear if Theagenes thought that Homer himself was an allegorist in the strong sense, that is, someone who consciously constructed his poems so that their apparent meaning refers to an "other" meaning.[42] To be sure, there is plenty in Homer and Hesiod that is arguably allegorical, not to mention the much-discussed observation that both Homer and Hesiod stress that the poet and the Muses are capable of reciting true and false stories. Before canvassing this further, I would like to return to the Milesians.

It is surprising the Milesians are generally passed over in silence when discussing Theagenes as the first recorded allegorist, that is, the first to practice allegoresis.[43] Indeed, it is the Milesian doctrine of the primary opposites to which the scholiast refers when he claims that Theagenes was the first to argue that the battle of the gods in Homer is really a description of the fight in nature between the primary elements and/or opposites. It seems clear—although scholars are loath to mention it—that Theagenes was more impressed with the Milesians than with Homer. It is as if Theagenes were a disciple of Anaximander. But if Theagenes endorsed the new naturalist vision of the universe and the arguments on which it is premised, just what position did he maintain with regard to Homer?[44] Did he believe, as commonly supposed, that Homer as a poet (if not *the* poet) was a prophet directly inspired by the gods? From this perspective, Theagenes would have seen Homer as one of the famous "masters of truth,"[45] that is, a "master of truth" who was already *aware* that the universe functioned according to "natural laws," but laws that were hidden from the masses (aristocratic and nonaristocratic alike). The Milesians had now discovered these divine secrets through their *historia*.

While it seems clear that Theagenes' measures were "defensive" in that he wanted to rescue Homer from charges of irreverence and intellectual simplicity, the argument has also been made that the origins of allegory were "positive" and "exegetical," that is, a way of claiming the poets' authority for the interpreter's own doctrines, and thus chronologically *prior* to the initial attacks on the two poets (e.g., Feeney 1991, 10–12; Struck 2004, 14–15). In his entry on Greek allegory in the *Oxford Classical Dictionary* (third ed.), Michael Trapp states that it is difficult to know what the "balance" was between the positive and the defensive possibilities. The positive was first argued by Jonathan Tate in a series of articles in the first half of the last century. He contended that allegoresis could not have originated with Theagenes' reaction to Xenophanes because it was already practiced by earlier figures like Pherecydes of Syros (see further on). Tate also argued that the early philosophers (by whom he means Xenophanes, Heraclitus, Parmenides, and Empedocles, and not the Milesians, whom he never mentions) were students of Homer and Hesiod *before* they became philosophers (1934, 106; see also Tate 1927 and 1929, cited further on). Because they were nurtured with the notion that the poets were divinely inspired, as speculative thought developed, so did the conviction that the poets had expressed profound truths that were difficult to define in "scientific language." Because of the enormous prestige of the poets, on the one hand, and the profound conviction that the myths were expressions of the same philosophical truths that they were now defining in scientific terms, on the other, the early philosophers wanted to appropriate these myths through allegory. From this perspective, allegory was originally a positive exegetical endeavor (and thus again in Long's strong sense). Furthermore, this interpretation helps explain why the early philosophers wrote in verse or, in the case of Heraclitus, in an obscure oracular prose.

Kathryn Morgan (2000, 64–65) has argued (contra Tate) that one cannot appropriate a tradition without first interpreting it, and, since allegorical interpretation is contingent on textual interpretation, "Any allegorical or symbolic treatment, whether its aim is to defend or to appropriate, is subsequent to the critique of myth and language." For Morgan, philosophy, before employing "myth" in a symbolic way, would have had to reject myth; otherwise a philosophical account of the world could not have set itself up as an alternative but would only have competed with myth *inside* the framework of mythical discourse. The textualization of the poetic tradition led to textual interpretation (that is, the objectification of the text) and then to criticism (and not the contrary, as Tate suggests), which she suggests is behind the origins of philosophy (2000, 24).[46] She thus follows Havelock, for whom it was a dissatisfaction with the accessible linguistic resources that led the pre-Socratics beginning with Xenophanes to polemicize.[47] I tend to concur with Morgan on the importance of textual interpretation in the rise of philosophy, but the situation seems somewhat more complex on the subject of allegory.[48]

Tate (1927, 214; 1934, 105), to support his position that allegoresis antecedes Theagenes, contends that Pherecydes of Syros, one of the first prose writers, already allegorized Homer in a positive sense in the early sixth century BC (Schibli 1990, 1–2, dates Pherecydes *flourit* to c. 544).[49] Tate has had some major supporters. In a recent work, *Birth of the Symbol*, Peter Struck (2004, 27) actually goes further than Tate when he contends: "What we can say without speculation (following DK 7B5) is that Pherecydes had an interest in Homer's poem as a source of wisdom about the fundamental structure of the cosmos."[50] In fact, few would contend (contra Schibli and Pfeiffer) that Pherecydes' prose theogony does not have allegorical and/or symbolical passages (see Ford 2002, 69). As we see in his opening sentence: "Zas [Zeus] and Chronos were forever and Chthonie" (DK 7B1), all names consciously contain etymological and symbolical intimations (life, time, and underworld). And is it plausible to consider the wedding of Zas and Chthonie and the embroidering of the cloth (DK 7B2) as anything but allegory?[51] But is Homer Pherecydes' only source, or even major source, of inspiration? The fact that he explicitly states that his three primordial entities always existed (*ēsan aei* B1) seems to challenge Hesiod's theogonical overture (*Theogony* 116–20; see also Schibli 1990, 15; Kahn 2003, 144), in which the primordial entities (which are themselves allegorized) are said to have come into being (*geneto*).[52] On the other hand, Pherecydes' contention that the primordial entities forever existed suggests the influence of Milesian philosophy (Schibli 1990, 15; Kahn 2003, 144).[53] There in fact are a number of parallels with Anaximander in Pherecydes (Schibli 1990, 29–33).[54] However, the differences between the two early prose writers are nonetheless substantial. While Pherecdyes' rationalized theogony is an advance over Hesiod's, Anaximander's *historia* is entirely devoid of supernatural entities. The universe functions according to natural laws based on rational argument. Although they both made a conscious decision to write in prose, their respective accounts are still miles apart. Another notable difference is that while Anaximander's account is transparent and his language unequivocal, Pherecydes' account demands interpretation.[55]

A few words are in order on *allegory*. The Greek word *allegoria*, from the Greek *allos* "other" and *agoreuein* "to speak," literally means "speaking other" or "speaking otherwise than one seems to speak" (*OED*).[56] The word *allegory* denotes, of course, two corresponding procedures: a way of composing a work and a way of interpreting it. To compose allegorically is to construct a work so that its apparent sense refers to an "other" sense. To interpret allegorically ("allegoresis") is to explain a work as if there is an "other" sense to it.[57] In my view, this may be the cause of some confusion with regard to the development of the notion, since it seems evident from a modern perspective that Pherecydes is "consciously" allegorizing (and thus allegorizing in Long's strong sense), while Homer is not.[58]

Plutarch (*On How to Listen to Poetry* 19e–f), writing in the first century AD, indicates that the word *allēgoria* had replaced in his day *huponoia*, which literally denotes an "under-meaning" or "under-sight or thought" or more precisely "to discover a hidden meaning under or behind the apparent meaning/thought/sight."[59] This is the term employed by Plato in the *Republic* (2.378d), when he refuses the allegorical defenses of Homer concerning the gods. And Xenophon employs the term in a similar sense in his *Symposium* 3.6 (see also Euripides, *The Phoenicians* 1133). Plutarch prefers the word *ainigma* (enigma or riddle—a riddle, of course, is something intentionally worded in a dark, puzzling way) and the verb *ainittest-hai* (to speak in hints), and this may have been the term employed by Theagenes if one considers that in Pherecydes' account we hear of caves, doors, and gates speaking in riddles (*ainittomenou*, DK 7B6).[60] More importantly, in the late fifth century BC, we find in the Derveni Papyrus, which contains a systematic allegori-cal interpretation in the form of a running commentary on an Orphic theogonic poem, no trace of *huponoia* and its cognates but rather the verb *ainittesthai* and its cognates (including *ainigmatōdēs*, "allegorically," *ainos*, and *ainigma*).[61] Ford (1999, 40) has reasonably conjectured that *ainittesthai* must have been "the operant term for expressing oneself allegorically before it became *huponoiein* and then *allegorein*." In conjunction with this, he plausibly argues that the root of *ainittesthai* is trace-able to the term *ainos*, which connotes an "ambiguous speech" discernable by a select audience that can decode the message.[62] This is already manifest in Hesiod (*Works and Days* 202), when he calls the story of the nightingale and the hawk an *ainos* that the nobles will understand. Homer employs *ainos* in *Odyssey* 14.508 in the sense of a "hint"—Eumaeus the swineherd takes the hint and acts accord-ingly. This may explain why *ainoi* were sung among aristocratic coteries in times of political unrest.[63] From this perspective, as Ford (1999, 42) argues, "the rise of epic allegoresis may be reinterpreted as the assimilation of the Homeric poems to the *ainos*." This position was already noted with regard to Theagenes.[64]

It is difficult to know if Theagenes' allegorical exegesis of Homer was simply a defensive reply on the part of a Homeric commentator to Xenophanes and his cohorts or whether it was intended to establish an exclusive and secretive club similar to and in competition with the Pythagoreans and/or Orphics, who were active in the same geographical area.[65] From this perspective, Homer's ever-popular and panhellenic epic was converted into "an esoteric text" (Ford 2002, 76). In Aeschylus (*Prometheus Bound* 609–11), *ainigmata* appears to be associated with antidemocratic elements. If allegorizing Homerists took pride in their exclusiveness, they were also alienating themselves from the masses and thus from democratic ideals. This would make Euthyphro's literal interpretation of myths all the more "popular" and thus all the more democratic. It is not as if the democratic elements were opposed to "mysteries," but the preference was for "mysteries" that were open to "all," as in the case of the ever-popular Eleusinian Mysteries.

When we turn to Homer and Hesiod themselves, we can see that at least some passages in Homer and Hesiod are easily allegorized. Félix Buffière (1973) provides numerous examples of passages in both poets that were prime targets of allegorical exegesis in antiquity. He conjectures (1973, 2–3) that for the first allegorists, allegorical exegesis began with Theagenes, and that, since the gods in Hesiod's cosmogony were so obviously allegorized (in particular, Chaos, Eros, Aither, Ocean, Ouranos, and Gaia), the allegorists must have concluded by analogy that the corresponding gods in Homer were identical, that is, the gods corresponded to elements. Thus the couple Zeus-Hera is a pair of elements like Ouranos and Gaia or, again, gloomy Hades is the same as Hesiod's black Night, which designates the immense and obscure depth of air (1973, 81). In sum, "the gods of the *Iliad*, as those of the *Theogony*, are personified natural forces" (Buffière 1973, 82). Because Homer's myths were so obscure, they were better suited to the allegorical game (and thus count as allegory in Long's weak sense). Buffière (1973, 85–12) also examines the elements in the pre-Socratics and the corresponding passages in Homer that "later" allegorists (from Heraclitus the Allegorist to Sextus Empiricus) surmised to show that the pre-Socratics, beginning with Thales, copied from Homer (e.g., Ocean as the source of all things; Zeus as associated with *aither*; Hera with air; the division of the world between Zeus, Hades, and Poseidon with the common earth in *Iliad* 15.193ff. corresponding to the famous doctrine of the four elements).

In his classic *Anaximander and the Origins of Greek Cosmology* (1960, 119–65), Charles Kahn provides an excellent analysis of the origin of elements, opposites, and members of the world in Homer and Hesiod. He notes that the division of the world (the famous *dasmoi*) in the poetic tradition into Earth, Sea, Under-world, and Heaven and its correlation with the four elements would be "familiar to every Greek schoolboy through the recitations of Homer and Hesiod" (1960, 136–37)—and that this would explain why it met with such consent. But as Kahn also observes, there is nonetheless a deep gulf between the old poetic scheme in Homer and Hesiod and the classical theory. The Milesian notions of fire and air have no counterparts in the poetic scheme, where *aither* is associated with celestial brightness and *aēr* with dark mist (e.g., *Il.* 16.300). The discovery of the elemental notions of fire and air (that is, air as a universal force or principle and the invisible air we breathe) must therefore be credited to the Milesians, Anaximander and Anaximenes (1960, 148). Kahn (1960, 152–53) concludes nonetheless (out of the blue, for no reference to allegory was previously made) that while the poetic conceptions of *aither* and *aēr* do not correspond to the Milesian notions of *pur* and *aēr*, Anaximander may have already been "fond" (like his successors) "Of discovering 'hints' (*huponoiai*) of the latest philosophical doctrines beneath the surface of the Homeric text." Kahn then goes on to cite several of Anaximander's pre-Socratic successors who make explicit references to Homer.

As Tate noted without mentioning the Milesians, the first philosophers must have been also nurtured on Homer and Hesiod. While there is no trace of this in Anaximander and Anaximenes, there is, I suppose, nothing to exclude it. But on Kahn's suggestion, Anaximander would fall into the "positive" rather than the "defensive" camp. And the implication of this is that Anaximander would have believed that Homer did have access to "truthful knowledge" about the physical universe. Moreover, it suggests that his own theories were somehow previously announced by Homer. It would also imply, I think, that Anaximander needed Homer's prestige to endorse his own position. While Anaximander may have seen Homer as a transmitter of the past, in particular as it concerns the prehistory of Greece, his own *historia* on the origin and development of the universe and humanity would exclude a privileged position for the poet, unless we see him as arguing for a cyclical view of history as we see in Aristotle (see later in this chapter).[66] In the final analysis, I see no plausible argument that the Milesians, like Xenophanes and Heraclitus, saw the poems of Homer and Hesiod as anything but transparent.

It is, however, difficult to know whether Anaximander, Anaximenes, Xenophanes, Pythagoras, or Heraclitus believed that the gods of traditional religion were fictions pure and simple, or whether they thought that there was an element of truth to the myths that Homer and Hesiod related about the gods, just as they thought it was true that the Trojan War had indeed occurred. Xenophanes, in fact, replaced traditional mythological gods with a radical "new" conception of the divinity that has similarities with Anaximander's *apeiron* and Anaximenes' *aēr* (and Heraclitus's *logos*) insofar as these basic principles are also said to "govern" all things (see Naddaf 2005, 66–67).

On the other hand, I believe that there is evidence to show that all the subsequent philosophers we characterize as pre-Socratic either composed some of their verses allegorically, as in the case of Parmenides and Empedocles, or interpreted allegorically as in the case of Anaxagoras, Diogenes of Apollonia, Democritus, and other minor figures (not to mention the Derveni Papyrus).[67] Most of the pre-Socratic references make implicit, if not explicit, allusions to Homer in particular as an allegorist. And where Homer is not the explicit focal point, as in the case of the Derveni Papyrus, it seems that all are contending that Homer had insights that conform to their own theories. There is little to indicate that these positions could be invariably characterized as "positive" or "defensive" following our previous analyses. So what are these pre-Socratics claiming? Some appear to suggest that the allegorical references in Homer are unintentional and thus allegorical in the weak sense, while others suggest that they are deliberative and thus allegorical in the strong sense, to employ the alternatives presented by Boys-Stones (2003, 190) and Long (1992, 42–43) respectively. Let us turn to the pre-Socratics beginning with Parmenides of Elea.

The Pre-Socratic Approach to Allegory

Parmenides, the father of deductive logic, not only composed in hexameter verse and claimed to be divinely inspired, but his "revelation" was delivered by a goddess in the form of a *muthos* or story on the hidden nature of being (DK

28B2.1). More to the point, Parmenides' proem is heavily allegorized and was the subject of considerable controversy (read: exegesis) even in antiquity.[68] There can be no doubt that Parmenides was familiar with Theagenes' interpretation of Homer, not to mention the competing Pythagorean and Orphic mysteries. On a number of occasions, Parmenides borrows expressions from Homer. A case at point is his preference for the Homeric term *aither* (DK 28B10.1; 1.2; see also B8.9, 9 and 11) to designate the upper sky in which the stars are located rather than the Milesian *pur* and/or *aēr*.[69] However, whatever the expressions that Parmenides borrowed from Homer and/or Hesiod and whatever the influences he underwent, I would argue that Parmenides saw his method as "objective" and the "truth" he espouses as his own discovery.[70] But this does not exclude that Parmenides may have had a "hidden" political agenda behind the poem (or have composed the poem in part as a political "riddle") if we consider the references to a democratic sociopolitical value system and the fact that he was politically engaged (see Naddaf 2005, 139). As for his allegorical approach strictly speaking, Parmenides is difficult to categorize. There is a sense in which he is allegorizing in the strong and deliberative sense in the proem, for example, but there is also a sense in which he is using the weak and unintentional sense as in his references to Homer and/or Hesiod.

Empedocles, like Parmenides, also propounded his philosophy of nature in hexameters and contended that they are derived straight from a god (*theou para muthos*, DK 31B23.11). As many have pointed out, Empedocles was a curious mixture of shaman and natural philosopher. He is often credited as the originator of the doctrine of the four elements of earth, air, fire, and water. These elements are aligned with the Homeric divinities: Zeus, Hera, Aidoneus, and Nestis (DK 31B6; 96, 98).[71] Whatever our interpretation of these correspondences, they could suggest that Empedocles was imitating Homer when he gives the elements divine names (see Buffière 1956, 98; see also Heraclitus the Allegorist, chap. 24). It was also considered that Empedocles borrowed his two antagonistic cosmic forces, Love and Strife, from Homer and Hesiod (in particular Achilles' famous shield).[72] In fact, Empedocles personifies and/or allegorizes a large number of divinities that are also found in Homer and Hesiod, including Aphrodite, Harmonia, Beauty, Ugliness, Murder, Anger, Truth, and Death (DK 31B118, 119, 120, 122, 124). Although no one questions the profound Pythagorean influence, the question is: to what degree did Empedocles' readings of Homer influence his own account and/or lead to a rationalizing of Homer? Empedocles' doctrine of metempsychosis would elicit an affirmative response, for it would suggest that he knew Homer in a previous existence. And in conjunction with this, prophets (*manteis*) and bards (*humnopoloi*) appear first and second in his order of succession in the best forms of reincarnation (DK 31B146, 147). More importantly, Empedocles was well aware that had he not written in a poetic form imitative of Homer, he would not have met with such success (see Most 1999, 356).[73] The evidence that we have suggests that he may have used Homer to foster his own prestige. He would thus fall into what Tate characterized as the positive and exegetical camp.

The relation of Anaxagoras to Homer appears somewhat different from what we find in Parmenides and Empedocles. According to Favorinus of Arles, Anaxagoras was "the first to demonstrate that Homer's poetry was about virtue and justice."[74] This could suggest that Anaxagoras believed that Homer's poems were to be understood not literally but allegorically, if the accent is on moral allegory rather than on the physical.[75] Indeed, it suggests that Anaxagoras thought that Homer composed his poems allegorically in the *strong* sense—a point that is reinforced by his disciple Metrodorus of Lampsacus (see further on in the chapter).[76] It seems disconcerting that one of the great figures of the Greek Enlightenment would have defended Homer contra Xenophanes. Given the popularity of Homer, this may have been one way for Anaxagoras to avoid an accusation of impiety. However, given that Anaxagoras' cosmic *nous* has knowledge of all things past and future (DK 59B12) and given that humans participate in this *nous*, it is theoretically possible for a human being to understand the "will" of the cosmic *nous*. From this perspective, Anaxagoras may have argued that Homer's "divine dispensation" enabled him to understand that the universe exhibits the same moral order that we associate with Anaxagoras in light of Euripides' famous fragment 910 (Nauck = DK 59A30): "Blessed is he who has devoted his life to scientific research, for he will neither malign nor harm his fellow citizens, but observing the ageless order of immortal nature, will enquire from what source it was composed and in what way. Such men would never take part in shameful deeds."

Democritus, for his part, is said to have practiced psychological allegory in his interpretation of Homer. Diogenes Laertius (DK 68A33) provides an example of his explanation of Athena's title Tritogeneia (e.g., *Iliad* 4.515, 8.39; see also Hesiod *Theogony* 895, 924) as referring to the threefold nature of *phronēsis* or wisdom: reflection, speech, and action (DK 68B2).[77] Another instance of allegory appears to be Democritus's comparison of the ancient notion of Zeus with the then modern notion of air (DK 68B30). This suggests, as we will also see with Diogenes of Apollonia, that Democritus believed that the ancient poets had a privileged access to the composition of the universe. In conjunction with this, the founder of Greek atomic theory was a strong believer in poetic inspiration (*enthousiasmos*), and it was, as he notes, precisely this that enabled Homer to build a *kosmos* of varied verse (DK 68B17, 18, 21; see Ford 2002, 169). Moreover, Democritus also believed in god-images or *eidōla* (DK 68A78) and that these gods, these atomic compounds, were not only living and intelligent but that they also, in contrast to Epicurus, play a role in human affairs.[78] He believed that these gods could "reveal the future by appearing and speaking" (DK 68B166 = Sextus 9.19), although they did not create the physical universe, nor, despite their intelligence, do they organize or control it. The evidence strongly suggests that Democritus believed that Homer was indeed a visionary sage with a privileged utterance that he intentionally transmitted allegorically. To be sure, this does not detract from Democritus's own originality, but it appears, in my view, inconsistent and disconcerting given his place in the pantheon of Ionian rationalism.[79]

Metrodorus of Lampsacus, a pupil of Anaxagoras, is well known as a Homeric expert and convinced allegorist/exegete. Metrodorus interpreted the gods and heroes of the *Iliad* as parts of the universe and as parts of the human body (DK 61A3–4). It is possible that he wanted Homer's poem to conform to Anaxagoras's description of the macrocosm and the microcosm or again to his own theories. However, the fundamental point here is not so much that Metrodorus was interpreting Homer allegorically (see Plato *Ion* 530c), but the fact that Anaxagoras's pupil was contending, as did Democritus, that Homer was a visionary sage, the precursor, if not the founder, of Ionian rationalism. In sum, there are no "new" ideas; everything that could be said was already said by Homer. Thus, Metrodorus interprets Homer allegorically in the strong, intentional sense.

Diogenes of Apollonia (c. 460–400), a younger contemporary of Anaxagoras, who argued that air, the *archē* of all things, is both intelligent and divine (DK 61B5–7), seems to lean in the same direction when he contends that Homer was speaking not mythically but truly in his description of Zeus (DK 61A8 = text from Philodemus's *On Piety* 6b). Of course, Diogenes had a coherent "scientific" approach to the subject of the relation between air and intelligence and so he may only mean here that Homer was correct to consider Zeus as all-knowing—air is Zeus because Zeus, like intelligent air, is all knowing. However, the evidence suggests he understood Homer as speaking truthfully (*alēthēs*)—that is, that Homer had a *correct* understanding of the universe, including its basic causes and intentions.[80] Diogenes thus also appears to interpret Homer allegorically in the strong sense.

My own reading here is confirmed somewhat by the Derveni Papyrus, a running commentary on an Orphic theogony, which is dated to late fifth century BC, but which clearly antedates this period given the number of pre-Socratic allusions (the Orphic text itself may have originated in the sixth century).[81] On the one hand, the text shows that there were in fact a number of competing "secretive" religious doctrines (the author says that it is not for the "many")[82] and that their very essence was grounded in a form of allegory.[83] On the other hand, it is also clear that the author believes that Orpheus (as Homer) was an allegorist who had access to truths about the universe that he covered in enigmas and that it was his task as an exegete to demonstrate Orpheus's knowledge of philosophical truths. In other words, the Derveni author is saying that Orphic theogony and pre-Socratic philosophy (notably that of Anaxagoras and Diogenes of Apollonia, but there are also clear references to Heraclitus, Parmenides, Empedocles, Democritus, and, of course, the Milesians) are saying the *same* thing.[84] As with Homer and Hesiod, the scandalous stories that Orpheus was understood to have expressed about the gods in his theogonies were again only descriptions of the physical universe, anticipations of unnamed pre-Socratic philosophers. But leaving aside the relation between

Orpheus and the pre-Socratics, the Derveni author is, as Betegh notes (2004, 132n1), treating the Orphic poem as allegorical in the strong sense.

There is also an ambiguity with regard to allegorizing Homer found among the sophists, "the prime movers," as Guthrie (1971, 48) notes, of the Age of Enlightenment in ancient Greece (see also Ford 2002, 80). Gorgias, to be sure, was more interested in the persuasive and enchanting effects of Homeric poetry and was engaged in providing a "rational" account of its effects. On the other hand, Protagoras's use of myth in the *Protagoras* is a perfect instance of his endorsement of the allegorical method, albeit in defense of the democratic state. If the sophists were an elite group and professed to teach another elite group, for a fee, the sine qua non of political success, the ultimate *aretē*, the older sophists were nonetheless clear proponents of democratic ideals. In both the *Protagoras* (316d) and the *Theaetetus* (180c–d), what distinguishes the sophists from the early poets is that they have nothing to hide. Thus Protagoras sees Homer and other early poets as using poetry (and in the case of Orpheus and Musaeus, mystery religions and prophecy) as a "disguise" for their real end: the practice of the art of sophistry (*Protagoras* 316d; note that the accent is on "intentionality" of the poets).[85] When Protagoras comments to Socrates in the *Protagoras* (339a) that "the greatest part of a man's education is to be in command of poetry," that is, "the ability to understand the words of the poet," this is going a long way in explicitly recognizing that the spell of Homer and other older poets was a formidable challenge to the sophists' pretension to teach their own version of *aretē*. Prodicus of Ceos, for his part, argued that at an earlier stage of civilization primitive man personified the natural substances that provided for the amelioration of life: Demeter with bread; Dionysius with wine; Poseidon with water; Hephaestus with fire, and so forth.[86] While these divinities are also the gods of Homeric myth, it is unclear if Prodicus thought that Homer himself (who is not mentioned by name) had "consciously" allegorized the gifts of nature (DK 85B5). However, the sophists were in stiff competition with the Homerics and so it would be difficult to see them conceding that Homer was indeed a visionary sage with privileged access to the divine.

When Antisthenes, a disciple of Socrates, contends that Homer said some things according to opinion (*doxa*) and some things according to truth (*alētheia*),[87] he appears to be advocating an allegorical interpretation of Homer. But what type of allegorical interpretation? In Xenophon's *Symposium* (3.5–7), the rhapsodes are ridiculed by Antisthenes because they do not know the *huponoia* of Homeric poetry; that is, I assume, that they understand Homer literally, as in the case of Euthypro. Niceratus, the son of Nicias, who boasts that he has learned by heart all of the *Iliad* and the *Odyssey* in order to become an *anēr agathos* or gentleman, has also been initiated into the *huponoia* by some Homeric professors for a fee. This suggests that there were numerous different interpreters of Homer. Indeed, if there was some concession that the wisdom of the poets was of ancient and divine origin, at least among the intelligentsia, it was open to numerous competing interpretive claims, as we see in the case of Simonides in Plato's *Protagoras*

(339a–347a) and *Republic* (1.331d–335e). As Socrates notes, the poets speak "in riddles" (*Republic* 1.332b) and riddles can be interpreted in various ways.

Aristotle has a great admiration for Homer and argues that there are many lessons to be learned from the great poet. But he sees the poems as making "fiction" or "the marvelous possible" (*Poetics* 1460a18ff.). This is not unlike what we find in Pindar, who himself likes to create myths and is fully aware of their power. Aristotle, however, goes much further than this. As Brisson (2004, 38) observes, *Metaphysics* 1074b1–14 shows that for Aristotle the initial or pre-anthropomorphic notion of the divinity that was handed down in the form of myth (*en muthou schēmati*) and that identified the primary natural forces or substances with gods, must have been divinely inspired (*theiōs eirēsthai*), for it constitutes the germ that culminated in his own philosophical theology. More important, Aristotle (*Movement of Animals* 699b35ff.), as so many others, provides with his own notion of the Unmoved Mover an allegorical exegesis of the famous scene in Homer's *Iliad* 7 in which Zeus describes his formidable power in the form of suspending *all* the other gods, and thus the entire universe, from a golden chain. This is akin to Plato's contention in the *Theaetetus* (152b) that Heraclitus's famous *panta rei* was borrowed from Homer. The contention was to come full circle when the Alexandrine scholar Ammonius (second century BC) wrote a work entitled *Plato's Debt to Homer*. It is difficult to say when the phenomenon of attributing lines in Homer's poems to later philosophical claims began, but it may have been implicit in the very first counterattacks of Homer's supporters like Theagenes of Rhegium and to have later convinced even a number of prominent pre-Socratics, including the likes of Anaxagoras and Democritus, albeit in a more contained manner, that is, analogous to Aristotle's claim that the "germs" of his philosophical system can be discerned in Homer. The reasoning behind Aristotle's own contention, as Boys-Stones (2003, 191) correctly observes, is grounded in his notion that human civilizations are repeatedly developed and periodically destroyed by natural catastrophes. However, as in Plato's *Laws* 3, Aristotle believes that some humans do in fact survive and these retain some fragments of antediluvian wisdom. This suggests that Aristotle is interpreting Homer in the weak and nondeliberate sense. To be sure, it is at times difficult to distinguish between deliberate and nondeliberate allegory, between the strong and the weak senses. What seems clear is that philosophy and allegory are not only intimately connected from the inception of philosophy, but also that allegory both enlivened and complicated the ancient quarrel between philosophy and poetry.[88]

Notes

1. See, for example, John Burnet, *Early Greek Philosophy*, third ed. (London: Adam and Charles Black, 1920), v. For a synopsis of works on the subject of the movement from *muthos* to *logos*, see Kathryn Morgan, *Myth and Philosophy from the Presocratics to*

Plato (Cambridge: Cambridge University Press, 2000), 30–36. For a brilliant account not mentioned by Morgan, see Glenn Most, "From Logos to Mythos," in Richard Buxton, ed., *From Myth to Reason? Studies in the Development of Greek Thought* (Oxford: Oxford University Press, 1999), 25–47.

2. This has been well documented by Luc Brisson, *How Philosophers Saved Myths: Allegorical Interpretation and Classical Mythology*, translated by Catherine Tihanyi (Chicago: University of Chicago Press, 2004). However, Brisson does not focus on the early history of allegory and its relation to philosophy. Nor does he raise the issue as to how Homer and Hesiod became the educators of Greece, which is important, in my view, to understand the correlation between philosophy and allegory. The thesis I develop here is thus quite independent of Brisson's, as my bibliography would make clear. Meanwhile, Brisson suggests that it was essentially "after" Plato (and indeed because of Plato) that philosophers began to use the allegorical method to elucidate myth. Indeed, if "reason" could only assert itself in opposition to myth (and Plato, for Brisson, is the first explicit representative of this), philosophers quickly realized that if they remained exclusively within the realm of the rational, they could never discuss the most important things—in particular, God, the soul, and its destiny after death. This explains the necessity of making a place for myth next to reason. The old myths (notably those of Homer and Hesiod) are thus reread and readapted. They are seen as discerning a primitive truth emanating from God. In sum, allegory enables the translation of myth in rational terms.

3. A recent exception is Morgan 2000. I will discuss her position later. There are a number of recent works on ancient literary criticism that examine the origins of allegory—e.g., D. C. Feeney, *The Gods in Epic: Poets and Critics of the Classical Tradition* (Oxford: Clarendon Press, 1991); Robert Lamberton and John Keaney, eds., *Homer's Ancient Readers* (Princeton: Princeton University Press, 1992); Andrew Ford, *The Origins of Criticism: Literary Culture and Poetic Theory in Classical Greece* (Princeton: Princeton University Press, 2002); Peter Struck, *Birth of the Symbol* (Princeton: Princeton University Press, 2004); G. R. Boys-Stones, "The Stoics' Two Types of Allegory," in G. R. Boys-Stones, ed., *Metaphor, Allegory and the Classical Tradition* (Oxford: Oxford University Press, 2003); Jean Pépin, *Mythe et allégorie* (Paris: Aubier Montaigne, 1958); Félix Buffière, *Les Mythes d'Homère* (Paris: Les Belles Lettres, 1956/1973); to mention only a few. For a recent list, see Struck 2004, 6 n7. I discuss some of these further on.

4. Anthony Long, "Stoic Readings of Homer," in Lamberton and Keaney 1992, 41–66.

5. I find Robert Segal's recent *Myth: A Very Short History* (Oxford: Oxford University Press, 2004) an excellent introduction to the subject, though the position developed here is not covered in his book.

6. Following his study of the occurrences of *muthos* in the *Iliad*, Richard Martin has concluded that the word *muthos* in Homer expresses, contrary to *logos*, an undemonstrable truth; Richard Martin, *The Language of Heroes: Speech and Performance in the Iliad* (Ithaca: Cornell University Press, 1989). More precisely, it connotes an "authoritative, efficacious and performative speech." Kathryn Morgan, following Martin's study, concludes "that prior to the Presocratics the world of myth was characterized by undemonstrable truth and poetic authority" (Morgan 2000, 16). There is no conclusive evidence for this. Bruce Lincoln, in his contentious but interesting *Theorizing Myth: Narrative, Ideology, and Scholarship* (Chicago: University of Chicago Press, 1999), 3–18, not only draws a sharp

distinction between *muthos* and *logos* in Homer and Hesiod, but argues that *muthos* retained its "original" sense of a true and authoritative discourse until Plato. This position is less than dubious, as we can see in Herodotus (2.23; 2.45) or again in Thucydides (1.21, 22) to say nothing of Aesop, for whom the moral of the story is sometimes characterized as *muthos* and sometimes as *logos*, and the pre-Socratics, whom Lincoln cites "selectively." For a number of my own examples, see pp. vii–x in my introduction to Luc Brisson, *Plato the Myth Maker*, translated, edited, and with an introduction by Gerard Naddaf (Chicago: University of Chicago Press, 1998).

7. H. Fournier, *Les Verbes "dire" en grec ancien: Exemple de conjugaison supplétive* (Paris: Klincksieck, 1946), 53.

8. Pindar (c. 518–438) appears to have been the first to contrast *muthos* to *logos* with respect to traditional stories about the gods, but he still terms his own version of traditional stories a *logos* (e.g., *Olympian* 7.21; *Nemean* 1.34).

9. For a synopsis, see Brisson 1998. For another opinion, see Marcel Detienne, *The Creation of Mythology* (Chicago: University of Chicago Press, 1986).

10. In conjunction with the definition of myth proposed here, it appears that myth provides both an (causal) explanation for the present social (and natural) order and a guarantee (through a sort of ritualistic/mimetic process) that the present order (social and natural) will remain as it is. Myth thus unifies a number of diverse functions including, religious, cultural, historical, social, and political. For a recent useful synopsis, see Segal 2004.

11. As Emily Kearns correctly notes on p. 524, even new theological and philosophical systems incorporated the traditional pantheon depicted by the two great poets; Emily Kearns, "Order, Interaction, Authority: Ways of Looking at Greek Religion," in Anton Powell, ed., *The Greek World* (London/New York: Routledge, 1995), 511–29.

12. At *Critias* 110a3–6, Plato contends that *muthologia* commences with the advent of literacy.

13. G. S. Kirk, *The Nature of Greek Myths* (Harmondsworth: Penguin Books, 1974), 22.

14. However, this potential critical evaluation does not mean that Homer or Hesiod thought that they could rationally demonstrate their choices. Rather, it remains at the level of poetic authority. To judge whether a claim was true or not, that is, to provide a *logos* (based on what G. E. R. Lloyd characterizes as a self-conscious methodology) originates with the first philosophers; G. E. R. Lloyd, *Magic, Reason and Experience: Studies in the Origins and Development of Greek Science* (Cambridge: Cambridge University Press, 1979), 229–34. From this perspective, Kathryn Morgan is correct, I believe, to point out that Homer and Hesiod did not themselves have criteria to enable them to judge whether a claim was true or not—this originates with the deconstruction of poetic authority by the first philosophers; Morgan 2000, 21–23. Consequently, as she notes, when Hesiod claims that the Muses know how to say falsehoods as well as true things (*Theogony* 24–28), it is not a value judgment on a truth claim about myth, but the undemonstrable claim that one mythological account is superior to another, that is, more unforgettable. But the notion here, I think, is a little more complicated. When Odysseus says of the divine (Muse-inspired) bard Demodocus that he sings of the fate of the Achaeans as though he himself had been there or had heard it from another who was (*Od.* 8.491), the Homeric bard is not seen as a creator but as a reciter/singer of a true story of which the audience is well aware. His *alētheia* or "truth" is precisely the absence of forgetfulness, *a-lētheia*, as Detienne correctly

noted many years ago; Marcel Detienne, *Les Maîtres de la vérité dans la Grèce archaïque* (Paris: Maspéo, 1967). Whence the Muse who *knows* all as the teacher and source of his inspiration (e.g., *Od.* 8.476ff.).

15. Although Thucydides does not provide a date for the Trojan War, the great chronographers Eratosthenes and Apollodorus took Homer as the first feasible historical source and began their chronographies with the fall of Troy in 1184/3 (see *FGH* 241F1, 244F61). The fall of Troy thus marks the beginning of Greek history; it marks the dividing line between mythical time and historical time, between the immortals and the mortals; see James Porter, "Homer: The History of an Idea," in Robert Fowler, ed., *The Cambridge Companion to Homer* (Cambridge: Cambridge University Press, 2004), 324–43.

16. Walter Burkert, *Greek Religion* (Cambridge: Harvard University Press, 1985), 249.

17. David Furley, "The Figure of Euthyphro in Plato's Dialogue," *Phronesis* 30 (1985), 201–08. Furley's position appears to be reinforced by Richard Janko's position that during the great religious crisis of 415 BC, brought about by the mutilation of the statues of Hermes on the eve of the Sicilian expedition, even those who applied allegory to Homer and Orpheus were hunted down; Richard Janko, "The Derveni Papyrus (Diagoras of Melos, *Apopyrgizontes Logoi?*): A New Translation," *Classical Philology* 96 (2001), 1–32.

18. For a different interpretation of Euthyphro, see Charles Kahn, "Was Euthyphro the Author of the Derveni Papyrus," in A. Laks and G. Most, eds., *Studies on the Derveni Papyrus*, (Oxford: Clarendon Press, 1997), 55–63. However, there can be little doubt that the Greeks were as gullible as most, as we see in Herodotus's famous account (1.60.3–5) of Peisistratos arranging a pseudo-epiphany (dressing a tall, striking woman in a suit of armor to resemble Athena) to regain his tyranny after his initial exile. Assuredly the belief in oracles appears no less naïve to us. The examples could be multiplied, but so could contemporary examples.

19. On the quarrel, see Ford 2002, 46–66; and Ramona Naddaff, *Exiling the Poets: The Production of Censorship in Plato's Republic* (Chicago: University of Chicago Press, 2002), 121ff. Of course, works abound on the subject. I will touch on this in more detail later.

20. Gregory Vlastos, *Plato's Universe* (Seattle: Washington University Press, 1970), 24.

21. For a more detailed account of what philosophy consisted in for the pre-Socratics, see my review article "What Is Presocratic Philosophy?" *Ancient Philosophy* 26 (2006), 161–79. In what follows, I begin with Anaximander and Anaximenes rather than Thales, since we possess enough information to reconstruct their respective theories on nature. But it is worth noting that Aristotle considers Thales in the *Metaphysics* as the founder of the earliest school of philosophy (*philosophia*; *Meta.* 983b7; b21). In conjunction with this, it is interesting to note that what preceded *philosophia* according to Aristotle was the *philomuthia* (*Meta.* 982b19) of the poets or *theologoi*. The fundamental difference between the two for Aristotle is that Thales' position was based on observation and argument, while the poetic contention was based on chance (*tetuchēken ousa*; 983a1). For an analysis of this passage and related passages notably in Aristotle's *Metaphysics* in the context of allegory, see André Laks, "L'allégorie, et les débuts de la philosphie," in Brigitte Pérez-Jean and Patricia Eichek-Lojkine, eds., *L'allégorie de l'antiquité à la renaissance* (Paris: Honoré Champion, 2004), 211–20.

22. This germ contains the two primary opposites hot and cold, which, in turn, are inseparable from the opposites of dry and wet. The germ of hot and cold develops into in a sphere of flames (the hot and the dry) enclosing a cold and wet center (like bark grows round a tree). The action of the hot (and dry) on the cold (and wet) center then causes a third concentric layer composed of air/mist (*aēr*) to develop (presumably through evaporation) between the two other layers. The pressure of this intermediary layer of air/mist finally breaks the coherent unity by causing the ball of flame to burst and in the process forms the celestial bodies. The subsequent action of the heat (from the sun) causes the wet and dry on the earth to separate into land and sea. This description is confirmed by other doxographies. See Gerard Naddaf, *The Greek Concept of Nature* (Albany: State University of New York Press, 2005), 73–74.

23. In my view, it is the Milesian explanation of meteorological phenomena that must have appeared so overwhelmingly superior to anything that the poets had to offer: the correlation between fire (the sun) and air explain the origin of wind, which in turn is behind a number of other meteorological phenomena. According to Anaximander, winds (*anemoi*) occur when the finest particles of air are separated off by the heat of the sun. Thunder and lightning are caused by the active agent of the wind (under the influence of the sun). More precisely, wind is like an inflammable air current trapped in a cloud like air in a balloon. When its heat or innate motion causes it to expand, the envelope is torn and the wind shoots out and bursts into flame; see Charles Kahn, *Anaximander and the Origins of Greek Cosmology* (Indianapolis: Hackett, 1960/1994), 101ff. and the corresponding doxographies. As for rain, it originates from vapor raised by the sun and concentrated in the clouds. Rain and wind thus represent opposite products of air.

24. The explanation that Anaximander gives us of the origin of humanity and of the other living beings is, as in the case of his cosmology, the first naturalistic explanation in this domain. As one might expect, his explanation is entirely consistent with his cosmological system. Indeed, the same natural processes are at work (DK 12A27). Living beings emerge from a sort of primeval moisture or slime (*ex hugrou*), which is activated by the heat of the sun after the initial formation of the universe (see, for example, Hippolytus 12A11; Alexander 12A27; Aetius 12A27, 30; Aristotle 12A27; Censorinus 12A30). Life thus results from the action of the hot and the dry on the cold and the wet. For a more detailed description, see Naddaf 2005, 88–92.

25. Given that Aristotle is referring to Anaximander here, it seems clear that the Milesian is identifying the four basic opposites with the four basic elements. This would strongly suggest that Theagenes of Rhegium is referring to Anaximander and/or the Milesians in general in his reference to the four elements in Homer mentioned further on. Meanwhile in *Generation and Corruption* 330a30–331a1, Aristotle provides a more complex account of the relation between the primary opposites and the four elements. According to this scheme, which may also go back to Anaximander, each element has one attribute in common and one in opposition to its acquaintance on either side. Thus: fire is hot and dry; air is hot and wet; water is cold and wet; earth is cold and dry. From this perspective, Anaximander would be the precursor to Empedocles and his insistence that the four elements are the roots of all things. Although on Aristotle's account, the Stagirite would side with Anaximander since the primary opposites are more basic than the four elements. For a detailed discussion in perspective, see Kahn 1960, 126–33.

26. Xenophanes is, in fact, the first to mention the two Greek icons by name (DK 21B11).

27. See also DK 21B14, where Xenophanes explicitly states that humans conceive of the gods as resembling men and women in clothing, speech, and body.

28. As James Lesher notes, "the poets undermine the mutual trust and honesty essential to a healthy society" (84); J. H. Lesher, *Xenophanes of Colophon: Fragments: A Text and Translation with Commentary* (Toronto: University of Toronto Press, 1992). This position is developed in more detail in Ford 2002, 53–66.

29. As with Lesher 1992, 81–82, I agree that *ex archēs* here suggests "from the beginning of one's life" rather than "from the beginning of Greek culture." There is a consensus that Xenophanes' complaint here is about the influence of Homer (as later with Plato) on the customary educational and religious practices of the Greeks.

30. Diogenes Laertius (*Lives* 8.1.21) reports that when Pythagoras (c. 570–500) descended into Hades, he saw the souls of Homer and Hesiod receiving an exemplary punishment for the crimes they attributed to the gods. Heraclitus also mentions the poet Archilochus in the same fragment.

31. The respective truth claims of Xenophanes and Heraclitus are based on self-conscious (and critical) methodologies that employ both the mind and the senses, both empirical and non-empirical evidence, to arrive at their respective conclusions. Moreover, they can and do distinguish between truth and opinion, between *alētheia* and *doxa*; between what is possible and what is not possible when it comes to truth claims.

32. But they also read and reflected on the naturalistic accounts of the Milesians. In fact, despite their own respective originalities, both Xenophanes and Heraclitus were inspired by Milesian naturalism. I have shown elsewhere that it is entirely plausible that Xenophanes may have studied with them; Gerard Naddaf (with Dirk Couprie and Robert Hahn), *Anaximander in Context: New Studies in the Origins of Greek Philosophy* (Albany: State University of New York Press, 2003).

33. Harvey Yunis, "Writing for Reading: Thucydides, Plato, and the Emergence of the Critical Reader," in Harvey Yunis, ed., *Written Texts and the Rise of Culture in Ancient Greece* (Cambridge: Cambridge University Press, 2003), 194; Charles Kahn, "Writing Philosophy: Prose and Poetry from Thales to Plato," in Yunis 2003, 153–55; Ford 2002, 75. Note that Heraclitus (DK 22B93) was nonetheless well aware that the intention of a text, like an oracle, may need to be discerned when it is ambiguous (whence his comment on the Sibyl with the raving mouth, DK 22B92). However, he does not describe Homer and Hesiod as having this type of divine power and/or speaking in an ambiguous way, as Kahn correctly notes; Charles Kahn, *The Art and Thought of Heraclitus: An Edition of the Fragments with Translation and Commentary* (Cambridge: Cambridge University Press, 1979), 125–26. Plato holds a similar position in the sense that he contends that we cannot ask Homer with what intention he composed his work; see Richard Hunter, "Homer and Greek Literature," in Robert Fowler 2004, 235–53. Aristotle (*Poetics* 1460b36–61a1), for his part, would reply to Xenophanes that while it may be true that Homer's tales about the gods are neither true nor appropriate, the fact remains that the stories accord with public opinion. There is also no evidence that Xenophanes and Heraclitus were interested, as with the Western Greeks, with life after death.

34. Rhegium was a city in southern Italy that was close to Xenophanes' sphere of influence, but also to that of Pythagoras; Ford 2002, 69.

35. Porphyry was himself convinced that the ancient poets "intentionally" allegorized their texts, as we see in his famous *Cave of the Nymphs.*

36. For Athena as wisdom in Homer and the contradictions it raises, see Jon Whitman, *Allegory: The Dynamics of the Ancient and Medieval Technique* (Oxford: Clarendon Press, 1987), 15–16.

37. Scholium to Venetus B on *Iliad* 20.67ff. My translation is based on Schraeder (1880, 240.14–241.12), which is reproduced in DK 8.2. This scholium is attributed/traced to Porphyry (*Homeric Questions* I; see DK 8.2, in which P examines previous solutions to allegorical exegesis), the third-century AD Neoplatonist philosopher and Homeric commentator. It is worth noting that there is an eight-hundred-year hiatus between Porphyry and Theagenes. This suggests that Theagenes wrote some kind of commentary on Homer, parts of which survived at least until the time of Porphyry. D. C. Feeney contends that "the author of this passage knows nothing at first hand of Theagenes' writings, and is only aware of a tradition that he was the first to use this sort of defense" (Feeney 1991, 91); see also Rudolph Pfeiffer, *History of Classical Scholarship: From the Beginnings to the End of the Hellenistic Age* (Oxford: Clarendon Press, 1968), 10–11. But there is no reason, I believe, that the author/Porphyry did not have access to some passages from Theagenes' commentary, as we see in passages of the pre-Socratics not to mention the author of the Derveni Papyrus. This would also seem to reinforce the thesis that verbatim quotes from Theagenes were still in circulation.

38. Compare Heraclitus the Allegorist (c. AD 100), who explicitly states at the opening of his book *Homeric Problems* that if Homer were not an allegorist, that is, if his apparent meaning about the gods were the true meaning, then he would be completely impious. He thus interprets the famous theomachy in Homer in a manner similar to Theagenes. In sum, he interprets Homer as a strong and deliberate allegorist.

39. See Ford 2002, 70; Pfeiffer 1986, 1–11; Jesper Svenbro, *La parole et le marbre. Aux origines de la poétique grecque* (Lund: Studenlitteratur, 1976), 84.

40. Contrast Dirk Obbink, for whom it was associated with ritual and religion, but the purpose was not to describe the author's meaning, but rather to apply that meaning to a contemporary situation; Dirk Obbink, "Allegory and Exegesis in the Derveni Papyrus: The Origin of Greek Scholarship," in G. R. Boys-Stones, ed., *Metaphor, Allegory, and the Classical Tradition,* (Oxford: Oxford University Press, 2003), 177–88. Obbink's argument is on p. 177.

41. On the 1,000, see G. Rispoli, "Teagene o dell'allegoria," *Vichiana* 9 (1980), 243–57.

42. But Andrew Ford sees rhapsodes like Theagenes as different from the other rhapsodes, who were controlled by the clan from Chios or again by the Athenians; Ford 2002, 80–81. He argues that the sophists profited from this position and had no personal objection to allegory (85). For the antidemocratic position expressed in Plato with regard to allegory, see p. 87; the allegorists are, by nature, antidemocratic since their success depends on disconnecting their publics from the masses. Ford also notes how there were competing ways of seeking hidden meanings, and in the final analysis there was little difference in the Sophistic manner of explaining a passage of Homer through etymologizing or the allegorical method (87).

43. See, for example, Pfeiffer 1968, 10–11; Feeney 1991, 8–10, 19–20; Most 1999, 340; Morgan 2000, 63–64; Ford 2002, 68–72; Struck 2004, 29; and Jonathan Tate, "On the History of Allegorism," *Classical Quarterly* 28 (1934), 105–19. Buffière 1956/1973 is

an exception; he does not explicitly mention the Milesians in his analysis of Theagenes (101–05) but in a previous discussion (82, 85–92).

44. To say nothing of his position on the traditional gods, which is invariably passed over in silence by scholars.

45. Struck draws his inspiration, as he notes, from Marcel Detienne, for whom the allegorical approach is intimately connected with the archaic view of the poet as "a master of truth" (Detienne 1967). Indeed, in this view the poet has "access to an extraordinary range of knowledge through a kind of panoptic sight" (Struck 2004, 50 n65; see also Tate 1934, 12).

46. Charles Kahn appears to move in the opposite direction when he writes in a recent article: "Alphabetic literacy may have been a facilitator, but this concept is no more explanatory of the rise of Greek rationalism than it is able to explain the extraordinary power of Greek poetry and drama" (141); Kahn 2003, 139–61.

47. Morgan 2000, 27; Eric Havelock, *The Literate Revolution in Greece and Its Cultural Consequences* (Princeton: Princeton University Press, 1983), 15–21.

48. Kathryn Morgan appears so convinced that literacy (or textualization) is a "sufficient cause" to account for the rise of philosophy that she suggests that Xenophanes and Heraclitus should be considered as the first philosophers because they are the first to argue that prior thinkers had misused language. It is thus not surprising that the Milesians are absent from her account; Morgan 2000, 26–30, 39.

49. The passages under consideration are *Iliad* 1.590 and 15.18 (see also Hesiod *Theogony* 729ff.), in which Homer describes the portion of Tartaros below the earth (Pherecydes DK 7B5). Tate contends that here Pherecydes understood the verses of *Iliad* as the words of god to matter: that is, matter do so and so; Jonathan Tate, "On the Beginnings of Greek Allegory," *Classical Review* 23 (1927), 214–15. Tate's argument is on p. 214. It is Celsus, according to Origen, who contends that Pherecydes is commenting on this passage from Homer. For a discussion, see Hermann Schibli, *Pherekydes of Syros* (Oxford: Clarendon Press, 1990), 39–40.

50. Tate's position is somewhat more nuanced than Morgan presents it; Tate 1934, 107. He argues that Pherecydes *seems* to be employing these passages to recast the Homeric myths for his own purpose; that is, what Homer is saying can be interpreted as follows: God ordered that the universe be "constructed" in the following way, a way that can be interpreted as already evident in Homer. Homer is thus employed in a "positive" sense as a way of endorsing his own position. As Tate notes, this is more in line with a process of rationalizing Homer, but rationalizing in a way that can *later* be identified with an allegorical interpretation. From this perspective, Struck actually goes further than Tate; Struck 2004, 27. In contrast, Kahn is less generous, contending that "Pherecydes' theogony is a fantastic story of his own invention" (Kahn 2003, 144).

51. See G. S. Kirk, J. E. Raven, and M. Schofield, *The Presocratic Philosophers*, second ed. (Cambridge: Cambridge University Press, 1983), 61.

52. Although clearly all four (Chaos, Gaia, Tartaros, and Eros) existed from the beginning. (See Naddaf 2005, 48–51.) Is Pherecydes' also challenging the contention, as Xenophanes did later (DK 21B14; A11), that it is impious to speak of gods being born?

53. Of course, he could also be challenging another Hesiodic pretender, the Spartan lyric poet Alcman (c. 600), who also wrote a theogonical cosmogony that was later the subject of much interpretation. See Kirk, Raven, and Schofield 1983, 47.

54. A case at point is in DK 7A8, in which Damascius states that for Pherecydes Chronos produces from his own seed (*ek tou gonou heautou*) fire, air/breath (*pheuma*), and water.

55. But an equally strong case could also be made for Hesiod, Alcman of Sparta, or the author of the Orphic text in the Derveni Papyrus as the inspiration behind Pherecydes' allegorizing. His motive could thus be religious, that is, "I have been divinely inspired, and should you want to understand my message, you will have to interpret me allegorically." On the other hand, given the dates and the parallels, it could be plausibly argued that Pherecydes is allegorizing Anaximander. Perhaps he wanted to emulate his brilliance in an enigmatic way with some "material" borrowed from Homer and/or Hesiod for good measure? I hope to develop the possibilities pertaining to Pherecydes in a future study.

56. More precisely, *agoreuein* means "to speak publicly." It is thus connected with *agora*, "the people's assembly," which in turn is connected with the verb *ageirein*, "to assemble." From this perspective, an allegory is a speech that is not meant for the "public." Indeed, it is not expressed in an immediate direct sense; see Alain Moreau, "Allégorie Eschyleenne: De l'abstraction à la créature de chair et de sang," in Brigitte Pérez-Jean and Patricia Eichek-Lojkine, eds., *L'allégorie de l'antiquité à la renaissance* (Paris: Honoré Champion, 2004), 115–27. As we shall see later, there may have been a "political" motive behind the origin of allegory. For a history of the word *allegoria*, see Pierre Chiron, "Allégorie et langue, allégorie et style, allégorie et persuasion: le témoignage des traités de rhétorique," in Pérez-Jean and Eichek-Lojkine 2004, 41–73.

57. Jon Whitman, "Allegory," in Alex Preminger and T. V. F. Brogan, eds., *The New Princeton Encyclopaedia of Poetry and Poetics* (Princeton: Princeton University Press, 1993), 31–35.

58. It must also be noted that as reading and writing became more popular among the intelligentsia, some of the old Homeric idioms may have appeared enigmatic and thus have elicited attempts at clarification; see Feeney 1991, 20; see also Pfeiffer 1968, 5, although he gives the impression that there were only rare words and phrases.

59. Plutarch (*Essay on the Life and Poetry of Homer*) was convinced that Homer is the source of all previous knowledge. In fact, he suggests that previous thinkers (all of whom read Homer) borrowed their ideas from him. The famous Neoplatonist Porphyry (c. 233–305) held, of course, a similar position on Homer. In his commentary *On the Cave of the Nymphs* on the cave of the nymphs episode in *Odyssey* 13.96–112, he employs all of the major terms of allegoresis (*allegoria*, *huponoia*, *ainigma*, and *sumbolon*) in his attempt to figure out Homer's meaning. This is beyond the scope of the present essay.

60. Theogonis completes an allegory of the "ship of state" with the contention "let these things be riddling utterances (*inikētē*) hidden by me for the noble. / No one can be aware even of future misfortune if one is skilled" (681–82). For text and translation, see Gregory Nagy (pp. 26ff.) in "Theogonis and Megara: A Poet's Vision of His City," in T. J. Figueira and Gregory Nagy, eds., *Theogonis of Megara: Poetry and the Polis* (Baltimore: Johns Hopkins University Press, 1985), 22–82; and Gregory Nagy, *Pindar's Homer: The Lyric Possession of an Epic Past* (Baltimore: John Hopkins University Press, 1990), 145.

61. See Martin West, *The Orphic Poems* (Oxford: Clarendon Press, 1983), 78 n.14; Feeney 1991; Andrew Ford, "Performing Interpretation: Early Allegorical Exegesis of Homer," in Margaret Beissinger, Jane Tylus, and Susanne Wofford, eds., *Epic Traditions in the Contemporary World: The Poetics of Community* (Berkeley: University of California Press, 1999),

39; Gábor Betegh, *The Derveni Papyrus: Cosmology, Theology and Interpretation* (Cambridge: Cambridge University Press, 2004), 396.

62. Ford 1999, 41, following Gregory Nagy, *The Best of the Achaeans* (Baltimore: The Johns Hopkins University Press, 1979), 222–41; and Nagy 1990, 148.

63. This appears to be the case for Archilochus, Alcaeus, Theogonis, and Stesichorus, among others; Ford 1999, 42.

64. In conjunction with this, and in guise of a conclusion, Andrew Ford notes that epic should be seen through the eyes of the interpreters as a social performance and thus from an ethnologist's perspective; Ford 1999, 46.

65. Also, the fact that the Pythagoreans ascribed all new doctrines to the master may explain why Homer's allegorists attempted to show through the allegorical exegesis of his poems that the pre-Socratics borrowed their ideas from Homer. So Theagenes decided to do for Homer what the Pythagoreans did for Pythagoras.

66. In my view, extensive travels notably to Egypt appear to have been a primary factor in early philosophers arriving at the conclusion that humanity and civilization were far older than one could conclude from reading Homer. I have argued at length elsewhere that Egyptians were seen as early as Anaximander as the most ancient people and Egypt itself as the cradle of civilization; Naddaf 2003 and Naddaf 2005. Geology, geography, and history were all employed in support of this claim.

67. There is evidence, I believe, that *all* the pre-Socratic philosophers had an ambiguous relation with the two great poets (and in particular, Homer) and that this ambiguity is reflected in their respective allegorical references. In fact, the only pre-Platonic "defensive" positions vis-à-vis the poets seems to come from nonphilosophers, as we see with Theagenes and the author of the Derveni Papyrus. The philosophers appear, with the exception of Xenophanes and Heraclitus, to have a "positive" attitude. But even in the case of Heraclitus, one must ask why he chose to compose in such an opaque oracular prose.

68. For a list of contemporary scholars who have referenced the debts to Homer and Hesiod and undertook a detailed analysis of the allegorical interpretations, see Most 1999, 354 n27.

69. As Kahn observes, both Parmenides (e.g., DK 28B8.56, B9, B11, B10.1, B11.2) and Anaxagoras (e.g., B1, B12) employ *aither* to refer to celestial fire and "consciously" do so in order "to reconcile the new philosophic conceptions with the Homeric terminology" (Kahn 1960, 148 n3).

70. Glenn Most argues the contrary: that "only a god [for Parmenides] could possibly be the source of a set of transcendent truths to which a mere mortal, if left to his own devices, would have had no access" (Most 1999, 353–55).

71. Empedocles, like Parmenides, has a preference in some passages for the Homeric *aither* over the Milesian *aēr*; e.g., DK 31B17.17–18, 53.

72. See Buffière 1956/1973, 159, citing Heraclitus the Allegorist, chap. 49; see also Brad Inwood, *The Poem of Empedocles: A Text and Translation with an Introduction*, rev. ed. (Toronto: University of Toronto Press, 2001), 173–74.

73. Although Aristotle famously notes in *Poetics* 1447b17–20 that Homer and Empedocles have nothing in common but meter and therefore it is right to call one a poet and the other a natural philosopher, he still suggests that Empedocles was an admirable poet (e.g., *Rhetoric* 1407a34).

74. Diogenes Laertius 2.11 = DK 59A1. This position would tend to endorse Finkelberg's position on the fundamental aim of the Homeric poems, although her position seems to be that the poems are "transparently" so; Margalit Finkelberg, "Homer as a Foundation Text," in Margalit Finkelberg and Gedaliaho Stroumsa, eds., *Homer, the Bible, and Beyond: Literary and Religious Canons in the Ancient World*, (Leiden: Brill, 2003), 75–96.

75. Also Aristotle notes in the *Protrepticus* (fr. 61 Rose) that "mind is the god in all of us and mortal life contains a portion of some god." See also Gábor Betegh, *The Derveni Papyrus: Cosmology, Theology and Interpretation* (Cambridge: Cambridge University Press, 2004), 309 n14.

76. Jonathan Tate contends that the origin and development of allegory suggests that speculative figures attempted to appropriate "for their own use some at least of the mythical traditions" (142); Jonathan Tate, "Plato and Allegorical Interpretation," *Classical Quarterly* 24 (1929), 142–54. He continues that in the fifth century it was still "the philosophers" who played the leading role *beginning* with Anaxagoras (and his disciples, including Metrodorus and Diogenes), for whom Homer's poetry was "about virtue and justice," if interpreted correctly. Tate believes that these philosophers were trying not to defend Homer but to find illustrations and support for their own work and thus interpreted Homer "positively"; Tate 1929, 144.

77. Kahn contends that a similar rationalization of epic was pursued by Democritus in his Homeric studies; for example, Democritus (DK 68B25) postulates that ambrosia is the vapor from which the sun is nourished; Kahn 1960, 153 n1. See also B2 and B142 on etymologies. For a good discussion on the role of etymologies in the present context, see Susan Levin, *The Ancient Quarrel Between Philosophy and Poetry Revisited* (Oxford: Oxford University Press, 2001). There is no doubt in my view that etymologies played a crucial role in early allegory. I hope to deal with this issue in a future study.

78. Taylor argues that the gods or *eidōla* for Democritus are parts of the objective world that can cause psychological states through their impact on physical minds; C. C. W. Taylor, *The Atomists: Leucippus and Democritus: A Text and Translation with a Commentary* (Toronto: University of Toronto Press, 1999), 211n45, 215. He argues that the doxographical evidence suggest that *eidōla*, which can be either harmful or beneficial, act "intentionally" and this, in turn, explains the origin of prophecy; Taylor 1999, 214.

79. For another perspective, see Ford 2002, 165–72.

80. As Betegh notes, "the evidence from Philodemus makes it likely (contra Laks) that Diogenes not only was ready to theologize his air, but also tried to allow some communication with the traditional representations of gods and accordingly agreed to some degree of allegory" (Betegh 2004, 309). It is also worth noting that if Diogenes does not mention Anaximenes, it may suggest that he also drew his inspiration from Homer.

81. On the pre-Socratic references, see Alberto Bernabé, "Orphisme et Présocratiques: bilan et perspectives d'un dialogue complexe," in André Laks and Claire Louguet, eds., *Qu'est-ce que la Philosophie Présocratique?* Cahiers de Philologie vol. 20 (Villeneuve d'Ascq: Presses Universitaires du Septentrion, 2002), 205–47; and Betegh 2004. For a succinct summary of Orphism in context, see Robert Parker, "Early Orphism," in Anton Powell, ed., *The Greek World*, (London: Routledge, 1995), 483–510.

82. The author may have been a priestly figure; remember how certain Hippocratic doctors followed pre-Socratic positions (see Betegh 2004, 345).

83. The author of the commentary notes that the "entire poem is spoken in the way of a riddle (*ainigma*)" (7.3–4 L–M). See Martin West, *The Orphic Poems* (Oxford: Clarendon Press, 1983), 78; and André Laks, "Between Religion and Philosophy: The Function of Allegory in the Derveni Papyrus," *Phronesis* 42 (1997), 121–42. Laks's argument is on p. 123.

84. For an excellent discussion, see Laks 1997, 121–42. Laks notes that it is unclear if the author of the Derveni Papyrus saw the Orphic theogony as an authoritative text. Laks is correct, I believe, to note that none of the pre-Socratic authors would have considered allegorizing their texts, at least not in the sense in which Homer and Orpheus were *thought* to have done; Laks 1997, 139. Richard Janko argues that the author of the Derveni Papyrus is none other than the infamous atheist Diogoras of Melos; Janko 2001, 1–32. Janko attempts to show that Diagoras attempted to make the Orphic poems conform to Ionian physics rather than the contrary. For a number of other interpretations and commentaries on the Derveni Papyrus, see André Laks and Glenn Most, eds., *Studies in the Derveni Papyrus* (Oxford: Oxford University Press, 1997). For a study, see Betegh 2004. Betegh concludes that "the author is trying to make Orpheus's teaching up to date by providing it with an allegorical interpretation involving the conceptual and explanatory frameworks of the late Presocratic speculations" (Betegh 2004, 372). See also Obbink, who observes that the true concern for the author is "for private mysteries and social moralizing" (Obbink 2003, 187). In conjunction with this, Betegh notes correctly, in my view, that the Derveni Papyrus shares certain features with Hippocratic texts, to wit: "a conscious use of concepts and explanatory methods developed in the 'inquiry into nature' tradition, among which first and foremost, there is a unifying concept of nature" (Betegh 2004, 355). Moreover, Betegh notes that certain representatives of the priestly *technē* felt that "their explanatory accounts have to satisfy such criteria in order to retain their persuasive power" (359). The Derveni author nonetheless assumed that this text contains not only the truth but also something of supreme importance: the key to the understanding of the world and our situation in it. Orpheus, however, covered his meaning in "riddles" (366); the comparison that Betegh uses is the interpretation of oracles, as we see in Heraclitus and Herodotus, rather than the traditional categories of natural and moral allegory (368). In the final analysis, however, none of these positions would have been endorsed by Xenophanes or Heraclitus. If they had thought that they had closed Pandora's box, it soon reopened.

85. If this *is* Protagoras's position, it is a staggering assertion, for it amounts to saying that there is *no* historical change, which would be a rather stark contrast with the position he appears to be advocating in the *muthos* on the origin and development of society that Plato attributes to him in the *Protagoras*.

86. Prodicus is thus the precursor of Euhemerus (c. 250 BC), for whom the gods and heroes were *real* people who were deified in recognition of their great services to humanity; this was actually a different twist in the allegory saga.

87. F. Decleva Caizzi, *Antisthenes Fragmenta* (Milan: Instituto editoriale Cisalpino, 1966), frag. 58 = Dio Chrysostom, *Discourses* 53.4.

88. Since completing this essay, I have been working on an equally important phenomenon that I did not address here: the notion of divine inspiration. For whether one had a literal or an allegorical interpretation of the works of Homer and Hesiod, it seems that there was never any doubt that their iconic poems were inspired by the Muses. The famous pre-Socratic philosophers Parmenides and Empedocles invoked the Muses and claimed

inspiration as the source of their own works. Others, like Democritus, despite his material-ist approach to philosophy, still argued that the great poets were somehow infused with a supernatural force. In this forthcoming essay, based on historical and linguistic analysis, I explore the relation between inspiration and allegorical interpretation at the nascent stage of its development and why it is critical to gain an understanding of this interplay in order to better comprehend Plato's attitude toward the poets, and thus some of the highly controversial positions in this area. I hope to show that Plato's often ambiguous attitude toward these very phenomena help to explain his ambiguous attitude toward his cultural and "musical" rivals, the great poets of the past, and why Plato insists that he can, and must, compose an even "higher" music or [*sic*] poetry and with it, the fulfillment of God's plan.

6

Philosophical Readings of Homer

Ancient and Contemporary Insights

CATHERINE COLLOBERT

On us Zeus has brought an evil doom, so that even in days to come we may
be a song for men that are yet to be.

—*Iliad* 6.357–58

Personally, I say that the cruel law of art is that human beings die and that
we ourselves die after exhausting all the forms of suffering, so that not the
grass of oblivion may grow, but the grass of eternal life, the vigorous grass of
fruitful works of art, on which future generations will come, heedless of those
asleep beneath it, to have their *déjeuner sur l'herbe*.

—Marcel Proust, *In Search of Lost Time*

The relationship between poetry and philosophy is not necessarily that of a quarrel. Poetry has been subject to philosophical inquiries and judgments since the
latter's beginnings. This was because at its origin philosophy had to distinguish
itself from other types of discourse in order to establish itself as a new and specific
discourse. Philosophers undertook to differentiate their discourse from the poet's
in two primary but opposite ways: a critical and conflictual way on the one hand,
and a constructive and positive way on the other. These two ways explain to a
large degree the philosophical reception of poetry. Because of its significance in
the Greek curriculum, Homeric poetry has played a key role in the history of
this reception.[1]

This chapter aims to examine the positive philosophical reception of Homer.[2]
By reducing Homeric poetry to the level of philosophical rationality, any philosophical

133

interpretation makes commensurate two types of language a priori irreducible: the conceptual language of philosophy and the allusive and evocative language of poetry. In fact, a philosophical reading of poetry consists first and foremost in translating poetry into philosophical language. It follows that philosophical interpretations have tended to ignore or minimize the poetic qualities of the Homeric epics. In contrast, a classicist strives to take these qualities into account and seeks to explain the Homeric world and worldview with historical and philological devices. He aims to retrieve the past, to form a historical construction. For the most part, this is achieved by avoiding the so-called pitfall of anachronism. This may be done by hunting down modern prejudices, of which scholars are sometimes not aware.[3]

I shall first consider three main types of philosophical readings, which I shall define according to their chief hermeneutical principles and ends. This will occupy the first two-thirds of the chapter. After this, I shall offer my own philosophical interpretation and justify its hermeneutical principles. There are in fact three general hermeneutical principles in which most philosophical readings of Homer are grounded. The first asserts that there is an implicit philosophy in the Homeric epics; the second that the epics set the ground for philosophy; a third related principle deals with the poet's intention, which may or not be philosophical. These principles allow us to categorize Homer's interpreters. The first is based on the claim that Homer has a philosophical intent, and therefore is a philosopher. The second and third types dismiss a philosophical intention on Homer's part, but instead support a weak form of textualism, which is based upon textual meaning.[4] The two latter types differ from one another with regard to their ends, as I shall specify.

The Philosophical Decipherment of Poetry: Poetry as a Riddle

There are several strategies for interpreting poetry in general and Homeric poetry in particular. The first type of philosophical interpretation assumes that poetry makes deliberately implicit philosophical assertions. It rests upon the claim that poetry contains philosophical truths poetically expressed. This first type is instantiated by allegoresis.[5] The allegorical reading of Homeric poetry starts, according to one tradition, with Theagenes of Rhegium (sixth century BC), followed by Metrodorus of Lampsacus,[6] the Stoics,[7] and Heraclitus[8] (first century AD—"not the Obscure, but the one who set out to make us believe unbelievable stories," as Eustathius puts it; 1504, 55). They are followed by Pseudo-Plutarch, the Neoplatonists,[9] and finally by the Christians of the Middle Ages.

This first interpretation is the result of four primary motives: 1) to provide an explanation for episodes and descriptions regarded as unclear and puzzling;[10] 2) to defend Homer against his belittlers; the defense consisting of giving a rational basis for implausible stories and inconsistencies in Homer,[11] in particular regarding the gods (this is the explicit aim of Heraclitus, as I shall make plain);

3) to use Homer for theological purposes, that is, as a wall against Christianity (the Neoplatonists); 4) to make Homer a contemporary for pedagogical purposes (Pseudo-Plutarch,[12] Eustathius during the Byzantine period).[13]

I shall focus on the interpretations by Heraclitus the Allegorist and Pseudo-Plutarch on the grounds, first, that they are exclusively allegorists, and second, because the Stoics and the Neoplatonists have a different agenda. The Stoics use Homer as an authority upon which they rely to put forward their own doctrines (Tate 1929), while the Neoplatonists seek to reconcile Homer and Plato. In this respect, the allegorists are first and foremost Homerists and not affiliated with any philosophical school.

Although the allegorical reading is not immediately offered as a defense, it always serves as one to some degree. Thus, one need not distinguish between two types of allegoresis: on the one hand, a "defensive," and on the other hand, a "positive" form.[14] All allegory is indeed panegyric.[15] As Heraclitus puts it, "if Homer did not allegorize, he would be impious" (*Homeric Questions* 1). Impiety or allegory: these are the two alternatives. But it is not reasonable to suppose that Homer was impious,[16] given both his significance in Greek education and the pleasure one feels while reading him. Thus, it is because of both Homer's influence and greatness that Heraclitus justifies an allegorical interpretation of Homer.

We can elucidate the hermeneutical presupposition of the allegorical reading by clarifying its procedure. I distinguish three primary steps: 1) searching for hidden philosophical truths; 2) translating symbols, images, the gods' names, and metaphors into concepts; 3) laying out Homeric doctrines. These entail that any passage of Homer may possess an implicit philosophical meaning beyond its fictionality. It is this that the allegorist aims to disclose. Though present in and carried through the text, the philosophical truths of Homer's statements do not appear immediately, that is, they are not on the surface of the text. The true meaning is concealed within stories that often seem improbable, like the Olympians fighting in the Trojan plain (cf. Porphyry, 8.2 DK); indeed, implausibility is a poetic device to hide truths. The idea is that behind—or more precisely under (*hupo*)—the literary meaning lies hidden truths.[17]

The primary reason why poetry requires an allegorical reading is poetry itself, which the allegorist regards as cryptic in essence.[18] In other words, it is the very conception of poetry that is at stake here. The idea that truths are deliberately hidden leads to a conception of poetry as a riddle[19] deliberately elaborated by the poet who *ainittetai* (Heraclitus, *Homeric Questions* 26.3). It is taken for granted that the poet riddles, that is, that he deliberately obscures his thought, and this is precisely what his greatness is all about. At the same time, his intention, considered as philosophical (*Homeric Allegories* 4.3), is regarded as obliquely expressed, and in consequence, "problematic," as Lamberton puts it.[20] The interpreter then undertakes to recover the authorial intention by answering the question: "What does Homer mean in this particular image or episode?"[21] The lack of clarity is in fact to be expected from the poet, as the commentator of the Derveni Papyrus claims,[22] making the art of poetry an art of disguise.[23] The allegorist subscribes to the view that the mob should not have access to truths that they do not understand (*The Life and Poetry of Homer* 92).[24]

The sophistication of poetry does not allow everyone to solve its enigmas and to enjoy its truths, that is, to be rewarded for his effort to decipher poetic riddles. As Struck (2004, 160) puts it: "The poet communicates in code in order that the wise may have the pleasure of cracking it, and be left wanting more." There is a claim on the part of the allegorist to a form of esotericism.[25]

Heraclitus's justification for Homer's use of allegory to express philosophical doctrines rests upon both the philosophical practice of some philosophers, for example, the pre-Socratics, and upon an elitist conception of knowledge. Far from being exclusively used by the poets, allegory is a trope used by the philosophers themselves. Take for instance Empedocles and Heraclitus the pre-Socratic philosopher[26]—"all that he says about nature is said through enigmatic allegories" (24.5).[27] Why should one refuse the poet the use of allegory while those who regard themselves as philosophers use it? In raising this issue, Heraclitus the Allegorist addresses two objections: first, language is not a sufficient criterion to discriminate philosophy from nonphilosophy, since philosophers, too, express their thoughts in a poetical way;[28] second, and in consequence, being a poet does not necessarily exclude one from being a philosopher. Since there are philosophers that are poets, there could be poets that are philosophers. It is worth pointing out that Heraclitus's argument is based solely on the way poets and philosophers express their thoughts. In this regard, the similarity of expression is a sufficient condition for arguing for the similarity of purpose and activity.[29] The reasoning amounts to saying (with Maximus of Tyre) that poetry and philosophy are similar; in other words, poetry is philosophy, though the converse does not necessarily hold.

Homer allegorizes, and therefore philosophizes insofar as the former amounts to the latter. In this way, the presence of allegories in Homer guarantees his philosophical intention, and allows Heraclitus to claim the existence of a Homeric philosophy, and that therefore Homer is a philosopher. The epics comprise a double language that mirrors a double reality. On the one hand, there is a story, for instance that of the Trojan War, and on the other hand, philosophical theories. Rather than an opportunity to philosophize, the story constitutes the vehicle of philosophical doctrines. In this respect, any poet who couches in his poetry these kinds of doctrines is entitled to be counted as a philosopher.

The gods play an important role in the allegorist's interpretation because poetry is the perfect medium to speak about them.[30] Some gods embody natural elements, for example, Zeus-Aether, Hera-air,[31] others moral notions like Aphrodite and Ares. For instance, according to Heraclitus, the episode of their love possesses a philosophical truth that was stated by Empedocles. Homer confirms Empedocles' theory beforehand insofar as Ares and Aphrodite are synonymous with War and

Love, whose union gives birth to Harmony, that is, the harmony of the world (69, 3, 7–10). Similarly, the episode of the Deception of Zeus is understood as a physical process; the Theomachy (*Il.* 20) is meant to be a struggle between natural forces.

From this perspective, there is a kind of philosophical rationality in poetry that makes it consistent and coherent. However, because such rationality is not straightforwardly given, bringing these doctrines to light requires translation—this is the second step. Poetic language is figurative language that needs to be translated into a philosophical language. What is translated are symbols that are supposed to be in the text. Once the symbols are identified,[32] the allegorist rationalizes them by transforming them into concepts. The obvious case of translation is the name of the gods translated into natural elements, as we have already seen. As Murrin (1980, 8) puts it, "severed from religion, Homer's gods function rather as technical vocabulary."

The idea of the symbol is crucial in the allegorical reading. The symbol is a result of a conception of poetry as using cryptic language to mask truths from the neophyte. A symbol consists in a shift of referent, like an allegory (*Homeric Questions* 26.2). It is the result of a gap between what is said and what is meant. Therefore, the symbol is a form of enigma.[33] It is in fact enigmatic language that is translated into a philosophical language, where translation constitutes the process through which the enigmas are solved. Translating and solving the riddles are two faces of the same coin. The translation consists of a philosophical rationalization, that is, a conceptualization, whose purpose is to disclose a philosophy that is implicit because darkened (*Homeric Allegories* 24.1). The disclosure rests upon the claim that Homer is the source of all philosophy. All philosophers are indebted to Homer, as if no philosophy would have been possible had Homer not existed.[34]

This brings us to the third step, the laying out of Homeric doctrines. The allegorist's method consists of bringing in doctrines of philosophers in the course of the explanation. However, it is accomplished in a way devoid of any polemical tone. The purpose is not to demonstrate that the Homeric text possesses truths unknown by the philosophers, but rather that the truths stated by subsequent philosophers were already present in Homer. Homer inspired and anticipated most philosophers, who sometimes even plagiarize him. The strategy of the reading is obvious. It consists of fitting Homer's sayings to philosophical doctrines. The idea behind it is that Homer possesses universal knowledge, and accordingly, that the epics are an encyclopedia.[35] In order to demonstrate the universality of Homeric knowledge, the allegorist introduces in a general way the doctrines the poet discloses in the epics. He presents a sort of theoretical overview and basic theoretical insights that makes him a kind of doxographer.[36] The universal knowledge that the allegorist grants to Homer prevents him from affiliating Homer with any philosophical school, making Homer the original and ultimate syncretic philosopher. Homer is the touchstone of true doctrines in that he validates Stoic and pre-Socratic doctrines.[37] Paralleling

Homer's sayings to doctrines from various philosophical schools allows the allegorist, on the one hand, to exhibit the philosophical solution of the Homeric riddles,[38] and on the other hand, to demonstrate that Homer is the greatest not only among the poets, but also among the greatest philosophers.[39]

Even though poetry is equated with philosophy, in order to read poetry as a philosophical treatise, poetry must be deciphered. Heraclitus's interpretation is not always convincing and sometimes appears far-fetched. Moreover, assuming that Homer intended to be a philosopher raises more problems than it solves. In fact, the allegorist is committed to the view that, on the one hand, authorial meaning equates with the meaning he *makes*, and on the other hand, the equation is the justification of his interpretation. This sounds like a circular argument. There is another difficulty: How is it possible that Homer intended to be a philosopher when there were no philosophers in his time? There would, however, be nothing amiss in saying that, even though Homer does not intend to philosophize, his poetry is a work of philosophy insofar as the textual meaning may go beyond any authorial intent. This is in fact the path taken by the second form of interpretation, to which I shall now turn.

Interpreting the Epics as a Work of Philosophy

The second form of rationalization rests upon the hermeneutical principle that there is an implicit philosophy in Homer, who, however, is not regarded as being a philosopher himself. The interpreter both maintains that the epics implicitly convey a philosophy, but acknowledges that Homer does not have a philosophical intent. His claim for a philosophical reading is that Homeric poetry can be a work of philosophy even though it was not intended as such. Unlike allegoresis, an implicit philosophical interpretation does not consist of asking what the poet means.

I shall delve into two readings that epitomize this interpretation, that is, those of the classicist Robert Rutherford and of the French historian of philosophy, Marcel Conche. Their approach rests on four claims: (1) Homer intends to provide the moral insights found in his poetry; (2) these moral insights constitute a moral philosophy; (3) Homeric moral philosophy is devoid of irrational elements; (4) but Homer is not a philosopher since he does not deliberately philosophize. It follows that Homer unintentionally offers a philosophy through moral insights that are intentionally provided. Moral insights deliberately couched in the epics are not meant to be philosophical, but are so nevertheless. It follows that this interpretation rests upon two chief hermeneutical principles: (1) there are allegories in a weak sense in the epics; (2) there is no philosophical intention.

Let us first clarify the weak sense of allegory. According to Long, there are two senses of allegory: a strong type and weak type (Long 1992, 60). The former is concerned with works that have been deliberately composed as allegories such as *The Divine Comedy*.[40] The latter sense bears on work that "invites interpretation in ways that go beyond its surface or so-called literal meaning," such as Pandora's box in Hesiod interpreted as describing the human condition (Long 1992, 43).[41] Rutherford and Conche are both committed to the latter sense of allegory, and regard the epics as comprehending a kind of moral philosophy; accordingly, both endorse the thesis that a work of literature, and poetry specifically, can be a work of moral philosophy. The thesis nonetheless implies a specific understanding of what philosophy—and moral philosophy in particular—is. A work of philosophy need not necessarily imply theorization and conceptualization. Instances of this kind of work in the history of philosophy are well known, from Plato to Kierkegaard, to Nietzsche to Wittgenstein. The epics may therefore be an instance of moral philosophy that does not furnish arguments or display philosophical reasoning. Thus, Conche argues, "the first philosophy of the Greeks is that of Homer. Without yet any speculation, without any theoretical or conceptual addition, it explains the primary truth of life."[42]

The task of the interpreter, then, is to make up for the lack of philosophical devices by retrieving moral insights from the epics. The rationalization of poetry consists not in deciphering poetry, but in bringing to philosophical light truths veiled by the poetic language. Explanation bears first and foremost on moral behavior; as Rutherford puts it, the epics are "a moral tale" that conveys ethical principles. Even though Homer is not a moral philosopher, it remains the case that he intends to bring in moral insight. In this regard, "character and experiences of Odysseus are a central concern of the poet."[43]

One must ask, however (as Rutherford and Conche do), whether lifting the poetic veil is sufficient for philosophical truth to appear. Moral insight does not necessarily constitute a moral philosophy. A moral philosophy is made up of moral principles that cohere and are, if not demonstrated, at least argued for. It requires consistency and unity, and that it be devoid of any form of irrationalism. The former point is advocated by Rutherford (1986, 150), who speaks of the epics as a "structured whole" where conflicting viewpoints are organized so as to obtain a "carefully organized, unified structure." The latter point is emphasized both by Conche and Rutherford, although in different ways. Rutherford dwells on the problem of the gods' role in the overall moral picture. The gods do not appear as paragons of virtue. "Frivolous, selfish and vindictive," as he puts it, they are moreover not reliable.[44] However, insofar as they play a relatively weak role in the *Odyssey*—contrary to the *Iliad*—it is possible to draw out a Homeric moral philosophy from the *Odyssey* without taking them into account. In other words, the gods' behavior does not impact Homer's moral philosophy in a crucial way. Conche adopts a slightly different strategy, seeming to be more sensitive to irrational elements in the epics. He then tackles various issues from divination to Zeus's politics to Homer's dialectic and rationalism. Consider, for instance, the conclusion of his chapter bearing on rationalism: "For the deeply ironic spirit of

Homer distrusts frenzy and irrationality, without nonetheless deluding himself with the power of reflection and reason" (Conche 2002, 62, my translation).

However the interpreter may be committed to the idea that moral insight counts as a moral philosophy under some description, he cannot avoid to some degree the need for allegorizing. Rutherford (1986, 146) alludes to the presence of allegories in Homer when he argues that the allegorist "saw something fundamental to the poem." The claim, although germane to the claim for philosophizing, does not necessarily equate with it, as I shall make plain.[45]

Here it is worth dwelling for a moment on Conche's interpretation of Achilles' shield. Conche (2002, 146) starts by criticizing the pertinence of the cosmologic interpretation of Heraclitus the Allegorist. He argues that this interpretation is contrary to what Homer asserts in *Iliad*, book 8. The argument is interesting insofar as it is from within the text that Heraclitus's interpretation is rejected.[46] However, the rejection is not of allegory as such, since Conche offers his own allegorical reading of the shield. According to him, Homer's purpose consists of depicting human events of a happy life, at least happiness as attainable by human beings. A cyclical conception of time is deduced from various elements like the round of the dancers. The shield is meant to be the allegory[47] of the human condition[48] made up of peace and war, life and death, and so forth. This leads Conche (2002, 159) to conclude that, "Heraclitus' thought—avant la lettre—is here, present." Note in Conche's interpretation the same tendency as the allegorist to regard Homer as the father of philosophy. However, according to Conche's interpretation, since it is based on weak allegory, as we have already seen, Homer's intention to allegorize does not equate with an intention to philosophize.

This brings me to the second principle, that there is no philosophical intent on the part of Homer. Along with Monroe Beardsley, the interpreter holds that the intentional meaning is of no significance: what matters is what the text means for us.[49] The lack of knowledge about Homer's biography, the composition of his poetry, and its overall context certainly constitutes an argument for a non-intentionalist reading. A further argument that one may bring forward is that a poem's meaning always goes beyond the poet's intention. In this sense, there is a discrepancy between Homer's intention and the epics' meaning.[50] Homer did not aim to convey philosophical ideas in his poetry, but it remains the case that an interpreter is justified to look for such ideas in the epics.

For this reason, when Conche argues that Homer understood reality dialectically, the legitimacy of his interpretation does not depend upon whether Homer had a clue about the concept of dialectic.[51] From a textualist perspective, there is nothing amiss in stating that even though Homer does not intend to produce a philosophical work, he did so nonetheless. The epics are a work of philosophy, although of a specific sort. This is what allows both Conche and Rutherford to argue that the interpretive task is to find the philosophical meaning that lies in the epics. It is worth invoking at this point a distinction between finding and construing a text's meaning.[52] Finding a philosophical meaning entails that it lies in the text, while construing it considers the text as "an occasion for meaning," as Eric Hirsch puts it.[53] If the epics are not an occasion for philosophical meaning because the meaning inheres in the text—insofar as it is a work of philosophy—it follows that Rutherford and Conche are guilty of holding two contradictory principles. First, the principle of the weak sense of allegorizing entails regarding the text as an occasion for philosophizing, which implies construing philosophical meaning; but second, the principle of inherent meaning—let us call it the principle of inherence—implies that a meaning is found.

The difficulty with this interpretation does not consist in making Homer an unconscious proto-philosopher or an unconscious cryptic philosopher, but rather in assuming that the epics are in some sense a work of philosophy after all. In fact, maintaining that the epics are open to a philosophical interpretation is different from claiming that the epics are essentially philosophical. In other words, a philosophical understanding of the epics does not necessarily force one to regard poetry as amounting to philosophy. Even though the poet invites us to think about his insights, and intends for us to do so, it does not make him a philosopher or his poetry a work of philosophy. A philosophical interpretation aims to understand philosophical properties in the epics. However, for the aim to be achieved, ascribing to the epics philosophical properties—thereby considering it to be a work of philosophy—is not necessary.[54] A philosophical interpretation of Homer must reject the existence of an intrinsic philosophical meaning for fear of inconsistency, arguing that philosophical properties do not belong to the text, but are the construct of the interpreter. The philosophic interpreter is left with one alternative: philosophically understanding the epics without claiming that any philosophy is couched in the epics. This is in fact the basis upon which the third form of interpretation rests.

Interpreting Homer as an Understanding of the Western Tradition

The third form of interpretation considers the epics from a philosophical stand-point, but uses a preexistent rather than a tailor-made philosophical framework.[55] Its aim is not to grasp the epics' meaning for its own sake or to explain the text. Interpretation is a worthy task insofar as it contributes to an understanding of the big picture, that is, the modern Western world. Understanding the big picture requires an understanding of its parts, and Homer constitutes one of them (although with qualifications). Homer is first and foremost regarded as a starting point of the history of the Western world.

This form of interpretation is exemplified by the readings of Castoriadis and Williams. Their approach is based upon the assumption that Homer is the kernel of the Western tradition. As Castoriadis puts it, "the birth of our tradition lies in the Homeric world."[56] The assumption stems from a philosophy of history in which the past is regarded as shedding light upon the current state of the West. Their readings seek to grasp the Homeric worldview in order to show how the Western world has been influenced by it. Reflecting on Homer amounts to reflecting on the conditions that have made the Western world possible. Consequently, understanding the Western tradition requires understanding Homer.

Williams's and Castoriadis's purpose does not consist merely in understanding the modern world, but of better understanding ourselves. The first step toward such an improved self-understanding is grasping the Greek world in general, and Homer's in particular. For Williams,[57] "When the Ancients speak, they do not merely tell us about themselves, they tell us about us." The improvement consists of a richer and subtler understanding that helps "to free us of misunderstandings of ourselves" (Williams 1993, 11). Many of these misunderstandings are due to misunderstandings of the Greeks, the chief cause of which lies in progressivism. Getting rid of both sorts of misunderstandings calls for rejecting progressivism.

Progressivism rests upon a modern prejudice according to which the historical development of the West begins with the Greeks, which as its first moment is regarded as its childhood.[58] According to progressivism, the past is gone and cannot be retrieved; it has ceased to be a living part of the present. Because of this, there is a gap between the past and the present—between the Greeks and modernity—that cannot be bridged. The gap is the outcome of the shaping of modernity, whose roots are viewed as Christian rather than Greek. Even though Christianity has over the centuries been heavily influenced in some respects by the Greeks, it remains the case that in other respects it has been built up in opposition to them.[59] Regarding the Greek past as irretrievable amounts to highlighting the opposition, of which moreover modernity is taken to be the outcome. The opposition carries the sense of otherness; the Greeks' otherness is emphasized in a way that makes the Greeks and Homer primitive.[60]

The picture is misleading, however, insofar as "the Greek past is specially the past of modernity" (Williams 1993, 3), and therefore should be rejected. But the rejection raises the question as to how one should consider the Greeks and Homer to be a starting point. There are various ways of appreciating it that basically depend upon a conception of history, more specifically, upon the meaning of the past, that is, upon how one defines the relationship between past and present. The relation between past and present should not be regarded as between that which no longer exists and that which does. Many take for granted that the modern world incorporates its past; the disagreement arises as to whether this past is irretrievably gone or still living. According to Castoriadis and Williams, the Greek world is not bygone, but still alive. It is "helping (often in hidden ways) to keep us alive," as Williams (1993, 7) puts it, while according to Castoriadis, the Greeks and Homer are a source that continues to exert an influence on the modern world. This is the case, as Williams (1993, 3) rightly states, because the Greeks are our "cultural ancestors," or in Castoriadis's words, because there is a genealogical link that binds Homer's world with ours. Note that the link does not amount to a historical causality, however, since the modern world is not a necessary effect of the Greek world in general, or of the Homeric world in particular. In this sense, the Western world could have had other faces.

It follows that for the goal of better understanding ourselves to be met, we have to regard the Greeks as close to us; in other words, to set closeness against otherness. The claim for closeness with qualification constitutes the primary hermeneutical principle of this form of interpretation. At the same time, however, Castoriadis warns us against the pitfall of *Selbstverständlichkeit*. The Homeric world is indeed different from ours; filling the gap may hinder all comprehension, what Castoriadis calls, "a false comprehension due to false closeness."[61] In this sense, not ignoring Homeric otherness is a key to grasping "the spirit and meanings of the texts," (2004a, 89). From this perspective, for the task to be completed, one should not dismiss the existence of otherness.

Let us elucidate the kind of grasp that both Williams and Castoriadis support. It is of a specific sort because of what we share with Homer's world, a sharing made possible by the aforementioned genealogical connection. According to Castoriadis, the grasp equates with a reappropriation, which means a new representation based upon the idea that that which has once existed (behavior, discourses, language) can be represented again.[62] Even though any culture allows for a reappropriation, in Homer's case the reappropriation is different in nature because of what is shared. At the same time, grasping the closeness of Homer's meaning allows us to highlight the differences between us and Homer, which must also be approved and valued, as Williams argues (1993, 7). In others words, the grasp is richer and more fruitful in that it brings out both differences and similarities. The differences appear nonetheless contrapuntally, so to speak.

This interpretation not only challenges the core of the progressivist's claim, but is also intended to pinpoint "some of our illusions about the modern world" (Williams 1993, 7). According to Williams, the illusions lie in thinking that many of the modern world's achievements in ethical matters were out of reach for Homer and the Greeks. The issues at stake include those of centers of agency, shame, responsibility, and autonomy. The two latter in particular are falsely considered to be the acquisitions of the modern world—thanks to Christianity.[63] For this reason, making sense of Homer is a necessary step toward making sense of these ethical concepts insofar as they originate in Homer.

Castoriadis and Williams do not endorse the thesis that philosophical properties are to be found in the epics, or that the epics implicitly convey a philosophy. Williams (1993, 4) attempts to offer a "philosophical description of an historical reality." The description is philosophical in the first place because of the way its object, the structures of thought and experience, are set forth, and second, because it interrogates the values of these structures to us (1993, 4). From this perspective, his method primarily consists in extracting "argumentative structures," and in restructuring the texts (1993, 13). Taken to be a work of literature that pictures "human action and experience," Williams asserts that the epics allow the interpreter to ask a set of specifically philosophical questions (1993, 15).

We may use the idea of shame as the most pertinent way to get at what Williams's interpretation intends.[64] He argues that "there is perhaps no single question on which an understanding of the Greeks can join more helpfully with reflection on our own experience" (1993, 92). He calls into question the widely shared view according to which Homeric society is a culture based exclusively on shame in contrast to our modern society based upon guilt. According to this view, the idea of shame conveys notions of heteronomy and egoism, ideas that are supposed to encapsulate the chief components of the Homeric ethical outlook. Williams argues that this is actually in marked contrast to what we find in Homer. He points to two basic albeit common mistakes about the mechanisms of shame: first, "to overlook the importance of the imagined other," and second, to pay no attention to "the identity and attitudes" of the observer (1993, 82). These mistakes are conducive to emphasizing heteronomy, and to assuming that shame is not entitled to be a moral emotion.

Williams convincingly demonstrates that guilt, too, plays a role in Homeric society, although in a different way than in ours, and that shame still impacts our ethical life and so should be taken as falling under the category of morality.[65] By examining afresh the Homeric concept of shame in comparison to the modern concept of guilt, Williams makes plain that some Greek values square with ours, and some do not. He concludes, "shame continues to work for us, as it worked for the Greeks, in essential ways" (1993, 102). The conclusion makes plain both that some alleged gaps can be bridged, and that some Greek ethical views are still pertinent to our moral outlook.

Castoriadis is also committed to the idea that Western distinctiveness has its roots in the Greek worldview, and more specifically, the Homeric worldview. Castoriadis aims to demonstrate that the Homeric worldview is that which makes possible the critical enterprise, which stems from a capacity to call into question what has been instituted, such as values and norms. For the task to be accomplished, he selects six themes in the epics: *moira*, freedom, individuation, universality, the *aristeia*, and the political community. It is worth pointing out that the selection is no accident since the themes are connected to that which in one way or another defines what is distinctive about the Western outlook. I shall focus on just one theme, *moira*, to show why according to Castoriadis the Homeric worldview comprehends a critical enterprise that is the precondition for philosophy.

Castoriadis rightly regards *moira* as linked with death, arguing that *moira* does not mean absolute predetermination and predestination.[66] In this way, he finds room for freedom: a hero makes decisions that shape his life (as Williams, too, makes plain).[67] Thus, without arguing that Homer is a moral philosopher,

Castoriadis regards the epics as conveying a critical moral insight. The insight works as one of the chief conditions for the birth of philosophy. He recognizes that this is a contentious issue. Even though philosophy is defined as a critical enterprise, not all critical enterprises are necessarily philosophic. In fact, such an enterprise manifests itself in other forms—crucially in poetry, albeit not in the same way as philosophy. Even though poetry has no room for argumentation, and does not offer a conceptual framework, it may offer a worldview that qualifies or serves as a critical enterprise.[68] It follows that, though poetry does not necessarily lead to philosophy, it could nonetheless set the ground for it.

Focusing on closeness rather than otherness certainly makes the dialogue with Homer richer and more productive. The idea that lies behind the claim of closeness is both a rejection of progressivism and in a way a critique of modernity, as modernity usually regards itself. Castoriadis's and Williams's interpretations of Homer are interesting in many respects in that they demonstrate that the epics' meaning is tied to the overall meaning of the Western tradition, and redress some false impressions about the understanding of the West. In this sense both Williams's and Castoriadis's readings of Homer are instrumental in getting a better grasp of our modernity, and in pinpointing, in Williams's case, certain weaknesses in our modern ethical outlook, with the former being in fact conducive to the latter.[69] Furthermore, their approach implies an understanding of Homer that is better than how he understood himself insofar as he could not be aware of his founding role in Western world history.[70]

Williams's and Castoriadis's interpretation focuses not so much on explaining Homer as on understanding the Western tradition, concerning which they already have philosophical views. These views act as a kind of guiding principle in this interpretation. But an interpretation of Homer based upon a ready-made philosophical framework, which has as its purpose a better understanding of the Western tradition, will at best capture part of Homer's meaning. This is the case because the interpretation misses the point about the very end and nature of epic poetry, as I shall make plain. Let us now turn to the fourth form of rationalization, which I advocate.

Interpreting Homer as a Philosophical Reappropriation of the Epics

In light of the various problems raised by the philosophical interpretations that I have considered, it seems safe to base an interpretation of Homer upon the three following claims: (1) Homer is not and does not intend to be a philosopher (contra Heraclitus the Allegorist); (2) the epics are not philosophical works (contra Heraclitus the Allegorist, Rutherford, and Conche); (3) the epics do not have a favored relation with philosophy (contra Castoriadis and Williams). I shall argue that the way to arrive at the most fruitful and also the most complete philosophical interpretation of Homer is to ground it in his conception of poetry. With the exception of Heraclitus the Allegorist, none of the interpreters takes this into account. I shall advocate a weak form of intentionalism where the interpretive task consists, first, of coming to grips with what the poet means when composing his poetry, that is, to approximate the authorial meaning; second, to make sense of it by imputing a philosophical meaning to it. My approach is different from Castoriadis's and Williams's in that on the one hand, I partly ground my interpretation on Homer's intention. I retrieve this intention by elucidating his conception of poetry, which, as I shall argue, inheres in the text. On the other hand, I aim to construct a philosophical framework based on this elucidation.

We should first explain the nature of a philosophical construct of Homer based on a weak intentionalism. First, it assumes that there is an original meaning or authorial intention to the extent that this meaning works as a kind of regulative principle. On the other hand, I take it that insofar as the authorial intention is not, strictly speaking, reachable, the interpreter can only approximate it. The approximation is meant to be a partial grasp of the authorial intention, and requires an explanation of two types of property: intrinsic and relational. I shall in the first place argue that understanding the poet's conception of poetry is instrumental to grasp the authorial meaning insofar as this conception elicits the nature and ends of poetry as the poet regards it, and that the elements of the poet's conception are laid down in the epics. These elements are intrinsic properties. In this sense, I agree with Heraclitus the Allegorist that the Homeric conception of poetry constitutes the first and primary step toward understanding the epics. I shall deal in the second place with the relational properties, which depend upon the historical circumstances surrounding the epics.

Epic poetry is the art through which the best men live on after death through the memories of their deeds. It is an activity through which the deeds of the past (the wrath of Achilles or the wanderings of Odysseus) are handed down and kept alive through narrative. In this respect, since the poet's function consists of recollecting the past, the epics have as their ends the preservation and immortalization of the deeds of the past. As an art of preservation, the epics comprise a set of selected memories. Note however that it is only concerned with those who accomplished great deeds, that is, the best of human beings, those who had an outstanding destiny.[71] Furthermore, it is worth pointing out that the poet and his audience considered Achilles, Odysseus, Helen, and other heroes to be actual individuals that therefore are appropriated by the poet.

As an art of immortalization, epic poetry converts rumor into glory.[72] This is why only the poet can give human beings immortality. "On us Zeus has brought an evil doom, so that even in days to come we may be a song for men that are yet to be" (*Il.* 6.357–58). Helen has an extraordinary life, which allows her to be a character in the epics, therefore to have an epic destiny (*Il.* 6.357–58, *Od.* 8.578) through which she gains immortality. To satisfy his desire for immortality, a hero must reach an imperishable fame (*kleos*), which he does by accomplishing great deeds and enduring terrible experiences. This constitutes the end of his life and gives life its meaning. In fact a hero fights ultimately for immortal glory—even though battle may be thrilling and desirable—as the dialogue between Glaucos and Sarpedon makes plain. "Ah friend, if once escaped from this battle we were for ever to be ageless and immortal, neither should I fight myself among the foremost, nor should I send you into battle where men win glory" (*Il.*12.322–25, trans. A. T. Murray).[73] The search for glory, which is tantamount to the search for immortality, is one of the primary keys to understanding heroic actions and motives.

Epic poetry is regarded as justifying an ethics grounded in fame, which exists only through the poet's song. Homer's poetical intention is to immortalize individuals as heroes, and in the process, both epic poetry and himself.[74] The clue to account for Homer's intention is the idea that surfaces in the epics according to which time is for human beings a destructive force. In this sense, in giving individuals immortality, epic poetry is conceived of as a *pharmakon*, a response to the human mortal condition. It follows that epic poetry is based upon and depends on a specific view of time, and accordingly, that the end of heroic ethics, that is, glory, is structured around this view.

This brings me to formulate a philosophical hypothesis, namely that our human relationship to time forces upon us a certain ethical outlook. By "time" I mean time as temporalized by human beings, time on a human scale, the time into which we fit our projects, ambitions, and desires. This time is the time of our lives; consequently, the idea of death also plays a decisive role in it as its limit. Epic immortality is understood as the negation of time's destructive force, which manifests itself in human life as the process of aging and death.[75]

Let us make clear that the Homeric conception of poetry as defined here is a construction insofar as, strictly speaking, there is no theory of poetry as such to be found in the epics. The conception is the outcome of both collecting and gathering elements in the text and making sense of them in a coherent way. However, as Gaut (1993, 603) puts it: "Some properties of works have necessary and sufficient conditions for their ascriptions which are fixed by the artist's realized intentions." I take it that this is the case for the Homeric conception of poetry I put forward (for which there is moreover a sort of consensus among scholars nowadays).

As we have seen, Heraclitus's construct of a Homeric conception of poetry is drastically different from this conception, and accordingly, implies a significantly different interpretation. Recall that his interpretation pretends to retrieve Homer's intention, which consists of hiding philosophical thoughts. Furthermore, his argument is mainly concerned with an alleged impiety regarded as necessarily foreign to Homer's intention. But it is highly doubtful that Homer possesses an idea of impiety, as Heraclitus understands it. Nothing in the epics could ground it better than the idea of poetry as a puzzle, which is meant to be a consequence of the alleged intent. It follows that Heraclitus does not retrieve the authorial meaning, but rather constructs it, as I have already made plain. In other words, he does not deal with the actual Homer but with a fictional or imagined Homer to whom he imputes an intention. This leads to a kind of arbitrariness and confusion between authorial intent and textual meaning[76] that makes his interpretation a false intentionalism, or even an unconscious textualism.

By contrast, the interpretation I advocate has as one of its chief principles the principle of inherence, according to which the approximate authorial meaning is found through an explanation of intrinsic and relational properties. The explanation of intrinsic properties, that is, properties that are found in the text, is achieved on the one hand by focusing on the words and their occurrences that express the key notions around which the philosophical interpretation is structured and, on the other hand, by closely examining episodes and words used by the poet and his heroes.[77] However, intrinsic properties are not sufficient to get at the approximate authorial meaning. It must be supplemented by an explanation of relational properties. These properties are found by inquiring into the epics' historical context broadly speaking—their cultural, political, and religious background, and by relying on historical evidence. Explaining these properties is sometimes crucial to understanding the epics' meaning, as the following example will make plain. If one grants that Homer lived around 700 BC, and so at the age of the rise of the *polis*, important consequences follow for analyzing the political organization of Troy, Scheria, and Ithaca, and accordingly, for grasping the nature of relationships between heroes.[78] The importance of relational properties is due to the fact that as a creation of a historical individual, a piece of art and literature possesses a historical dimension. In this sense, the epics are historically determined, and must be understood partly albeit not solely in their historical context.

On the other hand, since any philosophical meaning of Homer is clearly constructed, I acknowledge what I call a principle of externality—attributing properties that are foreign to the text, that is, neither intentional nor relational, in this case philosophical properties. The principle is based upon the idea that these properties are foreign to the approximate authorial meaning, and so are imputed to the text. It does not follow, however, that they totally conflict with the authorial meaning. The two principles are complementary in that the construction is the outcome of the finding. In fact, the philosophical properties are construed on the basis of properties that are found in the text—views on poetry, on time, and on human frailty, and so forth.

The interpretive task turns out to be philosophical insofar as it consists in validating the aforementioned hypothesis, first, by analyzing the Homeric conception of time, and second, by examining heroic ethics. My interpretation consists of a rationalization chiefly based on a conceptualization of time, which the epics clearly do not express. Even though one of the primary requirements of a philosophical interpretation is its consistency, the rationalization is not achieved by shifting irrational elements to rational. Consistency and rationality are not rules with which the poet always complies—*pace* the allegorists and Conche—because as parts of the poetic picture, they pervade the epics. This leads me to acknowledge that there are elements for which it is not possible to account. In consequence, for the interpreter to aim at a coherent and rational construction, rather than twisting the irrational elements, he should simply not take them into account; in other words, he should ignore them. The task of philosophical interpretation requires selectively choosing elements relevant for its purpose in order to produce a coherent explanation. It therefore supports a kind of decontextualization whereby the emphasis is put on specific lines that are extracted from their context, sometimes to the detriment of the literary quality of the text.

It follows that in philosophizing from the epics, the interpretive task I define goes beyond Homer. In fact, I would claim that Homeric poetry is an opportunity to philosophize, though the interpretation must be achieved within a philosophical framework relevant to the nature of the epics—which was not, as Andrew Ford reminds us, thought to be "a cryptic text."[79] For this reason, going beyond Homer does not equate with understanding Homer better than he understood himself, to put it in Kant's words,[80] but differently than he understood himself.[81] This is the case because a text is open to meanings different from the authorial meaning. In other words, the epics are much richer than Homer intended them to be. He would certainly be surprised to hear about the various interpretations of him that have been put forward over centuries, but he could not deny that his epics have legitimately provoked them.

For this reason, no interpretation of Homer is immune from anachronism. It is impossible for an interpreter to be rid of her historical idiosyncrasy. Yet even though we are doomed to anachronistic meanings—on account of our historicity—some sorts of agreement among interpreters over centuries should be noted. Heraclitus the Allegorist in the first century and Aldo Lo Sciavo (*Omero filosofo* [Firenze: F. Le Monnier, 1983]) in the twentieth century share the same view not only of Homer's intent, but also and accordingly, of the epics' overall meaning.[82] It would seem that our understanding is not entirely historical, after all. However, a philosophical interpreter who acknowledges that Homer was not a philosopher must first support a kind of anachronism, and second, must be committed to the idea that it is not possible to reach a truly historical and scientific interpretation, in Schleiermacher's sense, or at least that it is not her purpose. Philosophical interpretation consists, then, in a reappropriation that entails a degree of anachronism that, though pointless to disregard or deny, can be reduced as much as possible.

Let us recap. The overall procedure of my philosophical interpretation comprises four steps: (1) abstracting and collecting elements from various descriptions, dialogues, and so forth, and putting them into a historical perspective that equates with explaining intrinsic and relational properties; (2) grasping the Homeric conception of poetry; (3) drawing conclusions from it in order to formulate a philosophical hypothesis; (4) validating the hypothesis by constructing a philosophical meaning for the epics. Furthermore, I take it that combining the principles of inherence and of externality is instrumental to avoid arbitrariness, and works as a safeguard conducive to a less partial, therefore biased, interpretation—as I take the interpretations that I have examined here to be. This is the case because, first, the meaning constructed is a plausible outcome of the meaning found, as we have seen, and second, because explaining the intrinsic and relational properties is a requirement to approximating the authorial meaning and so to circumscribing the literary identity of the epics.[83] The procedure I have put forward makes the interpretation necessarily consistent with the properties found.[84] In contrast to Castoriadis's and Williams's interpretations, my philosophical interpretation follows from the identification of these properties. The hypothesis then is not extraneous, nor is it imposed upon the text. Even though Homer has no intention to write a philosophical work, the epics are compatible with philosophical interpretations. The compatibility requires, nonetheless, that an interpretation rest upon hermeneutic principles that are conducive to a clear distinction and coherence between the properties found, that is, between intrinsic and relational properties, and the constructed philosophical properties. The first two philosophical interpretations of the epics that I have considered fail to meet these requirements.

Conclusion

I would like to conclude this chapter by answering the following question: why offer a philosophical interpretation of Homer today? The various philosophical interpretations are the outcome of a positive prejudice in favor of Homer due to his place in the Western tradition. Let us make clear, however, that Homer has significance for us not as a starting-point of Western culture. One has to avoid the illusion of a search for origins. Origins are instituted. They are chosen in order to make sense of history. This does not imply, however, that I dismiss any deep connection between the Western tradition and Homer. I rather mean that when one decides to set the Homeric epics as the foundational text of the Western world, this compels the way history is written. Some may decide to regard the Bible as the beginning of the Western world, and the Greeks as the heralds of the Christian message. From this perspective, any decision about that matter is a decision about the way *we* understand the tradition, that is, its meaning for us.

It is true that Homer to some degree helps us to better understand our tradition, albeit not so much because he is the spirit of Greece as because he is both a synthesis of the Greek world and a crucial influence on its shape. In this sense, Homer is both the witness to and the craftsman of the Greek spirit. This, I would say, is the idea that lies behind the Platonic assertion that Homer is the educator of the Greeks. I would note, however, that this is the case both because the epics have never stopped being subject to various constructions since the pre-Socratics, and because the epics were regarded as *the* textbook.[85]

The philosophical interpretations that we have examined have in common addressing in a text philosophical problems that are necessarily contemporary to the interpreter. Every philosophical interpretation, then, assumes a kind of anachronism. For this reason, the methodology and presuppositions about Homer's intent and the nature of the text vary from one interpreter to another, as we have seen. However, it remains the case that what is at stake in these philosophical interpretations is to make Homer either a contemporary—as Heraclitus the Allegorist means to do—or an interlocutor who can respond to contemporary questions—as Conche argues—or who can help us to better understand the current state of the Western world—as Castoriadis and Williams claim.

By contrast, in offering a philosophical interpretation of Homer I do not intend to better understand the Western tradition, although my interpretation indirectly participates in it. My primary and chief aim is to shed light on the concept of time and its connection to a value system. Interpreting Homer is especially pertinent to this task both because his worldview revolves around an idea of time as a destructive force, and because as managing access to immortality, his art is conceived of as a response to time. This conception of art and literature ultimately rests upon the idea that art saves us from nothingness. The idea has indeed a long history and has been shared by many writers over the centuries. In modern French literature the writer who expresses it the most deeply is undoubtedly Proust.

Notes

1. For an overview of the reception, see Howard W. Clarke, *Homer's Readers: A Historical Introduction to the Iliad and the Odyssey* (Newark: University of Delaware Press, 1981).

2. The chapter does not deal with the broader history of the reception, which starts with Xenophanes and Heraclitus, or the various influences of Homer on philosophers. See Jean Pépin, *Mythe et Allégorie: les origines grecques et les contestations judéo-chrétiennes* (Paris: Études augustiniennes, 1976), and Gerard Naddaf's chapter in this volume.

3. A good example of this type of scholarship is Christopher Gill's book, *Personality in Greek Epic: Tragedy, and Philosophy: The Self in Dialogue* (Oxford: Clarendon Press, 1996).

4. I shall return to this point in due course.

5. Jonathan Tate, "On the History of Allegorism," *Classical Quarterly* 28 (1934), 105–15; at 109–10, he calls this the "historic" or "pseudo-historic." The interpretation of Orphic poetry as laid out in the Derveni Papyrus exemplifies it; see Gàbor Betegh, ed., *The Derveni Papyrus* (Cambridge: Cambridge University Press, 2004).

6. See Nicholas J. Richardson, "Homeric Professors in the Age of the Sophists," *Proceedings of the Cambridge Philosophical Association* 21 (1975), 65–81; 68ff.

7. Anthony A. Long, "Stoic Readings of Homer," in Robert Lamberton and John J. Keaney, eds., *Homer's Ancient Readers: The Hermeneutics of Greek Epic's Earliest Exegetes*, (Princeton: Princeton University Press, 1992), 58–84, claims that the Stoics did not in fact allegorize. His position is at odds with many commentators. See George A. Kennedy, "Hellenistic Literary and Philosophical Scholarship," in George A. Kennedy, ed., *The Cambridge History of Literary Criticism*, (Cambridge: Cambridge University Press, 1989), 200–19; Peter T. Struck, *Birth of the Symbol: Ancient Readers and the Limits of Their Texts* (Princeton: Princeton University Press, 2004), 113–14.

8. Along with Félix Buffière, *Les Mythes d'Homère et la pensée grecque* (Paris: Les Belles Lettres, 1956) and Long 1992, I do not consider Heraclitus to be a Stoic philosopher.

9. For the Neoplatonist reception of Homer, see Robert Lamberton, *Homer the Theologian: Neoplatonist Allegorical Reading and the Growth of the Epic Tradition* (Berkeley and Los Angeles: University of California Press, 1989).

10. See Porphyry's interpretation of the cave of the nymphs.

11. See Aristotle, fr. 142–79 (Rose); Porphyry, *Homeric Questions*.

12. His motive is "simultaneously praising and making more accessible the language and thought of the poet," as Lamberton 1996, 9, states.

13. As Tate 1934 argues, the motives are not only defensive but also positive and exegetic; see also Jonathan Tate, "Plato and Allegorical Interpretation," *Classical Quarterly* 23 (1929), 142–54.

14. As Michael B. Trapp, "Allegory, Greek," in Simon Hornblower and Antony Spawforth, eds., *The Oxford Classical Dictionary*, third ed. (Oxford: Oxford University Press, 2003) argues. For a discussion of the distinction, see Struck 2004, 14–15.

15. As Maureen Quilligan, *The Language of Allegory: Defining the Genre* (Ithaca: Cornell University Press, 1977), 28, observes, "the absurdity of the surface of a text is the necessary signal for the existence of allegory."

16. See Plutarch who dismisses allegory precisely because it is a way of defending Homer against impiety (*Essays on the Study and Use of Poetry* 19–20). See Rudolf Pfeiffer, *History of Classical Scholarship from the Beginnings to the End of the Hellenistic Age* (Oxford: Clarendon Press, 1968).

17. According to Plutarch, *huponoia* was the word used by the ancient Greeks that gave way to *allegoria* (*Moralia* 19e). The former word means first "conjecture, suspicion, guess" (LSJ), an underlying meaning, while the latter consists of a figure or trope that "says one thing but that means something other than what one says" (*Homeric Questions* 26.2). See also Pseudo-Plutarch, *The Life and Poetry of Homer* 24. However, Plutarch's picture is misleading since Pseudo-Plutarch keeps using *huponoia* (e.g., *The Life and Poetry of Homer* 92). See Pépin 1976, 85–92.

18. See Pseudo-Plutarch, *The Life and Poetry of Homer* 92.

19. See Philodemus, *Rhet.* I, 164, 174, 181 (Sudhaus); Demetrius, *On Style* 99ff.; Cicero, *Or.* 94, 166.

20. See Robert Lamberton and John J. Keaney, ed., [Plutarch] *Essay on the Life and Poetry of Homer* (Atlanta: Scholars Press, 1996), 13.

21. Note the various questions Porphyry asks (*On the Cave of the Nymphs* 3), for example, "What does the cave in Ithaca mean (*ainitteta*) for Homer?" (2).

22. See the Derveni Papyrus, line 5, column 13.

23. Plato ironically argues that the art of poetry is the art of enigmas (*Alc.* 2, 147b).

24. The idea that the poets conceal their thought is indeed not new, and was ironically stated by Plato (e.g., *Theaet.* 180c2).

25. See Giovanni Boccaccio, *Boccaccio on Poetry: Being the Preface and the Fourteenth and Fifteenth Books of Boccaccio's Genealogia Deorum Gentilium*, trans. C. G. Osgood (New York: Liberal Arts Press, 1956), 59–60; George Chapman, "A Free & Offenceless Justification of Andromeda Liberata," in Phyllis Brooks Bartlett, ed., *The Poems of George Chapman* (New York: Oxford University Press, 1941), 327, endorsed the same view, quoted by Quilligan 1979, 27.

26. See fr. 32 DK and 94 DK.

27. Note that in the same vein the commentator of the Derveni Papyrus regards Heraclitus as a mythmaker (column 4).

28. This has been already noted by Aristotle in order to differentiate the poet from the philosopher (*Poetics* 1447b15–20). For the anti-allegorical project of Aristotle see Struck 2004; Denis C. Feeney, *The Gods in Epic: Poets and Critics of the Classical Tradition* (Oxford: Clarendon Press, 1991).

29. The similarity was plausible in that, as Michael Murrin, *The Allegorical Epic: Essays in Its Rise and Decline* (Chicago: University of Chicago Press, 1980), 10, puts it, "the boundaries between philosophy and poetry were often blurred, and many writers could be classed in this twilight zone."

30. See Cleanthes, *SVF* 1.486.

31. One finds in Plato the same allegorical etymology (*Crat.* 404c). As Walter Burkert, "La genèse des choses et des mots: le papyrus de Derveni entre Anaxagore et Cratyle," *Les études philosophiques* 25 (1970), 443–455, 450, notices, allegory is an etymologized narration.

32. Note that Plato refers to the identification of a hidden sense (*Rep.* 378d 5–6).

33. The Homeric use of enigmas may be traced to Pherecydes, as Struck 2004 argues. For an analysis of the symbol, see also Buffière 1956; Northrop Frye, *Anatomy of Criticism: Four Essays* (Princeton: Princeton University Press, 1957).

34. This is in fact clearly stated by Pseudo-Plutarch: "Thus Homer was the first to philosophize in the areas of ethics and physics" (*The Life and Poetry of Homer* 144). See also 93, 122, 124, 127, 130, 143.

35. The idea is not new and seems to have been widespread in the fifth and fourth centuries BC, see Xenophon, *Symp.* 4–6. Plato's charge against Homer partly revolves around it (see *Ion* 531c, 537a, *Rep.* 598 e1–3).

36. As Lamberton and Keaney 1996, 13, note, H. Diels "devoted a chapter to the essay [*The Life and Poetry of Homer*] in his *Doxographi Graeci*."

37. Heraclitus states that Homer "seems to confirm the ideas of the Sicilian school and the Empedoclean theory" (*Homeric Allegories* 69.8).

38. See Pseudo-Plutarch who recognizes an Aristotelian statement in *Od.* 12.385–86 (*The Life and Poetry of Homer* 105, 114).

39. See Pseudo-Plutarch, *The Life and Poetry of Homer* 120, 152.

40. Dante (reprinted in Mark Musa, ed., *Essays on Dante* [Bloomington: Indiana University Press, 1964], 37) informs us that his *Commedia* has four different levels of meaning.

41. What is worth pointing out in Long's words (1992, 60), is that in the case of weak allegories, "the allegorizing is a contribution by us, the readers, and not something that we know to be present in the text as originally constructed. In some sense, all literary interpretation is weak allegorizing."

42. M. Conche, *Essais sur Homère* (Paris: PUF, 2002), 215–16. See also Pseudo-Plutarch, *The Life and Poetry of Homer* 106. In the same vein, David D. Raphael, "Can Literature Be Moral Philosophy?" *New Literary History* 15 (1983), 1–12, argues that Attic tragedy "is presented as the outcome of a new perspective, in a form of persuasion that can fairly be called rational although not reducible to rules of inference like logic" (4).

43. R. Rutherford, "The Philosophy of the *Odyssey*," *Journal of Hellenic Studies* 106 (1986), 145–62. See 147–48.

44. Note in contrast that according to the allegorist, the gods' behavior constitutes a reason for justifying allegories in Homer.

45. It is interesting to notice in passing that Arthur Danto, *Philosophizing Art* (Berkeley and Los Angeles: University of California Press, 1990), 63, appeals to such an equation in the case of Warhol in advocating that the artist is a philosopher.

46. In the same vein, see Porphyry, *Homeric Questions* 1.

47. Note however that Conche does not use the word.

48. In the same vein, see Rutherford 1986. The reading of the epics as a picture of the human condition is the most frequent nowadays.

49. Monroe Beardsley, *Aesthetics: Problems in the Philosophy of Criticism* (New York: Harcourt, Brace and World, 1959). To pursue this point fully would go beyond the scope of my immediate concern.

50. By the same token, one may injure someone without meaning it.

51. As Berys Gaut, "Interpreting the Arts: The Patchwork Theory," *The Journal of Aesthetics and Art Criticism* 51:4 (1993), 507–609, 606, puts it: "Most 'primitive' societies lacked the concept of art, and therefore any maker of artifacts in them could not have intended her works as works of art, nor could she have intended there to be a range of properties which were relevant for the interpretation of her works as works of art."

52. Note that some intentionalists and nonintentionalists share the view that a text's meaning is not found but construed by the interpreter. See Eric Hirsch, "Three Dimensions of Hermeneutics," *New Literary History* 3 (1972), 245–61; M. Beardsley, *The Possibility of Criticism* (Detroit: Wayne State University, 1970).

53. Hirsch 1972, 246.

54. I do not aim to advocate pluralism, although I support a form of it by which an interpretation is conceived of as one possible way among others to understand a work of literature. Homeric epics are open to a wide range of interpretations, as I have already noted. Pluralism in fact pervades Homeric studies. From this perspective, a Homeric scholar is bound to acknowledge that there are a variety of plausible and legitimate ways to interpret Homer. Note however that pluralism is not relativism. There are obviously interpretations that are not right. It raises the question of defining criteria for rightness. I leave aside the debating question between pluralism and monism insofar as I am only concerned with examining the strengths and weaknesses of philosophical interpretations of Homer. I shall address the question of their plausibility in due course. Both monism and pluralism have their defenders and opponents. See Michael Krausz, ed., *Is There a Single Right Interpretation?* (University Park, Penn.: Penn State Press, 2002). For a defense of pluralism, see Beardsley 1959; Michael Krausz, *Rightness and Reasons: Interpretation in Cultural Practices* (Ithaca: Cornell University Press, 1993); Gaut 1993. For a defense of monism, see E. Hirsch, *Validity in Interpretation* (New Haven and London: Yale University Press,

1967); Alexander Nehamas, "The Postulated Author: Critical Monism as a Regulative Ideal," *Critical Inquiry* 8 (1981), 133–49.

55. I shall clarify the latter framework in due course.

56. H. Castoriadis, "Séminaire du 24 novembre 1982," *Ce qui fait la Grèce, 1: D'Homère à Héraclite* (Paris: Seuil, 2004b), 65–84, 73.

57. B. Williams, *Shame and Necessity* (Berkeley and Los Angeles: University of California Press, 1993), 19–20.

58. Cf. Castoriadis's critique of progressivism, "Séminaire du 1er décembre 1982," *Ce qui fait la Grèce, 1. D'Homère à Héraclite* (Paris: Seuil, 2004c), 85–106, 85. Cf. Georg W. F. Hegel, *The Philosophy of History*, trans. J. Sibree (New York: Barnes and Noble Books, 2004).

59. As Williams 1993, 12, reminds us (quoting Peter Brown, *The Body and Society: Men, Women, and Sexual Renunciation in Early Christianity* [New York: Columbia University Press, 1988], 86): "the new way of thinking that emerged in Christian circles in the course of the second century shifted the centre of gravity of thought on the nature of human frailty from death to sexuality."

60. As an example of this type of reading, see Bruno Snell, *The Discovery of the Mind: The Greek Origin of European Thought*, English trans. (Oxford: Blackwell, 1953). Both Williams 1993, chap. 2, and Castoriadis 2004c, 87, strongly criticize Snell's position.

61. See Castoriadis, "Séminaire du 10 novembre 1982," in *Ce qui fait la Grèce, 1: D'Homère à Héraclite* (Paris: Seuil, 2004a), 35–46.

62. Note in passing that the reappropriation is not that of Gadamer's hermeneutics, which entails a fusion of horizons. On the issue of reappropriation of the Greeks, see Roger-Pol Droit, ed., *Les Grecs, les Romains et nous: L'Antiquité est-elle moderne?* (Paris: Le Monde Éditions, 1991); Barbara Cassin, ed., *Nos Grecs et leurs modernes: Les stratégies d'appropriation de l'Antiquité* (Paris: Seuil, 1992); Giuseppe Cambiano, *Le retour des Anciens*, French trans. (Paris: Belin, 1994); Maria Daraki, ed., *La Grèce pour penser l'avenir* (Paris: L'Harmattan, 2000); Catherine Collobert, ed., *L'avenir de la philosophie est-il grec?* (Montréal: Fides, 2002); Simon Goldhill, *Who Needs Greek? Contests in the Cultural History of Hellenism* (Cambridge: Cambridge University Press, 2002).

63. See Williams 1993, chaps. 3 and 4.

64. See Williams 1993, 75–102, 219–23.

65. I shall not elucidate his line of argument fully, which would go beyond the scope of my immediate concern.

66. Castoriadis, "Séminaire du 15 décembre 1982," in *Ce qui fait la Grèce, 1: D'Homère à Héraclite* (Paris: Seuil, 2004d), 107–22, 113.

67. Achilles chooses his death: he chooses to die in Troy rather than going back to Phtia because a "*bios atimetos* or *akleies* is not viable," as Castoriadis (2004c, 103) states. See Williams 1993, 21–49.

68. It would go beyond the scope of my immediate concern to demonstrate to what extent there is such a critical view in Homer.

69. See, in the same vein, Alasdair MacIntyre, *After Virtue: A Study in Moral Theory*, second ed. (Notre Dame: University of Notre Dame Press, 1984), 11, who aims, as he puts it, "to construe a true historical narrative." By the same token, Adorno and Horkheimer's interpretation of the *Odyssey* "Excursus 1: Odysseus or Myth and Enlightenment," in

Dialectic of Enlightenment: Philosophical Fragments, trans. E. Jephcott (Stanford, Calif.: Stanford University Press, 2002), 35–62, 35, rests upon the idea that history amounts to the process of the formation of subjectivity. The authors' chief thesis, stemming from a Marxist framework, is that Odysseus is "the prototype of the bourgeois individual." They argue that by fighting against the force of nature, the hero makes his way toward self-consciousness. In this sense, subjectivity manifests itself in flying from "the mythical powers" (37). Myth and enlightenment constitute the two opposing elements that allow one to make sense of Homer in the Western world.

70. I shall return to this point in due course.

71. "It is hateful and accursed to be forgotten by the Muses, the memory given by songs is most joyful for men sustaining life's short path," Sophocles says (fr. 145N).

72. See Gregory Nagy, *The Best of the Achaeans: Concepts of the Hero in Archaic Greek Poetry* (Baltimore: Johns Hopkins University Press, 1979), 16; Egbert Bakker, *Poetry in Speech: Orality and Homeric Discourse* (Ithaca: Cornell University Press, 1997), 166.

73. The dialogue alludes to a kind of duty on the part of a king toward his followers. Winning glory is attached to a kingly function because the immortal renown that the king acquires in battle is reflected upon his people. This function requires a young king to learn to "excel always and to fight among the foremost Trojans" (*Il.* 6.444–45).

74. In fact, the poet and his hero are inseparable and complementary in the process of immortalization; Homer immortalizes Odysseus just as Odysseus immortalizes Homer. In this sense, both of them are *periklutos* (*Od.* 1.325–28).

75. It is worth quoting the lines: "Just as are the generations of leaves, such are those also of men" (*Il.* 6.147).

76. See Nehamas 1981. For a critique of Nehamas's position, see Robert Stecker, "Apparent, Implied, and Postulated Authors," *Philosophy and Literature* 11 (1987), 258–71; Paisley Livingston, "Intentionalism in Aesthetics," *New Literary History* 29:4 (1998), 831–46; Gaut 1993.

77. This constitutes in fact the principle that the Greeks called *lusis ek prosopou*. This principle was anticipated by Antisthenes, according to Richardson 1975, 78.

78. Witness the vast literature on the various types of communities in the epics. See Victor Ehrenberg, *The Greek State* (London: Methuen, 1969); Moses Finley, *The World of Odysseus*, seventh ed. (New York: New York Review Books, 2002); Kurt A. Raaflaub, "Poets, Lawgivers, and the Beginnings of Political Reflection in Archaic Greece," in Christopher Rowe and Malcolm Schofield, eds., *The Cambridge History of Greek and Roman Political Thought*, (Cambridge: Cambridge University Press, 2000), 23–57; Peter W. Rose, "Ideology in the *Iliad*: Polis, *Basileus, Theoi,*" *Arethusa* 30 (1997), 151–99; Richard Seaford, *Reciprocity and Ritual: Homer and Tragedy in the Developing City-State*, second ed. (Oxford: Clarendon Press, 1999); Dean Hammer, *The Iliad as Politics, The Performance of Political Thought* (Norman: University of Oklahoma Press, 2002).

79. Andrew Ford, *The Origins of Criticism: Literary Culture and Poetic Theory in Classical Greece* (Princeton: Princeton University Press, 2002), 75.

80. Immanuel Kant, *The Critique of Pure Reason*, ed. Paul Guyer and Allen Wood (Cambridge: Cambridge University Press, 1998), B 370–A 440. See F. Schleiermacher, in Hanz Kimmerle, ed., *Hermeneutik, nach den Handschriften* (Heidelberg: C. Winter, 1959), I, 50.

81. See Hans-Georg Gadamer, *Truth and Method*, trans. J. Weinsheimer and D. G. Marshall (London and New York: Continuum, 2004), 301–02.

82. As Hirsch 1972, 253, rightly states, "Obviously, the pre-given historical world cannot be the decisive factor that accounts in such cases for the similarities between different periods or the irreconcilable differences of interpretation within the same period."

83. See Peter Lamarque, "Objects of Interpretation," *Metaphilosophy* 31 (2000), 95–124.

84. See Livingston 1998, 834.

85. See Robert Lamberton, "Homeric Allegory and Homeric Rhetoric in Ancient Pedagogy," in Franco Montanari, ed., *Omero Tremila Anni Dopo* (Rome: Edizioni di storia e letteratura, 2002), 185–205.

PART II

Philosophy and Tragedy

7

Violence and Vulnerability
in Aeschylus's *Suppliants*

SARA BRILL

The drama of the suppliant is triangulated, occurring as it does between hunter, hunted, and a host who must choose one of two sides. Suppliants are often also travelers, and the dramas of supplication frequently invoke the powerful tension between the familiar and the foreign, between kin and stranger. Of course, myriad variations on this theme exist in the realm of classical tragedy. What a suppliant drama is uniquely situated to present is the tension between a seemingly clear power structure (powerful host and enemy, powerless suppliant) and the forces that undergird it, the uncovering of which serves to complicate the very structures they enable. In short, the suppliant dramas of classical tragedy all play upon an equivocation between power and powerlessness, strength and vulnerability, precisely because they all present the curious and fragile power that belongs to the suppliant.[1] They are thus deeply political dramas; in these tragedies not just individuals but entire structures of power, entire regimes, are put on stage and examined.

In the following pages I would like to delve into Aeschylus's exploration of the curious power of the suppliant. More specifically, I hope to show how, in his *Suppliants*, Aeschylus's construction of the act of supplication contributes to the inquiry into the foundations of authority and the ever-shifting bases of power and vulnerability that this tragedy provides. In the *Suppliants* this inquiry into authority extends into both public and private spheres. At the level of the public, Aeschylus's *Suppliants* presents to its audience the collision between two forms of rule and their corresponding regimes: a democratic rule by persuasion and a tyrannical rule by force. At the level of the private, this tragedy draws attention to the complicated play between vulnerability and violence that is so often at work in desire and the institutions built upon it. As I hope to show, Aeschylus's characterization of the act of supplication provides a connective tissue between these two levels; it does so by highlighting the tension between a hatred of violence and a propensity for violence that is internal to his suppliant chorus, the Danaids. This internal tension is illustrated by the Danaids' ambivalent employment of the *muthos* of their ancestor Io. The act of supplication proves indispensable for Aeschylus's treatment of *kratos* in this play.[2] Thus, by investigating Aeschylus's handling of supplication we are both afforded a profound meditation on the ambivalent nature of power, *kratos*, itself and are provoked to consider the specific role of myth in the legitimization of authority.

Aeschylus's *Suppliants* has long stood out as an odd tragedy. Up until the 1950s its eccentricities were explained by its presumed early date of composition and thus as a function of its close ties with the tradition of lyric poetry out of which, it was also presumed, tragedy emerged. However, the theory of its early composition was exploded by the publication of Oxyrhynchus Papyrus 2256 fr. 3 in 1952, and scholars were left in the wake caused by the disappearance of the easy explanation this theory provided. In the introduction to his translation of the *Suppliants*, Peter Burian puts the state of affairs as follows: "Take away primacy of date, and what is left is a Greek tragedy that resolutely refuses to include most of the elements we expect of Greek tragedy: no hero, no hamartia, no downfall or tragic conclusion of any kind."[3]

The action of the tragedy can be briefly summarized. The play opens with the arrival of a band of suppliants, daughters of Danaos, at a sacred altar just outside of the city Argos, having fled their homeland of Egypt in order to avoid being married off to their cousins, the sons of Aigyptos. During the parodos, the Danaids take their places around the images of the gods. When they are discovered by the king of Argos, Pelasgos, a tense debate ensues, during the course of which the Danaids accomplish two tasks: they convince Pelasgos of their Argive kinship, on the basis of their being the product of the union of Zeus and Argive Io, and they procure from him a promise to protect them from the pursuing band of the sons of Aigyptos. Pelasgos in turn persuades them that the best way to attain this protection is to have the will of the Argive people behind them and so he sends Danaos to win support in Argos and himself advocates for the Danaids with his people. Egyptian ships are then sighted on the shore and shortly thereafter a herald accompanied by a group of armed men attempts to remove the Danaids from the altar of the gods, first by verbal threats and then by physical force. Pelasgos intervenes, and the play ends with the Danaids' descent into the city and an anticipation of a bloody battle to come.

The two companion plays of the trilogy, the *Aigyptioi* and the *Danaids*, and the accompanying satyr play *Amymone* are lost. On the basis of what little evidence remains,[4] scholars suspect that the subsequent plays of the trilogy involved a violent encounter between Argives and Aigyptids, the establishment of Danaos as *tyrranos* in Argos, the eventual marriage of the Danaids to the Aigyptids, and the bloody slaughter of all but one of the Egyptian grooms by their brides on the night of their wedding. One Danaid, Hypermnestra, has second thoughts and spares her husband Lynkeus. They ascend to the throne of Argos and create a line that would eventually produce the hero Heracles.

In what follows I will adopt as a first foothold into the text an assumption that seems warranted by the explosion of the theory that the tragedy was of early composition, namely, that Aeschylus was intentionally stretching the bounds of poetic convention by assigning to his Chorus of the Daughters of Danaos the dual roles of chorus and protagonist.[5] The tension between the individual and the collective that is so often presented in tragedy receives a startling treatment here; it is not an individual suppliant who faces a collective host, but a collective suppliant who faces a host who is both individual and collective, insofar as Pelasgos explicitly recognizes the seat of his power to lie with the consent of his people. Indeed, another unique feature of the *Suppliants* is its appeal to a democratic structure of power and its use, albeit offstage, of a vote of the people in order to determine a course of action.[6] Thus, the collectivity of the chorus, exemplifying both the strange power of the suppliant and the power structure from which it flees, is juxtaposed with the collectivity of the people of Argos, and the power structure they embody. More specifically, the two collectives provide the opportunity to present an encounter between democracy and tyranny, and all of the tensions such an encounter creates. In their defiance of their cousins, their rejection of marriage, and their eventual violence, Aeschylus's Danaids are particularly ambivalent protagonists.[7]

However, the collision between these two regimes can be presented in any number of contexts. What a suppliant drama adds is the play between violence and vulnerability *within* the character of the suppliant. This is particularly the case with Aeschylus's Danaids, whose fear of violence comes into direct conflict with their own propensity for violence. The exploration of this internal struggle provides the display of a *kratos* that is independent of any particular motive, aim, or desire, the recognition of which diminishes the distinction between violence and persuasion. Further, the mechanism by means of which Aeschylus reveals the Danaids' internal struggle is their own anxiety-laden interpretation of their mythic genealogy. Thus, in addition to the aforementioned display of *kratos*, we are afforded a sustained consideration of the use of *muthos* to legitimate action and the dangers that can accompany such uses.

In what follows I will attempt to support these claims by adopting the following structure: first, an investigation of the ritual of supplication in order to illustrate the broader cultural and religious context surrounding the act of supplication; second, a tracing out of Aeschylus's own construction of supplication and its effect on the encounter between Danaids and Argives; third, an examination of the internal conflict that the Danaids' peculiar practice of supplication engenders and their various means of dealing with this conflict.

Ritual Supplication

The Greek word for suppliant, *hiketes*, and its compounds, *hikesia*, "suppliant prayer," and *hiketeia*, "supplication," all stem from the verb *hikō*, which means "to come to" and when used of feelings or sufferings "to come upon."[8] There is some scholarly evidence that the prefix *ik-* connotes "to beseech" or "to plead," and that the sense of the root *hik-* is "reaching" or "gaining."[9] *Hiketeia* is thus associated with arrival in multiple senses: it suggests not only the movement of flight, in which the *hiketes* arrives as a stranger, but with the movement of persuasion, by means of which one's influence is exercised and one's aim is reached. A suppliant is one who arrives, frequently as a stranger, a *xenos*,[10] and does so specifically in order to ask for something. The success of the request lies in the capacity of the suppliant to convince the supplicated that it is in their best interest to do as the suppliant asks. Thus, like *xenia*, *hiketeia* is, to borrow a phrase from John Gould, a "ritualization of reciprocity."[11]

However, some important differences between *hiketeia* and *xenia* exist. For one, the terms of reciprocity are quite distinct. In *xenia*, where we have the visitation of one noble family by some member of another noble family, honor is bestowed upon the host by the very presence of the visitor; the visitor is then granted honor and protection by the host because the guest's promise of reciprocity is sufficient to constitute reciprocity. With the ritual of supplication, the power differential between host and suppliant is sufficiently great as to call into question the possibility of reciprocity. The only thing the suppliant has to offer are the very things with which the suppliant arrives: namely, his or her body and words alone. In order to forestall the possibility of the host taking possession of the body of the suppliant, the suppliant offers this body in advance by a display of self-abasement and humiliation. The suppliant repays the host in advance with the honor and flattery to his pride that is provided by the suppliant's performance of self-abasement. This performance is accomplished in deed—by the lowering of the body in order to provide a physical expression of the dominance of the host over the suppliant—and in word—in the use of stylized forms of address and belittling self-reference. A final element of the ritualistic act of supplication is the establishment of a physical contact between the suppliant and the supplicated, by grasping the hands, chin, or knees of the supplicated. So binding is this element of physical contact that every effort is made to entice the suppliant to break physical contact with the host rather than use force to do so. The prostrate suppliant can be guaranteed the obligation of the host so long as his or her body is in contact with that of the host.

The bond this physical contact establishes is one of mutual implication, and is similar to that bond that implicates both guest and host in *xenia*. However, the mechanism of this mutual implication is significantly different. The display of self-abasement by the suppliant establishes a context in which shame, *aidōs*, is the dominant tone. More specifically, the self-abasement of the suppliant is a form of payment in advance for the protection the suppliant seeks. Because payment has already been rendered, the host is inhibited by shame from refusing the request; such a refusal would be tantamount to stealing the honor the host had garnered from the suppliant. The very enactment, by means of self-abasement, of the suppliant's vulnerable and ignoble position constrains the actions of the host by making him indebted to the prestige this self-abasement affords him. Thus, the arrival of the suppliant and the enactment of supplication create a context in which all parties involved are constrained by the inhibiting force of shame.

Because of this mutually implicating context of shame, supplication constitutes a strangely aggressive act. It is by merit of the suppliant's willingness to publicly disavow status and dignity that the host's actions are constrained by shame. The very display of powerlessness grants the suppliant a means of determining the actions of the supplicated. Thus, the suppliants' capacity to enfold their host in a mutually implicating context of shame lies, paradoxically, in their display of their powerlessness. This display then becomes a means of constraining the actions of the host, thereby constituting a form of externally directed coercion by means of internally directed aggression. The act of supplication hinges upon a carefully orchestrated contradiction, as its performance confers upon it a condition the opposite to that of which it is a performance. Gould thus defines *hiketeia* as "a mime of aggressive symbolical significance, directed at what must be kept inviolate, but a mime whose aggressive implications are contradicted by the inversion of normal competitive behaviour-patterns which is also a definitive feature of the ritual, symbolized in action by the abject lowering of the body in kneeling or crouching, and in words by the self-abasement of language which accompanies the mime."[12] The efficacy of supplication lies precisely in its capacity to display the power differential between suppliant and supplicated, in its ability to render transparent the operation of power. Supplication puts power itself on stage, and for this reason it is uniquely suited as a vehicle to inquire into the foundations of authority.[13]

Our exploration of ritual supplication has revealed that the efficacy of the ritual hinges upon the suppliant's display of self-abasement. This display inaugurates a mutually implicating context of shame that constrains the actions of the host. Thus, the display of powerlessness exhibited by the suppliant actually functions as an operation of power such that the vulnerable becomes powerful by the very display of vulnerability. The suppliant literally inflicts his vulnerability upon the host. Thus, a certain aggression is inherent to the act of supplication, an aggression Aeschylus will hyperbolize in his Danaid chorus.

Aeschylus's Suppliant Chorus

When we turn to Aeschylus's portrayal of the Danaid chorus, we notice immediately the lack of resemblance they bear to the typical suppliant. Before the chorus speaks a single word, the future violence they will commit against their husbands hangs over their heads.[14] When they do speak, they begin by calling attention to the peculiarities of their status as suppliants. They are not exiles because of a terrible fate that drove them unwittingly and unwillingly from their land; rather, they have exiled themselves in order to avoid marrying their cousins (6–10).[15] Further, they must be instructed to adopt the proper attitude and countenance of a suppliant (191–203). Finally, they take the validity of their request for protection to be self-evident on the grounds that the violence their pursuers are willing to use against them is hubristic and without legitimacy (77–82, 418–37). In fact, the Danaids appear to equate violence with *hubris*, thereby posing the question of whether or not there is ever a justified use of violence. Thus, the question of the role of violence in authority is present whenever the Danaids speak of the conflict that motivates their flight to Argos.

At the same time, because the Danaids have set their hatred against their cousins' desire, the conflict between the Danaids and the Aigyptids is a power struggle between one group who would assert absolute domination over another group who claims the right to assert their autonomy and independence from, and thus their equality with, their would-be oppressors. By rejecting marriage, the Danaids assert an independence comparable to that enjoyed by their cousins and thus appear to desire and to identify with that same social status as their cousins.[16] The question of why the Danaids reject marriage with their cousins has been widely debated for centuries. I am persuaded by both Garvie's and Friis Johansen and Whittle's arguments that their motivation cannot be reduced solely to a general hatred for men or marriage, nor to a concern about incest; rather, as they argue, one must search for their motivation within the character of the Danaid chorus itself.[17] I would simply add that whether the Danaids initially reject sex and marriage as such, or just sex and marriage with their cousins, it is clear that the Aigyptids' response to their refusal to marry opens up the possibility that violent seizure is not only legitimate but perhaps even inextricably linked with sex and marriage. If we put aside considerations of motive that precede the events of the tragedy and remain within the confines of the tragedy itself, what emerges as the strongest determinant of the Danaids' actions is not the possibility of marriage as such, but the threat of violence. Whether or not the former necessarily entails the latter is precisely what is investigated within the tragedy, as we shall see; the Danaids' conception of marriage will be colored throughout the tragedy by its varying proximities to violence.

It is out of fear and hatred of this violence that the Danaids flee the Aigyptids; however, their flight does not remove their fear that the Aigyptids possess some means to justify their actions. And while the widely presumed conclusion of the trilogy, with its presentation of a character who welcomes marriage rather than rejects it, suggests that some alternative to violent seizure and forced marriage exists, this possibility does not, on its own, resolve the Danaids' fear about factors that legitimate such violence, nor does it occur before the Danaids themselves engage in increasingly violent behavior that will culminate, as the audience is well aware, in the murder of their husbands. The Danaids' struggle with violence is thus not simply an external struggle between them and their cousins. Ironically, as we shall see, while the Danaids flee their cousins, they bring with them, and act as the representatives of, the very power structure that has led to their predicament. The character of the chorus itself is a site of tension between the use of violence and the fear of violence.

In fact, it is the Danaids' own proclivity for violence that brings about a collision between democratic and tyrannical regimes, as we can see in the increasingly tense stichomythia that occurs between them and King Pelasgos in the first episode of the play. This episode begins with Danaos instructing his daughters in the proper behavior of a suppliant: "You must answer the strangers as strangers should, in piteous voices filled with sorrow and need. Say plainly that this exile is not stained by blood, but strike all boldness from your words, and all immodesty from your eyes; look downcast and gentle. Speak only when spoken to, but then don't be slow in reply. People here will be ready to take offence. You are refugees and in need: remember to be submissive. Proud speech is not for the weak" (196–203). When Pelasgos arrives, the exchange between him and the chorus is marked by his observations about the foreign appearance of the chorus (234–37), observations that make all the more baffling, so far as Pelasgos is concerned, the Danaids' claims to Argive ancestry. Throughout this early encounter, Pelasgos appears willing and eager to hear what the Danaids have to say. Most immediately, this willingness draws Pelasgos into a rapid-fire series of questions about his and the Danaids' ancestry. There is some contention as to who, in the first part of this stichomythia, asks and who answers the questions posed in this exchange;[18] however, regardless of the roles of inquirer and respondent, this volley of question and answer tells the mythic genealogy of both Pelasgos and the Danaids. By means of the recitation of this myth the Danaids indicate that they are in possession of knowledge about Pelasgos's ancestry, while Pelasgos in turn becomes implicated in their claims to kinship as his continued participation supplies tacit approval to their responses. When taken together, the exchange of question and answer serves as a litany that enacts and instantiates a shared heritage between Pelasgos and the Danaids. Thus, when one of the characters states, "Everything you say confirms my story" (310), it does not, in a certain sense, matter which character does so, as the message is precisely that the discourse establishes a shared genealogy.

Eventually, on the basis of this give and take, Pelasgos concedes that the Danaids are of distant Argive descent (325–26);[19] however, he is still unwilling to grant the Danaids protection from their cousins until he has better understood the nature of the flight. It is significant that even after their claim to Argive kinship has been accepted, their role as suppliants is maintained (333–35), precisely because distant kinship does not justify, at least as far as Pelasgos is concerned, going to war against the Aigyptids. Pelasgos will maintain this reserve regarding the civic status of the Danaids throughout the tragedy, referring to them later as *astoxenia* (356), a term that was for Aeschylus something of an oxymoron (although it would develop a more established meaning),[20] and finally settling upon granting them the status of metics (609).[21] Some institution other than kinship would need to be found if Pelasgos is going to risk the lives of his citizens for the sake of distant kin. Toward this end, he asks a question that draws what is for him a crucial distinction. He wonders if their flight from their cousins is because of their hatred of their cousins or because their cousins are acting unlawfully: *potera kat' echthran ē to mē themis legeis* (336). Presumably, without the sanction of the law, the Danaids would have a much more difficult time convincing Pelasgos that the actions of their cousins are unjust. The Danaids, however, do not ever claim justification for their actions on the basis of Egyptian law. Rather, the Danaids ground the validity of their actions in the dishonor and misery a forced marriage would bring to them, and appeal to the wrath of Zeus, god of suppliants, as providing a divine justification for their actions (335–47). The Danaids thus place what they take to be the will of Zeus over the binding force of law.

Pelasgos's concern for the law and the Danaids' claim of divine protection develop into a crisis about the nature of authority that increasingly centers on the character of Pelasgos himself. In a series of highly charged exchanges, the Danaids insist upon the divine power of the king and Pelasgos insists upon the importance of the consent of the people. Thus, as the Danaids call upon Themis and Zeus to protect them (360), Pelasgos responds by saying: "This is not my hearth where you sit. If the whole community risks infection, the people must find a cure together. I can promise nothing until I share the counsel of all my citizens" (365–69). The Danaids respond with the following lines, "You are citizens, you are the state! A king fears no judgment: your nod is vote enough to rule this altar, this common hearth; your throne and your scepter alone command in every need. Beware defilement!" (370–75). As Pelasgos continues to equivocate, he asks again for legal precedent to assist his decision, and the Danaids respond with threat: "May I never, never fall into men's hands, under men's power. My defense from this marriage I loathe is escape; I will find my own cure under the stars. Make justice your ally, my lord. Choose to honor the gods" (392–96). However, this veiled threat fails to sway Pelasgos, who again seeks to convince the Danaids that he must first gain the consent of his people. The Danaids' attempts to convince him to help them become increasingly urgent, and as the pressure from them builds, Pelasgos repeatedly calls out for some means of attaining clarity: "We must search deep for a thought that can save us, for an eye, clear-sighted and unblurred, to descend, like a diver combing the sea floor" (407–09). He then repeats, "We must search for a thought that can save us" (417). However, the saving grace of thought seems to have receded against the onslaught of the Danaids' pleas, and

Pelasgos is plunged deeper into crisis: "I have thought and thought, and am run aground on necessity's steep shoals" (438).

Against Pelasgos' paralysis, the Danaids become increasingly aggressive in a final attempt to goad him into action in their favor. This last attempt is pivotal for understanding the internal conflict that haunts the Danaids throughout the tragedy and thus deserves our careful attention:

Danaids: Hear the last of many righteous pleas.
Pelasgos: Speak! You may be certain I shall hear.[22]
Danaids: I have belts and sashes to tie my robes.
Pelasgos: Such things are suited to women. What of it?
Danaids: Well you see they give me a fine device [*mechanē kalē*].
Pelasgos: What kind of talk is this? Come, speak plainly.
Danaids: If you fail to make us a firm promise . . .
Pelasgos: How will your device of sashes serve?
Danaids: To adorn these images with strange new offerings.
Pelasgos: This is a riddle. Tell me what you mean.
Danaids: We mean to hang ourselves from these gods—right now!
Pelasgos: The words I hear are whipstrokes to my heart.
Danaids: Then you understand. I have opened your eyes and you see.
    (455–67).

A number of issues emerge out of this exchange that merit comment. First, we must deal with the Danaids' claim that they would rather destroy themselves than give in to the demand of their cousins.[23] The Danaids make evident at the start of the play that they are willing to resort to a threat of suicide (160). In the third stasimon, prior to being confronted by an abusive and threatening Aigyptid herald, they sing a series of stanzas in which they express a wish for death (784–91 and 800–07). Certainly, they do not carry out this wish. However, I take this choral ode as a sincere expression of duress that involves a serious consideration of self-inflicted violence as a means of liberation from an intolerable state of affairs. Such a consideration brings self-inflicted violence into the realm of possibility and leads the Danaids to consider their own bodies as material by means of which they may express a certain power, namely, their capacity for violence. Thus, in this threat of suicide we can see a tyrannical power structure turned inward and transformed into self-laceration. By means of this threat, the Danaids reveal themselves as having identified with the very violent tendencies possessed by their oppressors.

Second, the Danaids' threat of suicide, and the impurity such a suicide would visit upon the Argive people, functions as an act of violence designed to force the hand of a king held hostage by his own piety and concern for the well-being of his city. Thus, the Danaids' threat of self-aggression is itself an aggressive act against

Pelasgos and Argos. The Danaids have turned their vulnerability to strength by using their most vulnerable possession, namely their bodies, as weapons. It is not without irony that this suppliant chorus claims, in the parodos, that they come bearing no weapons but their suppliant branches: "What land would receive us more gently, armed as we are only with suppliants' weapons, these olive branches tufted with wool?" (19–22). In a sense, no other weapon is necessary because of the aggressive element that is inherent to the act of supplication. However, in this particular characterization of supplication, involving as it does not simply self-abasement but the threat of self-destruction, Aeschylus presents us with a hyperbolized supplication whose aggression is not limited to the realm of the symbolic.

At the same time, even this hyperbolized supplication depends for its efficacy upon the piety of the supplicated. It is therefore no accident that the suppliants call attention to their own dependence upon piety: "One altar shelters even the warworn, one refuge for exiles: awe of the gods" (83–85). It is significant that it is not until the Danaids make explicit the aggression inherent to the act of supplication, that Pelasgos finally concedes that the wrath of Zeus, god of suppliants, is of the utmost importance, and submits to the Danaids' will: "Yet the wrath of Zeus Lord of Suppliants commands our awe and reverence. His fear is highest" (478–79).

Third, Pelasgos's capitulation to Zeus god of suppliants is not the only concession he makes to the Danaids on the basis of Zeus. When the suppliants arrive in Argos, they seem to have at least two things working in their favor. First is their claim to kinship with the Argives that has its foundations in the mythic seizure of Io by Zeus. Second is the piety of Pelasgos and the Argive people. It is the combination of Pelasgos's reverence for Zeus, and Zeus's dual connection with the Danaids as both their progenitor and the god of suppliants that serves to provide the foundation for the efficacy of the Danaids' threat to commit suicide. On the basis of these two factors, Pelasgos is doubly bound to protect the Danaids, doubly obligated to look after their well-being. First, their kinship to him commits him to avoid the shedding of family blood upon his land. Second, his reverence for the gods, especially Zeus, commits him to do whatever he can to avoid the terrible desecration that the Danaids threaten. The Danaids are able to invoke both an obligation to family and an obligation to suppliants.

The dual obligation that makes Pelasgos vulnerable to the demands and threats of the Danaids, namely his kinship with them and his reverence for the rights of the suppliant, find their footholds in the figure of Zeus, who is not only god of suppliants but also progenitor of the Danaids themselves. Nor is Zeus's influence in this tragedy limited to these two aspects. We have identified the suppliants' willingness to kill themselves as a kind of internalized tyranny, as the inversion of the very power structure from which they were fleeing. Aeschylus goes out of his way to call attention to the distinction between this tyrannical power structure and the democratic regime of the Argives; however, what is particularly important for our purposes is that Zeus is specifically identified with *both* regimes. In the tense exchange about the nature of authority that occurs between the Danaids and Pelasgos, the absolute nature of authority as emphasized in the Danaids' characterization of Zeus is carefully juxtaposed with the contingent nature of Pelasgos's authority, insofar as Pelasgos rules by the consent of his people. While the Danaids ask Pelasgos to identify himself with Zeus, Pelasgos demands of himself respect, awe, and fear of, and therefore distance from, Zeus. Eventually, his respect for Zeus overrides his fear of war with the Aigyptids, but not without causing a crisis.

Thus, Zeus stands at the nexus of the overdetermined commitment Pelasgos has to the Danaids, a commitment that grants them their influence: the desire of Zeus created the line of the Danaids and thus supplied the foundation for their claims to kinship; the fear of Zeus on the part of Pelasgos provides the piety that the Danaids will use in their favor; and the absolute power of Zeus provides a model that supports the suppliants' use of force both on themselves and on Pelasgos. At the same time, while the Danaids are not concerned with the legal status of their actions, they do exhibit an unsurprising and perhaps even necessary ambivalence about the figure to whom they appeal as a higher authority for their flight from violent seizure and forced marriage. As we shall see, what runs through their discourse like a red thread is an anxiety about the possibility of a divine legitimization to the violence from which they have fled. This possibility haunts their characterization of Zeus, and while the Danaids go out of their way to conceal it, the anxiety it provokes creates a tension that runs in varying degrees of proximity to the surface of their utterances and threatens to break through.

In our investigation of the initial encounter between Pelasgos and the Danaids we have noted that Aeschylus plays upon and hyperbolizes the symbolic aggression that is inherent to the act of supplication. When the Danaids attempt to force Pelasgos's hand by threatening suicide, symbolic aggression becomes actual aggression, but aggression of a curious nature. After all, it is not as though the Danaids simply threaten Pelasgos or a member of his family. Rather, they put themselves at the mercy of his reverence at the same time that they attempt to manipulate that reverence in order to attain his protection. They also put themselves at the mercy of their own propensity for violence. Thus, the pursued and frightened Danaids become threats to their hosts, but not without also becoming threats to themselves by contemplating the possibility of an aggression that recoils against suppliant and supplicated alike. Aeschylus's use of the threat of self-inflicted violence blurs any easy distinction between oppressed and oppressor. Complicating matters further, the Danaids' willingness to use their vulnerability to their advantage comes with a toll whose effects, as we shall see, center around their relationship with the very figure who grants to their threat of suicide its efficacy: Zeus. Zeus appears as an ambivalent figure here to say the least, and at the heart of his web of influence resides his desire for the mortal Io. Because of the centrality of this motif for the tragedy, Aeschylus's treatment of the Zeus and Io myth deserves our particularly close attention.[24]

Zeus and Io

The myth of Io is a story fraught with surveillance and subterfuge. The mortal Io catches Zeus's eye and thereby also garners the attention of Hera. Every effort Zeus makes to conceal Io results in a countermovement on the part of Hera to survey Io. Zeus turns Io into a cow, Hera sends Argus, the many-eyed shepherd to watch over her. Zeus sends Hermes to kill Argus and Hera contrives a subtler means of surveillance: the gadfly that goads Io into exile and drives her mad. Eventually, after many years of wandering, Io arrives in Egypt, where Zeus finally sets her free, turning her back into a woman and, with his divine and fertile touch and breath, impregnating her with a child whom she will name Epaphos in honor of the touch (*haphein*) that produced him. That even the touch and breath of Zeus are fecund is a mythic testament to Zeus's power that well precedes Aeschylus. However, his suppliant chorus uses the themes of touch and breath in their version of Io's tale to punctuate the deep ambivalence that adheres to their recognition of Zeus's power. In the development of the themes of touch and breath we watch the Danaids struggle with their anxiety about the relationship between authority and violence. A profound commentary on the nature of power itself is opened through this struggle.

We are introduced to the themes of touch and breath at the same time that we are introduced to Io. In the tragedy's parodos the Danaids explain their presence in Argos as a function of their Argive ancestry: "We are Argive. We boast birth from the fly maddened heifer whose womb the touch and breath of Zeus filled—Io" (15–18). Note that Io's madness is associated with the goad sent by Hera, whereas her fertility is associated with Zeus. This initial passage inaugurates a series of associations between Io's impregnation by Zeus and the breath and touch of Zeus. Thus, just a few lines after the one cited here we encounter, "by the breath of Zeus, by the touch that ripened at the hour appointed for Io to give you birth, rightly called Epaphos, child of his touch" (44–46). Frequently, when this particular breath and touch are referred to, their gentleness is emphasized: "Look with kindness on women of a glorious line, renew the gentle tale of love for Io, whom your touch once made mother of us all" (531–35). The image of gentle breath is developed further in the direction of gentle wind: "breathe your mercy on us. Send sweet breezes" (28–29). It is clear from these references that the Danaids identify themselves with their ancestor Io, and specifically identify their flight from the Aigyptids with some element of Io's flight.[25]

But here is where things begin to get complicated. The Danaids initially appear to want to align their flight with the flight of Io and the Aigyptids from whom they flee with the gadfly that Hera sent to pursue and madden Io. In these two identifications, Zeus emerges as the figure capable of protecting the Danaids as he was capable of restoring Io. However, the Danaids' version of Io's story suppresses the fact that it was by merit of Zeus's desire for Io that Io was turned into a cow and pursued by the Hera-sent gadfly in the first place. Thus, the Danaids are afforded their appeals to Zeus as a savior by merit of overlooking the role he played in the plight of Io and by characterizing Hera as the antagonist. Then at the very place in the story when it would seem as though Zeus's desire would be most difficult to ignore, that point at which Io is turned back into a woman and impregnated, the Danaids euphemize Zeus's sexual encounter with Io by means of reference to his divine and gentle caress and breath. Thus, the Danaids' choice to selectively identify with Io wrests from them a somewhat tortured discourse that is predicated upon the denial of the possibility of Zeus's own role, on the basis of his desire, in Io's plight. Here we begin to see a tension between the genealogical function of the myth and the legitimating function of the myth. Earlier, the Danaids appealed to the myth of Io in order to substantiate their claims to Argive kinship (and protection). The genealogical function of the myth served to bind Pelasgos and the Danaids together. Now, the Danaids also attempt to use the myth to justify their flight from their cousins by identifying themselves with Io and their cousins with the gadfly; however, in order to do so they must repress certain elements of their own genesis, namely, Zeus's own seizure of Io.

What the Danaids must at all costs attempt to avoid is the identification between the Aigyptids and Zeus, yet it is this identification that is most warranted by their own identification with Io. Consequently, great effort is made by the Danaids to avoid both confronting the scene of Zeus's rape of Io and acknowledging their own debt to this very act of sexual violence. Thus, say the Danaids, "Zeus's will be done—though his desire [*himeros*] is hard to track and the paths of his mind stretch shadowed tangled in thickets where I cannot trace or guess" (86–95). It is hard to miss the straining irony suggested by these lines. In the story of Zeus and Io, Zeus's *desire* is the *least* obscure element.[26] The possibility that the very figure to whom they appeal for protection against violent seizure is their progenitor precisely because of such a violent seizure is truly terrifying, as is the accompanying possibility that some divine legitimization would exist for the actions and desires of the Aigyptids. Now we encounter most explicitly the tension between the genealogical function and the legitimating function of the myth. The Danaids' use of the myth for genealogical purposes commits them to a story that calls into question the capacity of the myth to legitimate their actions. They are thus forced to offer only a partial identification of the myth and to suppress certain parts of it. At the same time, the lengths to which the Danaids go to hide from these terrors indicate the presence of some awareness of them.

I must, on this point, take issue with Robert Murray's otherwise excellent treatment of the Io myth in this tragedy. He describes the Danaids' identification with Io variously as a "partial and incomplete understanding," as a perception of similarity that is "woefully limited and superficial" and as a "half sight."[27] As I hope to show in the following pages, the problem involved in the Danaids' identification with Io, as Aeschylus presents it, is not a function of a partial, superficial, or incomplete understanding. The Danaids suspect all too well what Zeus wanted from Io and how he went about getting it. This is, in fact, one of the reasons why the myth of Io is attractive to them. The Danaids have themselves identi-fied with their oppressors insofar as they have revealed themselves as harboring violent tendencies, and it is this identification that causes them unrest. The myth of Io provides a means for working out this unrest precisely because it provides a means to suppress the sexual violence that runs through it. The Danaids' relation-ship to this myth is as necessary as it is conflicted. On the one hand the myth provides them with a divine genealogy. On the other hand its capacity to do so is predicated upon the highly ambivalent role Zeus plays with respect to Io, a role that the Danaids themselves seem to identify with. The Danaids' solution is to rewrite the myth in such a manner that suppresses Zeus's role as sexual predator and casts him rather as liberator and healer. For all of its ambivalence, the myth of Io provides the Danaids with material that can be worked over and made into an image that they can desire without internal conflict. The Danaids attempt to do to the myth of Io what they cannot do to their psyches: erase any hint of a violence that takes itself to be legitimate. That their use of the myth will prove to be ultimately unsuccessful is not a function of their ignorance, but rather seems to be a comment on Aeschylus's part about selectively appropriating the past in order to legitimize the present.

One does not have to scratch far beneath the surface to see traces of the Danaids' awareness of Zeus's capacity for sexual violence, but perhaps the best example would be in a short line that occurs in episode 1. Pelasgos and the Dan-aids are at that point in their exchange where Pelasgos is the uncontested inquirer, desiring to know the name of the child of Zeus and Io. The Danaids respond: "Epaphos, named for the prize Zeus seized [*rhusiōn*]" (315). The word *rhusiōn* is deeply ambiguous in this context, having connotations of both the "pulling away" that can characterize rescue, and the "dragging away" that can characterize violent seizure of an explicitly sexual nature.[28] Its appearance here, in conjunction with Zeus and the child he created, serves to complicate the Danaids' own characterization of Zeus and opens up for us the possibility of Zeus's association with violent seizure. Throughout the rest of the play the word appears in association with the violence that the Aigyptids threaten. Thus, in this slippage in their characterization of Zeus, the Danaids further the association they are so eager to deny between Zeus and the Aigyptids, and provide us with an intimation of a Zeus who would be the least appropriate to appeal to for rescue from the unchecked desires of a suitor.

The Danaids' identification with Io the liberated mother and their refusal to identify with Io the rape victim collide with mounting intensity throughout the tragedy and serve to offer up increasingly complicated characterizations of Zeus. As an effect of the Danaids' own desire to provide a discourse about Zeus that is free from reference to his desires, we can see this discourse strain itself to pro-vide an image of perfect power.[29] "In the pure stillness where he thrones he wills thought to deed and the deed is done" (101–03). "His deeds are accomplished with the whisper of a word that brings to birth whatever his fertile mind wills" (598–99). In these lines Zeus's power is described as pure capacity, complete license, perfect deed, absolute efficacy. It is not bent to any will other than Zeus's own. This depiction of power at times borders on oxymoron and contradiction, producing an image of Zeus's power not as pure capacity but as pure impossibility: "From their heaven storming towers of hope Zeus hurls men to ruin, yet his strength wears no armor, his force is all ease" (96–100). "Zeus who rules all time caressed her with might, with tender breath freed Io from pain" (574–78).[30] "You who delivered Io from pain with hands of healing, making gentle your might" (1064–67).[31] Out of the paradoxical desire to be liberated from desire, the Danaids produce an image of a power that is perfect and without violence, a power that is perfectly effective but yet also completely at ease. A strength without armor. A might that is gentle. A violence that is capable of doing violence even to itself and thereby rendering itself gentle. It is with these terms of perfect capacity and logical impossibility that the Danaids strive to describe Zeus's power. Certainly, when they do, they open up for us what appears to be a contradiction residing within their conception of power, just as the tension between rule by force and rule by persuasion opens up for us an ambiguity residing within *kratos*. However, if we dismiss this portrait of power as simply contradictory we overlook precisely the profound dialectic to which it gives rise. Aeschylus's portrayal of power in the *Suppliants* suggests that ambiguity and contradiction, or perhaps what would be a better word here, ambivalence, is an irreducible component of *kratos*. Against the plurality of power that is given voice in the clash between a rule by force and a rule by persuasion, Aeschylus's Danaids offer us an image of a singular, unified *kratos*. The Danaids treat the conflict between the rule by force and the rule by persuasion not as a tension to be resolved, but as irresolvable precisely because in the final analysis they are two manifestations, two expressions, of a single *kratos*. Thus Danaos can say of the outcome of the vote in his and his daughters' favor, "Skillful turns of speech persuaded them, but Zeus put his seal on the outcome, too" (623–24).

Conclusion

We began this investigation of the role that the motif of Io plays for the Danaids by noting that the Danaids' acknowledgment of their own capacity for violence sparks a powerful internal conflict. The myth of Io acts not only as a legitimating genealogy but also as a manifestation of this very conflict; the Danaids' selective appropriation of the myth serves as an effort to resolve the tension of this conflict by legitimizing their flight from the Aigyptids and their threat of suicide. Provided that the Danaids suppress Zeus's role in contributing to the suffering of Io, the Danaids find in Zeus a benefactor able to defend their flight from their cousins and their request for aid. They are then allowed to dream of a homogeneous power, a power bereft of violence. In their anxious and tense discourse, Aeschylus's Danaids develop an image of a power made perfect in its capacity to tame even itself.

However, the Danaids' vision of a perfect power does not correspond well with a structure in which a lustful Zeus finds himself responding to a jealous Hera.[32] Nor does their partial identification with Io successfully serve their purposes. It fails precisely because the myth's role as a genealogy is at odds with its role as legitimizing the Danaids' flight. Ultimately, the Danaids cannot suppress their own knowledge of how Io became pregnant and what Zeus's role was in her flight and suffering. Their dream of a power bereft of violence remains a dream, and we are poised, by the end of the tragedy, on the brink of their descent into the city, into the realm of heterogeneous power, of warring kings and jealous gods, into a direct encounter with their own violence.

Throughout the tragedy, the act of supplication serves to punctuate the complex portrayal of *kratos* that Aeschylus offers us. It is by means of his characterization of supplication that we are privy to a view of the internalization of violence and the use of this very internalization as a weapon. Aeschylus thereby complicates any easy distinction between violent and violated. Further, his use of the act of supplication displays for us the internal conflict undergone by those who both hate violence and commit it. Finally, this in turn opens up for us a commentary on the problematic nature of the use of myth to legitimate present action. We are invited to compare the Danaids' rewriting of myth with the rewriting conducted by tragic poets themselves. Perhaps Aeschylus here presents the Danaids' selective deployment of myth as a means of suggesting the limitations and boundaries to the appropriation of myth within which a poet should operate. However, we should on this point be most cautious. The very autonomy or independence that Aeschylus's play claims for myth should serve to make us reticent to simply attribute to Aeschylus's own intentions a statement about the need for respect and humility in the face of the myth. What we can say is that there is displayed here for us, in the tension between genealogical and legitimating functions of the myth of Io, an illustration of the relationship between power and interpretation—when the Danaids turn to use the (suppressed and rewritten) myth to legitimate their own actions, they are called to task for doing so by their own implication in those elements of the myth they attempt to suppress.

Notes

A version of this chapter was delivered as a paper at the 2005 meeting of the Society for Ancient Greek Philosophy. I am indebted to the comments of several audience members, as well as to those of Ryan Drake, Hasana Sharp, Emmanuella Bianchi, and the editor of this volume.

1. I am construing suppliant dramas somewhat broadly here to include not only the plays entitled *Suppliants* by Aeschylus and Euripides, but also classical tragedies that

prominently feature one or more scenes of supplication. The plays of Euripides present the largest number of such instances; scenes of supplication can be found in his *Herakles* (240ff.), *Andromache* (309ff.), *Hecuba* (234ff.), *Medea* (324ff.), *Hippolytus* (324f.), and *Herakleidae* (10 f.).

2. That Aeschylus's presentation of *kratos* in the *Suppliants* is deeply and intentionally ambiguous has been most explicitly and effectively indicated by J. P. Vernant in his essay "Tensions and Ambiguities in Greek Tragedy," in J. P. Vernant and Pierre Vidal-Naquet, eds., *Myth and Tragedy in Ancient Greece*, trans. Janet Lloyd (New York: Zone Books 1990), 29–48; see especially 39. The interplay between political and erotic interests in the tragedy has been particularly well illustrated by Froma Zeitlin in "The Politics of Eros in the Danaid Trilogy of Aeschylus," in Froma Zeitlin, *Playing the Other: Gender and Society in Classical Greek Literature* (Chicago: University of Chicago Press, 1996) 123–71. What I hope to add to this discussion is a sense for the unique contribution that Aeschylus's characterization of supplication makes to his portrayal of *kratos* in the *Suppliants*.

3. Peter Burian, *Aeschylus: The Suppliants* (Princeton: Princeton University Press, 1991), xi.

4. See A. F. Garvie, *Aeschylus's Supplices Play and Trilogy* (Cambridge: Cambridge University Press, 1969), for the collection of sources, with additions by A. J. Podlecki, "Reconstructing an Aeschylean Trilogy," *BICS* 24 (1977), 67–82; Alan Sommerstein, "Notes on Aeschylus's *Suppliants*," *BICS* 22 (1975); and R. P. Winnington-Ingram, *Studies in Aeschylus* (Cambridge: Cambridge University Press, 1983), for a revised discussion of the trilogy (55–72).

5. One could make plausible the claim that Pelasgos is the protagonist of the play, as Burian does in "Pelasgos and Politics in Aeschylus's Danaid Trilogy," *Wiener Studien* 87(1974), 5–14; however, I follow Garvie 1969, 130, as does Burian himself 1974, 13, in reading the Danaids as the dramatic protagonist of the tragedy. Further, my claim that Aeschylus's use of the Danaid chorus is innovative does not preclude the possibility that it also reveals something about the relationship between lyric choruses and tragedy. For such an account see Sheila Murnaghan, "Women in Groups: Aeschylus's *Suppliants* and the Female Choruses of Greek Tragedy," in Victoria Pedrick and Steven M Oberhelman, eds., *The Soul of Tragedy: Essays on Athenian Drama* (Chicago: University of Chicago Press 2005), 183–98.

6. It is in fact believed to be the earliest extant reference to democratic voting; see Paul Cartledge, "Deep Plays: Theater as Process in Greek Civic Life," in P. E. Easterling, ed., *The Cambridge Companion to Greek Tragedy* (Cambridge: Cambridge University Press, 1997), 3–35; the passage is discussed on p. 20.

7. All of these actions serve to distance an Athenian audience from the Danaids. Athenian audiences would have at times sympathized with and at other times condemned the actions of the Danaids; it is likely that part of the dramatic force of the trilogy was found in its eventual reconciliation between audience and chorus by means of the Hypermnestra's acceptance of domestication.

8. LSJ s.v. *hikō.*

9. J. P. Gould, "*Hiketeia*," *The Journal of Hellenic Studies* 93 (1973), 74–103.

10. There are, of course, some significant difference between *xenia* and *hiketeia*, as we will note presently; however, in the final analysis, the difference between the two is often one of the circumstances of their arrival, as Gould notes; Gould 1973, 92 and n94a.

11. Ibid., 75.

12. Ibid., 100.

13. Given this structure, Aeschylus's *Suppliants* invites comparison with another of his investigations of the nature of power, namely, his *Prometheus Bound*. As we shall see, many points of comparison between the two plays exist, especially in their respective treatments of the myth of Io. A number of scholars have noted the significance of both of these plays for the larger Aeschylean inquiry into Zeus and the nature of Zeus's power. See, in particular, both Robert Murray, *The Motif of Io in Aeschylus' Suppliants* (Princeton: Princeton University Press, 1958), and Vernant's 1990 treatment of this issue.

14. T. Gantz, "Love and Death in the *Suppliants* of Aeschylus," *Phoenix* 32:4 (1978), 279–87, provides a concise illustration of the foreshadowing this violence receives in the *Suppliants*.

15. Textual references to the *Suppliants* are cited by line number from H. Friis Johansen and E. H. Whittle, *Aeschylus: The Suppliants*, 3 vols. (Copenhagen: Gyldendalske Boghandel, 1980), hereafter FJW. In cases where lengthy translated citation was necessary, I have preferred to use the translation of Peter Burian, making sure to note where Burian stakes a position on a controversial textual issue, and have also consulted the translations of Gilbert Murray, *Aeschylus: The Suppliant Women* (London: George Allen & Unwin, 1930) and T. G. Tucker, *The Supplices of Aeschylus* (London: Macmillan and Co, 1889).

16. By suggesting that the Danaids claim for themselves an autonomy akin to that enjoyed by their cousins, and thereby identify with the social status of their cousins, I am in partial disagreement with opinions such as that expressed by Robert Caldwell: "Nowhere in the text can we see any evidence for masculine behavior on the part of the Danaids, nor is there any evidence of their desire to compete with men on a sexual or non-sexual level" (R. Caldwell, "The Psychology of Aeschylus's *Supplices*," *Arethusa* 7:1 (Spring 1974), 45–70; I am quoting from p. 49. Caldwell in turn is writing against the assertion of that the Danaids have a "masculinity complex" by D. Kouretas, "Application de la psychanalyse à la mythologie: la nérvose sexuelle des Danaids d'apris les 'Supliantes' d'Eschyle," *Revue française de Psychanalyse* 21 (1975), 597–602, and calls our attention to the Danaids' own emphasis on their feminine appearance. While I agree with Caldwell that it is not simply the case that the Danaids want to be men, it is my opinion that the Danaids are comfortable neither in the aggressive attitudes of their male cousins nor in the passivity they believe to accompany femininity; according to this reading, while they may describe themselves as doves (223–24) and calves (350), they could also easily be described as hawks and wolves. This discomfort becomes increasingly pronounced throughout the tragedy as they recognize their possession of both sets of qualities and serves to generate the internal conflict that drives much of the play.

17. Garvie 1969, 221–24, and FJW 1980, 30–39. Such a claim also precludes reduction of their aversion to marriage to an attitude instilled by their father's fear of an oracle proclaiming that he would be murdered by a son-in-law. There is good reason to believe that Aeschylus makes use of this concern in his characterization of Danaos. On this issue see M. Sicherl, "Die Tragik der Danaiden," *Museum Helveticum* 43 (1986), 81–110, W. Roesler, "Der Schluss der 'Hiketiden' und die Danaiden-Trilogie," *Rheinisches Museum* 136 (1993), 1–22, and A. H. Sommerstein, *Aeschylean Tragedy* (Bari: Levante, 1996), 144–47; nevertheless, within the confines of Aeschylus's *Suppliants* the Danaids' opposition to marriage is not reducible to Danaos' concern alone.

18. The controversy hinges upon the possibility of a missing line at the start of the stichomythia, between lines 293 and 295, is born out in the current standard line numbering,

and has been debated among translators such that some editions attribute questions to Pelasgos and answers to the chorus leader throughout the entire stichomythia (293–347), while others, Burian included, begin with the chorus leader asking the questions and Pelasgos responding, and then reverse the roles after line 308. FJW maintain that Pelasgos asks the questions throughout the interchange (FJW *ad* 291–324, 295 and 309–11), while Martin West gives the first round of questions to the chorus, with Pelasgos acting as respondent: M. West, *Studies in Aeschylus* (Stuttgart: B. G. Teubner, 1990), 139–40. That it is Pelasgos who asks the questions after line 308 is without controversy. If all other issues were equal, having the chorus leader begin asking the questions is consistent with the more dominant strains in the Danaids' character, and does nicely illustrate, when they reverse roles, that a certain intertwining between Pelasgos and the Danaids has been accomplished by the end of the stichomythia.

19. With an emphasis on the distance, FJW *ad loc.*

20. FJW *ad loc* and *ad* 325–326. *Astoxenia* means most literally "citizen-stranger."

21. For a discussion of the status of *metoikia* in the *Suppliants*, see Geoffrey Bakewell, "*Metoikia* in the *Supplices* of Aeschylus," *Classical Antiquity* 16:2 (1997), 209–28.

22. Note the emphasis Aeschylus places on Pelasgos's willingness to listen.

23. The Danaids' willingness to threaten suicide, along with their refusal to justify the legality of their flight from the Aigyptids, has led some commentators to doubt the validity of the Danaids' status as suppliants on the grounds that their threat comprises an act of aggression against Pelasgos; see Burian 1974, 11, and more recently Chad Turner, "Perverted Supplication and Other Inversions in Aeschylus's Danaid Trilogy," *The Classical Journal* 97:1 (2001) 27–50. I maintain, on the contrary, that the Danaids' threat presents, in hyperbole to be sure, a kind of aggression that adheres to ritual supplication. In exaggerating this aggression, Aeschylus illustrates the *complexity* of power relations already at work in the institution of supplication. After all, the Danaids' aggression, insofar as it is directed both internally and externally, is not the same as the Aigyptids' aggression, but is nonetheless compelling.

24. In the following section I am indebted to Robert Murray's concise and illuminating study in Murray 1958.

25. E. W. Whittle locates the start of this identification with the Danaids' first mention of Io at line 16: "Two Notes on Aeschylus's *Supplices*," *The Classical Quarterly* 14:1 (1964), 24–31.

26. To be fair, as Friis Johansen and Whittle point out, no sexual connotation is necessarily inherent in the word *himeros*, however, as they also note, *himeros* more effectively conveys the force of Zeus's directed action, his capacity to achieve what he wants without effort or pain, than does *boulē* (FJW *ad* 87).

27. Murray 1958, 66 and 69.

28. As Vernant notes, *rhusios* "has two simultaneous and contradictory meanings: One is the brutal violence of rape, the other the gentle sweetness of deliverance"; Vernant 1990, 39. Whittle first described the use of *rhusiōn* here as an indication of the Danaids' awareness of sexual violence as an element in Io's story: "If *rhusiōn* in Supp. 315 means 'taking prize' it constitutes a sudden revelation that Zeus's handling of Io . . . was no gentle caressing but a violent seizure, a forceful act of possession. . . . By this unforeseeable disclosure Aeschylus opens the way for the development, by means of a series of verbal echoes, of an ironical parallel between Zeus's 'making prize' of his bride Io and the enforced marriage dreaded by their descendents, the Danaids"; E. W. Whittle, "An Ambiguity in Aeschylus: *Supplices* 315," *Classica et Mediaevelia* 25 (1964), 1–7, quoting from p. 4.

29. Zeitlin has maintained that in the Danaids' characterization of Zeus, and even within their own longing for death, we can see traces of a suppressed desire for sexual union with Zeus himself; Zeitlin 1996, 153–60. I find this claim compelling, and would only add that we also maintain the possibility that the Danaids' wish for death is, paradoxical though it may be, a wish for liberation from desire itself, both from their own desire to commit violence and from the desire (exemplified by both Zeus and the Aigyptids) that leads to the sexual violence they fear. The Danaids may *identify* with Zeus, that is to say they may want to enjoy the same unproblematic expression of power that they create for Zeus, without wanting to be *desired* by Zeus. Such a reading may help to clarify the enigmatic reference the Danaids make at 786 to being trapped by their father's watching.

30. This image of being caressed with might is particularly unsettling.

31. Friis Johansen and Whittle note how strongly connected lines 1064–67 are with lines 574–78. FJW *ad loc.*

32. Zeus's implication in two competing and mutually incompatible systems of power is a theme scholars have noticed throughout Aeschylus's extant work. See in particular the discussion of two Zeuses in Murray 1958, 58, and Vernant 1990, 40.

8

The *Agamemnon* and Human Knowledge

WILLIAM WIANS

> It is the observer rather than the victim who profits from the lesson.
>
> —Hugh Lloyd-Jones, *The Justice of Zeus*

The *Agamemnon* opens with a series of signs and portents. A watchman from the palace of King Agamemnon, perched on the roof like a loyal watchdog, longs to see the beacon telling of the fall of Troy. During long nights over many years, he has observed the silent procession of the blazing stars and learned what these natural beacons portend—the coming of summer's heat and winter's cold, the rise and fall of celestial dynasties (1–7). He is confident that he will correctly read the meaning of the manmade signal as well—the news that Troy has fallen (8–11). As if in answer to his prayers, a fire appears in the distance. He calls it a good auger, a harbinger of a new day shining forth with joyful celebration (21–23) (and so it shall be; but only after the deaths of Agamemnon, Cassandra, Aegisthus, and Clytemnestra, and the Furies' long pursuit of Orestes to Athens). For Clytemnestra, the beacon conveys a different message, that the time for her revenge draws near, even as those around her doubt she knows its meaning. For the chorus, the fire in the night is a confused symbol, a rumor, a woman's dream, the truth of which they deny and the meaning of which they cannot fathom even when they know its truth. They invoke Zeus, but immediately acknowledge that they do not know how the god is to be named. They know only that by means of hard experience Zeus corrects the minds of men.

The *Agamemnon* is a play about knowledge. More precisely, it is a play about the human failure to know. It offers a sustained exploration of the modes of human knowledge and error, assaying language, dreams, portents, prophecies, and eyewitness reports—all of which are sometimes partially understood and sometimes profoundly misunderstood. As human participants in a divinely appointed drama, the characters know both more and less than they can say. Humans must in the end be instructed by the gods, but the lessons that unfold are painful to endure, even if the truth ultimately learned is joyful and triumphant.

There is nothing new in saying that for Aeschylus humans are taught by Zeus through painful experience. The chorus' well-known lament, *ton pathei mathos* "learning comes through suffering" (177), has long been seen as practically the motto of Aeschylean tragedy.[1] My main point will emerge from a different though related direction. It is my intention to subject the *Agamemnon* to a philosophical analysis of a sort it has not received by focusing on its treatment of the possibility and nature of human knowledge. Hard experience is necessary because, as I shall show, Aeschylus systematically challenges and throws in doubt all the ways humans presume to know. "Systematically challenges" in that the failures of the characters to know serve more than the dramatic purposes of the plot. Doubt and error are central to the very meaning of the drama. The playwright uses the uncertainties surrounding the fall of Troy and the return of the Argive king to undercut the full range of modes of human knowing and to contrast human ignorance with an inevitable though dimly perceived divine plan.

The limits of human knowledge as traced out in the play bear importantly on philosophical discussions of early Greek interest in knowledge. Yet despite its preoccupation with the issue, the *Agamemnon* has been neglected by philosophers.[2] The result of attending to the problem of knowledge in the play will be to take what has been called the pessimism of the archaic poets (ca. 700–500 BCE) and extend it well into the classical age of fifth-century Athens. In fact, Aeschylus displays an attitude that in crucial respects is even more pessimistic than that of the archaic poets. Even when based on direct experience, human claims to know are surrounded by pervasive doubts and irremediable uncertainties that tend toward a virtual skepticism regarding knowledge of what Socrates called *ta megista*—the most important things.[3] At the same time, underscoring the limits of ordinary human knowledge serves to reinforce the poet's traditional role as teacher of society and to contrast the playwright with figures from the Greek enlightenment to whom he has been compared.

Poetic Pessimism

As with so many aspects of Greek culture, the problem of human knowledge goes back to Homer. Knowledge, whether human or divine, depends on direct personal experience. Snell called it a constant ratio of knowledge, "the wider the experience, the wider the knowledge."[4] The chief effect of the ratio is to emphasize how little humans know. The gods know everything, past, present, and future, precisely because they have seen and do see all. Human beings are creatures of a day, ephemera, not able or wise enough to look beyond the narrow scope of the present. The attitude is widely documented in literature after Homer, and expressions of it can be found in archaic poets from Hesiod to Theognis and Pindar. Lesher aptly labels it "poetic pessimism."[5]

In contrast to their poetic predecessors and contemporaries, natural philosophers in Ionia had by the sixth and fifth centuries come to believe that the cosmos was rationally organized and that the principles of its organization could be rationally apprehended. Indeed, Lesher finds the origins of philosophy precisely in an optimistic reaction against the pessimism of Homer and other poets.[6] The reaction had many aspects and took in all parts of the Homeric and archaic worldview, including what we would now distinguish as cosmology, theology, epistemology, geography, and history, and what began in Ionia quickly spread to the western Greek world in Magna Graecia.

The situation in Aeschylus's Athens was different. No philosopher of the Ionian stamp was active in Athens until well after the Persian invasions.[7] Indeed, one may question whether Aeschylus was aware of pre-Socratic thought at all. Various passages in the *Oresteia* and other Aeschylean plays have been said to show the influence of thinkers as diverse as Heraclitus, Xenophanes, Anaxagoras, and Empedocles, but such claims are more problematic than is often recognized.[8] The tetralogy to which the *Agamemnon* belongs (the three plays of the only surviving tragic trilogy *Oresteia*, plus the lost satyr play *Proteus*) won first prize in the drama festival of 458, when Aeschylus was sixty-six, two years before his death. The playwright himself (525–456), while younger than Xenophanes (born in 570) and Heraclitus (c. 545–480), was a contemporary of Parmenides (fl. 478), but belonged to the generation prior to Anaxagoras (500–428) and Empedocles (c. 492–432).[9] The first sophists, Protagoras (c. 492–421) and Gorgias (c. 480–376), did not appear on the scene until the second half of the fifth century (commentators can be vague about this), after the playwright's death.[10]

What is clear is that, unlike the optimistic pre-Socratics, Aeschylus does not reject the archaic view of knowledge. Many passages in the *Agamemnon* show unmistakably that the old pessimism persists, with a steady declination from the all-seeing and therefore all-knowing gods, through the special vision of divinely privileged seers, to the strict limits imposed on what ordinary humans may know.[11]

At the base of Aeschylus's epistemology is the commonsense core of the archaic view of knowledge that seeing is believing. Direct personal experience is taken—by the characters at least—to be veridical. The confidence felt by both the watchman and Clytemnestra upon seeing the fire in the night is the first and most obvious example. Somewhat later, a herald from the army of Agamemnon arrives to report firsthand the victory he has witnessed (489–680). Immediately we see the characters' reliance on the old archaic ratio. The old men of the chorus had doubted that Clytemnestra's signal fires were a true sign of the fall of Troy. Now they think they will soon have more certain proofs, for in the distance they spy a herald approaching, recognizing him as such by the olive wreath he wears and the dust on his feet. "Now we shall understand these torches and their shining," they say confidently (389), for they will learn from a human voice speaking outright, not by relying on smoke signals (493–95).[12] The herald quickly convinces them—they believe him because he himself was there (503ff; 582). Similarly, Cassandra is recognized as a mantic even before she speaks because of the distinctive robe and garlands she wears (1264–65). Upon his return to Argos, Agamemnon speaks confidently of knowing the difference between true and false friends: "I can speak, for I have seen, I know it well" (838; but note already an ironic skepticism—his confidence is fatally misplaced in his own wife). A short while later, Clytemnestra describes her painful years of loneliness. She can speak, for she knows it of her own experience, it is not something heard from another (858–60). Much later, Aegisthus offers a similar validation of his knowledge of the life of an exile: "Exiles feed on empty dreams of hope. I know it. I was one" (1668).

Conversely, not seeing leads to ignorance—or worse. In the *parodos*, the chorus, claiming inspiration from a god, vividly retells the course of events leading to the sacrifice of Iphigenia. But the murder itself they do not relate, saying that this they did not see (248). When the chorus asks the herald for news of Agamemnon's brother Menelaus, the herald confesses he does not know—a storm sent by some god hid Menelaus from sight (624–25). Only with the sunrise did the herald see the sea "blossoming with dead men" (653–660). More ominously, Agamemnon enters his bath with no thought of danger because he does not see Aegisthus, who is carefully hidden. So, too, years before, his uncle Thyestes unknowingly feasted on the flesh of his own children because he was served a "featureless meal" (*agnoiai labōn / esthei, boran asotōn*; 1596–97).[13]

The limits of human experience are contrasted with others who know more. Several times in the play, various characters invoke the godlike Sun, who enjoys a perspective and therefore a knowledge that human beings lack. After admitting that he does not know the fate of the still missing Menelaus, the herald says that only the Sun knows of his whereabouts (632–33; 674–76). Much later in the play, Cassandra goes to her death asking that it be avenged by the Sun, who from its high vantage point will witness the murders that the chorus and audience will not see (1323–26). Near the very end of the play, the chorus, confronting the regicides Clytemnestra and Aegisthus, wonders despairingly whether Orestes is still in the sunlight (1646). Once again, the old ratio of experience is at work. The Sun sees more, therefore the Sun knows more than human beings.

The other gods share with the divine Sun its comprehensive vision and knowledge. In Agamemnon's scene with Clytemnestra, he twice recalls to the mind of the audience the gods' far-seeing knowledge. Upon agreeing at last to tread on the purple carpet, Agamemnon wishes that no god's "eyes of hatred (*phthonos*) strike him from afar" (947). A few lines later, he urges the chorus and Clytemnestra to show kindness toward Cassandra, knowing that their actions will be "watched from far by the kind eyes of God" (953).[14]

One type of human being is permitted knowledge that extends further. As in the earliest Greek poetry, the seer or prophet is distinguished from other human beings by a privileged ability to see beyond the experience of ordinary mortals. The seer Calchas advises the Greek expedition when it is becalmed at Aulis. When two eagles appear overhead and swoop down to tear apart a pregnant hare, it is a portent clearly seen and watched by all (114–18). But only Calchas sees beyond the divided opinion of the army to know the omen's meaning; "and, seeing beyond, he spoke" (122–25). Most famous in this regard is the Trojan princess and war-prize Cassandra, condemned by Apollo, the god of prophecy, always to speak the truth about the future, but never to be believed by those yet to experience it (1212). Her scene, the longest in the play, traces the limits of human knowledge. At first, her prophetic powers win a kind of admiration. Even though she had only just been brought to Greece, Cassandra tells the chorus that the house of Atreus is cursed because of the horrible feast served to Thyestes. But she does not know this through hearsay. Rather, her prophetic powers allow her to see the murdered children, their father, and their murderer standing before her (1095–97; 114, 1125, 1214, 1217, 1221). The amazed chorus exclaims that her knowledge is "as if you had been there" (1201). But their amazement quickly turns to confusion when she warns that Agamemnon is about to be murdered. Now they cannot grasp her meaning, for this is a the truth they have yet to experience (1242–45). Cassandra can only say that soon they will know, for they "shall look on Agamemnon dead" (1246)—a prophecy Aeschylus brings back in the first words of Clytemnestra after the murders are revealed: "You see the truth in the future at last" (1567–68).[15] When at last Cassandra finishes her troubled prophecies, including that of her own death, the chorus marks the difference between prophetic and ordinary knowledge in visual terms:

> Is it, in cruel force of weight,
> Some divinity kneeling upon you brings
> The death song of your passionate suffering?
> I cannot see (*amēchanō*) the end. (1174–77)[16]

The scene ends by returning to the ratio between knowledge and experience, but with a turn of the screw. The chorus observes that Cassandra has endured much and is therefore wise (1295). But this is not spoken in admiration. Earlier they had asked, "from divination, what good has ever come to men?" (1132). Now they pity Cassandra, "for you see so clear" (*thesphatou morou*; 1321). Cassandra's clarity of vision may be marveled at, but the chorus has no wish to share in her prophetic powers. Aristotle's innate desire to know not withstanding, ordinary human beings caught up in the tragic immediacy of their existence may well prefer not to know.[17]

Tragic Skepticism

So far we have considered passages in which direct experience lies behind a character's claim to know. But in key passages and scenes, the playwright suggests that even direct experience gives no assurance of certainty. Instead of degrees of knowledge, with gods knowing more and human beings less of essentially the same things to the extent their experience affords them, these passages lead to a sharp separation between human and divine knowledge with regard to what human beings most want or need to know. By doing so, Aeschylus questions the ratio even as his characters assume its validity, and so deepens the pessimism of his poetic predecessors until it approaches a kind of skepticism.

The commonsense core of the archaic view of human knowledge grounds what one knows in what one has seen or experienced. But Aeschylus undercuts any easy equation between the two. In its second ode, the chorus tells of the despondent Menelaus, who in his longing for his unfaithful wife is plagued by images of her beauty that he reaches for but cannot touch (414–26). More significantly, when the watchman on the palace roof spots the long-awaited beacon, he is about to rush to report the sighting to his queen, confident that she will share his joy "if the beacon signals truly" (29). In one way, the signal is of course true. But his joy at seeing it reflects his limited perspective. For though seeing, the watchman both knows and doesn't know what the beacon signifies, just as seeing the procession of the stars he both knows and does not know what the passing of time will unfold. Though like a watchdog he longs to be loyal to his master and a threat to his enemies, he grasps only the signal's surface meaning, allowing Clytemnestra to use him as an instrument of her revenge. Similarly, when the herald convinces the chorus that Troy has fallen, both he and they have knowledge based on experience. But just as certainly, they do not grasp the full implications of what they take to be joyful news.

In another passage the playwright suggests that the very act of seeing may lead to not believing. As Clytemnestra leads Agamemnon into the palace and so to his death, the unknowing but prophetic chorus is filled with a sense of foreboding:

Why must this persistent fear
Beat its wings so ceaselessly
And so close against my mantic heart?
Why this strain unwanted, unrepaid, thus prophetic? (975–79)

Yet precisely because they have seen Agamemnon with their own eyes they resist their prophetic sense of doom:

Yet I have seen with these eyes
Agamemnon home again. (988–89)

Their firsthand experience has become a barrier to knowledge.

If the archaic ratio of knowledge depends on what is seen, then Aeschylus creates a subversive irony by turning the eyes themselves into a kind of evidence. Eyes form a running figure in the *Agamemnon*.[18] In the *parodos*, eyes speak when speaking is impossible. The chorus relates that as Iphigenia was brought forward to the sacrificial altar, the girl begged her father for her life so piteously that Agamemnon had her gagged. But still she speaks, now with only "the eyes' arrows of pity," as eloquently as she had once sung at the king's table (227–47). When in the first episode of the play Clytemnestra assures the chorus that Agamemnon will certainly return, they weep with joy. Aeschylus has the Queen draw attention to the quality of the evidence when she observes that their eyes speak of a loyal heart (271). Some five hundred lines later, when Agamemnon himself stands before them, the chorus again weeps. They excuse their tears as evidence of their loyalty: "the eyes of men cannot lie" (796). Agamemnon agrees, but is induced to ignore a more telling piece of evidence. Clytemnestra does not cry. Her eyes are dry. She smoothly explains that her tears have been exhausted by long nights crying for her absent husband, "the rippling springs that were my tears have dried / utterly up, nor left one drop within" (887–88). Only at the end of the play, when she openly proclaims that she killed Agamemnon with her own hand, does Clytemnestra no longer deny their evidence: "Through us he fell, / by us he died; we shall bury. / There will be no tears in this house for him" (1552–54).

The failure of characters to see what is before them points to a further way in which Aeschylus undercuts the ratio of experience. The playwright consistently draws attention to the intentional dimension of knowing. The *Agamemnon* is replete with examples of characters who refuse to believe what they see before them, or who willfully believe what they wish to be the case even in the absence of evidence.

At the moment of the murders of Agamemnon and Cassandra, the chorus twice hears the king cry out (1343ff.). At first, they take the evidence of their ears as doubtlessly true. But they immediately fall into bickering as to the proper course of action. Because they are reluctant to surrender their hope of the long-awaited homecoming, they begin to question the original evidence:

—Shall we, by no more proof (*tekmērioisin*) than that he cried in pain,
Be sure, as by divination (*manteusomestha*), that our lord is dead?
—Yes, we should know what is true (*saph' eidotas*) before we break our
 rage.
Here is sheer guessing and far different from sure knowledge (*saph' eidenai*).
 (1366–69)

But by this time, the only thing they learn is that Cassandra had spoken the truth. As the palace doors open, they look upon Agamemnon, dead in his bath.

A particularly rich example comes in the long episode following the *parodos* (258–354). There Clytemnestra is challenged by the chorus, who doubt the beacon's significance. She convinces them of what is in fact true—Troy has fallen—but does so in a way that is profoundly misleading.[19] From the beginning of the episode, Aeschylus focuses on the question of evidence. Clytemnestra has come onstage to prepare a sacrifice at an altar. The chorus, longing to know what to think (*euphrōn*), asks whether she is sacrificing because she has received some trustworthy word (*kednon*), some hopeful message (*euangeloisin elpisin*) that requires testing (*pepusmene*).[20] Clytemnestra answers with the truth:

> You shall know joy beyond all you ever hoped to hear.
> The men of Argos have taken Priam's citadel. (266–67)

The chorus is baffled; what she says is beyond belief (*pepheuge toupos ex apistias*; 268). They ask for some evidence (*tekmar*) that will persuade them. Has the queen put her trust in an image from a dream? Does she base her hope on a rumor (*phatis*)?[21] How could a messenger carry word from Troy so quickly (280)?

Clytemnestra answers that the god Hephaestus was the first to send forth the message.[22] The next thirty-six lines vividly describe what she did not see firsthand: how her "torchlight messengers" each ran their course, each beacon being lit in turn, carrying the fiery message from mountaintop to mountaintop, from Ida to the palace in Argos. She concludes:

> By such proof (*tekmar*) and such symbol (*symbolon*) I announce to you
> My lord at Troy has sent his messengers to me. (315–16)

Still, the chorus remains doubtful. They entreat her to repeat her story (*logous*). She answers with another vivid visualization of what she did not herself see, now describing the clashing voices of conqueror and conquered, seeing in her mind's eye the vanquished Trojans stooping over their dead and hearing the cries of despair coming from their mouths (320–29). The chorus, longing for an end to the war, is at last convinced:

> My lady, no grave man (*sōphron*) could speak with better grace (*euphronōs legeis*).
> I listened to your proofs (*tekmaria*), and I believe you (*pista*)
> And go to make my glad thanksgivings to the gods.
> This pleasure is not unworthy of the grief that gave it. (351–54)

There is no small irony in Clytemnestra's performance coming in response to the chorus's demand for proof (*tekmar*), as if they would accept only an objective demonstration. Her first proof, which might be compared (with some exaggeration to be sure) to the causal and empirical methods of the Ionian philosophers and geographers, does not convince them. Only the performance of an epic scene vividly imagining Troy's destruction wins their assent.[23] Their final praise of her proofs (*tekmaria*) and her gravity serves to reinforce the irony. For compelling as her performance is, her success is an inversion of the boast made by Hesiod's Muses. They may tell lies that look like the truth. By her skillful words spoken with the authority of an eyewitness, Clytemnestra uses the truth to conceal and to deceive.[24]

Homer and Hesiod were certainly aware of the possibility of deception, including self-deception.[25] But this did not for them become part of any systematic doubt.[26] In contrast, Aeschylus takes such possibilities and turns them into a corrosive agent, eating away at the common, everyday assurance that at the least humans know what they directly experience. As the playwright carefully shows, experience is too complex and intentional a thing for that simply to be true.

This brings us to the final dimension of the limits of human knowledge in the *Agamemnon*. It is not the result of one character's deceptive words or another's unwillingness to see what is before them. Rather, it is imposed by the very condition of being human. The foundational problem in the play—as in so much of Greek literature—is inextricably linked to the kind of knowledge being sought. This is not a knowledge of empirical facts or outcomes, but of what can be termed the moral dimension of events, the larger significance of characters' actions and lives in an order not of their own making. The characters of the *Agamemnon* consistently fail to grasp what they most need to know. From within the epistemological gap between human and divine there arises a problem of moral knowledge.

The limits of the human condition are often represented by the chorus.[27] Throughout the play, as they clamber along on staves, they remind us both in their words and in their appearance of the riddle of the sphinx (72–82).[28] Though as we've seen they are permitted on occasion to speak prophetically,[29] more often they serve to remind the audience of human frailty and limitation. At the midpoint of the great opening *parodos*, they pray to Zeus (160–82). But immediately they acknowledge their uncertainty as to how Zeus should be named. This is, of course, a well-known archaic way of avoiding offending a god.[30] But the invocation is immediately joined to a recognition of the profound limitation placed on human knowledge (which it surely is a reflection of, in any case):

I have pondered everything
Yet I cannot find a way,
Only Zeus, to cast this dead weight of ignorance
Finally from out my brain. (162–66)

The limits on human knowledge especially affect knowledge of the *dikē* of Zeus, the ability to discern divine justice and purposes. As the play suggests, it is

not readily apparent either to ordinary watchmen or messengers or even to gener-
als or royalty. The human chorus cannot find a way out of its perplexity unaided.
Only the god can dispel the weight of their ignorance.[31]

The justice of Zeus is the central theme of the odes sung by the chorus
throughout the play, but once again the *parodos* provides the best evidence. It
dwells on the problem of tracing out the justice behind the war and its aftermath.
The chorus's faith is perhaps unshakable; but it is hedged all around with doubts
engendered by their scant comprehension of its long arc. When at the beginning
of the *parodos*, the chorus speaks of the portent of the eagles, the spectacle is
recognized as an omen of a god driving toward justice. But which god—Apollo,
Pan, or Zeus—they do not know (55–59). They believe that the war is a punishment sent by Zeus (60–66) and that the end will be destiny unfolding (67–71).
But their hope is formless, expressed three times in the lamenting refrain, "Sing
sorrow, sorrow; but good win out in the end" (121, 139, 159). Similarly, as Iphigenia is brought forward for the sacrifice, the chorus knows the words of Calchas
are fulfilled (183–257). But why this terrible thing had to happen the chorus
does not know. It can only repeat its faith of a larger purpose behind the events,
pronouncing here what I have called the motto of Greek tragedy: justice so moves
that those only learn who suffer (250)—a faith that seems to offer scant comfort
even toward the end of the play:

> Alas, the bitter glory
> Of a doom that shall never be done with;
> And all through Zeus, Zeus,
> First cause, prime mover.
> For what thing without Zeus is done among mortals?
> What here is without God's blessing? (1481–88)

The inscrutability of divine purposes is why every major character in the
play confidently sees himself or herself as the instrument of divine justice and is
both right and not right to do so. Agamemnon sees the smoke rising above the
ruins of Troy as a sign that Priam's city deserved its fate and regards himself as
the divinely appointed punisher of Troy's hubris (811–28). And so he is—though
that does not excuse his own hubris in destroying the sacred altars of the city or
in treading on the carpet. Clytemnestra consistently represents her actions as just,
and just by divine and not merely human standards. She proclaims that the justice
of her actions will eventually be seen by all (349); that in inducing Agamemnon
to walk on the carpet, she acts with the gods' aid to accomplish what fate has
ordained (912–13); she sees herself as nothing less than the instrument for the
punishment of the sins in the house of Atreus (1394–98, 1431–44, 1497–1504,
1654–60). As late as the final line of the play, she still expects to order all things
for the good (1673). So too Aegisthus, looking on the dead Agamemnon, exults

that by his and Clytemnestra's actions the gods have brought just punishment (1577–82, 1603–11).[32]

The same theme unfolds over the course of the episode with the herald (immediately after the second choral ode, itself a meditation on the justice of Zeus). Almost overcome at the realization of his dream of returning to Argos, the herald confirms the fall of Troy and announces the imminent return of King Agamemnon. For the herald, as for the watchman in the play's prologue, this is a supremely optimistic moment. He speaks of daylight replacing the gloom of night, of the returning sun, of the now gracious gods Zeus and Apollo. So carried away is he that he does not hear the ominous overreaching in his praise of Agamemnon, who having destroyed Troy's altars and sacred places, is "fortunate to be honored far above all men / alive" (530–31).[33] Nor does he hear himself when he reminds the chorus that only the gods live without pain (553–54)—why pain and its lessons may be necessary for humans, neither he nor the chorus considers. He begins to recount his own sufferings on the long campaign (555–65), but soon stops himself and bids farewell to all their unhappiness, asserting that there is no point in reliving such grief (566–71). Instead, claiming the conqueror's right to boast, he predicts the glory to be enjoyed by the city and its leaders, and celebrates "the grace of God / . . . that did this" (581–82).

As if to confirm the tragedy of knowing and not knowing, Aeschylus brings Clytemnestra forward to address the herald. In another bravura performance, she proclaims her joy at the confirming report—a joy that is no doubt genuine in its own way (587–89). But rather than allowing the herald to repeat his tale to her as he is prepared to do, she commands him to return to Agamemnon and urge him to return home quickly. She shall hear the whole story (*panta logos*; 599) from Agamemnon himself. Echoing the chorus's praise of her vivid proofs of Troy's downfall, the herald praises the queen for a speech spoken so suitably (*hermeneusin euprepe logon*). In a few lines Clytemnestra has turned the bearer of a true report into a bearer of a murderously deceptive message.

Once again we have a scene that reinforces the power of Clytemnestra's authoritative performances. But I want now to emphasize a different point. Clytemnestra sends the herald away by saying that Agamemnon will tell her the whole story. But Agamemnon does not know the whole story, any more than does Clytemnestra or any other character.[34] One of the play's most acute ironies is that in acting in accordance with a private conception of justice, each character unwittingly serves a larger purpose stretching across generations. But the inverse is also true: though serving a larger purpose, each character labors from within circumscribed human experience that cannot be overcome. For all her devious use of the truth, Clytemnestra is deceived about her role in the larger history of events. Both she and Agamemnon are participants in a story still unfolding; both are the objects of a lesson being taught, the victims of Aeschylus's sacrificial drama, not those who are meant to benefit from it.[35]

After Clytemnestra leaves the stage, the chorus asks the herald for news of Menelaus (617–19). The presence of the long-ensuing discussion of the Spartan king's whereabouts (620–80) might puzzle the modern reader. Passing over dramatic reasons for its inclusion,[36] I would say its philosophical significance lies in its presenting the limits of human knowledge as it were in miniature. It isn't just that the Spartan king has "gone from human sight" (624), making knowledge of him impossible. He has been obscured from human sight by the action of the gods. It is they who sent the storm that led Menelaus adrift (634–35, 648–49). It is they who saved the herald's ship (661–66). It is they who will lead Menelaus home when it suits their purposes (677–79). Human knowledge depends not simply on what we experience, but on what the gods allow—or force—us to experience. As the chorus earlier remarked, it is Zeus who leads men to think (176). There is no method of patient inquiry a la Xenophanes, no Heraclitean unveiling of hidden nature. The ignorance of the fate of Menelaus is a potent reminder that human beings know nothing that is not taught to them by the gods.[37]

The Poet's Knowledge

The unrelenting erosion of both claims and means to know forces a final question, one that will lead to a more precise understanding of the relationship between Aeschylus and his poetic forebears. On what grounds does Aeschylus claim his knowledge of the moral order? It cannot be based on ordinary experience, for all the reasons explored in the play. If Aeschylus regards himself has having some special knowledge to impart, it must be grounded in some other way.

Does Aeschylus rely on poetic inspiration? The question is complicated because of an obvious but crucial difference between the forms of tragic and epic narrative. As noted as long ago as Plato in *Republic* II, in one kind of narrative the poet nowhere speaks in his own voice. In the other kind, the poet's voice will occasionally intrude. The latter kind of narrative (which Plato calls "mixed") is exemplified by Homer and Hesiod who, precisely in their invocations to the Muses, speak in their own voice. In tragedy, by contrast, the poet never speaks in his own voice, whether to invoke the Muses or for any other reason.[38] If I am right that the form of tragic narrative itself makes a direct invocation impossible, we need not worry that we have only seven of the ninety plays Aeschylus is said to have written. In no tragedy would such an intrusion have been permissible.[39] One cannot infer, of course, that just because direct invocation was impossible in tragedy that Aeschylus felt no debt to a higher power for his inspiration. One can note the number and variety of Plato's references to poetic madness and inspiration in the *Ion* and the *Phaedrus*, and the whole tenor of the speech of Agathon in the *Symposium*. These suggest that the belief that the poet was divinely inspired was widely held well into the fourth century at least. It is perfectly plausible that

Aeschylus shared such a belief. But rather than speculate further along these lines, I think we can make more progress on the question by returning to the *Agamemnon* and the theme of human knowledge.

In the *Agamemnon* a moral order pervades the universe, but the workings of the order are for a long time hidden, its operations only partially perceived. Zeus operates irresistibly, but the outlines of his plan can be traced out only after it has been played out in events: "You shall know the outcome when it has come" (252). It is not direct experience that yields the knowledge that is essential, but reflection long after the fact. This lesson is repeated in the second choral ode: "They have the stroke of Zeus to tell of . . . / This thing is clear and you may trace it . . . The curse on great daring / shines clear" (367–68, 374–75).

Experience is required to learn the lesson of being human, but it is nothing like proto-scientific or empirical experience. It is rather memory of what has been suffered that teaches human beings the limits of their humanity and the necessity to be moderate. The call for remembering the lessons of the past can be tinged with irony (as is so much in the play). The herald seeks to forget his years of hardship with the army. Agamemnon enters saying that the punishment of Troy's overreaching must be remembered, even though he has already forgotten its lesson, just as memories of injustices they have suffered drive the imperfect justice of Clytemnestra and Aegisthus. But the importance of memory in human life is anticipated without irony by the Watchman's prologue. As he is about to rush to report the sighting of the beacon to Clytemnestra, he pauses, reminded of a darker history: if the walls could speak, they would tell tales. But he remains silent. Some things that are known, he says, may not be spoken openly. Nor need they be spoken. To those who know, his intimations will be intelligible; to those who do not understand, it will be as if the past were forgotten (33–39). So too in the *parodos*, precisely at the point where they first pronounce Aeschylus's tragic motto, the chorus speaks of the grief of memory that teaches moderation (*sōphronein*; 179–81). It is not knowledge of the future that humans need if they are to live as they ought, but recollection of the past.

More precisely, it is the experience of events remembered and meditated on by the poets that have the power to teach. Though this too may be an obvious point, it is not the chorus that remembers the launching of the expedition and the events at Aulis, it is the playwright. Once the purposes of divine justice are accomplished, the lesson must be retold in stories and song. *Muthoi* (such as those provided by the playwright) trace patterns and purposes of what was previously experienced without full comprehension. Poetic *muthoi* supplement the limited vision of ordinary human beings who inevitably are immersed in the immediate. Here lies a role for the communal experience of the ritual of tragedy. The unique relationship of an audience with the action witnessed on stage lifts the audience out of the ordinary and makes them privileged observers of events, both involved but held at a critical distance. This is a shared reflection prompted and guided by the tragic playwright. By this means, moral knowledge can be attained after all.

While all tragic theater may claim to impart the moral lessons of the recollected past, the *Agamemnon* achieves something more. By making an exploration of the limits of human knowledge one of the play's central themes, Aeschylus both exhibits and justifies the poet's status as moral instructor of the city, allowing himself to assume the position of successor to his poetic forebears. Like the sophists of a later generation, Aeschylus displays a steady concern with the problems and limits of language. For Protagoras, Gorgias, and the teachers who came after them, this was reflected in the study of rhetoric, playing a central role in their relativism and agnosticism and serving to enhance their status as successors to the didactic authority of the poets. In Aeschylus, a similar concern leads to quite a different expression. In the *Agamemnon*, doubts regarding the possibility of human knowledge, including insecurity over language and communication, extend even more deeply than in Homer and the archaic poets. But the problem of human knowledge does not end in the sophists' relativism. By reflecting on *muthoi* drawn from the past, the playwright teaches the limits hedging round ordinary claims to know and the curbs under which human beings must live. In doing so, the play offers a profound understanding of the human condition. In the end, Aeschylus teaches his audience a tragically inflected Socratic ignorance: the wisest know only that they do not know.

Notes

1. H. D. F. Kitto, *Greek Tragedy* (London: Methuen, 1939), 70; W. Jaeger, *Paideia: The Ideals of Greek Culture*, Vol. 1 (Oxford: Oxford University Press, 1945), 266–67; A. Lesky, *A History of Greek Literature*, translated by J. Willis and C. de Heer (London: Methuen and Co., 1966), 258, 264; C. Collard, *Aeschylus Oresteia* (Oxford: Oxford University Press, 2002), xxx–xxxi. The idea is repeated later in the same choral ode as *tois men pathousin mathein* ("those only learn who suffer"; l. 250), with a near echo at lines 182–83: *daimonōn de pou charis biaiōs* ("from the gods . . . grace comes somehow violent"). In this chapter, the text cited is M. West, ed., *Aeschylus Agamemnon* (Stuttgart: Teubner, 1991). Translations are those of R. Lattimore, *Agamemnon*, in R. Lattimore and D. Grene, eds., *Complete Greek Tragedies* (Chicago: University of Chicago Press, 1953), occasionally modified in light of H. Lloyd-Jones, *Agamemnon* (Englewood Cliffs: Prentice-Hall, 1970), and Collard.

2. In fact, classicists have generally paid more attention to philosophical issues in the play than have philosophers. See especially two stimulating and insightful studies of the use of language in the *Oresteia* by Simon Goldhill: *Language, Sexuality, Narrative: The Oresteia* (Cambridge: Cambridge University Press, 1984), and *Reading Greek Tragedy* (Cambridge: Cambridge University Press, 1986). Exceptions to the play's neglect by philosophers are M. C. Nussbaum, *The Fragility of Goodness* (Cambridge: Cambridge University Press, 1986), and B. Williams, *Shame and Necessity* (Berkeley and Los Angeles: University of California Press, 1993), but both concentrate on ethical rather than epistemological issues. Also to be

noted is the phenomenologically informed study in M. Naas, *Turning: From Persuasion to Philosophy* (Atlantic Highlands, N.J.: Humanities Press, 1995).

3. The phrase appears at *Apology* 22d7, leading to Socrates' disavowal of a knowledge of such things. See further C. D. C. Reeve, *Socrates in the Apology* (Indianapolis: Hackett, 1989), 33–37.

4. B. Snell, *The Discovery of the Mind*, translated by T. G. Rosenmeyer (Cambridge: Harvard University Press, 1953), 137. Snell's thesis has been criticized by later scholars; see, for instance, E. Hussey, "The Beginnings of Epistemology," in S. Everson, ed., *Companions to Ancient Thought I: Epistemology* (Cambridge: Cambridge University Press, 1990), 11–38. Nevertheless, the basic idea behind the ratio of experience remains valid.

5. J. H. Lesher, "Early Interest in Knowledge," in A. A. Long, ed., *The Cambridge Companion to Early Greek Philosophy* (Cambridge: Cambridge University Press, 1999), 225–49. See also Lesher's contribution to this volume.

6. But the reaction is a complex one. See the excellent analysis in G. Most, "The Poetics of Early Greek Philosophy," in Long 1999, 332–62, and by Naddaf in this volume.

7. Anaxagoras could have come to the city as early as 480, at about the age of twenty, but may have arrived as late as 456; his peak philosophical activity may be dated between 470 and 460; see G. S. Kirk, J. E. Raven, and M. Schofield, *The Presocratic Philosophers* (Cambridge: Cambridge University Press, 1983), 352–55. The first native Athenian philosopher, the obscure Archelaus, said to be Anaxagoras's pupil and the teacher of Socrates, was probably not active before the middle of the century.

8. Arguing for influence, see B. Gladigow, "Aischylos und Heraklit," *Archiv für Geschichte der Philosophie* n.s. 44 (1962), 225–42 (for Heraclitus); Goldhill 1984, 7 n17 (Heraclitus and the sophists), 82 n133 (Xenophanes), and 121n32 (Empedocles); Kirk, Raven, and Schofield 1983, 354–55 (Anaxagoras). H. Lloyd-Jones, *The Justice of Zeus* (Berkeley and Los Angeles: University of California Press, 1971), 84–6, rejects any pre-Socratic influences: "If Aeschylus knew of modern thinkers like Xenophanes and Heraclitus, he refrained from obtruding his knowledge upon his audiences." At another extreme, Jaeger 1945, 244–45, sees Athenian tragedy as a pious repudiation of Ionian speculation.

9. Dates are from J. Brunschwig and G. E. R. Lloyd, eds., *Greek Thought: A Guide to Classical Knowledge* (Cambridge: Harvard University Press, 2000), 999–1000, supplemented by Kirk, Raven, and Schofield for Xenophanes. These dates make less plausible both a claim on behalf of Anaxagoras (about thirty-two at the time of the *Oresteia*) and Goldhill's argument for a "more involved interrelation between Aeschylus and the philosopher-poet" Empedocles, who was younger still. Interestingly, Kirk, Raven, and Schofield argue for Anaxagoras's influence on the playwright by using the same embryological "theory" at *Eumenides* 657–66 cited by Goldhill as evidence for the influence of Empedocles.

10. Protagoras first came to Athens around 450, Gorgias not until 427; see J. de Romilly, *The Great Sophists in Periclean Athens* (Oxford: Clarendon Press, 1992), 2; R. Wallace, "The Sophists in Athens," in D. Boedeker and K. Raaflaub, eds., *Democracy, Empire, and the Arts in Fifth-Century Athens* (Cambridge: Harvard University Press, 1998), 203–22. If Plato's report of Protagoras's visit to Athens at the height of his fame and in the company of the younger sophists Hippias and Prodicus is not a complete fiction, it took place around 433; see W. K. C. Guthrie, *Plato, Protagoras and Meno* (Baltimore: Penguin Books, 1956), 27; D. Nails, *The People of Plato* (Indianapolis: Hackett, 2002), 309–10. Aeschylus certainly anticipates the sophists' concern with language (see T. Rosenmeyer, "Gorgias, Aeschylus, and

Apate," *The American Journal of Philosophy* 76 (1955), 225–60; C. Segal, "Gorgias and the Psychology of the Logos," *Harvard Studies in Classical Philology* 66 (1962), 99–155; Goldhill 1984; Goldhill 1986. But given the chronological gap separating the playwright and the sophists, one should be careful to note that these "parallel investigators of the position of man in language and society" (Goldhill 1986, 229) were not precisely contemporaries.

11. My claim that Aeschylus extends archaic pessimism about human knowledge does not deny that the *Oresteia* reflects a shift from the archaic *oikos* to the classical *polis*. On the political dimensions of Aeschylus's thought, see C. W. Macleod, "Politics and the Oresteia," *The Journal of Hellenic Studies* 102 (1982), 124–44; A. H. Sommerstein, *Aeschylean Tragedy* (Bari: Levante Editori, 1996), 393–421; A. J. Podlecki, *The Political Background of Aeschylean Tragedy*, second ed. (Ann Arbor: University of Michigan Press, 1999).

12. I follow West, Lattimore, and Collard in assigning lines 489–502 to the chorus and not to Clytemnestra, as shown in the MSS and D. Page, ed., *Aeschuli. Septem quae supersunt tragoedias* (Oxford: Clarendon Press, 1972); see further O. Taplin, *The Stagecraft of Aeschylus* (Oxford: Oxford University Press, 1977), 294–97.

13. Note also the frequent linking of rumor to what has not been witnessed: 274–76, 475–78, 861–66.

14. So too in the trilogy's final lines, Zeus is praised for his all-seeing justice (*Eumenides* 1045).

15. See also the lines of Aegisthus: "whose curse works now before your eyes" (1598).

16. E. R. Dodds, *The Greeks and the Irrational* (Berkeley and Los Angeles: University of California Press, 1951), 29 and 50 n2, notes a heightened sense of *amēchania*, human insecurity and helplessness, in classical writers "who still preserve the archaic outlook."

17. This attitude is well expressed by Solon, fr. 1, 53–56: "Apollo the far-shooter, let another man be a prophet, / who, because of the gods' favor, / can see evil approaching in the distance. / But no bird signs or sacrifices can protect against what is fated."

18. See also Goldhill 1984.

19. See Goldhill 1986, 8–10, who carefully analyzes her manipulations of language and persuasion in the two accounts she gives to the chorus.

20. "Requiring an explanatory answer, and not merely assent or dissent" LSJ, q.v. *pusma*. The chorus takes her sacrifices as petitionary, not celebratory, as reflecting doubt, not certainty.

21. Note the implied contrast with the chorus's earlier *angelas*, news, at 83–85.

22. Though Hephaestus is often depersonalized simply as the name of fire (Collard 2000, 126), Aeschylus may be anticipating the idea that human beings possess no knowledge that is not derived from the gods.

23. See Collard 2000, 125 and 127; Lloyd-Jones 1970, 34. On the tension between truth as an authoritative poetic performance versus an objective demonstration, see M. Detienne, *The Masters of Truth in Archaic Greece* (New York: Zone Books, 1996), and K. Morgan, *Myth and Philosophy from the Presocratics to Plato* (Cambridge: Cambridge University Press, 2000), 15–24.

24. I therefore agree with Goldhill that Aeschylus reveals a keen awareness of the enormous power of language, even before the sophists come on the scene. We shall return at the end of the chapter to consider Aeschylus's attitude toward this power in relation to his poetic forebears.

25. To cite just the *Odyssey*, the praise by Antinous of Odysseus's storytelling abilities recognizes the caution necessary when listening to a skilled speaker, while the suitors and their mindless carousing is an example of those who are willfully ignorant.

26. The long-standing question of skepticism in Homer and Hesiod is addressed by Hussey 1990 and H. M. Zellner, "Scepticism in Homer?" *Classical Quarterly* 44 (1994), 308–15.

27. The "groping for truth that is the lot of all mortal men, choruses included" is the subject of T. Gantz, "The Chorus in Aischylos' *Agamemnon*," *Harvard Studies in Classical Philosophy* 87 (1983), 65–86.

28. An identification made tentatively by Collard 2000, 118, and forcefully by Lloyd-Jones 1970, 20.

29. In fact, they are able to relate the entire *parodos* only because they enjoy a prophetic gift (105–06). Having been left behind ten years before, they have no firsthand knowledge of the events they narrate.

30. Lloyd-Jones 1971, 85. Given the widespread cultural attitude the invocation reflects, the echo of Heraclitus need be no more than a coincidence.

31. Gantz 183, 78–79, calls the invocation "a cry of despair from men who are not yet ready to understand the workings of justice." See further the excellent analysis in A. Lebeck, *The Oresteia* (Washington: The Center for Hellenic Studies, 1971), 22–24.

32. On the contradictory dimensions of the pursuit of justice by different characters, see Collard 2002, xxxii–xxxiii.

33. The chorus should hear it but apparently does not, despite having sung barely seventy lines earlier of their fear of the man who, "fortunate beyond all right" (*tucheron ont' aneu dikas*; 463–4), would be pulled back into darkness for his excess.

34. The herald had used essentially the same words at the end of his report to the chorus (582) and again after adding the account of Menelaus and the storm (680). See further Goldhill 1986, 7–8.

35. Collard's otherwise excellent comments on the subject are limited to how the gods' will is learned by "tragic sufferers" within the play; Collard 2002, xxxi–xxxii.

36. Dramatically, Aeschylus prepares for the necessity of Orestes having to avenge his father's death without the aid of his absent uncle (Menelaus was said to have arrived in Argos shortly after Orestes had killed Aegisthus and Clytemnestra). More tantalizingly, the playwright sets the stage for the fourth play of the tetralogy, the lost satyr play *Proteus*. It was unusual for all four plays of a tetralogy to be based on a single myth, suggesting that the *Proteus* was something of an innovation (Collard 2002, xliii; see Sommerstein 1996, 189–90, for a speculative reconstruction). After being blown off course following the sack of Troy, Menelaus sails to Egypt. There, in order to learn his way home, Menelaus must wrestle the all-knowing, shape-shifting demigod Proteus. Trying to escape Menelaus' grasp, Proteus quickly changes his appearance from one thing to another—lion, snake, water, tree. But Menelaus eventually triumphs, forcing Proteus to return to his "true" shape. What could be the connection between this play and the tragedy of the *Oresteia*? Perhaps the play stood as a comic burlesque of the problem of human knowledge, complete with a "happy" ending. The truth can be grasped only by enduring the full range of shifting and deceptive appearances.

37. For a concise survey showing how the dependency extends far beyond the classical period, see L. Brisson, "Myth and Knowledge," in Brunschwig and Lloyd 2000, 39–50.

38. I would have said "in neither tragedy or comedy," but for the interlude in the *Clouds* when the leader of the chorus, presumably speaking for the playwright, addresses the judges directly and criticizes them for not giving the prize to an earlier version of the play. This exception, however, might be used to make the rule stronger. In a comedy, intentionally violating the prohibition of the author speaking in his own voice might well add to the overall comic effect.

39. Invocations by characters are still perfectly possible, of course, but provide no evidence in themselves for the attitude of the playwright.

9

Poetic *Peithō* as Original Speech

P. Christopher Smith

By turning to a radical example of poetic *peithō*, Cassandra's *amoibaion* or exchange with the chorus of Aeschylus's *Agamemnon* (1073–1172), this chapter seeks to penetrate behind the largely unquestioned understanding of reasoning that we in the West have taken over from the Greek philosophers. From Plato and Aristotle in particular we have accepted that the preferred kind of argument is *apodeixis*, which is to say, demonstration or conclusive inference starting from the inclusion in, or exclusion from, each other of clearly envisioned, stabilized ideas (*eidē*) or classes (*genē*) of things—as in "All human beings are mortal beings," and so forth, or "No human beings are immortal beings."[1] Drawing upon Heidegger's *Destruktion* of philosophical, metaphysical abstractions, the concern here will be to clarify the original (Heidegger: *ursprüngliches*) character of *peithō* or persuasive speech as this is preserved in Greek tragic poetry in resistance to philosophy's reconstruction of *peithō* as logical inference.[2] Finding herself, as Agamemnon's war prize, now before his palace, and knowing full well that entering it will mean Agamemnon's and her own murder at the hands of his wife Clytemnestra, the priestess Cassandra issues her bleak and horrifying prophecies in what she knows will be a vain effort to persuade the chorus of Argive elders to intervene. We will see that in sharp contrast to traditional logical argument, Cassandra's *peithō* remains firmly embedded in what Heidegger calls the lived, "factual" world and resists any of philosophy's attempts to suppress human "facticity's" basic features.[3]

In an extension of Heidegger's *Destruktion* of metaphysical thinking, however, this study adds another consideration. Though we have received it as a written drama, Aeschylus's *Agamemnon* displays important traits of a much earlier orality known to us from Homer's *Iliad* and *Odyssey*. First, its performance, like the performance of Homer, was not a reading, but the voiced enactment of memorized poetry. Second, and more importantly, it was conceived by the poet not visually but acoustically according to the sound of it. In fact, as the one who staged and choreographed his own dramas, Aeschylus would have instructed his actors and chorus orally and they, in turn, would have learned not from a script but by ear, much as we learn melodies still today. Hence an additional question to be addressed here concerns writing's role in the genesis of metaphysical philosophy and the suppression of oral poetry's original "facticity."

For our task will be to use Aeschylus' retention of orality as an access to a past before philosophy's reflective abstraction, literally, withdrawal, from the basis and ground of spoken poetic *peithō*. To this end, we will first explore some of the epistemological, ontological, and psychosomatic characteristics of Cassandra's poetic *peithō* and turn, then, to a close reading of her *amoibaion* with the chorus.

It is striking, first of all, that Cassandra's audience does not, and cannot, fully know just what it is that she is telling them about Agamemnon's and her own impending murder at the hands of Clytemnestra, and that this audience cannot, therefore, be fully persuaded by it. Demonstrative certainty is impossible here, for equivocation, indeterminacy, and inconclusiveness are inherent in everything she says. She is, to be sure, cursed by Apollo to foretell truly what will happen but never to persuade anyone of what she says. Even so, this mythical account of her failure to persuade displays a fundamental feature of all poetic *peithō*, namely, that concomitant conviction and lack of conviction, *pistis* and *apistia*, are the inevitable correlate in an audience, of the unstably oscillating "It could be this way, it could be that" in the things the speaker's words disclose to her listeners but simultaneously obscure as well.[4] Precisely as spoken, Cassandra's words are pluri*vocal* and poly*phonic*: rather than signifying stabilized intelligible realities, her voiced speech makes incompletely audible only disrupted resonances of motifs remembered, and anything she says recalls to mind not one thing but infinitely many things at once, often collapsing themes past, present, and/or future in a phantasmagoria of fractured images. Given the indefinite and opaque being of the things she is talking about, no audience could know for sure the truth of what she says. The uncertainty of the poetic word remains ultimate. Nothing is defined "clearly and distinctly," and everything remains in question: "It *is*, is it not?" The "argument" here, if one could call it an argument at all, is therefore unendingly inconclusive.

As we can already see, there is an ontological ground, or better, with Nietzsche, an ontological *Abgrund* or groundless abyss, that corresponds to this epistemological uncertainty. The temporal whirl of the past, present, and future events of which Cassandra tells—her encounter with Apollo in Troy, Thyestes' adulterous conniving with Atreus's wife Aerope, Atreus's serving Thyestes his own children for dinner in revenge, Aegisthus's and Clytemnestra's murder of Agamemnon and herself—cannot be brought to a standstill in order to found, base, or plot these events in some underlying structure of fixed *eidē*, the intelligible forms or "looks" of them. It is impossible to establish some *logos* or logical pattern in their appearance and disappearance, for they never "are" for us in the mode of being that Heidegger calls *ständige Anwesenheit* or static presence. Rather, their presence is always beset simultaneously by absence, their being, by their not-being-yet and not-being-any-longer what they are.

What is more, the voicing itself of what Cassandra says participates in the same unstable transience as the events she relates. Insofar as her words, as opposed to stationary, legible writing, are heard, there "is" for the speaker and her audience only their crescendo to audibility and diminuendo to silence with no discernible logic "beneath" or "behind" it. We hear in her song only the confusion of what was, what will be, and what is now as these are experienced while she and her audience remain under way (*unterwegs*) within the blur of their temporal occurrence. Hence, just as there is no charting or mapping of the things she sings about, no static grammar of her speech is available for the audience either.

There is a critical point here: we cannot underestimate the signal importance of mapmaking for the Milesian origins of philosophy more than a century before Aeschylus. In distinction from the Homeric poetic understanding still preserved in him, the derivative philosophical understanding saw itself as detached surveillance of what is, as *theōria*, spectating, looking on from above. It is no coincidence, therefore, that Anaximander is said to have made the first map, and that his Milesian compatriot, the logo*grapher* and forerunner of Herodotus, Hecataeus, is famed precisely for a map. For mapmaking, carto*graphy*, to happen, one's understanding of the world must have begun to shift away from Homeric poetry's story telling while underway within the events and things one speaks of, to a *theōrētikōs* thinking that surveys at a distance the things it has "arrayed before" it (Heidegger would say *vor-gestellt*). Only then can it proceed to graph them, to signify them with spatial markings (*graphai*), to "write" them (*graphein*) across a space. From Agathemerus we read that "Anaximander, the Milesian *auditor* of Thales' teachings (*akoustēs Thaleō*), was the first who dared to *draw* (*grapsai*) the known world on a tablet" (DK 12 A6), and from Themistius we read that "Anaximander was the first among the Greeks whom we know, with courage enough to publish a *written account* (*logon . . . suggegrammenon*) about the nature of things" (DK 12 A7). Thus to Heidegger, we add the suggestion that metaphysics' detached looking on at the statically present *logos* of things coincides with the new philosophical consciousness's turn away from listening and its turn to seeing its own markings across a space, to reading "writing." It is exactly this development that Aeschylus's later tragic poetry counteracts.

Now, it could be that like musicologists who can no longer just sing along inwardly to a performance of Mozart's delicious melodies but must simultaneously visualize or even read the score—there are illuminated desks at the back of Carnegie Hall for this sort of thing—we have all been seduced by Aristotle's application of philosophy's cartographical mentality to tragedy. One need only think in this regard of his dismissal of song in tragedy as a pleasurable accessory (*hedusmaton*), his emphasis instead on the composition (*sustasis*) of the plot with a logically connected beginning, middle, and end, and his comparison of tragedy to a visible, indeed, "easily overseen" (*eusunopton*), living organism of a specific spatial size (*megathos*).[5] It needs to be pointed out, therefore, that even if the audience for the *Agamemnon*, like the prophetic Cassandra, already "knows" what is coming and how the story will end, this is quite a different thing from construing the grammar, a written structure, a map, of what they hear. Like those listening to a familiar piece of music, and who have memorized by ear how it goes, the ancient audience hears the performance of the *Agamemnon*, but their experience remains primarily acoustical, not visual.[6] Unlike us, who must start from the written script, they have no over*view* and do not en*vision* any logic of what they are hearing.[7] Instead, they follow along with the melodies of the poetry as they are being played out, and they themselves are even drawn into the choral dance of their harmonies, rhythms, and meters. Precisely this being-under-way within the events, with no map of their supposed logic, radically opposes Cassandra's poetic sung speech and its listeners, to philosophical speech.[8]

With the mention of dance we have come, finally, to the psychosomatic unity of Cassandra's speech. We note that the experiences her words communicate are heard and felt physically rather than observed by some unaffected, disembodied Platonic *psuchē*.[9] Far from being purely intellectual, Cassandra's speech arises from, and rests in, somatic experience, which is to say, in *pathos* or what the body "feels" and "undergoes." Her speech, therefore, is fundamentally a language of dance and song that involves listeners physically, rather than some kind of instruction that allows detached onlookers to see and comprehend conceptually the logic of what she says. Hence psychologically, which here is also to say, somatically, her communication is determined, not so much by its cognitive content as by its affective tone or *pathos*: foreboding, despair and terror, *Angst*.

Indeed, the *amoibaion* we are considering consists of seven parings of strophe and antistrophe, most of which issue out of an initial cry. In taking over the role usually assigned to the singing and dancing chorus, Cassandra is actually not speaking but singing and dancing, and corresponding to the embeddedness of everything she says in *pathos*, we note the corporeal, *choreo*graphic dimension of "strophe" and "antistrophe" here. Prior to their technical use in plotting groups of written words on a surface, these words referred to a dance "turn" and "counterturn." What is more, we must not forget that not only the excited dochmiac meter in which Cassandra's physical movement becomes most frantic,[10] but all the meters Aeschylus employs here, are based in dance steps, the *thesis* or "placing" of the "foot" being on a long syllable, and *arsis* or "lifting," on a short one. Hence, in the written, and even in the recited text of the *amoibaion* we have only the barest skeleton of an actual performance. Silent, dead markings communicate no live *pathos* unless they are at least imagined acoustically. And, as opposed to the reader of writing, the singer of poetry's "verses" or "turns," cannot separate thought and word from the bodily experience of the feelings and their expression in dance movements. With these things in mind let us turn now to the *amoibaion* itself.

Importantly, it is introduced with Cassandra's persistent silence in response to Clytemnestra (1035–68), who up to this point has been able to persuade everyone to do what she wants, even a reluctant Agamemnon to commit the incriminating travesty of walking on the royal tapestries (914–72).[11] Nevertheless, she cannot now persuade Cassandra to join Agamemnon in coming into the palace, and she suffers thereby her first defeat in *peithō* or persuasion. "I shall waste no more words only to be put to shame," she says in exiting (1067).

Then, *out of Cassandra's silence*, we hear her first utterance, a startling cry with deep *pathos* and no *logos* significance at all: *otototototoi popoi dā*, followed still not by any kind of declarative statement, but by an invocation, "O Apollo, O Apollo!"[12] Thus begin the first strophe and its antistrophe (1072–73, 1076–77) in seven parings of these, most of which issue similarly out of her silence and then an initial cry. For Cassandra is dancing and singing here, not just speaking, and what she says arises, not from what she has conceived intellectually, but from what her body is undergoing.

In response to the questions and puzzlement of the chorus (or chorus leader), her second strophe at 1080–82 moves only now from the vocative "Apollo, Apollo," to a first fragment what we might call cognitive content: "Guide, my destroyer (*apollōn*)," she says, "Indeed, a second time you have destroyed (*apōlesas*) me completely (*ou molis*)." This cognitive content, however, has two characteristics that sharply distinguish her *peithō* from any philosophical argument. First, in oscillating unsteadily from one possible sense to another, her meaning is highly equivocal, as the chorus's continuing puzzlement makes evident: "It *seems* (*eoiken*)," they say, "she would prophesize about her own miseries" (1083).

Second, using mutable, vocal word-names (*onomata*) rather than stabilized word-signs (*sēmeia*) and by employing metonymic tropes,[13] her speech moves entirely within speech from one acoustical resonance to another. To be precise, by a "turn" of speech called polyptoton or "multiple inflection," Cassandra and her audience hear the name Apollo as it modulates into two forms of the verb *apollumi*, first the gerund *apollōn* or "the one destroying," and then the participial *apōlesas* or "you have destroyed."[14] And by the ironic figure litotes, *ou molis*, literally, "not scarcely," is heard to mean its opposite, "completely." Thus, it is not as if Cassandra writes "2" to designate and then communicate the *eidos* or intelligible "look" of duality she has seen and that "always is" "what it is"(*to aei on, ti estin*). In contrast to philosophical argument, by listening to where the spoken words lead them she and her audience follow along in the unsteady modulations of words into other words with new, and often contradictory, senses.

In answer to her own question what sort of house this is to which her destroyer Apollo has led her, strophe 3 of her song begins once again with a tone-setting cry, from which first arise dreadful ambiguous images of events either past or future, the banquet in which a cuckolded Atreus avenges his wife's seduction by serving Thyestes his children for dinner, or Agamemnon's murder by Clytemnestra:

Ah, Ah,
God-hated (*misōtheon*) indeed, much witnessing,
murder-of-one's-own (*autophōna*), evil, throat-slitting (*karatoma*)
man-slaughter-place (*androsphageīon*) and dripping-floor-place (*pedorrantērion*).
    (1090–92)

Again, we note how things are brought into view, not by designation of something clearly present as a whole before the spectator, but in wavering e-*voca*-tions: Vocal, voiced word-names (*onomata*) call up for listeners shifting shards of events. This acoustical conjuring moves entirely within the reverberations of speech with no indications of anything outside it. Communication of content is accomplished here by the fusion word-names into compounds, *miso-theon, auto-phona, kara-toma, andro-sphageion, pedo-rrantēr-ion*, all instances of the ways unstable meanings of poetic speech can proliferate endlessly within itself by the trope of polyptoton.

But more basic even than the productive instability of what we get to "see," if only in a blur, is the acoustical communication of the psychosomatic *pathos* out of which this envisioned content arises and which provides its ineliminable context. For in verse 1090, the first of Cassandra's agitated dochmaic meters has already begun to intrude: *misotheon men oun, polla sunistora* ("God-hated, indeed, much witnessing").[15] Indeed, the chorus's response lets us know just how erratic and frenzied the movements of her song-dance have become:

Keen-scented, the stranger seems to be like a dog
tracking down what it will find: murder. (1093–94)

In the antistrophe to strophe 3 Cassandra continues to evoke visual fragments of awful things, here Thyestes' banquet:

For by these witnesses there I am persuaded (*epipeithomai*):
Crying, these new-born, of slaughter and
roasted flesh, eaten up by the father. (1095–97)

To be sure, the chorus does share her own persuasion (note her *epepeithomai*) concerning these facets of past events, for it already knows about them (see 1098–99). It is astonished that Cassandra could know them, and it is persuaded thereby of her prophetic gift: "Indeed, we have heard of your fame as prophet," they respond. The chorus is not persuaded, however, when it comes to her prophesizing the future, to which she now turns (1100–04). For Apollo's "curse" is working—or should we say, the negative dynamic of any original *peithō*, its inevitable undecidability and the concurrence of doubt and conviction this evokes in the audience.

As before, what Cassandra says next bursts from silence into a cry: *Iō popoi*, upon which not a statement but a question follows: "Whatever is she [Clytemnestra] scheming?" (1100). And into the openness and indeterminacy of this question—Is it so or is it not?—comes Cassandra's *possible* answer, still in the interrogative, at first and, really, throughout, for nothing here is "clear and distinct," nothing settled conclusively:

Some new grief? Great (*mega*),
great (*meg'*) evil she is scheming in this house,
unbearable (*apherton*) for dear ones, hard to heal (*dusiaton*);
But defense—
it stays far away. (1101–04)

Indeed, nothing *could* be "clear and distinct" here, for there is no set underlying extra-linguistic substance, no *ousia* or primary being, of which this speech may be said to predicate many different qualities. Rather, for the speaker and audience "there is," *es gibt*, only the erratic play of the phenomenal qualities themselves, as these are named vocally, all the while their very indeterminacy and questionableness announces that in whatever we might be hearing there is as much undisclosed as there is disclosed. For instance, with the polyptotons or inflections—the *a* and *ton* added to the stem *pher* in *apherton* and the *dus* and *[t]on* to the stem *iat* in *dusiaton*—this speech, instead of signifying some preexistent being outside itself, once again expands its vocabulary within itself in order to call things into being, however indistinct and incoherent they may "be."[16]

We also note here the pleonastic doubling of *mega* or "great" (1101–02), which, of course, provides no new cognitive content at all, but which serves the much more basic function of communicating acoustically the sustaining *pathos* or feeling of ever-intensifying foreboding out of which the cognitive content originates. In keeping with this *pathos* the dochmiac meter of opening verse ("Whatever evil is she scheming"; 1100) of this fourth strophe, returns in the last verse *hekas apostatei* ("It stays far away"; 1104), a rhythmic change whose emotional impact is made even more intense by breaking the verse off from its subject in the previous verse, "But defense— / It stays far away" (1103–04). The trope or "turn of speech" here is an anacoluthon, namely, a rupture of the sentence structure in order to communicate a strong and even violent *pathos*.[17]

Cassandra's jagged, nonlinear speech, pervasively in the interrogative and not declarative mode, continues through the antistrophe to the fourth strophe and into in the fifth strophe and antistrophe, all cited here in Robert Fagles's splendid poetic rendering, here without the chorus's perplexed responses:

You, you godforsaken—you'd do *this*?
The lord of your bed (*ton homodemnion posin*),
you bathe him . . . his body glistens (*phaidrunasa*), then—
                    how to tell the climax?—
                              comes so quickly, see,
               hand over hand shoots out, hauling ropes—
                                   then lunge! (1107–11)

               No no (*e e papaī, papaī*), look there!—
what's that? some net (*diktuon ti*) flung out of hell—
     No, *she* is the snare,
the bedmate, deathmate murder's strong right arm! (*all' arkus hē xuneunos,*
hē xunaitia)
                    Let the insatiate discord in the race
rear up and shriek "Avenge the victim—stone them dead!" (*katololuxatō*
thumatos leusimou) (1114–18)

     Look out! look out! (*idou, idou*)—
ai (*aā*) drag the great bull from the mate!—
     a thrash of robes, she traps him (*en peploisin . . . laboūsa*)—
writhing—
               black horn glints, twists—
                                        she gores him through!
               and now he buckles, look, the bath swirls red—
There's stealth and murder in the cauldron (*dolophonou lebētos technan*), do
you hear? (1125–29)

     We note the polyptotons and word-fusions—the *homo-demnion* or "same-bedded" spouse (1108), the *phaidru-nasa* or "bright-washed" (1109), the *thumatos leus-imos* or "stoning-able sacrifice" of a victim (1118), the *dolo-phonou* or "sly-murderous" scheme of the bath (1129). Characteristic here, however, are the synedoches, the discontinuous naming of event-fragments in their happening, where each time the named part reverberates infinitely into other unnamed parts of an indefinite whole—*proteinei de cheir ek cheros oregmata* or "stretching forth hand over hand, striving" (1110–11) and *tuptei; pitnei d' en enudrō(i) teuchei* or "She strikes; he falls in the water-full tub" (1128). As is typical of poetic *peithō*, we have only the disjointed temporal sequence, now this, next this, then this, with none of philosophical argument's second level of explanatory causal connections along with (*meta*) this recounting: "She stabs, he falls": not "He falls because she stabs." Thus the *aitia* here in *he xuneunos, he xunaitia phonou* (1115–16) still has its original judicial meaning, "the co-guilt of murder," and not, as in medical science and philosophy, its derivative meaning of "cause."

We note further that the compound word-name *xunaitia* displays two distinctive features of original speech. First, by polyptoton or inflection the root word *aitia* acquires new sense in being "declined" with the prefix of *xun*, meaning "with." Second, by the trope of enallage, the substitution of one part of speech for another, the root word is made to function in an entirely new way: the noun *aitia*, "guilt," now serves in the place of the adjectival "bearing guilt" (*hoi xunaitian echontes*). Here again we hear speech bending, turning itself within itself, to call forth new senses.

Most striking in regard to the cognitive content here, however, are what by philosophical standards would be termed the mere metaphors of the bull/cow/horn, and the net/snare. In fact, however, these are not metaphors at all, if by "metaphor" is meant that some extra-linguistic thing, already known to the audience, is signified with the word-sign for some other thing different from it but like it in a crucial respect. Rather, in keeping with the language-immanence of this speech, *metapherein* here can only mean to "carry over" or "trans-fer" word-names into new ranges of sense in order to let things be heard, let them *be* for the audience, in new ways. Here metaphor is really metonymy, that is, a "renaming" that calls someone or something into being in a new way by naming it anew. In this way Clytemnestra herself comes into being for the audience as she *is*, as the "cow" (*boos*) and Agamemnon himself, as he *is*, as the "bull" (*tauros*). Or is it that Clytemnestra, assuming now her characteristic masculinity,[18] "is" the bull to be kept from Agamemnon, the "cow"? The reference, we observe, oscillates unsteadily, undecidably. The equivocation is resolved only once the knife with horn handle with which she stabs him *becomes*, takes on its being as, her "horn" with which she gores him. In this way Cassandra's word-names call something into being for the audience in a heretofore unheard of way: they do not *re*-present something, rather they make it present in the first place, in all its ambiguity as it *is* now for an audience.

Similarly, instead of indicating something outside of themselves, the two word-names "net" (*diktouon*) and "snare" (*arkus*) (1115–16) function as a kind of leitmotiv that, in reverberating across the entire drama's acoustical field and beyond, resonates with the first choral song's all-ensnaring "net" (*diktouon*) thrown over Troy (357) and with Clytemnestra's doubly allusive image of her husband as a "net" (*diktouon*), his body being perforated with war wounds at Troy in the past as well as by her own stab wounds at home in the future (868). But "net" and "snare" also resonate reciprocally with the *pepla*, the "weave" or woven robes, in which Clytemnestra catches him (1126–27).[19] These too, the net and the snare, are no mere metaphors; Clytemnestra, as she is made present here, *is* not *like* a net; she *is* not something or someone with her own being that may be compared *to* a net. As the "bed-mate" and one "co-guilty" of murder, she herself *is* the net, for this is how she becomes present now. For the audience of Cassandra's *peithō* there *is* no Clytemnestra as an extra-linguistic *ousia* or substance. There is no single, unified Clytemnestra *ontōs ousa*, no Clytemnestra as she "really is," that underlies the many ways she may be said to appear and that could be signified by a univocal sign.

As always, however, these original, pre-philosophical features of the content of Cassandra's attempts to persuade the chorus of the impending doom are sustained by an even more basic communication of *pathos*. Cursed as she is by Apollo, she is unable, of course, to persuade the chorus cognitively of the things she would have them believe, but she does communicate to them her perturbation and *Angst*, as we hear in their response, first, to her vivid net/snare imagery, but even more, to her invocation of the dreaded furies (1117; see the chorus's "Which Erynys in the house do you command to exult?" 1119–20).[20] For at 1121 the chorus breaks out in dochmiac bimeters of its own:

> *epi de kardian / edrame krokobaphēs*
> *stagōn, ate kai / dori ptōsimois*
> To my heart runs, yellow-died,
> my [every] drop [of blood], as also for those felled by spear
> (it comes to an end with the [last] rays of setting life). (1121–23)

And this choral stanza ends suddenly with the chorus's own foreboding:

> *tacheīa d' ata pelei.*
> But doom is sudden. (1124)[21]

In the sixth strophe Cassandra turns to her own dismal fate beginning with another dochmiac meter:

> *Iō iō talainas /*
> Oh, Oh, of the wretched, ([how] evil-fated the lots!) (1136)

and continuing with a dochmiac bimeter:

> *to gar emo throō / pathos epegcheai*
> My own I cry, [my] suffering I pour out. (1137)

Calling questions again to Apollo, Cassandra, to be sure, now falls back into more sober iambic trimeters:

> Why ever have you brought me, wretched one, here?
> For nothing but that I should die too. What else? (1138–39)

But the chorus's response is still infected with her earlier dochmiac meters:

Phrenomanēs tis ei / theophorētos, am-
phi d' autas throeis
nomon anomon, / hoia tis xoutha
One mad in thought your are; born by a god, a-
bout yourself you lament.
Song, no-song, like something tawny . . . (1140–42)

Here a verse in bacchiac tetrameter intervenes:
insatiable in crying, ah, its senses suffused with pains (1142)

followed, however, by three concluding dochmaic meters:

Itun Itun stenous' / amphithalē kakois
aēdōn bion.
Itys, Itys sobbing—flowered round by the bad,
the Nightingale, its life.[22] (1143–44)

Cassandra herself, reflecting on her own fate, answers in the sixth antistrophe in a mix of more steady meters including some iambic trimeters. As usual, however, she begins from a cry:

Oh oh (*iō iō*), the fate of the clear sounding Nightingale!
For they threw round her the form of flight,
the gods, and sweet times without tears;
But for me awaits the split of a spear that cuts both ways. (1146–48)

And the chorus follows her falling back into its own iambics, not, however, without a grating onomatopoeia in complaint about the frightening things she has said with a *dusphatōi klangai* or "dissonant ring" to them (1152). Even if they are no longer sung, its words, this is to say, are still embedded in a *pathos* or "feel" that they have about them and that they communicate prior to any cognitive content.

In Cassandra's seventh and final strophe, dochmiacs return:

. . . *patrion poton /*
tote men amphi sas / aionas talain'
ēnutoman trophais
(oh Scamander's) fatherly flow,
then around your banks for a time [I], wretched one,
came of age, well nurtured. . . . (1158–59)

And again this disturbed dochmiac "feel" to things, this *pathos*, is communicated to the chorus, which resumes its own dochmiac bimeters in response:

ti tode topon agan, / epos ephēmisō

. . .

peplēgmai d hupai / dēgmati phoiniō(i) /,
dusalgei tuxa(i) / minura threomenas,
thraumat' emoi kluein.

What [is] this too penetrating word you have voiced?

. . .

I am struck by a bloody bite
as you of your hard-pained fate in hushed tones complain,
horrible for me to hear. (1162–66)

To this, Cassandra's antistrophe, in which, temporally, the past of Troy and her own future coalesce, responds in plain but poignant verses, especially affecting because of their *p* alliterations:

Iō
ponoi ponoi poleos olomenas to pan
Iō propurgoi thusiai patros
polukaneis botōn poionomōn
Alas
for the sorrow, sorrow of the city all destroyed
alas for the father's sacrifices before the walls,
many slaughterings of livestock that grazed in pastures. (1167–69)

And she concludes, in sinking back into the matrix of despair from which all that she has said arose,

No remedy to ward off
a suffering such as it has now.
And I, still warm in spirit, will quickly be thrown to the dirt. (1169–72)

To be sure, in Cassandra's prophecies I have taken an extreme example, yet the very extremity of it serves us well, I think, in magnifying the essential features of poetic *peithō* and in highlighting its contrast with the derivative reasoning to which Platonic-Aristotelian philosophy has accustomed us. Indeed, I conclude that even in Cassandra's wildest utterances Aeschylus lets us hear how "reasoning" might have actually sounded a century before philosophy's abstraction from our original, oral communication with each other. For, to begin with, we do not write arguments for each other as disembodied minds removed from our factual situation. To begin with, our words are not written signs signifying some static, extra-linguistic being. Rather, in withstanding our inevitable perplexity and in tracing out the anticipations and remembrances of what we say aloud, we are moved by what we speak, mentally and physically, toward reaching an ever so precarious and tentative understanding with one another. Indeed, when compared to what we hear from Aeschylus's Cassandra, philosophy's written scientific language of word-signs supposedly designating a preexistent stable reality outside of itself turns out to be but the petrified sediment from poetry's fluid sung speech.

Notes

1. Argumentative demonstration is, of course, a later, derivative sense of *apodeixis*, which originally meant "showing forth," a deed in oral performance in order that the *kleos* or fame of the one who did it might be remembered and not lapse into oblivion. See Herodotus, *Histories*, I, 1–5. See also Gregory Nagy, *Pindar's Homer* (Baltimore: Johns Hopkins University Press, 1990), 217–24.

2. I will argue here that in his dramas Aeschylus perpetuates an earlier, oral understanding of speech even as *graphē*, writing and mathematical written sign systems, are continuing to spread through Greek education. We should keep in mind that though Homer had been standardized in written form some 250 years before, he was still learned by memory and sung by rhapsodists in Aeschylus's day and beyond. See Kevin Robb, *Literacy and Paideia in Ancient Greece* (Cambridge: Cambridge University Press, 1994), chap. 6, "The Epical Basis of Greek *Paideia* in the Late Fifth Century: *Ion* and *Euthyphro*," 159–82.

3. The idea of a lived, factual world is, of course, taken from the early Heidegger up to and including *Sein und Zeit* (Being and Time) (Tübingen: Niemeyer, 1927), but I will draw on many of Heidegger's later insights. Unless otherwise noted, all translations from the Greek and German will be my own.

4. See Heidegger, *Vom Wesen der Wahrheit* (On the Nature of Truth) (Freiburg lectures 1931–1932) Gesamtausgabe Band 34 (Frankfurt: Klostermann, 1988) on *a-lētheia* and the inevitable concomitance of *Verborgenheit* and *Unverborgenheit*, hiddenness and unhiddenness. However, I must enter a caveat concerning the applicability of Heidegger's language to the project at hand. I would note that in poetry *a-lētheia* does not mean "un-hiddenness" but "un-forgottenness," which is to say, whatever is rescued from oblivion by being remembered. The word *lēthē*, or oblivion, and its contrary, *anamnēsis*, or being remembered, have their roots in a culture of oral tale telling, where what is saved from oblivion is remembered, preserved in presence, each time in the poets' performances of their tales. See n1 on the original sense of *apodeixis*. With the advent of writing, of course, memory (*mnēmē*), as well as the performance (*hupokrisis*) of what is to be remembered, begins to lose its importance. For what is written and seen (read) now displaces what has been heard and thereby remembered. Heidegger, "phenomenologian" that he was, was concerned almost exclusively with what appears visually (*phainetai*) in the light (*phōs*). See, for example, his account of *die Lichtung*, the "clearing" or "light place" in the dark woods in which beings come to light, in *Holzwege* (On Blind Paths) (Frankfurt: Klostermann, 1951), "Der Ursprung des Kunstwerks" (The Origin of the Artwork) (1935), 41–44. He is, this is to say, very much in the tradition of Western ocularism and, *like* the metaphysical philosophy he would call

into question, completely removed from the origins of speech in a preliterate aural/oral culture. His mistranslation of *a-lētheia* is the result of this abstraction. Hence we must take his repeated references to "hearing" with a grain of salt.

5. See the *Poetics*, 1450b16 and 1450b24–1451a5. Nietzsche is very useful in reversing Aristotle's abstraction from the acoustical. See his *Die Geburt der Tragödie aus dem Geist der Music*, in particular §§5–6 on the importance of lyric poetry, Archilochus, Pindar, for the genesis of tragedy. See also my *The Hermeneutics of Original Argument* (Evanston: Northwestern University Press, 1998), (henceforth HOA), §6.5, "The Rise of the Visual and Demise of the Acoustical in Aristotle's Poetics," 271–90, and §7, "Nietzsche's Recovery of Original Acoustical Experience," 291–310.

6. This is not to say that there were no surprises for the audience at what was supposed to be the first and only performance of the *Oresteia*. Indeed, Elizabeth Vandiver points out that Aeschylus is a master of such surprises and that Cassandra's opening cry, for example, would have abruptly disabused the audience of their natural expectation that she would be a silent character. Hence, even if the audience knows how the story goes they could be shocked by Aeschylus's retelling of it. See Elizabeth Vandiver, *Greek Tragedy* (Chantilly, Va.: The Teaching Company, 2000), tape 7.

7. Just as there is a certain irony in Kierkegaard writing Hegelian philosophy books in order to demolish Hegelian philosophy, there is an irony in writing a theoretical paper to be read silently that applies static written concepts in order to free Aeschylus's oral poetry from the preconceptions inherited with literacy. Here it is worth remembering that not the Greeks but the Romans invented a grammar, that is, a written structural analysis of speech, this, in order to learn Greek as a *second* language. (Grammar, of course, comes from *grammē* or written mark.) We can safely assume, therefore, that Aeschylus was blissfully unaware of the terminology we are using, and that he composed by ear, not theory. The same could not be said of Cicero, however. Could it be that John Coltrane is different from Philip Glass in just this way?

8. I am indebted to Marcel Detienne for the expression "sung speech." See his remarkable *The Masters of Truth in Archaic Greece* (New York: Zone Books 1996), 39–52.

9. See Plato on "the self itself by itself" (*hē psuchē . . . autē kath' hautēn*; *Phaedo* 79cd).

10. For the analysis of the different meters in the *amoibaion* I am indebted to D. J. Connacher, *Aeschylus' Oresteia* (Toronto: University of Toronto Press, 1987), 40–43, and to Hugh Lloyd-Jones, *The Oresteia* (Berkeley: University of California Press, 1979), 87. There a many variations, but the basic form of the dochmiac dimeter is U — — U — / U — — U —, as in "the wise kang ga roos / re sist leath er shoes" (see Lloyd-Jones 1979, 87, for this mnemonic taken from Richard Jebb). Of course, the mood of this facetious example is completely wrong, even if the extra long syllable at the end of each foot, "roos," "shoes," displays the unstable, off-balance sound of this meter nicely. Hence I include the following necessary correction: "The staccato rhythm of dochmiacs makes them suitable for the expression of violent emotions, especially fear and despair. Here then we have one lyric meter which, unlike most of the others . . . , can be associated with a particular mood or sentiment"; J. Halporn, M. Ostwald, T. Rosenmeyer, *The Meters of Greek and Latin Poetry* (Indianapolis: Bobbs-Merrill, 1963), 51.

11. See especially Clytemnestra at 943: "Be persuaded (*pithou*). You remain the master, just freely follow me this once."

12. See, similarly, Cassandra's *Iou iou, ō ō kaka* at 1214, the last word of which does have incipient cognitive content, to be sure, but like the English "oh shit!" that might translate this verse, it serves more as a cry than a designation of something. See Nietzsche on the origin of the word in the cry in Friedrich Nietzsche, *Nachgelassene Fragemente 1869–1874*, KSA 7 (Berlin: de Gruyter, 1988), 63: "Speech (*Sprache*) developed from the scream (*Schrei*) with its accompanying gesture." See also my HOA 297–98.

13. See my HOA, 72–78, on the proliferation of meaning by the metonymic tropes.

14. Compare the play on "Helen" in the second stasimon, 687–89, where *Helena* modulates to *helenaus, helanandros, heleptolis* (destroyer of ships, destroyer of men, destroyer of cities). Far from witty punning, with these inflections Aeschylus brings Helen into being for us in some of the manifold ways she "is."

15. See n10.

16. I would contend that this proliferation is in the nature of original poetic speech, which, as the word *poiēsis* indicates, "makes" things be for us in the first place.

17. See n7.

18. See, for instance, the *gunaikos androboulon*, or "man-planning woman" at *Aga.* 11.

19. See also the chorus's *agreuma* in *morsimōn agreumatōn* ("of fated snares") 1048.

20. Though traditional, Fagle's translation of *stasis d' akoretos genei* in 1117 as "insatiate discord in the race" may be mistaken. For *stasis* originally means party or faction, in which case *stasis* and not *genei* is what refers to the Erynyes and *genei* would mean "for the clan [of Atridae]." See Nagy 1990, 366–69.

21. See Heidegger on *Sein* and *pelei* in the *Antigone's* first stasimon; M. Heidegger, *Hölderlins Hymne "Der Ister"* (GA 53) (Frankfurt: Klostermann, 1993), 87–88.

22. Itys was murdered by his mother, Procne, and her sister, Philomela, to avenge his father Tereus's, rape and mutilation of Philomela. The gods turned Procne into a nightingale so that she might mourn for her son. Here we have one of many instances of how the resonances become inter-mythical in radiating beyond even the whole trilogy of the *Oresteia* to other stories.

10

Luck and Virtue in Pindar, Aeschylus, and Sophocles

C. D. C. Reeve

This chapter is a discussion of some aspects of *Nemean* 8, *Agamemnon*, and *Antigone*. It was inspired in part by Martha Nussbaum, *The Fragility of Goodness*,[1] and so deals with one of her central themes—that of the vulnerability of virtue to luck. But it is an independent investigation, which responds to Nussbaum's important work, to the extent that it does, largely by implication. The questions on which it focuses are these: Do Pindar, Aeschylus, and Sophocles think that virtue is vulnerable to luck? And if so, what sort of virtue is at issue and what sort of vulnerability?

Virtue's Vulnerabilities

Virtues are largely defined by the well-known human liabilities, or "temptations," they combat or resist. One measure of their strength or degree—of *how* virtuous their possessor is—is how well they perform that role: someone is fairly courageous if he can handle quite a lot of fear (danger) without coming undone; very temperate if he can resist the strongest sexual temptation. Since people are usually vulnerable only to certain kinds of things—danger in one case, sensual pleasure in another—virtue may also be measured not just by how much of one kind of thing someone can withstand, but also by how many different kinds. Prima facie, it is possible to be very temperate but not very courageous.

Virtues relatively invulnerable to the things they are designed to combat, however, are vulnerable to other things that happen by luck, things like Alzheimer's disease, psychosurgery, brainwashing, and so on. No one is thought to be without virtue, or to have less than perfect virtue, because of *this* kind of vulnerability.

215

They are also vulnerable, at the formative stage, to the outcome of the genetic lottery, the shaping influence of parents, and the like.

A third kind of vulnerability is less direct. Here what is attacked is not virtue itself, but its exercise. We are just, we are ready and able to do the just thing, but the corrupt government, or the secret police, or the class structure prevents us from succeeding. Finally, there are attacks on virtue that are less direct still, such as attacks on the normal or expected *consequences* of virtue. We do the courageous thing but are cheated of the rewards.

One way to think of vulnerability, then, is in terms of its trajectory and target. Some vulnerabilities—temptations—meet virtues head on. Some—genetic disability, bad parents, Alzheimer's disease—prevent its development or destroy its roots. They attack from the rear, as it were. Some attack not virtue but its exercise. Some attack the normal consequences of its exercise.

Virtues come not just in degrees of strength, but also in those of development or maturity. *Nascent virtue* (or "natural virtue," as Aristotle sometimes calls it) is what someone has if he has virtuous habits but little or no insight into the reasons why it is good to have them. *Full virtue* is the degree of virtue the man of practical wisdom—the *phronimos*—and other insightful and reflective moral agents have: their habits are reliably virtuous and they understand the good such habits promote. *Philosophic virtue* is the almost superhuman degree of virtue that Stoic sages and Platonic philosopher-kings possess—an amalgam of heroic or saintly virtue with reflective understanding and wisdom.

Even in thinking about sages and philosopher-kings, however, it is important not to leave Earth entirely behind. Virtues, even of the most exalted sort, are like immune systems, they are designed to work well in most of the situations an agent (animal) is likely to encounter. No virtue, no achievable level of human wisdom, can be expected to deal well with absolutely every situation. The apparent ingenuity of luck, so to speak, may outpace the resources of even the most admirable agent.

Nemean 8

In the following lines of *Nemean* 8, Pindar seems to be saying that excellence or virtue flourishes among wise and good people, but not among foolish, envious, or bad ones:

> But excellence (*areta*) flourishes (*auxetai*) like a vine fed by the green dew,
> raised up among men who are wise (*sophois*) and just (*dikaios*) to the liquid
>   sky.
> Various are the uses of friends. Help in trouble is greatest,
> but joy (*terpsis*) also looks for a pledge of friendship that is clear in the
>   eyes. (40–44)[2]

The early part of the poem, which gives a powerful example of virtue not flourishing, helps us to understand what he intends. Ajax deserved the armor of Achilles, but, as a result of trickery, Odysseus was given it unjustly:

> Talking delights the envious,
> ever busy against the noble (*eslōn*), meddling not with smaller men.
> It was this that slaughtered the son of Telamon
> and bent him over his own sword.
> A quiet man, no talker, steadfast of heart, lies forgotten
> in the rage of dispute. The great prize is given to the supple liar.
> In their secret ballots the Danaans make much of Odysseus,
> and Ajax lost the golden armor and died struggling in his own blood.
> In truth, otherwise were the gashes that in the onset
> they tore in the warm flesh of their adversaries
> under the spears of defense about Achilles' body,
> in many another combat of those wasting
> days. But hate, even then, was there with its pretexts.
> It walks companion of beguiling words; it is sly and a spite that makes
>   evil;
> it violates the beautiful and brilliant
> to lift up out of things obscure a glory rotten at the heart. (21–34)

It isn't virtue or excellence itself that is fragile or dependent on others, then, but the *rewards* of virtue. Ajax died with his virtue intact. That is why he deserves to be praised by a poet who can set the record straight:

> Zeus father, may such never be my way;
> let me, walking always in the path
> of simplicity, make my life, and die thus, leaving
> to my children fame without reproach. Some pray for gold,
> some for lands
> without limit, but I to lay my limbs in the ground as one who
> gladdened his fellow-citizens,
> praising that which deserves it, scattering blame on the
> workers of evil. (34–39)

Pindar cannot bestow virtue; but he can ensure that it gets the praise, and vice the censure and blame, each deserves.

That this is indeed the poem's message is strongly suggested by the closing lines of its first part:

> Happiness (*olbos*) abides longer among men
> when it is planted by the hand of a god. (17)

For happiness is a reward of virtue, not virtue itself. What the poem seems to be saying, then, is that virtue needs the recognition of friends and—especially—the support of the gods if it is to result in happiness.

Virtue has such needs, moreover, in part because of the conception of happiness the poem endorses. Pindar is writing to celebrate the success of Deinias of Aigina in a race. But success is not just winning; it is being recognized as winning. Thus, while Ajax "won" the armor of Achilles (he deserved it), he wasn't given it. Hence his virtue, since it wasn't surrounded by wise and good men, but by envious ones, didn't flourish or receive the recognition or honor it deserved. It is this recognition that Pindar—as a divinely inspired agent of justice—bestows. All but explicitly, then, Pindar identifies happiness with merited or deserved honor—hardly surprising given the genre to which his poem belongs. That is why "delight (in victory) also seeks / To set its truth before the eyes of friends." Honor is the goal, but it depends on the recognition of others.

What the poem presents as vulnerable to luck isn't personal virtue or even its exercise, therefore, but the honor and prizes that are its normal consequences—consequences in which happiness is thought to consist. Ajax is unlucky not to live among virtuous people. That his virtue survives anyway is a measure of its heroic quality. Yet *Nemean* 8, by its very existence, implicitly acknowledges something else—something it is easy to overlook. Ajax—to put it in this somewhat misleading way—can the better accept his bad luck because poets like Pindar exist to set the record straight:

> The vaunt of reputation to come
> Alone controls the way men speak of those things that are gone, their life
>   in song and story . . .
> Happiness (*pathein eu*) is first of prizes,
> And good repute (*eu d'akouein*) has second place; the man who attains
> These two and grasps them in his hands
> Is given the uttermost garland. (*Pythian* 1.182–92)

In that respect, heroic poetry—the "undying ornament of the Muses" (Bacchylides 10.10)—functions like the promise of heaven for a virtuous Christian. But the very need for such a promise reveals an insufficiency or lack in virtue itself—especially virtue valued substantially for the sake of honor or happiness. It needs some consolation for what it recognizes luck can do, some basis for hope in face of the facts of life.

The *Agamemnon*

Agamemnon has murdered his daughter Iphigenia and sacked Troy. He returns home to Argos and his wife Clytemnestra. She invites him to enter his house treading on a path of purple embroideries and persuades him to accept (904–13). At issue in the scene is the soundness of Agamemnon's judgment (*phronein, gnomē*):

Agamemnon: Do not by strewing my path with raiment make it exposed
to envy. It is the gods you should honor with such things;
and to walk, being a mortal, on embroidered splendors
is impossible for me without fear.
I tell you to honor me with honors human, not divine.
Apart from footwipers and embroideries
the voice of fame resounds; and good sense (*to mē kakōs phronein*)
is the god's greatest gift. We must pronounce him fortunate
who has ended his life in the prosperity he cherishes;
and if in all things I may fare so, I do not lack confidence.
Clytemnestra: Come, tell me this, not against your judgment (*gnōmēn*).
Agamemnon: My judgment (*gnōmēn*), be assured, I shall not suppress.
Clytemnestra: Would you have vowed to the gods, in a moment of fear,
   that you would act after this fashion?
Agamemnon: Yes, if any with sure knowledge had prescribed this ritual.
   (920–34)[3]

The judgment at issue, which Agamemnon claims he will not suppress, is that it is wrong to step on the embroideries. It is to be compared to his earlier judgment that it is wrong to "massacre my daughter, the pride of my house" (208). What Clytemnestra's question reveals is the vulnerability of this judgment to fear. Out of fear, Agamemnon would promise to do what he knows will bring the envy of the gods. He doesn't ask, out of fear of what? He doesn't reflect that there are things one must not do even out of fear. He doesn't, for that matter, wonder whether the gods are likely to help people who undertake to do things they know are wrong.
   Clytemnestra's second question reveals a second such vulnerability:

Clytemnestra: What do you think Priam would have done, had he
   accomplished this?
Agamemnon: Indeed he would have walked upon embroideries, I think.
Clytemnestra: Then feel no scruple for the reproach of men.
Agamemnon: Yet talk in the mouths of the people has great power.
Clytemnestra: But he of whom none is jealous is not envied (*aphthonētos*).
   (935–39)

Even though Agamemnon knows that Priam has been punished by Zeus, he doesn't worry about emulating him. His concern about public opinion is quieted quickly by his desire to be envied. About the dangers of being envied—especially by the gods—he does not think.

The final step in the exchange shows us that Agamemnon is willing to abandon his judgment for the sake of something as trivial as satisfying his wife's whim:

Agamemnon: It is not a woman's part to desire contention.
Clytemnestra: But for the fortunate even to yield up victory is becoming.
Agamemnon: Do you in truth value victory in this contest?
Clytemnestra: Be persuaded, you are the winner, if willingly you leave all
    to me.
Agamemnon: Well, if this is your pleasure, let someone swiftly loose
My boots, which serve my feet as slaves;
And as I tread upon these purples of the gods,
Let no eye's envy strike me from afar.
For I feel much reluctance to waste the house's substance with my feet,
Ruining wealth and tissues bought with silver. (940–49)

Reluctant to waste the house's substance with his feet, Agamemnon removes his shoes, exhibiting in the process the concern for wealth that may itself lie behind the other traits Clytemnestra's questions have exposed. (Notice the terrible irony of "with my feet." In killing Iphigenia he has already wasted the true substance of his house with his hands.)

There is no doubt that Clytemnestra stages this scene to reveal to us what sort of man Agamemnon is. Her intention is to justify before the fact her own subsequent murder of him. Here he is, she says, a man deserving to die. Whether we follow her that far or not, she has certainly shown us a man whose virtue is compromised.

Was Agamemnon like that in Aulis? Did he kill his daughter because his judgment was fragile? Or was something else at issue there? Here is how the chorus describe his thinking on the matter:

How am I to become a deserter to my ships,
losing my allies?
For that they should long (*sph' epithumein*)
for a sacrifice to still the winds and for a maiden's blood
with a passion exceeding passion (*orga(i) periorgōs*)
is right in the eyes of heaven (*themis*). May all be for the best!
And when he had put on the yoke-strap of compulsion,
his spirit's wind veering to an impious blast,
impure, unholy, from that moment
his mind changed to a temper of utter ruthlessness.
For mortals are made reckless by the evil counsels
of merciless infatuation (*parakopa*), beginner of disaster.
And so he steeled himself to become the sacrificer

of his daughter, to aid a war
fought to avenge a woman's loss
and to pay beforehand for his ships. (212–27)

The allies' enthusiasm for virgin blood is fairly clearly a derivative enthusiasm. They want Iphigenia sacrificed as a means to getting out of Aulis and on to Troy. They want it, because they believe it to be *necessary* to achieving their goals. Agamemnon's coming to share their belief is what the chorus characterizes as his putting on "the yoke-strap of compulsion." And why does he put it on? Because he listens to "the evil counsels of merciless infatuation." He puts it on because he is mad for something—because, like his allies, he has a "passion exceeding passion." And that fits in nicely with the chorus's initial characterization of him as "letting his spirit go with the sudden blasts of fortune" (187). This excessive passion, which is his own, is the merciless infatuation that makes him reckless.

Agamemnon represents his passion as *themis*, as right in the eyes of heaven. But his claim receives no support in the play. It may be right to sacrifice Iphigenia—though we shall see reason to wonder even about this. But it isn't at all clear that it is right to be so enthusiastic about it, or for the enthusiasm to have the source we are about to discover it has. Indeed, the chorus unequivocally condemns Agamemnon's passion as "impure" and "unholy," and describes its effects in terms that leave no doubt at all that their words are wholly appropriate:

And her prayers and cries of "Father!"
and her maiden years they let go for nothing,
those arbiters eager for battle;
and her father told his servants after a prayer
to lift her face downwards like a goat above the altar,
as she fell about his robes to implore him with all her heart,
and by gagging her lovely mouth
to stifle a cry
that would have brought a curse upon his house;
using violence, and the bridle's stifling power. (228–37)

Even in this somewhat deflationary translation it is a brutal scene.

Why are the allies so eager to be off to Troy, so eager that they have a "passion exceeding passion" to sacrifice Iphigenia in order to do it? The official reason is to punish Troy for offending against the Zeus-supported laws of guest-friendship by condoning Paris's abduction of Helen. But the desire for justice is not usually so passionate, so willing to stop at nothing (not even more injustice), as that. We must suspect that it is cover for another motive. What could that be? Clytemnestra, in a speech we shall look at further on, suggests one: the love of gain. The allies are so eager because they have their eyes on Troy's wealth. (This doesn't mean, of course, that they don't have the motive of justice at all, only that it gets much of its force and heat from the motive of gain.)

Agamemnon's destruction of Troy raises similar issues. In her second long speech to the chorus, Clytemnestra warns about the consequences for Agamemnon and the allies if they have been overzealous:

> If they reverence the city-keeping gods
> of the conquered land and the divinities' abodes,
> then the conquerors shall not be conquered in their turn.
> But may no longing (*erōs*) first come on the army
> to ravage what they should not ravage, vanquished by love of gain!
> For they still need to win their way safe home,
> to round in due course the second bend of the racecourse.
> And even if the army should return without offense against the gods,
> the agony of the dead might awaken;
> may it wreak no sudden havoc. (338–47)

A little later we learn from Agamemnon's herald that Clytemnestra's worst fears (or best hopes) have been fulfilled, and that heaven has already been moved to wrath:

> and now with . . .
> honor welcome the king after long lapse of time.
> For he is come, bringing light in darkness to you
> and to all present here together, the lord Agamemnon.
> Come, give him good greeting, for it is proper,
> him who has uprooted Troy with the mattock of Zeus who does justice
> with which the soil has been worked over.
> And the altars and the seats of the gods are vanished,
> and the seed is perishing from all that land . . .
> how shall I mix good with bad, telling
> of the storm that afflicted the Achaeans, not without the wrath of heaven?
> (520–649)

Later still, Agamemnon himself describes what he has done to Troy, and justifies it as the will of Zeus.

> First Argos and the gods of the land,
> it is right that I address,
> they that have a share in
> my safe return and in the satisfaction exacted
> from Priam's city. For by no spoken word the gods

heard their parties' pleas, and in no uncertain fashion
their votes for the death of men and the ruin of Ilium
they put into the urn of blood; and to the opposite vessel
hope of a hand approached, but the vessel was not filled.
And even now the smoke marks out the conquered city.
Destruction's storms have life; and dying with the city
the embers waft forth rich breaths of wealth.
For this must the gods with very mindful gratitude
be paid, since their arrogant rapine
has been avenged, and for a woman's sake
their city has been ground to the dust by the Argive monster,
the offspring of a horse, the shield-bearing army,
which launched its leap as the Pleiads set. (810–26)[4]

Like his earlier description of the sacrifice of Iphigenia, we know that this one goes too far. It is fairly certainly the will of Zeus that Troy fall. But it is not his will that it be raped, its altars and seats of the gods destroyed. "On him who is gentle in the use of power," Agamemnon himself tells us a little later, "the god from afar looks favorably" (951–52).

Just as in Argos, then, we have Agamemnon's sacrifice of Iphigenia, and his subsequent immoderate treatment of Troy, represented as a failure of judgment or virtue to withstand desire. Hence, the appropriateness of the chorus's great ode, which immediately precedes their description of the sacrifice of Iphigenia:

But he who gladly sings the triumph of Zeus
shall hit full on the target of understanding (*phrenōn*):
of Zeus who put men on the way to wisdom (*phronein*)
by making it a valid law
that by suffering they shall learn (*pathei mathos*).
There drips before the heart instead of sleep
pain that reminds them of their wounds;
and against their will there comes discretion (*sōphronein*). (174–81)

The wise man, it is implied, understands that injustice is not to be done; the foolish man, who fails to understand this ahead of time, will learn when disaster teaches him.

At Aulis, but not at Argos, it might be responded, Agamemnon faces a moral dilemma: he is caught between the conflicting demands of Zeus and Artemis, with no way out. He must defeat Troy. Zeus has ordered it. So he must get Artemis to release his becalmed fleet. So he must sacrifice Iphigenia. Though this is a common view, it would be surprising if it were correct, since it would seriously disrupt the parallels between what Agamemnon does at Aulis, what he does at Troy, and what he does at Argos that so much else in the play strives to establish. And, in fact, there are independent grounds for thinking it is not correct.

A person caught between an apparently fated rock and an ethically hard place is certainly in a bad situation. But Agamemnon should not be seen in quite that light. When Clytemnestra is trying to persuade him to show his true colors by walking on the embroideries, he tells her that he would walk on them "if any with sure knowledge had prescribed this ritual." We are bound to be reminded—and are surely intended to be—of the prophet Calchas and his prescription of the ritual sacrifice of Iphigenia as what alone will free the fleet. Agamemnon accepts Calchas's prescription without demurral, and we are apt to do the same. But a puzzling remark of the chorus's should give us pause. They characterize Agamemnon as "blaming no prophet (*mantin outina psegōn*)" (186). The clear suggestion—to put it no stronger than that—is that this was something he could and perhaps should have done.

That he could have done it—could have done it, that is to say, without putting himself in the wrong or violating any social or religious norms—is clear from *Iliad* 24. There Priam tells his wife Hecuba how he might have responded to the suggestion that he try to ransom back the body of Hector from Achilles, had the messenger been a human being instead of the goddess Iris:

If it had been some other who ordered me, one of the mortals,
one of those who are prophets (*manties*), or priests, or diviners,
I might have called it a lie and we might rather have rejected it. (220–22)[5]

And this, in turn, forces us to ask why Agamemnon did not do what it was open to him to do. Why didn't he call it a lie and explore other options? Why didn't he send to Delphi for advice? We already know the chorus's answer. His judgment was overcome by a passion exceeding passion for Troy's "rich breaths of wealth." If their answer is right, there was no dilemma, just an apparent failure in virtue or judgment caused by greed.

It is possible that I have put too much weight on the three words of line 186. So let us leave them aside. Let us suppose that there was no third course of action open to Agamemnon, that he really had to kill Iphigenia or disobey Zeus. Nonetheless, I still think he would be culpable not just for killing Iphigenia in so brutal a fashion, or for thinking that the passions that provoked him to that brutality were just, but for putting her to death *simpliciter*. Even if he had done it gently, full of remorse or regret, he would still have been fully culpable for doing it at all.

The sacrifice of Iphigenia is required to assuage the fleet-becalming anger of Artemis. But her anger is obviously proleptic or forward looking. She is angry not because some eagles have killed a pregnant hare—that way lies lunacy—but because of what Agamemnon *will do* in Troy, something that is *symbolized* by what the eagles have already done to the hare (109–39). So she vents her anger by arranging a situation that will expose to view the very trait of his character that will be responsible for his treatment of Troy. Hence, if Agamemnon hadn't been a man like that—a man whose judgment can be overcome by his passion—he wouldn't have aroused the proleptic anger of Artemis by his (then) future rape of Troy, he wouldn't be in the situation of having to choose between his daughter and Troy, and he wouldn't have had to sacrifice his daughter. Thus the situation in which he finds himself results from his own character and future actions, not simply from things outside his character that are the result of luck.

Throughout the play, indeed, Agamemnon is portrayed as someone whose judgment—whose moderation, good sense, or *sophrosunē*—is overcome not just by extraordinary pressures of the sort that only heroic or philosophic virtue could withstand, but by relatively ordinary ones. Perhaps (just perhaps) only a philosopher-king or Stoic sage could have dealt well with what happened in Aulis, but in Argos, in facing Clytemnestra and her symbolic embroideries, a normally virtuous person—a person with normal good judgment—could surely have done better.

Agamemnon apparently stands condemned, then, not as an exemplar of the vulnerability of mature virtue to frontal assaults by luck, but as someone of inadequate virtue. If we simply stop there, however, we ignore something important—we isolate Agamemnon from the "house of the Atreidae," mentioned significantly in the play's opening lines (1–3), and from the workings of a fate in which all in that house are embroiled. In the following insightful passage, Jean-Pierre Vernant describes the consequent effects on deliberation and planning:

> In the tragic perspective, acting, being an agent, has a double character. On the one side it consists in taking council with oneself, weighing the for and against and doing the best one can to foresee the order of means and ends. On the other hand, it is to make a bet on the unknown and the incomprehensible and to take a risk on a terrain that remains impenetrable to you. It involves entering the play of supernatural forces . . . where one does not know whether they are preparing success or disaster.[6]

But it matters, too, that one is so embroiled even before one's birth, that one's very ancestry—one's genetic inheritance as we would say—and one's early character-shaping upbringing also depend on the play of such forces. Luck, in that larger sense, has attacked Agamemnon's virtue from the rear before *he* was even on the scene. The house of the Atreidae, we know, was not a healthy home environment for a child! Men like Agamemnon are born and made in such homes.

Antigone

Prone as we are to seeing vulnerability to luck as a bad thing, we are prone, too, to imagining strategies for reducing it. One such strategy is minimalism: make yourself a smaller target by caring about fewer things, by making your happiness depend on less. In an extreme form, which recognizes only what a rational agent can control as truly valuable, this is the strategy a Stoic (or, in the special case of moral value, a Kantian) recommends. Maximalism is a matter of eliminating luck as much as possible by extending one's own—or reason's—control. As Aristotle puts it in *Magna Moralia*: "Where there is most understanding (*nous*) and reason (*logos*) there is the least luck, and where there is the most luck there is the least understanding" (1207a4–6). Plato's *Republic* might serve (cautiously) as a blueprint. There selective breeding, dismantling of family structure, appropriate education and training, rule by virtuous kings with secure knowledge of the good, control by temperate and courageous soldier-police (guardians), give as much immunity to luck as one can imagine—though far from complete immunity (545c ff.).

In Sophocles' *Antigone*, Creon can readily be represented as either an aspiring minimalist or an aspiring maximalist. If we imagine him as pruning his set of commitments so as to eliminate those arising from family, we see him as the former. But if we see him focusing on his political commitments, we can just as easily see him as the latter:

> Whoever places a friend (*philon*)
> Above the good of his own country (*patras*), he is nothing:
> I have no use for him. Zeus my witness,
> Zeus who sees all things, always—
> I could never stand by silent, watching destruction
> March against our city, putting safety to rout,
> Nor could I ever make a man a friend of mine
> Who menaces our country. Remember this:
> Our country *is* our safety.
> Only while she voyages true on course
> Can we establish friendships, truer than blood itself.
> Such are my standards. They make our city great. (182–91)[7]

The city—and only it—keeps us safe from luck. No friendships—no bonds of family—can be secure outside it. Pruning of commitments isn't the issue now, but control and an awareness—akin to the *Republic*'s—that its scope must extend to something larger and closer to self-sufficiency than the household.

In the theater, as in real life, however, we need to distinguish between what people say or believe their values or commitments are and what they actually are. We also need to distinguish between what people say or believe their values are in certain situations—for example, when a strong emotion has been aroused—from what they say or believe when they are calm. It is these thoughts, among many others, of course, that the *Antigone* urges us to mobilize—not just in the case of Creon, on whom I shall focus, but in that of Antigone herself. And once they are mobilized, minimalism and maximalism emerge more as protective fantasies than effective strategies.

I begin by putting together three suggestive passages. In (a) and (b), Creon is the sole speaker; in (c), Haemon also speaks:

(a)
I am not the man, not now: she is the man
if this victory goes to her and she goes free. (484–85)
. . . while I'm alive,
no woman is going to lord it (*arzei*) over me. (525)
From now on they'll act like women. (578–79)

(b)
Oh Haemon,
Never lose your sense of judgment (*tas phrenas*) over a woman.
The warmth the rush of pleasure, it all goes cold
in your arms, I warn you . . . a worthless woman (*gunē kakē*)
in your house, a misery in your bed.
What wound cuts deeper than a loved one
turned against you (*philos kakos*)? Spit her out,
like a mortal enemy—let the girl go.
Let her find a husband down among the dead. (648–54)

(c)
Creon: [*To Haemon.*] Better to fall from power, if fall we must,
at the hands of a man—never be rated
inferior to a woman, never. (679–80) . . .
Creon: [*To the Chorus.*] This boy, I do believe,
is fighting on her side, the woman's side.
Haemon: If you are a woman, yes—
My concern is all for you.
Creon: Why you degenerate (*pangkakiste*)—bandying accusations,
threatening me with justice, your own father! (740–42) . . .
Creon: Don't flatter me with Father—you woman's slave. (756)

The passages listed under (a), surprising in themselves, lead up to (b) and prepare us for it. The passage in (b) is complex—ironical, too, because Creon himself is losing his judgment over a woman—and needs careful analysis. The three passages in (c) shows us how deep-seated Creon's feelings are.

In (a), Creon might seem to be speaking with the voice of experience, so that the pathology we see in operation in it—but more explicitly in (b)—must be taken to be rooted in his own sexual life with Eurydice: he abandoned his family and turned to the state because he found home life cold. But this way of thinking forces us to ask why he found it cold. Was it just that he picked a bad wife? The difficulty of answering that question in a promising way gives us an incentive to turn in a different direction. Creon sees Antigone as a bad wife because she disobeys him (*him*, the exemplar of reason), and because he sees a good and loving wife as necessarily an obedient one. This throws us back on *his* character.

Creon explicitly connects his role in the family with his role in the state:

Show me the man who rules his household well:
I'll show you someone fit to rule the state. (661–62)

Since there is pathology in operation in his role as husband and father, we would expect it to carry over into his political role too. It is useful, therefore, to hear Creon's remarks about the city as if they are remarks about the household or family, and vice versa. In the speech in which we first meet him, he says:

Of course you cannot know a man completely,
his character (*psuchēn*), his principles (*phronēma*), sense of judgment
   (*gnomēn*),
not till he's shown his colors, ruling the people,
making laws. Experience, there's the test.
As I see it, whoever assumes the task of setting the city's course,
and refuses to adopt the soundest policies (*aristōn bouleumatōn*)
but fearing someone (*ek phobou*), keeps his lips locked tight,
he's utterly worthless (*kakistos*). So I rate him now,
I always have. And whoever places a friend
above the good of his own country, he is nothing. (175–83)

Like many politicians, Creon speaks in favor of character, principles, judgment (compare Agamemnon), and of action as their test, and is contemptuous of weakness of will or judgment. When you've reached the best decision, he says, you shouldn't abandon it out of fear. That may seem reasonable enough. But it soon becomes clear that he means something by it that isn't reasonable at all, namely, that when *he* has made up his mind, that must be the best decision. If he were subsequently to abandon it, that couldn't be because he had been persuaded rightly that a different one is better, but only because of some weakness.

In this strange idea both pathology and argument intertwine. A husband in a traditional Greek family might feel that his judgment is the important one, since the others in the family are women, children, and slaves:

> So,
> Men our age, we're to be lectured are we?—
> schooled by a boy his age. (726–27)

Hence he might with *some* justification think that his judgment alone had genuine authority, and that its blind acceptance by his family was an example of reason in action:

> Are you coming now, raving against your father?
> Or do you love me no matter what I do? (633–34)

It doesn't take much to see how dangerous it would be to transfer this line of thought from the domestic to the political sphere (see 736–39). But even in the domestic one, it has its problems. For one thing, it results in the enforced infantilism of the children, as we see in the case of Haemon, who is denied any judgment of his own. Obviously, it isn't good to grow up as the child of such a father. But there are also other less obvious consequences. A father whose judgment is absolute condemns his wife to fear, and frightened wives are, no doubt, cold comfort.[8] Herein may lie an explanation of why Creon thinks it is particularly *fear* that causes people to abandon their judgment: it is fear that makes them accept his.

A little later in the same opening speech, we learn what, in the case of the burial of Polynices, that judgment is:

> But as for his blood brother, Polynices,
> who returned from exile, home to his father-city
> and the gods of his race, consumed with one desire—
> to burn them roof to roots—who thirsted to drink
> his kinsmen's blood and sell the rest to slavery:
> that man—a proclamation has forbidden the city
> to dignify him with burial, mourn him at all.
> No, he must be left unburied, his corpse
> carrion for the birds and dogs to tear,
> and obscenity for the citizens to behold.
> These are my principles. (198–206)

That the judgment is harsh, we see at once. But why? Creon's principles do not tell us, anymore than Antigone's principles tell us why she buried Polynices—her famously confused speech as she is herself about to be buried alive attests to that (904–14). As far as principles are concerned, Creon could simply have had the body buried without civic honor outside Theban territory. One suspects, therefore, that the harshness has another source. And a plausible one is suggested in (b): "What wound cuts deeper than a loved one turned against you"—a bad loved one (*philos kakos*)? Polynices is Creon's *philos*, after all, the son of his sister Jocasta.

Creon overreacts to Polynices' attack on Thebes; he overreacts to Antigone's disobedience; he overreacts to Haemon's initially very diplomatic attempts to get him to change his verdict on Antigone. This pattern of overreaction to disobedience in family members,[9] I have tried to suggest, is a symptom of an underlying pathology that produces powerful feelings. It is no surprise, therefore, that when passion cools, when the anger produced by disobedience interpreted as a failure of love has subsided, Creon has second thoughts. "It's a dreadful thing to yield" (1096–97). But yield he does. It is no surprise, either, that when he discovers what his passion has done, he finds all too alive within him the very commitments and loves it hid from him. With his wife and child dead as a result of his own "stupidity," his own bad judgments (*dusbouliais*; 1269), the joy of his life is gone (1275) and he has become "nothing" (1325; cf. 183), a "living corpse" (1167).

When we meet Creon, he has been thwarted. A precipitating event (Antigone's burial of Polynices) has aroused a passion that reveals itself in a distortion of judgment and speech. He is brought to say things the play reveals he does not mean. This is the chorus's diagnosis. In the ode immediately before Haemon arrives to try to change his father's mind, they sing:

Blest, they are the truly blest who all their lives
Have never tasted devastation. For others, once
The gods have rocked a house to its foundations
The ruin will never cease, cresting on and on
From one generation on throughout the race—
Like a great mounting tide . . .
And now the light, the hope
Springing up from the late last root
In the house of Oedipus, that hope's cut down in turn
By the long, bloody knife swung by the gods of death
By a senseless word (*logou t'anoia*)
By fury in the heart (*phrenōn Erinus*). (582–603)

To be sure, they also see the hand of Zeus in all of this:

Zeus,
Yours is the power, Zeus, what man on earth
Can override it, who can hold it back? (604–05)

But whether divine plan or fate or just blind luck, the fact remains that the house of Oedipus (and so of Jocasta and Creon), in which Creon's character was forged and his emotions shaped, has left him vulnerable not, of course, to just anything, but to the unlucky situation in which he finds himself, where it is the opposition of members of his own family that he, as political ruler, must everywhere confront.

Conclusion

None of the ancient writers I have discussed focuses on the vulnerability of virtue to head-on attack by luck. In part this is because the latter tends simply to measure or diagnose virtue's degree or quality: to be undone by *that* amount of fear or danger shows not that one's courage is vulnerable, but that it is weak or, anyway, unheroic. Nor does any of these writers make a positive virtue of virtue's vulnerability to less direct attacks. We are not better off because our virtue is in various ways fragile, though we may be curiously noble, curiously interesting: divine wisdom is something enviable in part just because it is invulnerable. The causal web in which we are enmeshed, and of which we are largely ignorant, stretches backward and forward in time. It makes us, affects what we do, and, try as we may, breaks us. We don't any of us get out of it alive. Yet the *Antigone*'s great choral ode on man is more optimistic than the play itself, or than the *Agamemnon* or *Nemean* 8, in claiming that "from Death alone will man find no escape" (351–52). There is no real escape from luck either, from the vast play of forces. Learning so is itself a bit of—tragic—wisdom.

Notes

I am grateful to William Wians, Patrick Miller, and Richard Kraut for their very helpful comments.

1. M. C. Nussbaum, *The Fragility of Goodness* (Cambridge: Cambridge University Press, 1986; revised edition 2001).

2. Translations are based on C. M. Bowra, *The Odes of Pindar* (Harmondsworth: Penguin Books, 1969); Richmond Lattimore, *The Odes of Pindar* (Chicago: University of Chicago Press, 1947); and John Sandys, *Pindar* (Cambridge: Loeb Classical Library, 1937).

3. Translations are from Hugh Lloyd-Jones, *Aeschylus: Oresteia* (London: Duckworth, 1979).

4. Note the "rich breaths of wealth."

5. Richmond Lattimore, *The Iliad of Homer* (Chicago: University of Chicago Press, 1951). Cf. 1.106–08, 12. 237–43. The powerful feeling created in the play that no one reliably knows the will of Zeus is also no doubt relevant here.

6. Quoted and translated by Bernard Williams, *Shame and Necessity* (Berkeley and Los Angeles: University of California Press, 1993), 19, who comments: "In this

passage, one might be left with a fairly lively sense of tragic if one merely deleted the word 'supernatural.' "

7. Translations are from Robert Fagles, *Sophocles: The Three Theban Plays* (Harmondsworth: Penguin Books, 1982).

8. Naguib Mafouz, *The Palace Walk* (New York: Doubleday, 1990), is in part a meditation on this fact.

9. Since Creon identifies the state with the family, he also overreacts to disobedience in citizens—witness his treatment of the sentry (304ff.), the chorus (280ff.), and Tiresias (988ff.).

11

Sophocles' Humanism

Paul Woodruff

The invention of the human, says Harold Bloom, is due to Shakespeare.[1] He means that the Bard invented a certain way of showing personality in his characters, and that Shakespeare's has become the modern way of representing human beings in fiction. Bloom does not define personality, and he says all too little about the alternatives—about what it is to depict people as more or less than human. He leaves those of us who are not as self-centered as Bloom's favorite personalities—Hamlet or Falstaff—to wonder whether we are capable of being seen as human at all.

I would prefer to give first credit to the poet who wrote of Hector, the tamer of horses—the warrior hero who lives at home, who fights for his people, who takes affectionate leave from wife and child, who will be mourned by mother and father. Hector is not divine; he makes mistakes and will die. But he is a thoroughly human character, unlike Achilles, who has a goddess for a mother and lives in a temporary shelter with his warrior friend and a stolen woman, likening himself on an especially brutal occasion to a wolf.[2] Gods live on Olympus, beasts roam or bed down in dens, but Hector is at home in a city. And, to poet and audience alike, Hector is a foreigner, released from cultural boundaries by the poet's imagination. True, this imagination makes the Trojan warrior Greek, but it is plainly reaching for what is universally human, the city dweller who is neither a wild animal nor an even wilder god. The inventor of the human (in the European tradition) wrote the *Iliad*.

After Homer, Sophocles. Sophocles is the first writer of the European tradition to pick out human action as his subject and to keep it distinct from the divine. Unlike Aeschylus and Euripides, Sophocles does not surrender his plots to divine intervention. The human world rarely connects with the divine one at the level of human understanding.[3] This is the more remarkable because Sophocles—unlike some of his more up-to-date contemporaries—welcomes the idea that gods are everywhere in human events.[4]

Reverent Humanism

As a religious humanist, Sophocles is bracketed on the religious side by Euripides, whose plays show gods actively engaged in developing their plots,[5] and on the humanist side by Thucydides, who explains the course of history through a kind of social science, in terms of universal human drives and desires.[6] Thucydides is truly a godless writer (as we shall see), but Sophocles is godly.

The thesis of this chapter is that Sophocles—more than other poets of his day—writes from a humanistic understanding of human action. For every action he puts on his stage he shows a human cause. For example, Deianeira (the faithful old wife) decides to try to recover her husband's love from his new trophy wife, even though she understands how a new passion can seize a man. When she asks (line 546), "Who'd share her own marriage?" we in the audience agree that even a generous-minded woman would probably feel as she does, and this feeling of hers (not the deep-laid plan of Zeus) drives what we see of the plot. Action in Sophocles falls consistently (though implicitly) under the kinds of generalizations Aristotle requires of a good plot.[7]

Sophocles nevertheless shows almost nothing but the fruition of divine plans foretold in oracles. His characters are convinced that the causes of human calamity are gods who have been offended by human arrogance. What these characters say is not the same as what Sophocles shows, however. None of his surviving plays uses a *deus ex machina* to resolve a plot, and the divine events to which the plays refer take place before or after the staged action of the drama.[8] Sophocles occupies an uneasy position between the new humanism of the sophists and traditional beliefs about the gods.

Sophocles' humanism, then, is a reverent humanism. Hyllus may well be speaking for his author when he concludes the *Women of Trachis* with these lines:

> You have seen majesty in death, and novelty,
> Much suffering, and suffering in new forms,
> And nothing in this is not Zeus. (*Trach.* 1276–78)[9]

On the other hand, when Athena herself is asked the cause of Ajax's insane rage against his commanders, she does not claim credit, but assigns it to a human cause:

> Odysseus: So why was he so irrational in his assault?
> Athena: He was unbalanced by his anger . . . (*Ajax* 40–41)

The most striking evidence of humanist influence on Sophocles is often referred to as the "Ode to Man":[10]

Many wonders, many terrors,
But none more wonderful than the human race,
  Or more dangerous. (*Antig.* 332–34)

And why are we humans dangerous? Because in this choral ode human beings
are given the role traditionally assigned by this myth to Prometheus. Navigation,
agriculture, building shelters and wearing clothes, hunting and fishing, domesticat-
ing animals, using language, living in cities, curing illnesses—all these arts human
beings have taught themselves:

These he has taught himself
. . .
He has the means to handle every need,
Never steps towards the future without the means. (*Antig.* 356, 360–61)

This was probably not altogether a new idea when Sophocles wrote the play around
442; earlier anthropologists had already been working out such explanations for
the origins of society and human technology.[11] Still, it is a new idea, and a godless
one, though the ode containing it ends with a warning to those who disregard the
law of the land and the justice of the gods:[12]

If he honors the law of the land
And the oath-bound justice of the gods,
Then his city shall stand high.
But no city for him if he turns shameless, out of daring . . . (*Antig.* 369–
  72)

In the *Prometheus Bound* (*PV*), probably by Aeschylus and highly likely to be an
earlier text than *Antigone*, Prometheus makes the following famous claim, reflecting the traditional idea that human beings could never have invented the arts for
themselves: "All mortal skills come from Prometheus,"[13] he says, after listing many
of the arts that will appear as human inventions in Sophocles' "Ode to Man." In
Aeschylus, the arts have a supernatural origin; not so in Sophocles' chorus.[14]
    This choral passage in the *Antigone* shows that Sophocles was aware of the
new godless anthropology, but it does not license us to suppose that Sophocles
adopted such a theory as his own. Some choruses may speak for the playwright, but
a Sophoclean chorus acts so often as participating in the drama, given to error and
contradiction and the changing of minds, that we have no good way of knowing
when the chorus really gives its own considered opinion, let alone their author's.[15]
My case will rest not on this but on Sophocles' construction of plot.

Learning from Plot Construction

All playwrights construct speeches that are opposed to one another, and ancient Greek audiences apparently delighted in set-piece debates. Sophocles often writes opposed speeches, and since he does not write in his own persona, he does not reveal himself directly to his audience. Perhaps one character or another speaks for him, but how are we to know which are the ones who do so? Some readers have thought that his choruses speak for him, but that can't be right.

In only one way does Sophocles disclose himself: in his selection and arrangement of events to be enacted on stage. Epic poets and other playwrights use the same material; Sophocles uses it differently. From the differences we may learn something about the mind of the author. No other method is defensible, I think. And yet even this gives limited results. Consider an example:

The *Ajax* limits Athena's intervention sharply; all she does in this play is to divert Ajax by madness from killing the commanders of the Greek army, and then to "make sport" of him afterward.[16] His murderous rage, his refusal to submit to authority, his choice of suicide over dishonor—these all come from him while he is in his senses, and not from the goddess, or even from him in the madness that the goddess sent him. His actions are easy to understand in human terms, as flowing in predictable ways from his combination of character and circumstance. He is powerful, violent, self-absorbed, and brilliantly successful for most of his life; now he has fallen into a shamefully ridiculous situation. Such men in such circumstances are likely to prefer self-destruction to submission. No goddess need apply to bring about a catastrophe.

What conclusions may we draw from this about Sophocles? Reinhardt rightly infers from similar evidence that Sophocles thinks "the causes of human suffering are human"—although Reinhardt assigns this view only to the Sophocles of plays he thinks were written long after the *Ajax*.[17] But we would like to know more: Does Sophocles restrict the role of Athena because, like Thucydides, he believes that there are repeatable patterns in human action, and that these are sufficient to explain human outcomes? Or does Sophocles restrict her role because he has found that showing purely human action makes for more powerful theater? Both are probably true: Sophocles learned to study human causes of human behavior from the early humanist anthropologists (as we learn from the "Ode to Man"); and he learned in the school of theater that the most compelling scenes are those that seem to emerge naturally from character and circumstance—and not supernaturally from divine intervention. Sophoclean theater is powerful because of its focus on human action. He is too good a playwright to dampen the emotional impact of a scene by letting his protagonist be seen as a victim.[18]

We have seen that Sophocles apparently rejects the Prometheus myth. We shall see that he does not commit himself in the *Electra* to the story that Apollo commanded the death of Clytemnestra. Would he deny other traditional stories about the supernatural?[19] He could have done so on humanist theoretical grounds. He could also have done so out of a strong sense of reverence that divided the divine world from the human.[20]

My method cannot answer that sort of question. We will never know for sure why Sophocles does what he does. To make matters worse, we will never know all that he did, since we have only seven of the one hundred twenty or so plays he wrote. Our sample may represent a principle of selection for a Hellenistic textbook, rather than the general principles of Sophocles' dramaturgy.

What Sophocles does as a playwright in the surviving plays, however, in contrast to what epic poets and other playwrights have done with the same material—that we can study, with interesting results. To study plot construction as such we must exclude elements that do not belong strictly to the plot—that is, elements that are not part of the sequence of events that is shown on stage. Here are two elements I believe we should exclude:

First, the characters' own interpretations of events in assessing plot construction. We are shown that Haemon repudiates his father; the chorus thinks Aphrodite is the cause, but we do not know whom Sophocles holds responsible for the event. The development of the scene suggests that other causes move Haemon, besides love, and that one of them is Creon's insult.

Second, the larger background of myth, known to the audience from other sources. Much of what we associate with Sophocles' characters happens outside the plots of his plays—the curse on Oedipus's father, for example, is outside the plot. That curse may be quietly at work behind the scenes, but we are unaware of it for the duration of the play, and it does not directly affect what we see in any scene. The curse that actually animates the plot is the one Oedipus calls down—during the play—on the killer of Laius, not the one that came from the gods.[21]

I do not exclude offstage events that belong to the plot and are reported by messengers as occurring during the sequence of staged actions. Oedipus's self-blinding happens offstage, of course, but it is an essential part of the plot, because it affects subsequent scenes: we will see him return with blood streaming from his eyes.

These distinctions are essential to understanding the limited role gods have in the stories Sophocles uses. Most of the divine interventions, relating to his material and known through myth, are outside the plots of his plays, though some, like the voice of the god in *Oedipus at Colonus* (*OC*), are merely off stage. Gods may take larger parts in plays known to us only through fragments, but in the absence of complete texts we cannot deliver a verdict on those plays.

The method I propose is to look at the structure of events Sophocles either shows on stage or includes in the plot as contemporaneously affecting the events on stage. These events consist mainly of actions, as we shall see. The very concept of action in theater implies human or humanlike agency. To see an event as an action is to see it as arising from human choice.[22]

Godly Theater

Godly narrative begins with Homer, who engages the gods to break particular helmet straps, or to direct particular heroes the wrong way for safety, showing gods in workmanlike behavior, taking anthropomorphic roles. Sophocles never uses such a story in the plot of what he shows on stage. It would not have been reverent for him to narrow the gap in this way between the human and divine.

Theater may be godly in more stage-appropriate ways than is Homeric narrative. It may approach the subject of the gods with reverence, as Sophoclean theater does. Or it may show kinds of scenes that Sophocles avoids—epiphany and intervention. By "epiphanic theater" I mean theater that aims to make a divine power present in performance—literally present and not through mimesis. The Christian Mass, in which God comes to be in bread and wine, through transubstantiation, is a paradigm of epiphanic theater. Many cultures use dance to try to make a divine power present in one of the performers; such dances are known to achieve a kind of possession. Ancient Greek theater may have aimed at epiphany in certain scenes; audiences may have thought they felt the presence of Dionysus during the parodos of the *Bacchae*, for example, or at the terrible denouement.

Sophoclean theater is not epiphanic, however; Sophocles' choruses yearn for absent gods, and his scenes move an audience without giving them a sense that a god is suddenly now with them.

Intervention, by contrast, can be represented through mimesis. Writers of narrative or drama employ divine intervention when they show supernatural powers changing the course of events. A power is plainly supernatural when it knows what human beings cannot know or when it can achieve results denied to human beings. The *deus ex machina* in ancient Greek theater is represented as flying into the scene (human beings can't do that) and resolving a complicated plot by such moves as telling the future (which we can't know) or facing down other supernatural powers (which we can't do). Sophocles does not use such a device.

The traditional view, from which I think Sophocles has shifted, is that gods or other supernatural beings intervene directly to affect human events, and that their intervention is necessary to the outcome. A good example is the Promethean gift, laid out in detail in *PV* 439–506 (quoted in brief previously). This is a clear case of intervention because the following counterfactual is true according to the myth: Had Prometheus (or some other supernatural being) *not* given the arts to humankind, our ancestors would have had to make do without the arts, and would probably have perished. The story is that his gift saved the human race, and this story is not merely reported from outside the plot. It is essential to the plot as the immediate antecedent for the action. If this counterfactual were not true Prometheus would not have been punished:

> I dared to rescue mortals
> From destruction and an end in Hades.
> Therefore I am bowed down by these woes . . . (*PV* 235–37)[23]

Another good example of intervention is the crazed enthusiasm of the women of Thebes in Euripides' *Bacchae*, for which no explanation is offered other than the intervention of a vengeful god. We may imagine that Euripides has in mind a deeper psychological explanation, but the play does nothing to bring this possibility out, and we are left with the reasonable conclusion that if Dionysus had only stayed away from Greece, Pentheus would have enjoyed a peaceful reign, undisturbed by reports of his mother carrying on in the mountains with other women away from the sight of men.

In Sophocles, generally, we do not need to appeal to the gods to understand what happens.[24] News comes to Heracles' wife, in Sophocles' *Women of Trachis*, that her husband is on his way home after a great victory, bringing a trophy wife. She attributes the trophy wife to the influence of Eros; doing so gives her some comfort and allows herself, in her conscious mind at least, to exonerate her two-timing husband:

> And as for Love—anyone who challenges Him,
> To an exchange of blows, is out of his mind.
> Love rules by his own whim; he rules over gods,
> He rules over me. Why not over women who are like me?
> So if I blamed my husband for catching this disease
> I'd be a lunatic. And the same for her.
> What could she be responsible for, even along with him? (*Trach.* 441–47)

Is Heracles' trophy hunt due to a tyrant god or to a disease? Or is it simply due to love, the familiar human passion, which is like both a tyrant god and a disease? Surely no supernatural explanation is needed; successful men take trophy wives often enough.

Just so, in the case of Haemon in *Antigone*, the chorus blames the boy's rebellion on his infatuation, which they identify with Aphrodite. But that was Creon's idea—that Haemon has lost his wits by letting himself be ruled by a woman—and it is not obviously correct. In any case, this is love, and does not need to be understood as a god. A metaphor does not make an intervention—it only makes for better understanding.

Other cases are harder to place. When Dionysus in the *Bacchae* tempts Pentheus to put on woman's clothes, is this an intervention? Or is Dionysus releasing a desire that is already in Pentheus? We cannot say for sure. One of the delights of Euripides is that he leaves us swaying between supernatural and psychological explanations for events. We are not uncertain in Sophocles; the causes of human suffering are human, but the gods are behind the whole human story. For contrast, we should look in more detail at a totally ungodly form of humanism.

Thucydides: A Benchmark for Godless Writing

The sophists swam at the crest of one of several waves of new ideas that inundated Athenian intellectuals in the second half of the fifth century. The new medical thinkers were at the crest of another. Where were the poets? Though firmly anchored in the tradition that became literary with Homer, fifth-century Athenian poets were affected by the new learning. But of all the writers of surviving works who are not considered sophists, the one who most clearly reflects the new learning is Thucydides.

Because his subject is human events, Thucydides' history will serve me as a benchmark, and I will ask how closely other texts compare with it. Specifically, in Thucydides:

Concerning gods:

1. The gods do not intervene directly in human affairs. They are not part of the history.

2. Explanations of events (such as wars) or natural phenomena (such as plagues), if they may be given at all, do not refer to the gods. In some cases, such as plague, Thucydides prudently offers no theory, saying that it defied explanation, as indeed it did. He had no rational way to account for it and avoided speculation (2.50).

3. Divination is not reliable. Oracles can be interpreted to fit the events after the fact (2.54), and soothsayers can give fatal advice (5.103, 7.50).

Concerning human beings:

4. Human passions explain human actions, and human actions explain human reactions. For example, the Athenians took imperial control of the Delian league and expanded it into an empire because of fear, ambition, and greed; the Spartans and their allies launched preemptive war out of fear caused by Athenian expansion.

5. Human events fall into roughly repeating patterns.[25] To say that the patterns are "roughly repeating" is merely to paraphrase Thucydides' "will recur in the future, either in the same fashion or nearly so."

6. Good judgment depends on the cautious use of *eikos* (reasonable expectation) in paired arguments, because determinate knowledge of the future of human events is denied us. Oracles are worthless, and science cannot predict human events with certainty. Reasonable expectations must be honestly debated and vigorously tested, or they too will lead people astray.[26]

7. Sequences of human events are not governed by necessity, though people engaged in them may believe so. The Athenians felt compelled by necessity to run their league of states like a tyranny, and the Spartans felt compelled by fear to start a war rather than wait for arbitration. But both were wrong, as Thucydides shows through the use of foils: the Spartan league was not a tyranny, and not all Spartans felt the need to make war. The wise king Archidamus knew better.

8. Human events cannot be predicted with certainty because they are not determined by *anankē* or by a fixed human nature. Thucydides' patterns of history are empirical and hold only for the most part.[27]

In Sophocles, by contrast, gods do intervene from time to time in the larger myths from which he works. And oracles in Sophocles are always true. Often a plot turns on the question of how a character's chosen actions will fulfill an oracle—not whether. As for necessity, Sophocles, like Thucydides, shows through the behavior of foils that the main characters' actions are not necessary: similar characters in similar circumstances act otherwise.

Sophocles' Dramaturgy

Sophocles generally constructs a plot as Aristotle, later, would want a good playwright to do; we should not be surprised that he is Aristotle's prime example. Aristotle's advice on plot is excellent, I think, and it is to Sophocles' credit that he followed it long before it was presented. Coherent human action is what most captivates an audience, and coherent action is action that springs plausibly from character and circumstance.

Aristotle's advice on plot, however, has seemed to some modern critics to be incompatible with the godliness of all ancient theater, even Sophocles. Halliwell rightly remarks that Aristotle does not pay enough attention to the role of the gods in these plays. His criticism of Aristotle's *Poetics*, he says, depends

only on the fundamental proposition that the universe portrayed in all the Greek tragedies we know, including those which Aristotle himself cites most frequently, is one in which significant human action is never regarded as

PAUL WOODRUFF

wholly autonomous or independent of larger, non-human powers. By contrast with this, Aristotle's own understanding of dramatic action posits, it seems to me, nothing other than intrinsic and purely human criteria of plausibility and causal intelligibility.[28]

The argument of this chapter is that Sophocles was able to satisfy humanistic criteria without any disrespect for the background of divine sovereignty. He makes the particulars of human behavior explicable in human terms without displacing the larger explanation of all human events with reference to the gods. He is like a modern religious teacher of evolution, who shows the cause of each change, and then says, "but God is behind it all." But even this analogy fails: Sophocles' gods are closer to human events than that.

In Sophoclean theater, the characters act in ways that are understandable because they fit familiar patterns of human behavior. The actions are, almost always, *eikos*—in conformity with reasonable expectation. This does not mean that people always act in character, because Sophocles' people respond to each other, and they respond to events, more often than they simply play out certain traits. We may reasonably expect different kinds of behavior from the same person in different circumstances. Fresh from his tutorial with the devious Odysseus, truth-loving Neoptolemus tells a lie. It is not "in character" as we would say, but it is *eikos*.

If I am right about Sophocles' dramaturgy, sequences of events do not exhibit necessity (*eikos* is weaker than *anankē*),[29] and are not driven by fate or by the intrusive hands of the gods. We understand certain events around Oedipus as his actions, coming from him, precisely because they are *eikos* and not *anankē*. Make them necessary, and we, the audience, would begin to doubt that he is the agent.

I studied *Oedipus Tyrannus* (*OT*) in high school with a teacher who was marvelously helpful on other texts, but his account of *OT* was terribly wrong. He told us to imagine a hero walking blindfolded across the surface of a huge slab of Swiss cheese, falling into one hole after another, through no fault of his own. The hero would be as incapable of making choices or of taking action as is a small animal that has become the toy of a household cat. I can imagine a play written on this image (or a film made *of* the image), but I think it would be either very short or very boring, and if it were interesting, it would only be so for its *pathos*. Watching victims being victimized is dull sport, unless the villains take the foreground. The cat would be worth watching, but not the mouse.[30]

Sophocles' play is nothing like that. People who are attracted to such images of fate are mistaking the background myth for the play. Sophocles did not dramatize the background myth. In *OT*, Oedipus is in charge of the action of the play from the first scene till almost the last—and even then he is trying to stay in control. The action of the play concerns his assault on the mystery of the death of Laius, and nowhere in the play is there the slightest sign that a god or fate is directing the process. Everything Oedipus does is the sort of thing we would expect him to do—the grand promise, the magnificent curse, the hasty conclusions, unwarranted fears, sudden furies, and unrelenting curiosity. They all go together with the character we have heard about, who killed an old man in an episode of road rage, solved a mystery that had baffled the prophets, and seized an opportunity to rule a land that (he thought) was not his own. It all fits.

One couplet has suggested to some readers that the gods are at work. Tiresias responds with these words to threats from Oedipus:

> My fate will not fall because of you;
> Apollo will be sufficient, and he has it well in hand. (*OT* 376–77)

The plain meaning of this, as argued persuasively by Knox,[31] is that Tiresias, being a servant of Apollo, belongs to the god. Only the god—and never Oedipus—could bring him down. Long ago, however, the text was emended by Brunck, who switched the pronouns around to read, "It is not I who will cause your downfall...." On that reading, Tiresias is telling Oedipus (and the audience) that Apollo is in the process of bringing Oedipus down. In the immediate dramatic context, that seems to make sense, but it is a poor reading (though orthographically plausible). Generally one should make the best of a *difficilior lectio* (the harder reading) if sense can be made of it, as here. And in the broader context, the emended line makes no sense. At no point have we seen evidence of Apollo's hand in the events presented on stage. And, in the long run, Oedipus will not be brought low by anyone other than himself, certainly not by Apollo. He will soon blind himself and try to sentence himself to exile. He has already unwittingly cursed himself. He will never fall lower than he is at the moment of this exchange with Tiresias. Already a father-killer, already a man who has impregnated his own mother, he is beyond the human pale. But he does not yet know it. He will, by his own efforts, find this out. And then, much later, far from bringing him down, the gods will exalt him. On the emended reading, Tiresias is making a threat to Oedipus that we know is false.

Tiresias is always right, however, and so he cannot have meant to say that his god would bring Oedipus low. True, the oracle that Oedipus has already fulfilled came from Apollo; but the Greeks do not appear to believe that divine foreknowledge of an event causes that event. True again, the chorus prays to Zeus for the fulfillment of oracles (end of second stasimon). And perhaps they speak for Sophocles here. But by what means are the oracles to be fulfilled? The story as it is staged by Sophocles is the working out of a plausible pattern of events. It is, as the orators would say, *eikos*, that is, it fits reasonable expectation. Oedipus *would* find out his own story in a flurry of threats and curses.

Reinhardt has made a similar point about Creon in *Antigone*: it is like Creon to resist the truth, to spend time dithering, and to arrive too late to save his niece and his son from death. Reinhardt contrasts that with the "too late" scene in the *Ajax*; but of course that action really is very like Ajax. Why should we be surprised to see that the blunt hero of many battles falls on his sword, before his friends and loved ones can arrive to prevent it. They are not dilatory; he has always been precipitate.[32]

Sophocles' approach to dramaturgy makes for good theater. We care about Oedipus because he takes action, and we can understand him as taking action because his actions fit a reasonable pattern. We would not know what to make of him if he acted at random, and we would not much care for him if he had been taken over by a higher power and was being controlled like a TV by a laser-operated device. In that case, we would be more interested in the operator of the device than we would be in Oedipus (the character).

Generally, except in epiphanic theater, what we see on stage draws our attention to human actions, or representations of human actions, because these deserve our attention more than a sequence of events that are not actions. Actions require human agents, and agents must exercise some power of choice.[33]

Sophocles stages human events in natural patterns (as Thucydides does), but his way of doing this honors the gods. Sophocles leaves a place for the gods on the margins of his stories, not as specific activators of his plots, but as mysterious powers behind the scenes. These gods are more remote than Homer's or Euripides', but they inspire more awe.

The Unexpected in Sophocles

"Truly, everything is possible when the skill of a god is at work," says Odysseus about Athena's promise to prevent Ajax from seeing him (*Ajax* 86). And since the gods are always reported to be at work behind the scenes in Sophocles' plays, we would expect to see this often confirmed on stage. Strange things should happen. And if those things are strange enough, then they could not fit into a pattern of reasonable expectation. They would be "not *eikos*," and my account of Sophocles' dramaturgy would be wrong.

Indeed, the unexpected does happen often on Sophocles' stage, and it captivates us: plain-spoken, blunt Ajax tells a complicated lie to the woman who loves him; Neoptolemus, whose nature is to tell the truth, tells a whopper to Philoctetes; Oedipus at the height of his powers, justly proud of his skill at solving riddles, blows the most important case of his career; good-boy Haemon, the loyal son, spits at his father and goes after him with a sword; old, blind, lame Oedipus rises from his seat and leads a procession across rocky terrain.

These scenes are startling reminders that anything can happen on Sophocles' stage. Yet none of them shows the gods at work, and none of them defies reasonable expectation. In all but the last case, a reasonable human explanation stares us in the face. We are surprised because we had not expected a change to defeat our earlier expectation. It is reasonable to expect people to do extraordinary things when they are in extraordinary circumstances.

Ajax must lie in order to take his life, which he feels he must do in order to avoid dishonor; that fits his character, and it defeats the expectation that he always tell the truth. Neoptolemus's good nature has fallen prey to an unscrupulous teacher; such things happen to good youths in bad company. Oedipus's last riddle had an answer too painful for him to contemplate; some truths are. Haemon was stung by his father's insults and was transformed into a rebel; we've seen that sort of transformation in our own children. Sophocles does not labor these explanations, but he devises scenes that present them: we actually see Odysseus corrupting Neoptolemus, for example, and Creon goading his son into rebellion. These things happen on stage, and they happen without active intervention of the gods.

Only the last case—Oedipus's rising to guide the sighted into a sacred space—seems humanly impossible and therefore invites a supernatural explanation, but Sophocles does not give it. Only moments before the old man walked alone, we saw that he was helplessly dependent on his daughter to guide him; now we do not see what gives him the power. We, and the chorus, have recently heard thunder three times. We believe that Oedipus has heard more, but we do not know what he heard or how it enabled him to walk unaided. The miracle is a mystery. Later, when the god urges Oedipus to make no further delay, Oedipus is not the only one to hear it. But *we* do not hear it. The voice was heard only off stage.

The two hardest cases for my account are *Philoctetes* and *Women of Trachis*. At the end of the play named after him, Philoctetes changes his mind and decides to go back to war. He doesn't have to. Odysseus's plan to use a combination of deception and force has fallen through. At the last moment, however, Heracles appears and advises the two men to return to war. Some scholars take this as Sophocles' one known use of the *deus ex machina* to unravel a plot—a device he would have learned from Euripides. But where in this case is the supernatural power? Heracles does not know anything that the others do not already know. He does not do anything that others have not already done. He does not thunder or spray with lightning bolts. He says what has been said before. He is persuasive because Philoctetes trusts him as an old friend, and this trust arises from an earlier connection between them. After all, the bow Philoctetes carries came to him from Heracles. So we do not need the machine, we do not need the majesty and glory of the gods, we do not need their special powers. We need only a known and honored friend of Philoctetes. This is not, then, a normal use of Euripides' device; although we are witnessing the miracle of a dead man appearing to his friend, we do not see him appearing as a god, wielding divine power or exhibiting divine knowledge.[34]

Consider also that Heracles is played by the actor who played Odysseus, that his face is covered by a mask, and that we have (probably) already seen Odysseus disguised as a merchant, trying to hornswoggle our hero. Could it be that this Heracles is another of Odysseus's many wiles? We cannot rule it out, if Heracles is not brought in on a machine. In a recent production by Peter Meineck, the offstage voice of Heracles was taken by many in the audience as a trick of Odysseus.

Speaking of surprises, we must admit that Sophocles' world allows for magic. The extraordinary bow of Heracles seems to have magical powers, for example. And Deianeira believes that the love potion she prepares for her husband is magical. It is not really out of the ordinary, however, for it turns out to be the recycled poison that Heracles used to make his arrows toxic.

"In the *Trachinian Women* the humanist view of Sophocles as a dramatist of the emotions and of character meets its greatest stumbling block," writes the greatest Sophocles scholar of recent years, Charles Segal. Dark powers out of ancient myth surge through the plot. And yet the beauty of the play is the triumph of the human over the bestial, as Segal later points out.[35] Deianeira's motive is an intensely human combination of fear and jealousy. Heracles is stung by desire for a woman younger than his wife. That is not surprising in a hero; is it any more surprising that as he approaches death he furiously tries to take control over his own passing? And that, at the very end, he accepts his fate to the extent that he controls his beastlike outbursts of anger and pain?

Fulfilling Oracles

Oracles are huge in importance in the surviving plays of Sophocles. And yet they do not ever cause an event that Sophocles shows on stage. Sophocles evidently holds that the gods are able to know what human beings will do without depriving them of choice.

Still, the oracles must come true. The second stasimon (choral ode) of *Oedipus Tyrannus* concludes:

> No longer will I go in reverence
> To the sacred navel of the world—
> Not to Delphi, not to Abai,
> Or the temple at Olympia,
> If the words of god do not come true
> For all humanity to see.
> Ruler of all, O Zeus our lord,
> If that be your name, do not let this escape
> Your notice or your undying power:
> The word of god to Laius long ago
> Is withering, it is already lost.

Now Apollo's fame and honor die away,
And everything divine departs. (*OT* 896–910)

They need not pray for the outcome they want; Apollo's oracle is already true. The remaining action of the play concerns the human discovery of that truth, and the human reaction to this terrible knowledge.

Orestes follows an oracle like an instruction manual in *Electra*. Philoctetes learns, from Heracles' instructions, to take the action that allows him to fulfill an oracle. Ajax unwittingly fulfills an oracle. Oedipus, long before the staged action of *Oedipus Tyrannus*, was trying to not fulfill an oracle, but did so anyway—as if he could not help it.

In *Oedipus at Colonus*, the situation is the reverse. Oedipus knows what the oracle has said of his future—the burial at Colonus, the gift to Athens—and is determined to fulfill that oracle. But he is subjected to a series of temptations that might divert him from his predicted destiny—first on behalf of his city, and then on behalf of his family. He resists both temptations, but not because of the oracle.

The causes are before us: How could Oedipus be moved to save his city, when he knows that he has no city? He has never truly had a city at all; he left Corinth before becoming an adult citizen there, and he arrived at Thebes as a hero, never having been properly initiated into either place. And now the Thebans will not allow him inside their borders; they fear too greatly the pollution he carries. All they want is the protection he might offer *at* their border. It is no mystery or miracle that Oedipus sees through Creon on this point.

As for the temptation of family, represented by Polynices, Oedipus's resistance is easy enough to understand.[36] His sons have abdicated family responsibility, leaving him to the care of his daughter. Now they threaten to destroy both their family and their city by quarreling (and the quarrel is their fault).[37] Sophocles has changed the received story, according to which Oedipus's curse, pronounced much earlier than the action of the play, caused the quarrel between his sons. The change is one of many ways that Sophocles has made the story more human than the myth he had received.[38] We have known for a long time that Oedipus is a man capable of lethal anger, and now we see it again. His anger has run both ways across generations; long ago it killed his father, now it will kill his sons.

In resisting these temptations Oedipus knows he is fulfilling oracles, but he is still conscious of his own active power to refuse, made visual throughout the play by his defiance in sitting on, or at the edge of, sacred ground. On the positive side, he uses his powers of persuasion to bring over Theseus, and ultimately he will take the lead in the procession that leads to the oracle's fulfillment. All of this fits the pattern of Oedipus's life, though we are left to wonder how he has found—or been given—the ability to find his way at the end.

"And none of it is not Zeus"

Sophocles' was reverent. That is one of the few facts about his life that is attested on all sides, and not merely inferred from his plays. The ancient *Life* tells us he was "uniquely god-loved" (12), favored by Heracles, and held the priesthood of Halon. Other testimony tells us that he was the Athenian who welcomed Asclepius into Athens and was therefore revered in cult after his death under the title "Receiver."[39]

In his surviving plays the theme rises again and again to the surface: be reverent. Respect holy places, do not believe you can succeed without the gods, remember that men are born to die, fear the overconfidence that leads to blindness.[40] In the minds of Sophocles' characters and choruses—aside from heroes in their blind passions—the influence of the gods is felt everywhere, but especially when people have gone wrong. Creon at first seems to pin the blame on "some god" for Haemon's death, likening himself to a draft horse under the control of a more powerful being:

> Some god leapt full force onto my head
> And steered me onto a wild path, shaking my reins,
> And I have trampled joy with sharp hooves. (*Antig.* 1273–75)

But later, when responding to the report that his dying wife put the blame on him, he accepts her verdict:

> I'll never pin the blame on anyone else that's human.
> I was the one, I killed you, poor child.
> I did it. It is all true. (*Antig.* 1318–20)

Reinhardt writes: "It makes no difference whether he blames his own stupidity, or a god: here the daimon's work does as little to make Creon innocent as it does in *Oedipus Tyrannus* to make Oedipus guilty."[41] But if this is so, we have to ask what is the daimon's work in these plays. Sophocles does not tell us.

Charles Segal captures the point elegantly:

> In tragedy the violence that exists in our world is not only a divine power, a manifestation of Eros or Aphrodite or Zeus's will, as it is in archaic epic or lyric. It is a numinous power and simultaneously something within us; it is both a part of ourselves and a mysterious visitation of something beyond ourselves. . . . Sophocles is the great master of commingling these two ways of accounting for the violence and suffering in human life, internal and external, psychological and religious.[42]

Commingling of human and divine causes is nothing new in the Greek tradition; we find it in Homer, whose epic poetry makes the actions of the gods part of the story—without thereby detracting from the actions of his heroes, which are as good or as bad as they would be had no god intervened. The difference in Sophocles is that whatever the gods are doing behind the scenes is not part of the plot that is staged.

Sophocles is reverent, and he treats his gods reverently. Somehow, he believes, the gods' influence is everywhere, but he does not presume to show how it operates in particular cases. Sophocles' cautious and creative mind approaches the mystery and pulls back in silence.

Notes

This chapter was first presented as a paper at the conference on ancient philosophy at Princeton University, December 7, 2002. I am grateful for comments given me at that time by Alexander Nehamas, and for advice from the editor and readers for this volume.

1. Harold Bloom, *Shakespeare: The Invention of the Human* (New York: Riverhead Books, 1998). The title tells the tale with which I wish to quarrel. Bloom does concede that Sophocles is among our sources for "the idea . . . of the self as moral agent" (4), but he thinks Shakespeare first brought into literature the idea of the self as a personality that can change by reconceiving itself (xix). That is very well, but I disagree with him that this ability is central to being human.

2. Before their final battle, when Hector proposes that they make a pact for the winner to respect the loser's body, Achilles replies, "Hector, I can never forgive you. Don't speak to me of agreements; there are no oaths you can trust between lions and men; wolves and lambs can never have like minds," likening himself to lion and wolf (*Il.* 22.261–63).

3. "Sophocles' aim is not to mystify divine power as incomprehensible; rather, he explores what it means to be human and mortal in the interconnected world of gods, city, and nature"; Charles Segal, *Sophocles' Tragic World: Divinity, Nature, Society* (Cambridge: Harvard University Press, 1995), 15.

4. "And nothing in this is not Zeus"—last line of the *Women of Trachis*. See also Segal 1995, 5.

5. In the *Bacchae*, for example, he shows Dionysus in disguise as a human, working out his revenge, by causing people to take actions they would, apparently, not otherwise take. Philosophers were critical of the *deus ex machina* (Plato, *Cratylus* 425d; Aristotle, *Poetics* 15.)

6. See further on, and also C. D. C. Reeve, "Thucydides on Human Nature," *Political Theory* 27 (1999), 435–46.

7. Such generalizations are defeasible, as we would say: people of a certain kind behave in a certain way, unless a change in circumstances explains the exception, thus defeating the generalization. Aristotle says such generalizations fall under *eikos*, which means "reasonable expectation" or "probability"; Aristotle, *Poetics* 15.

8. In *Ajax*, Athena tells us what she did before the play began to prevent Ajax from murdering the commanders of the Achaean army. In *Philoctetes*, Heracles arrives to persuade his old friend Philoctetes and Neoptolemus not to abandon the army at Troy. Whether this is a true case of *deus ex machina* is debated by scholars. Heracles may have arrived by machine, as a god would do, but he acts as a human being. Instead of applying

divine power, he speaks as a friend, citing Zeus's plan—which has already been made known through oracles. Heracles' voice merely adds credibility to the prophecy that Philoctetes will be healed and win glory at Troy. For the controversy among scholars, see n34.

9. Unless otherwise indicated, all translations are my own: Paul Woodruff, *Sophocles: Antigone*, with an introduction by Paul Woodruff (Indianapolis: Hackett Publishing Co., 2001); Peter Meineck and Paul Woodruff, *Sophocles: Oedipus Tyrannus*, with an introduction by Paul Woodruff (Indianapolis: Hackett Publishing Co., 2000); for a complete Sophocles, see Peter Meineck and Paul Woodruff, *Sophocles: Theban Plays*, with an introduction by Paul Woodruff (Indianapolis: Hackett Publishing Co., 2003) and *Sophocles: Four Tragedies*, with an introduction by Paul Woodruff (Indianapolis: Hackett Publishing Co., 2007).

10. This is the first stasimon of the *Antigone*.

11. For a collection of the relevant texts, see W. K. C. Guthrie, *The Sophists* (Cambridge: Cambridge University Press, 1971), 79–84.

12. Of the warning, Ehrenberg writes: "Man is shown in his complete independence, both when he conquers nature and when he follows his own laws. From it results his greatness as well as his doom"; Victor Ehrenberg, *Sophocles and Pericles* (Oxford: Basil Blackwell, 1954), 64.

13. *Prometheus Bound*, line 506, concluding 439–506.

14. Sophocles may have taken the idea from the sophist Protagoras, as Ehrenberg suggests, but it was so widely disseminated at the time that speculation on the source is pointless (ibid.).

15. We do not know, for example, at whom the chorus directs the first stasimon of *Antigone*; for this and other reasons we do not know how the chorus stands at this point on the main issues of the play.

16. See Karl Reinhardt, *Sophocles*, third ed., trans. by Hazel Harvey and David Harvey. With an introduction by Hugh Lloyd-Jones (Oxford: Blackwell, 1947/1979), 13 and 236 n5. Page numbers refer to the 1979 edition.

17. "Just as in the *Electra* and *Philoctetes*, so too in the second *Oedipus* the causes of suffering are entirely human. And more and more, as the human takes the place of the divine as the cause of suffering, so the divine becomes something that stoops down to man from above, at the last moment, to guide and reconcile." Reinhardt 1947/1979, 207. Reinhardt's method for dating the plays is not defensible; we have no good reason to think *Ajax* is early.

18. The point holds for dramaturgy in general. The art of theater focuses on human action (or at least on action that resembles human action), because that is what best commands our attention. Passivity is boring. For the general point, see Paul Woodruff, *The Necessity of Theater: The Art of Watching and Being Watched* (New York: Oxford University Press, 2008), chapter 5.

19. Sophocles has been called "the tragic Homer" in ancient and modern times (Ehrenberg 1954, 25, citing Diogenes Laertius 4.20), but his beliefs about the gods do not seem to be entirely conventional for his time. His gods are not the ethically sanitized powers that Plato would like to find in poetry. Athena, in the *Ajax*, invites Odysseus to laugh at the shame of his enemy, but Odysseus—too humanly wise to be arrogant after a victory—declines (79–80). This is one of several scenes in which Sophocles goes beyond conventional help-friends-hurt-enemies doctrine—but without treading on myth or theology. On the ethical issue, see M. W. Blundell, *Helping Friends and Harming Enemies* (Cambridge: Cambridge University Press, 1989).

20. Tragic reverence emphasizes the awe-inspiring aspect of the gods, rather than the more human aspect of the gods that we sometimes encounter in Homer. For the concept of reverence, see Paul Woodruff, *Reverence, Renewing a Forgotten Virtue* (New York: Oxford University Press. 2001).

21. Aristotle advises playwrights to leave the supernatural out of the plot in this way; *Poetics* 15, 1454a37–b8.

22. Events in which human beings are shown as passive lack theatrical merit. In *Prometheus Bound*, remarkably, the playwright shows his hero not as a passive victim but as one who is actively planning and speaking against the power that oppresses him. See Woodruff 2008, 75–92, for the general argument connecting theater, action, and choice.

23. The case is slightly muddied by the suggestion in *Prometheus Bound*, line 254, that humans learned the arts from having the gift of fire, which could be consistent with the invention story. But the center of the story's gravity is on the idea of a supernatural gift.

24. See, however, the exceptions discussed previously in n8.

25. "This history may not be the most delightful to hear, since there is no mythology in it. But those who want to look into the truth of what was done in the past—which, given the human condition, will recur in the future, either in the same fashion or nearly so—those readers will find this *History* valuable enough, as it was composed to be a lasting possession and not be heard for a prize at the moment of a contest" (1.22). See also 3.82 (with Reeve's interpretation, 1999): "Civil war brought many atrocities to the cities, such as happen and will always happen as long as human nature is the same, although they may be more or less violent or take different forms, depending on the circumstances in each case. In peace and prosperity, cities and private individuals alike are better minded because they are not plunged into the necessity of doing anything against their will; but war is a violent teacher: it gives most people impulses that are as bad as their situation when it takes away the easy supply of what they need for daily life."

26. This is a technical point that requires much explanation. *Eikos*-based explanation is defeasible; that is, in order to use it wisely, one must be on the watch for defeating circumstances. See Paul Woodruff, "*Eikos* and Bad Faith in the Paired Speeches of Thucydides," in John Cleary and William Wians, eds., *Proceedings of the Boston Area Colloquium in Ancient Philosophy* X (1994), 115–45.

27. Athens was confident that the Syracusans would surrender as other cities had done, to an Athenian siege, owing to internal divisions. But this was not the necessary result, and the Athenian expectation was defeated by an important fact about Syracuse: the city was not so badly divided as earlier target cities had been. See Woodruff 1994.

28. Stephen Halliwell, *The Poetics of Aristotle: Translation and Commentary* (Chapel Hill, N.C.: University of North Carolina Press, and London: Duckworth, 1987), 13.

29. To see the difference, compare the opening speeches in Plato's *Phaedrus*: Lysias's argument against the lover is based on *eikos* (what a lover may be expected to do); Socrates' is based on *ananke* (what a lover must do, by necessity of definition). And consider which kind of argument would be best illustrated by a powerful drama. The character who is what he is by definition has a place in comedy, perhaps, but not in Sophoclean tragedy.

30. The general view I reject is well represented by Ehrenberg, who writes often of human fate, which makes us victims: "Man, although often admirable, is the victim of stronger forces" (Ehrenberg 1954, 27). See also Lloyd-Jones, introducing Reinhardt: "The gods control the action quite as firmly as they do in Homer or in Aeschylus" (1979, xxv). This may well be true of the larger story of Oedipus (though we are not told in

the plays how it is true); but it is certainly not true of the story that is staged in *OT*. Similarly, Reinhardt describes Ajax as a "victim of fate" in contrast with Odysseus, who is "well-adjusted to his fate" (1947/1979, 15). Ajax is certainly shown in the play to be in conflict, but the conflict is with Agamemnon and Menelaus, not with fate, and once the commanders appear on stage we see why Ajax resents them. They are odious control freaks, dominated by the tyrannical desire to rule by means of fear. Of Creon in *Antigone*, Reinhardt rightly says: "His own narrowness drives him on, the captive of his own oath, and subject to his own proclamation." And then on the same page Reinhardt damages the point by insisting that the conflict in which he is entangled is between the divine and the human (1947/1979, 77).

31. Bernard Knox, *Oedipus at Thebes: Sophocles' Tragic Hero and His Time* (New Haven: Yale University Press, 1998), vii and 7–8. Augmented edition of 1957 original.

32. Reinhardt 1947/1979, 91.

33. Aristotle, in his *Poetics*, calls attention to this, I think, by calling characters "agents." See also Woodruff 2008, 101–03.

34. The appearance of Heracles at the end of the *Philoctetes* has been a subject of scholarly controversy. Reinhardt writes of the importance here of the divine perspective, but it is hard to see how Heracles' perspective differs from Odysseus's in this play (1947/1979, 190–91). Webster points to the difference between this and the Euripidean *deus ex machina*. See T. B. L. Webster, *Sophocles Philoctetes* (Cambridge: Cambridge University Press, 1970), 156. Roisman reviews the attractive possibility that the audience sees that Heracles is really Odysseus (whom they have probably seen eavesdropping up to now) in disguise; nevertheless, she argues for the importance of the religious element that Heracles carries with him. See Hanna M. Roisman, *Sophocles: Philoctetes* (London: Duckworth, 2005), 106–11.

35. Segal 1995, 26 and 67.

36. For a corrective to Knox and others who see "superhuman power developing in Oedipus in the course of the play," see P. E. Easterling, "Oedipus and Polynices," *Proceedings of the Cambridge Philological Society* 13 (1967), 1–13: "The trouble with this theory here, it seems to me, is that Sophocles throughout the play takes pains to present Oedipus *as a man*, a man who behaves in a characteristically human way" (2). And indeed the passionate anger, the curses, the powerful love Oedipus shows are not unusual in Sophoclean heroes (or in life). But Knox is surely right that Oedipus is developing the power to pronounce curses that actually work (the boys will kill each other) and give blessings that actually protect (Athens will be saved from a Theban incursion).

37. Some editors, starting with Campbell (1879), wrongly suppose that Oedipus, at *OC* 1375, refers to has own curse as causing the quarrel, but Jebb (1899) and others have this right. Oedipus' curse is caused by the quarrel, not vice versa. See Jebb's note on line 1375, where *prosthe* refers to lines 421–27 and 451f. Lewis Campbell, *Sophocles, edited with English Notes and Introduction*, second ed., revised (Oxford: Clarendon Press, 1879) and Richard Jebb, *Sophocles: The Plays and Fragments, with Critical Notes, Commentary, and Translation; Part II, The Oedipus Coloneus*, third ed. 1889 (Reprinted Amsterdam: Hakkert, 1962), notes *ad loc.*

38. *Thebaid* fragments 2 and 3 tell the older version. Of the change, Wilson writes: "In so doing he very nearly eliminates supernatural elements from the play entirely. Instead, Oedipus' curse on Polyneices and Eteocles is presented as a function of intelligence and

understanding, not magic"; See Joseph P. Wilson, *The Hero and the City: An Interpretation of Sophocles' Oedipus at Colonus* (Ann Arbor: University of Michigan Press, 1997), 153.

39. See R. Buxton, *Sophocles* (Oxford: Clarendon Press, 1984), 4–5 with notes.

40. See especially the opening of the second stasimon of *Oedipus Tyrannus.*

41. Reinhardt 1947/1979, 92.

42. Charles Segal, *Tragedy and Civilization: An Interpretation of Sophocles* (Cambridge, Mass.: Harvard University Press. 1981), 7, drawing on the insights of René Girard.

12

The Fake That Launched a Thousand Ships

The Question of Identity in Euripides' Helen

MICHAEL DAVIS

For Aristotle, tragedy as a form of poetry is a paradigm for human nature, plot or story is "the first principle and like the soul of tragedy," and the best stories require what he calls recognition.[1] If he is correct, tragic recognition should provide a portal to self-understanding. Now, Euripides' *Helen* is a play so teeming with mistaken identities that lead to recognitions or false recognitions that it ought to be to be a virtual primer on human nature. That a play by Euripides should be a tool for self-knowledge is no surprise, for the tradition tells us that his plays were "patched up by Socrates" (*Sōkratogomphoi*).[2] And Socrates, of course, is the philosopher especially fervent in the pursuit of self-knowledge.

In search of ourselves, then, we hurry expectantly to Euripides' *Helen*, but when we arrive we are perplexed. What exactly is this play? It was first produced at a tragic festival in 412 BC; so mustn't it be a tragedy? Yet in modern times, when not harshly judged and dismissed out of hand, it has received mixed reviews.[3] The *Helen* has been called "an elegant romance," "a parody of tragedy," "frankly funny," and "nearer to comedy and operetta than high tragedy" "though filled with unpleasantness and meaningless cynicism," a farce, a tragicomedy, a tragedy *manquée*, "in no possible sense a tragedy," "a brilliant failure," *un tragédie roman-esque*, a "drama of ideas," and like the *Magic Flute* "a half-lyrical, half-philosophical romance."[4] The identity of the *Helen* is thus something of a question.

The conceit of Euripides' play, borrowed in part from the lyric poet Ste-sichorus and in part from Herodotus, is that Helen never really went to Troy. She was neither abducted by Paris nor did she run off with him willingly. True,

255

she was promised to Paris as a bribe to name Aphrodite more beautiful than Hera and Athena in the famous Judgment of Paris, but before Aphrodite can pay this debt, Hera substitutes for Helen a phantom, an *eidōlon*, a perfect copy fashioned out of air. The real Helen is then concealed in a cloud by Zeus, who tells Hermes to deposit her for safekeeping at the court of King Proteus of Egypt, where she remains for the ten-year duration of the war and for the seven-year period in which Menelaus attempts to return home from Troy. During this time Proteus dies, and his son, Theoclymenus, who is smitten with Helen, plans to make her his wife. He begins killing any Greeks who come to Egypt—presumably in the hope of preserving the secret that Helen still lives (although, since the chorus is made up of captive Greek women, it is not so clear that he hasn't been raiding Greek cities—for what reason, we are left in doubt). When Menelaus, with the phantom Helen, and his crew shipwreck in Egypt, he comes to the house of Proteus begging and is told by a philhellene porter to leave before he gets killed. He runs into Helen, who has just heard from another Greek, Teucer, that Menelaus is presumed dead and then from Theoclymenus's sister, the seer Theonoë, that he is not only alive but nearby. After considerable confusion including a report that the phantom Helen has suddenly vanished into the air, they recognize each other and plan an escape. They convince Theonoë to conceal Menelaus's presence from her brother. Then Helen tells Theoclymenus that she has heard from one of Menelaus's companions (in fact the real Menelaus) that her husband is dead. She agrees to marry Theoclymenus if only he will allow a symbolic burial, a cenotaph, of Menelaus at sea. Menelaus's companion will officiate and she must be present. The cenotaph, Theoclymenus is told, must be lavish and will require that a ship carry a suit of empty armor out to sea with a sacrificial animal and produce of the earth—in other words provisions for a journey. Well, you know the rest. They collect his shipwrecked crew, take over the ship, and sail away. Theoclymenus is about to send men to chase them and kill his sister in anger when Helen's dead twin brothers, now gods in heaven, intervene (a typical Euripidean *deus ex machina*) to stop him and tell us that after they die Helen will become a god and Menelaus will live among the gods.

Now the play does seem to end happily—although this is not at all unusual for Euripides. Still more strikingly untragic are the characters themselves. When we first encounter Menelaus shipwrecked in Egypt he seems rather too worried about the state of his clothing lest "the sacker of Troy" be mistaken for a homeless man (415ff.). As part of Helen's escape plan involves faking the death of Menelaus, she tells us (1085) that she is going into the house to cut her hair, change into black, and rake her nails across her cheeks—all this to look the part of a grieving widow. A hundred lines later she reenters having cut her hair and wearing black, but we hear nothing more of scratches. Apparently Helen could not bring herself to mar her beautiful face—*the* beautiful face. Early in the play she had contemplated suicide with these words:

To die is best. How would I die not beautifully?
It's unseemly to hang by the neck,
and deemed inappropriate by the slaves.
But they hold cutting the throat to be something noble and beautiful,
and the moment for the flesh to be released from life is brief. (298–302)[5]

So "shockingly out of place" and inappropriate for us is Helen's curiously self-centered comparison of the relative beauty of ways to die, that the authenticity of the passage has been regularly called into question.[6] Helen and Menelaus seem perfectly paired. He is *the* sacker of Troy (although he seems to have forgotten how much help he needed—remember that Homer even calls him a "soft spearman" at *Iliad* 17.587), and she is the most beautiful woman in the world (although in this play she is the only one ever to comment explicitly on her beauty). At first glance, then, these unusually vain and superficial people seem rather the stuff of soap opera or light comedy than of tragedy.

But what we are to call the *Helen* is an identity crisis that pales to insignificance beside the question of what we are to call Helen herself. As Helen and Menelaus have a daughter, Hermione, they must have been married for at least a year before she was abducted, but it does not seem more than, say, three years, for if Helen were married at sixteen, this would make her thirty-seven when the play opens, and, since everyone seems to think she looks the same as she did seventeen years ago, it would be hard for her to be much older than this. So we have a woman who was married to a man for perhaps three years seventeen years ago. Meanwhile, the phantom Helen slept with Paris for ten years, then, when rescued, slept with Menelaus for seven more, and at no time did either of them doubt her identity. So why is the real Helen the real Helen? Because the phantom was made of air? But how was Helen "made"? One version has it that Zeus took the form of a swan fleeing from an eagle, swooped down on Helen's mother, Leda, and impregnated her. Helen was born from an egg, a story so implausible that even Helen can bring herself to believe it only about half the time (20–21, 257–529). Would such a fabulous story, in any event, make her reality more believable than the phantom's? This is an issue of considerable importance, for everything in the play depends on what it means for Helen to be real, and so on which Helen is real—the one hibernating in Egypt or the one who actually did what Helen is so famous for having done and thereby made possible the war that established what it means to be Greek over and against barbarian. One is reminded of the old joke that Shakespeare's plays were not written by Shakespeare but by another man of the same name. Our puzzle might be put in the following way. In the prologue of the *Helen* a character steps on stage and says, "This is Egypt" and "I am Helen." Of course, it is not Egypt but the *skēnē* of the theater of Dionysus on the slope of the Acropolis in Athens, and "she" is really a male actor wearing a large mask. Why do we accept her claim? We suspend disbelief for the sake of the story—the *muthos*. This, of course, makes Helen not so very different from her phantom; both are who they are by virtue of being embedded in a story.

Helen's is not the only identity question in play. The second half of the prologue is her meeting with Teucer, the half-brother of Ajax exiled by his father from their home in Salamis for having failed to prevent his brother's suicide at Troy. Teucer comes to Egypt to ask the seer Theonoë for directions to Cyprus where Apollo's oracle has told him he is destined to found a new Salamis. In a strange inversion of the main story, Teucer takes the real Helen to be a look-alike, an image. At first he is overcome with anger and hates her for the destruction she has caused. He relents only when he considers that she is not real (it is not altogether clear why he is so sure she cannot be the real Helen, since he admittedly doesn't know precisely where she is other than with Menelaus, who is himself just about to make an appearance in Egypt). Only the bracketing of Helen's reality, seeing her as an image or phantom, allows him to see her as she really is. She, in turn, does not recognize him, although the tradition regularly places him among her original suitors. When she asks who he is, he first responds with a generic description—"one of the wretched Achaeans" (84). Then he says, "Our name is Teucer, the father giving me life is Telemon, Salamis is the fatherland which nurtured me" (87–88). The expression "our name" (although it is certainly not uncommon in Greek to use a first person plural pronoun as a singular) hints that many are called "Teucer" (it is, for example, the name of a legendary king of Troy). Teucer himself is the son of one of Priam's daughters. We know as well that Telemon sired another son and that Teucer is about to found a city bearing the same name as his fatherland. Teucer thus fails to describe himself in an altogether distinctive way, for every common noun by virtue of being common applies in principle to many individuals. We are moved to name things to overcome this generic character of language, but while we may name babies to honor their uniqueness, we also have books in which prospective parents shop for the perfect name. Telemon exiles his son for failing to protect Ajax, who committed suicide because he was not awarded the armor of the dead Achilles as a sign that he was now the best of the Greek warriors.[7] Apparently, for Ajax to be recognized as unique among the Greeks means for him to wear the armor of Achilles. To look like Achilles is the measure of uniqueness.[8] Accordingly, a name, like armor, is of necessity inadequate to its task, for it is an exterior mark of identity designed to render what is interior—a shell of armor posing as the inimitable core of a man. A name does not confer identity.

Several things emerge in the subsequent conversation between Helen and Teucer. Troy was sacked and set afire "so that not even a trace of its walls is manifest" (108). There is thus no external sign remaining of the war, which therefore might as well have been an illusion or phantom—something in a poem. Teucer says that he saw Menelaus carry off Helen "with my own eyes, just as I see you—no less" (118) and then, when questioned about whether "this seeming seems steadfast" (121), he replies "I myself saw with my eyes; and mind sees too" (122). He confidently takes sight to be the gold standard for identification at the very moment that he misidentifies what is before his eyes. At the same time, even after pressing Teucer to distinguish between what he saw and what he heard (117), after asking about the fate of her family, Helen too quickly jumps from a report of Menelaus's death to the fact of that death. Later she will announce to the chorus that Teucer "said clearly that her husband was destroyed" (308). Even had Teucer said this, why would she believe him? Helen is surely not shy of declaring how wrong others can be in the face of apparently decisive evidence. Teucer only repeats a report of Menelaus's death; are there not also many reports that Helen ran off with Paris to Troy? The explanation of the chorus, that fear leads us to assume the worst (312), is just a sign of how much mind determines what we think we see. Sight does not reveal identity.

Finally, Teucer becomes impatient with stories (*muthoi*—143) and presses on to his own business in Egypt; he has come to find the way to Cyprus. Apollo had prophesied that he would found a new Salamis there, but Teucer doesn't know where to start. He has been told his story, but it has no contact point with reality. Helen tells him that "the journey itself will signify" (151). The story must suffice, for there is no way to anchor it to reality. Teucer replies that she has spoken beautifully (*kalōs*—158); beauty apparently need not be connected to the real. Identity, what something really is, is neither a question of body nor a matter of name. It might be thought to be established by context—the story in which something is embedded. But with no connection to reality, a story may well be mere poetic fancy. The report of Menelaus's death is as false here as it will be at the end of the play when Helen uses it as a ruse to effect her escape.

No one can claim an unproblematic identity in the *Helen*. Menelaus is shocked that the old woman who is the gatekeeper at the house of King Proteus does not recognize the "Sacker of Troy" even though he has just finished lamenting how perfectly awful he looks. Still, he thinks himself "not unknown in any land" (504). Helen, who announces to the chorus that she has just been told by the seer Theonoë that her husband is not dead and in fact is in Egypt (528–40), immediately turns her head and discovers a man she does not recognize to be Menelaus.

Then there are the Egyptians. Proteus shares a name with a sea god described in *Odyssey* book 4. There Menelaus is describing how his ship was becalmed at an island off the shore of Egypt. In order to learn how to get away he must lay hold of Proteus, who has the power to change into anything, and hold on until Proteus becomes himself. The identity of the god whose name means "first" is to be somehow all things. His namesake is a king of Egypt who is said to "dwell in this house" (460) but turns out to have died sometime before the play opens. His tomb sits conspicuously before the house, and his son Theoclymenus, now king, regularly greets him when entering and leaving (1165–68). Hermes left

Helen in the safekeeping of Proteus, and now in order to avoid the advances of Theoclymenus she takes refuge at the tomb as though in a temple. Since Proteus still protects Helen, it is not altogether clear what the distinction between living and dead means in Egypt. His body is after all still there—entombed at the entrance of his house.

The Menelaus of the *Odyssey* learns how to seize the sea god Proteus from his daughter, Eidotheia, whose name means something like the look or shape of a god. The Proteus of the *Helen* also has a daughter. At first her name was Eido—either form understood as shape or form understood as a principle of knowledge—but upon reaching puberty (apparently you must be named what you are in Egypt), she acquired the power to understand "all the divine things that are and will be" (13–14) and thereafter was named—"god-knowing." Euripides thus splits Homer's Eidotheia into the problematic identity of the preadolescent Eido and the grownup but still virginal seer Theonoë. Theoclymenus, whose name means "listening to god" or "obeying god," also has a namesake—a fugitive and a prophet who becomes a friend and ally to Odysseus's son Telemachus (*Odyssey* book 15).

To summarize, there are two Proteuses—two "firsts." The one not in our play is a god whose identity it is not to have a fixed identity. The identity of the one in our play is thoroughly ambiguous. He is dead and yet not. He sires two children; the name of one means to know the gods, of the other to obey the gods (Euripides thereby invents the tension between Athens and Jerusalem). Theonoë, the knower, divides into what she was in her youth—something to be known—and what she is now—someone who knows. The action of this play ends when her brother conforms to his name and obeys the gods; his namesake, of course, like his sister, was a seer.

That the identities of everyone and of many things in the *Helen* are doubled is paradigmatically manifest in Helen's twin brothers—Castor and Pollux. They are called the Dioscuri—the sons of Zeus. Like Helen, however, it is not clear what this means, for we are repeatedly told that Tyndareus may also be their father (137). When Helen asks about them Teucer says, "They are dead, and they are not dead; there is a pair of stories (*logō*)" (138). Either they killed themselves out of shame over Helen, or they have become "most like stars and are a pair of gods" (140). These twins alternate appearances in the night sky, since Zeus granted each immortality only every other day.[9] It is, of course, hard to know what this means. What would it mean for two identical beings to alternate existence in the very same place? Why wouldn't the two simply be one? At the end of the play when the Dioscuri address Theoclymenus to forbid him to kill his sister they say, "*We* the twin Dioscuri call you" (1643–44). Then they turn to address Helen and say "*I* speak to my sibling" (1662) (emphasis mine). The *Helen* is a play in which no one seems to recognize anyone else—apparently for good reason. That immortal twins should appear on alternate days in the heavens as gods signals how problematic Euripides has made the question of identity in this play. The ambiguity of twins who are both two and one, alive and dead, god and mortal, bodily and not, is somehow paradigmatic for the ambiguity at the core of our being.

Let us see if we can unravel some of these difficulties. Like many Greek tragedies, the Helen has a conspicuous "recognition scene." Since recognition must turn on the question of identity, perhaps we can gain some clarity by looking closely at the scene in which Helen recognizes Menelaus. Helen has just returned from following the advice of the chorus and asking Theonoë about the fate of her husband. She has learned that he is alive and even "somewhere near this land" (538). Addressing him in his absence, Helen says "When will you come? How far would you come?" (540). Then she turns her head, sees Menelaus, and utters her next line: "Oh, who is this?" (541). Although the groundwork for the recognition has been rather well prepared, Helen does not take the bait. He, on the other hand, recognizes her body, but knows that she cannot be Helen—"Never have I seen a body more similar" (559). The moment of recognition itself is rather strange and surprisingly difficult to pin down. It begins with a sentence that no one translates literally because it is just too odd. Helen looks at Menelaus and says, "O gods—for even (or also) to recognize friends (or those dear) is a god!" (560). We are first puzzled and then inclined to think that the sentence must mean something like "What a divine thing to recognize a friend!" But the immediate sequel makes this difficult.

> Menelaus: Are you a Greek or a woman of the country?
> Helen: Greek, but I would learn yours too.
> Menelaus: Woman, I see that you are especially like to Helen.
> Helen: And you indeed to Menelaus; I do not even grasp what I'm
> saying.
> Menelaus: You have rightly recognized a most unhappy man.
> Helen: O, after a long time you have come into your wife's arms. (561–
> 66)

Now, when Helen says that it is even a god to recognize friends this cannot be an exclamation of joy over having recognized Menelaus, for then her next line would be altogether unintelligible. Are we to believe that she recognizes the husband she hasn't seen for seventeen years in one line and in the next asks him what country he is from? Accordingly, the recognition must occur later when she makes it explicit at line 566. Menelaus, on the other hand, does not accept her as Helen until after the messenger arrives to tell him that the phantom Helen disappeared into the air (605–21). So, despite never having seen "a body more similar," Menelaus doesn't trust his eyes. The general point might be put this way. Helen "recognizes" Menelaus at 566 because she expects him; not until he expects her to be Helen does he recognize her. The problem is once again the relation between the eyes and the mind; expectation, whether dread or longing, shapes our thoughts and determines what we "see."[10] Menelaus gives expression to this connection when he responds to Helen's claim to be his wife by saying, "Am I to suppose I do not think well? Are my eyes diseased?" (575). Helen responds, "Who else will teach you but your eyes?" (580). Were this correct, of course, the phantom Helen would be the real Helen.

Let's begin again. Why doesn't Helen recognize Menelaus immediately? It has been seventeen years. She may have agelessly retained her beauty (I think of her as Sophia Loren rather than Elizabeth Taylor, but I am no doubt dating myself), but Menelaus has changed. Helen knows who he is *supposed* to be but cannot quite believe her eyes. Menelaus's name has remained constant, but he changes. The odd sentence at 560, then, does not mean it is divine to recognize a friend. Rather, Helen is disappointed. You may always believe that you will know the one who is dear—*philos*—but even with those closest to you it is as impossible to grasp the unchanging core as it is to recognize a god. To recognize friends *is* a god, for only a being with the power to see within others could genuinely know them.

Were Helen and Menelaus *philtatoi*—most dear to one another—they would see into each other so as to know each other perfectly. Yet the relation between them is thoroughly cynical; they use each other. Menelaus does not recognize Helen in a moment of divine insight but acknowledges that she is Helen only when he learns that the phantom Helen has vanished. Now, there is no reason in principle why he should accept the existence of a phantom at all. The two Helens are never seen together; as soon as one disappears the other appears. There is no temporal difficulty, for Helen could have made her way to the house of Proteus while Menelaus was making his way. The slave who arrives to announce that "your wife has gone soaring up invisible to the air" (605) eleven lines later says, "Greetings daughter of Leda, were you here then?" (616). Menelaus now accepts her as his wife because he needs *some* Helen lest he have to return home embarrassingly empty-handed after ten years of war and seven years of wandering; he needs her to justify the plot line of his life. At first Menelaus refused to acknowledge her because he needed to justify another plot line—"the greatness of toils there [Troy] persuades me, not you" (593). He cannot afford to have the great deed of his life reinterpreted as the pursuit of a phantom.[11] At the same time, neither does Helen exactly recognize Menelaus. She needs him, for without him "never again will I come to Greece, my fatherland" (595–96).[12] And she tells him what she knows in stages, revealing only as much as she believes necessary to persuade him of her identity, for example feigning complete ignorance of the phantom (572, 574) and springing it on him only when it is clear that she has no other choice (582). Trying one tack and then another, Helen behaves exactly as she would if she were an imposter. When the two finally agree to acknowledge one another, then, it is not because they trust each other but because they need each other. They see what their minds tell them they must see.

If really to recognize friends is a god, what sort of being is a god, and how can it be a verb? When Menelaus first hears from the gatekeeper that Helen, the daughter of Zeus or perhaps of Tyndareus, she who once lived in Sparta, is now living in the house of Proteus (470–472), he is perplexed: "What am I to say? What am I to think?" (483). That the two are not simply the same for him suggests a distinction between internal cause and external manifestation. That there could be living on the Nile another woman named Helen born of a man named Zeus (a man because it is clear that in heaven there is only one Zeus), that there could be another Tyndareus and another Sparta, these all seem unlikely to Menelaus. Still, "it is likely that in so much space many have the same names, both city with city and woman with woman; this is nothing to wonder at" (497–99). What is obviously left out here—so obviously that one intelligent translator, Richmond Lattimore, simply supplies it anyway—is the claim that the world also contains many *men* with the same name. But Menelaus balks at this conclusion, for he cannot quite admit that there could be another Menelaus somewhere. His whole reflection on the possibility of doubled names has as its purpose to find a way to explain his own singularity and uniqueness as the "Sacker of Troy." This sheds some light on why Menelaus has been so careful to indicate that while there might be another *man* named Zeus, there was only one Zeus in heaven. There cannot be two Zeuses, one in Egypt and one in Greece, because to be a god means to be a universal particular. Ares may be a god of war whose name sometimes simply means war, but he is also unique—a person who gets caught sleeping with Aphrodite. Gods are combinations of significance (they mean something) and individuality (they are something).[13] Menelaus longs for this status and believes it belongs to him as "Sacker of Troy" as it belongs to Helen as the "face that launched a thousand ships." Apparently not only is the recognizing of friends possible only *for* a god; what it means to *be* a god is to be the sort of being that cannot itself be recognized—a being that consists of the impossible combination of perfect intelligibility and intelligence. Gods are simply perfect representations of what we mean by souls.

We long to be gods but do so at our own peril, for, if Ares stands for war, then he is a kind, and as a kind he is something that has instances—he can be duplicated. If Menelaus is not careful, then, he will turn into an *onoma*, a name or a noun—something fashioned out of air that, because it stands for one thing, can also stand for something else and so is necessarily detachable from the thing it identifies. In principle no name is unique even though it is meant to be our personal ID tag, for a sign of uniqueness cannot itself be unique. This problem is present from the very first line of Helen's opening speech. *Neilou men haide kalliparthenoi roai* may refer either to the Nile's beautiful virginal streams, presumably virginal because receiving water only from melting snow and not from tributaries, or to the beautiful virgins, nymphs—personifications of the streams of the Nile.

The streams of the Nile are either gods to be named or things to be described by godlike adjectives; the language does not permit us to settle the issue. Helen goes on to speak of Proteus, his wife Psamathe (sand), Theoclymenus, Eido, and Theonoë, all of whom share this doubleness; they are both names and nouns.

The crucial action of the *Helen* occurs before it begins when Paris judges Aphrodite to be the most beautiful of the goddesses. Suppose Hera had won. Would she not then have been the most beautiful of the goddesses, and so the goddess of beauty, and so Aphrodite? Remember the joke about Shakespeare. The Judgment of Paris makes sense only when we put together universal quality with particular identity. *Ouranos* means sky and *gaia* means earth. At the same time they are the names of specific gods. When the two couple they produce a generation of gods—among them a son Kronos, whose name is very close to *khronos*—time. Kronos castrates Uranus and a new generation of gods takes over. At the same time, time deprives space of its unrivaled dominion. The coupling of *ouranos* and *gaia*, on the one hand sexual, on the other, describes the fact that the two cannot exist without being together. There can be no earth without something enveloping it, and there can be no envelope without something inside. To recognize friends, kin, those most dear and most loved, is a god. To recognize what we most love involves the togetherness of universal and particular, even though we regularly identify what we most love as unique—my one and only. Aphrodite is the combination of universal significance in a particular individual. In the *Helen* Euripides has experimented with the separation of these two elements. The phantom Helen is a symbol for everything that led the Greeks to Troy. The particular individual Helen is hidden in Egypt. Euripides has in this respect simply taken a hint from Homer. In the *Iliad* the Trojan elders admire the sight of Helen at the city wall saying that "there is no cause for indignation for Trojans and well-greaved Achaeans to suffer for so long a time for a woman like her; in her face she resembles in an uncanny way the deathless goddesses" (3.156–58). Later Helen tells Hektor that the whole war has occurred for her sake and for that of Paris "so that we may be made subjects of song by men of times to come" (6.356–57). Homer's Helen is likened to a god and understands herself as a figure of solely poetic significance. She thus testifies to her own unreality.

What then would it mean that the Greeks unwittingly went to Troy and fought for ten years for the sake of a breathing phantom made of the sky (34), a cloud (706), what was only a name or word (43)? That the Trojan War was undertaken in the name of something unreal would seem to compromise not only the name of Helen as the face that launched a thousand ships and that of Menelaus as the sacker of Troy but also to call into question the significance of the single most important event in the history of the Greeks—their greatest deed, indeed what constituted them as Greek as opposed to barbarian.[14] On the one hand, it seems preposterous to have gone to war with Troy for a phantom. On the other hand, were Helen only a particular being it would have been equally preposterous; it is not as though Helen herself would have been restored to each member of the army. As accounts of human behavior, both idealism and realism fail; they make our lives tragically ridiculous.

Before this play begins, we believe there is only one Helen. The recognition comedy calls this into question and forces us to ask whether we can ever be sure of another's identity, or for that matter our own identity. This applies most obviously to those we most think we know—those we love, our friends, and those we hate, our enemies. Helen may say, "O gods, for even to recognize friends is a god," but, upon first seeing and "recognizing" her as the Helen he hates, Teucer says, "O gods, what sight have I seen? Do I see the most hateful deadly likeness of a woman who destroyed me and all the Achaeans?" (72–74). We not only invoke the gods to say "thank god" but also when we say "goddamn." The most common Greek definition of justice is helping friends and harming enemies. Our inability to recognize friends would, therefore, call into question our ability to be just.[15] This, in turn, calls into question the justice of the Trojan War, a war that begins with a violation of the laws of *xenia*—guest-friendship.

The question might be put somewhat differently: short of recognizing friends, how is it possible to share with them, since friends are supposed to hold all things in common? It is not uninteresting that when Menelaus's slave arrives to inform him of the disappearance of the phantom Helen and is then convinced of the identity of the real Helen, he asks to share Menelaus's pleasure (700).[16] Menelaus replies with "Indeed, old one, share in speeches (*logoi*)" (701). Speech serves as the limit of sharing. In mediating between us it is simultaneously the sign that there is no perfect us. The slave then begins a long reflection on causality (711–33). The god is the cause of everything, but nevertheless everything has the appearance of chance. There is thus a split between what happens and its significance. The slave first had respect for the events of Helen's wedding, but after her disgrace he lamented them; now, when her reputation is cleared, he has renewed respect. But of course the events of the wedding did not change—only their significance. Life unfolds in time as if it were a tragedy—the significance of its events only intelligible in light of the end of the story. The slave uses himself as an example. A good slave, he says, shares the goods and ills of his master and so is like his master. He may be named a slave but he is noble by nature—his spirit is free. In other words, this slave dares to claim that he shares in Helen's plight. Like her, chance (*tuchē*) has plagued him with a bad appearance that conceals a good inside. What she thinks of as her extraordinary fate or destiny (*tuchē*) is really the ordinary and necessary discrepancy in every human being between what they seem to be and what they really are. Real friendship means sharing pleasures (700), faring well (736), and luck (*tuchē*; 738). It means "joining in one fortune (*tuchē*)" (742). If the necessary condition for a common life together is sharing pleasure and toil, then political life requires something that is strictly speaking impossible. The existence of the phantom Helen brings to the surface the inner distrust that plagues Helen and

Menelaus, but in revealing the hollowness of the Trojan War, it also brings to light the deeply problematic status of political life.

The story of the Trojan War, whether the traditional version or in Euripides' revisionist account of Helen, begins with the Judgment of Paris, a judgment about which of the gods is most beautiful. Our experience of something beautiful is complicated, for on the one hand we experience it as in a class by itself, as unique, and at the same time as in some way paradigmatic of the class which, in its beauty, it is threatening to surpass. This is even more telling in Greek, where *to kalon* means not only the beautiful in the sense in which it attaches to Helen but also the noble in the sense in which it attaches to Achilles (and in which Menelaus wishes that it attached to him). The *Iliad* is therefore a poem about the beautiful across its whole range. Now, if experience of the beautiful combines in itself an experience of what is particular with an experience of something universal, then it might seem to be a model for what it means to combine the two when we identifying something. This experience, while showing up most powerfully in beautiful things, would really point to our underlying ability to see anything at all as apart from other things—as one. However, *the* premise of the *Helen*—the phantom—means to show that this powerful urge is a mistake. Accordingly, every recognition in the *Helen* is in some way defective. *To kalon* is a general name for what shows up in each of the gods—the illusion of the unity of universal principle with particular being.

In its concern for identifying the beautiful, the Judgment of Paris lays the groundwork for all trials. Any judgment has two parts—a universal principle of right and the particulars of the case. What is the crime, and did he do it? Accordingly, perfect justice would require that the one judged both be an individual, and therefore deserving of praise or blame, and fit perfectly under a universal rule, and so be a type. The shifting meaning of the Greek *tuchē* in the *Helen* points perfectly to this doubleness, for it may mean either chance or destiny. From the perspective of the one I am free and hence responsible; from the perspective of the other my fate is sealed.[17] This is the meaning of Paris's choice of Aphrodite; all gods somehow embody this tension, but Aphrodite as *the* beautiful is the exemplar of it.

There are two trials in the *Helen*. They occur simultaneously and deal with the same issue—whether Helen and Menelaus will be allowed to leave Egypt. Zeus is the judge in one case, Theonoë in the other. Here is Theonoë's description:

> On this day in an assembly before the seat of Zeus there will be strife among the gods concerning you. On the one hand, Hera, who was ill-disposed toward you before, is now well-disposed and wants you to be safe in your fatherland with this one here [Helen], in order that Greece may learn that Cypris's [Aphrodite's] gift of a bride to Alexander [Paris] was false. Cypris, on the other hand, wants your homecoming to be wrecked, so that it will be neither argued nor manifest how she bought beauty on account of Helen

for a vain marriage. The end is with us, either what Cypris wishes, I will destroy you by telling my brother that you are here, or again siding with Hera, I will save your life, concealing you from my sibling, who ordered me to say when you should chance to come to this land on your journey home. (878–91)

So Zeus will hear this case and decide between Hera's wish to reveal that Aphrodite cheated and Aphrodite's wish to cover it all up. And yet Theonoë goes on to say that she will decide the case of Helen and Menelaus and proceeds to listen to their arguments on their own behalf. How can both of these be true? While we do know that Zeus will decide, we do not know what he decides. Much in the same way, we can preserve our freedom of action in particular while believing in general in destiny. This tension is preserved within the human side of the case in the quite different arguments given by Helen and by Menelaus. Helen urges Theonoë to lie to her brother and say that Menelaus is not in Egypt. Her reasons are curious. She turns herself into a piece of property belonging originally to Menelaus and about to be stolen without right by Theoclymenus (this is of course meant to remind us of the abduction of Helen by Paris). So important is this right of ownership that even "a rich man (*ploutos*) who is unjust must be let be" (905). Helen never asks how the rich man first got his property. Her example is of interest since *Ploutos* has been once used in this play as a name for Hades (69)—the god of that place, or the place itself, where the issue of first ownership cannot come up because there is no time.[18] Helen can have such a clear-cut notion of justice only because she stops the clock at a certain time; this is appropriate enough for the gods perhaps and for Hades, and it may well be appropriate for the Egypt where Helen has remained frozen in time for seventeen years, but it cannot really hold for a human being. Helen's argument posits absolutely fixed and unchanging ownership—a first owner. Not only does she forfeit any freedom for herself, but her insistence on fixity describes a world governed from a first beginning by a necessary order. Menelaus, on the other hand, argues that Proteus made an agreement to keep Helen safe until the war was over and she could be taken home. An agreement is an agreement; when a man indicates his will, that is all there is to it. In Menelaus's world nothing counts but freedom. Soul can exist only in the uneasy combination of these two. Perfect soul—a god—would be the impossible total reconciliation of the two.

The story of the *Helen* is about an escape from Egypt. Why Egypt? The king's name is Proteus—first. Despite his death he is still called king. His tomb is outside his house, and his son regularly talks to him. His daughter "recognizes gods" and wants to remain a virgin—that is, not participate in generation. The main feature of the country itself is the Nile—the very first word of the play. Its streams are virginal; they come from a first source and are not part of a larger motion. When Menelaus first sees the house of Proteus he calls it one of the "houses of the rich (*plousiōn*)" (432). The word is very close to *Ploutōn*—an alternate name for Hades, the god of the dead. Egypt is where things stay put; they are what they are, and so the names of people are the nouns that describe them. There is no difference between the universal and the particular. Egypt is Hades in which Helen has "lived" for seventeen years without changing, which is to say she has not lived at all. Herodotus points out that the Egyptians have such contempt for the impermanence of the human body, its susceptibility to change and decay, that they worship what is other than it. This leads to some strange practices, for in their rejection of the human, they turn to animal worship (despite the fact that animals, too, change and die), and in their attempt to stabilize the body they mummify corpses, leading them to the odd contradictory practice of having contempt for living body on the one hand and worshipping dead body on the other. But the principle underlying these practices is always traceable back to an attempt to find something within the bodily realm that has permanence—to find a first thing. Egypt is thus a place where a particular individual gets transformed into a universal principle. Menelaus and Helen, who have each in their way achieved a certain permanence as phantoms, want to go home. But to go home means they must escape Egypt, which is simply another version of the longing for permanence.

Their escape proves to require three things. First, Theonoë must lie. Teucer had come to Egypt to consult her even though he already had an oracle from Apollo (144–50). Theonoë is apparently a better seer. She is less ambiguous. She tells it straight. However, once she lies for the sake of justice she will no longer be simply believable. Egypt will cease to be the Egypt where things simply are what they are. Put differently, really to tell the future would mean that there is no future. For human beings, having a future means not knowing, not being a finished product, not having an already settled identity, being a verb rather than a noun. Second, Menelaus must "die." He must put the Sacker of Troy behind him. Third, Helen must cut her hair, wear black, and scar her face; she must put behind her the Face That Launched a Thousand Ships. Of course it turns out that Menelaus does not really die; he simply reasserts himself as the hero of a new story. And Helen cannot bear to scratch her face. So, in order to escape being characters in a poem, phantoms, nouns rather than real human beings, Menelaus and Helen have to launch a plan that turns them into characters in a new poem, the *Helen*. It is therefore no surprise that at the end the twin brothers who when they become gods become indistinguishable from each other tell us exactly what is in store for Helen and Menelaus. Helen will become a god, and Menelaus will live among the gods on the isle of the blessed. It is appropriate that on the basis of a very fanciful and forced etymology, they rename the island that guards the place where she was stolen away by Hermes Helenē, saying that it derives from *klepsas*—taking by stealth. Euripides thus makes Helen meaningful and a goddess.

One of the peculiarities of the *Helen* is its use of choral odes—stasima. Ordinarily in Greek tragedy (although the practice is by no means strictly adhered to) after a prologue, the chorus enters singing an ode, the parodos. An episode follows made up of dialogue among the characters; this, in turn, is followed by a stasimon. Episodes and stasima alternate until the end of the play, which ends in an exit song, an exodos. In the *Helen*, a kommos, a sung interchange between the chorus and a character, occurs where one would "ordinarily" find the first stasimon. The next ode, the first stasimon, is so abbreviated as scarcely to be a stasimon at all; it is only thirteen lines long (515–27). The first real stasimon in the play, therefore, does not occur until line 1107—two-thirds of the way through the *Helen*, and by some three hundred lines further into the play than any other first stasimon in Euripides. The upshot of all of this is that the appearance of the more "poetic" part of tragedy is delayed for quite a long time. When the stasima do find their way into the play, they turn out to seem formulaic—as though Euripides pulled stock songs out of his repertoire and inserted them with only the slimmest connection to the plot of the *Helen*. The choral exodos, their exit song, turns out to be something Euripides uses word for word as the exodos for three other tragedies (the *Alcestis*, *Andromache*, and *Bacchantes*) and with only a slight variation for the *Medea*. Now, as it turns out this is only deceivingly haphazard, for Euripides has a thematic purpose in mind. The second stasimon is perhaps most striking in this regard. For apparently no reason, Euripides introduces the story of Demeter, Persephone, and Hades—Persephone, the daughter of the goddess Demeter, is taken away to Hades for half the year each year. Her mother mourns her loss and the earth goes infertile. This is the mythic account of the change of seasons. But in the version in this stasimon, no proper names are used; we are left to infer the identities of the characters in this plot from its action. And it is a story about the tension between permanence and generation, at the end of which we are puzzled to find Helen compared not to the mourning Demeter (Helen, after all, has several times mentioned the fate of her daughter Hermione) but to the permanent virgin, Persephone. We are given a generic account of the loss of the daughter by the mother, and Helen is somehow blamed in terms of this relation. She sinned against the mother by being so preoccupied with her own beauty—the sign of her permanence. Despite affirming her own reality over and against that of the phantom, Helen wants her name back. In the *Helen*, the poetic, the symbolic, is the realm of the phantom. It comes back late in the play as the real Helen, despite her own self-understanding, is about to once again become a poetic fiction. Euripides knows that poetry necessarily detaches its characters from the real; it beautifies them and turns them into proper names—*eidōla*. It is thus not accidental that the stasimon that attacks this process should have within it no proper names. The phantom Helen, who did go to Troy, was an image in a Greek poem. Greek poetry embodies the ideal. At first it seems that the *Helen* means to solve this problem—to be a poem about the real in its opposition to the ideal. It turns out, however, that Egypt, which may first seem to be a sign of this resurrection of the real, in fact idealizes the body. The *Helen* is the story of a woman who, to avoid becoming a phantom image, becomes a mummy.

Euripides writes a play concerned with the problem of identity—of things, of other human beings, and finally of ourselves. He shows that recognition or identifying requires fixing something or stabilizing it and so necessarily lifting it out of time. He shows as well that while we do long for such fixity, at the same time we want to be alive and so changing. This perfectly expresses the impulse to deify. The double character of our longing is described by alternate translations of a biblical sentence: I am what I am, and I will be what I will be.[19] Menelaus and Helen, each in a way having gotten only half of what they long for, want out. So they devise a way to escape. But the escape proves to be a reenactment of what they are escaping from, for to do anything human beings must set before themselves models—ideals. As ideal, these objects of longing are of necessity not real; they are shadows—beautiful *eidōla*. The *Helen* is in the end a tragedy because Helen and Menelaus do not realize that their attempt to penetrate the *kalon*—the beautiful or noble—for what is real and good—the dear or *philon*—necessarily involves them in a projection that idealizes and is itself an illusion. Or, when Helen utters her now famous sentence, "O gods, for even to recognize friends is a god," she may be expressing her doubt in the reality of the gods, but in order to do so she has had to begin by making an appeal to them.

Notes

1. See Aristotle *On Poetics* 1450a29–39.

2. The phrase belongs to Mnesimachus; it is quoted by Diogenes Laertius (*Lives and Opinions of Eminent Philosophers* 2.18).

3. For the harshness see, for example, Ulrich von Wilamowitz-Moellendorff, *Analecta Euripidea* (Berlin: Berolini, 1875) 241, 244–45.

4. See Richmond Lattimore, *Euripides II* (Chicago: University of Chicago Press, 1956), 263; A. W. Verrall, *Essays on Four Plays of Euripides* (Cambridge: Cambridge University Press, 1905), 43–133; G. M. A. Grube, *The Drama of Euripides* (London: Methuen, 1941), 352, 337; Anne Pippin, "Euripides' *Helen*: A Comedy of Ideas," *Classical Philology* 55:3 (1960), 151; Cedric H. Whitman, *Euripides and the Full Circle of Myth* (Cambridge: Harvard University Press, 1974), 35, 68; Gilbert Norwood, *Greek Tragedy* (New York: Hill and Wang, 1960), 260; M. Patin, *Euripide II* (Paris: Hatchette et Cie., 1883), 75.

5. Throughout I have quoted Gilbert Murray's text as reproduced in A. M. Dale's *Euripides' Helen* (Oxford: Clarendon Press, 1967). The translations are my own.

6. See Dale 1967, 86.

7. Compare 40–41.

8. Consider in this regard the fate of Patroklos in Homer's *Iliad* 16.

9. See *Cypria* 1.

10. This problem is the theme of Helen's kommos with the chorus at 330–85. Anticipation leads us to poeticize our world and endow its particulars and those of ourselves with more significance than they deserve. We suppress chance at the cost of reality.

11. Even after he acknowledges who Helen is, Menelaus expresses doubts about her fidelity (794). That is, even when he identifies her, he admits that he cannot know her. This occurs directly after Helen has called into question Menelaus's claim that when he came to

the door of the house of Proteus begging, he did it in deed but not in name. She does not automatically accept his understanding of his inner nobility, the nobility that allows him to denounce crying to Theonoë at 948 after having "eyes wet with tears" at 456.

12. Helen knows how deeply those who are held captive long for home; later, to insure their cooperation, she will make a promise to rescue the Greek slave women at the court of Theoclymenus with absolutely no explanation of how or whether she plans to keep it (1385–89).

13. In this way the question *quid sit deus* is the same as the question *ti to on*. In the latter case the question of being constantly moves between two poles. On the one hand the being of a thing is its permanent and unchanging form—its *eidos*; on the other hand, the being of a thing is whatever makes it particular—its *tode ti*. The latter clearly has something to do with body, but oddly cannot simply be identified with body. The *locus classicus* for this problem is Aristotle's *Metaphysics Z*. The problem of this duplicity of being is also thematic in the sister play of the *Helen*, Euripides' *Iphigenia Among the Taurians*, as well as in the comparison Herodotus invites between book 2 on Egypt and book 4 on Scythia and Libya. In addition, see my "Euripides Among the Athenians," in *The St. John's Review* 44:2 (1998), 61–81, and Seth Benardete, *Herodotean Inquiries* (The Hague: Martinus Nijhoff, 1969), 128.

14. The importance of the Trojan War is acknowledged in an interestingly backhanded way by Thucydides, who wants to make the case that the Peloponnesian War between Athens and Sparta is the "greatest motion that has come to be among the Greeks and some part of the barbarians, and in a word, among most human beings" (*The Peloponnesian War* 1.1.2) but cannot do so until he dispenses with the prior claim of the Trojan War.

15. See, for example, Plato's *Republic* 332a–c.

16. The slave addresses Menelaus in either the dual or the plural; in either case it is peculiar unless it is meant to go back to 646 where the chorus use the dual to call Helen and Menelaus a pair.

17. This is just the double perspective of all tragedy, which Aristotle refers to as the likely and the necessary. See *On Poetics* chapters 7–8 with my *The Poetry of Philosophy* (South Bend, Ind.: St. Augustine's Press, 1999) 52–54.

18. That we are meant to think of Hades is also clear from the reference to Persephone at 913.

19. See Exodus 3:13.

Contributors

Sara Brill is Assistant Professor of Philosophy and Classical Studies at Fairfield University. She is the author of articles on Plato, tragedy, and ancient medicine and is currently working on a book about the roles of law and myth in the discussions of psyche in Plato's *Phaedo*, *Republic*, and *Laws*.

Rose Cherubin is Associate Professor of Philosophy at George Mason University. Her current research focuses on the relationships between *dikē* (justice), what is, and the possibility of knowledge in Greek thought through the fifth century BCE. Her recent publications have concentrated on Parmenides and his intellectual context.

Catherine Collobert is Professor of Philosophy and Chair of the Department of Philosophy at the University of Ottawa. She is currently working on a book entitled *A Philosophical Reading of Homer*. She has published numerous books and papers in ancient philosophy.

Michael Davis is Professor of Philosophy at Sarah Lawrence College and the author many books, including *Ancient Tragedy and the Origins of Modern Science* (1988), *The Poetry of Philosophy: On Aristotle's Poetics* (1992), *The Politics of Philosophy: A Commentary on Aristotle's Politics* (1996), *The Autobiography of Philosophy: Rousseau's* The Reveries of the Solitary Walker (1999), and *Wonderlust: Ruminations on Liberal Education* (2006).

J. H. Lesher is a member of the Department of Philosophy at the University of North Carolina, Chapel Hill. He is the author of *Xenophanes of Colophon: Fragments* (1992), *The Greek Philosophers: Greek Texts with Notes and Commentary* (1998), *Plato's Symposium: Issues in Interpretation and Reception* (coedited with Debra Nails and Frisbee Sheffield, 2006), and many articles on aspects of ancient Greek philosophy.

Fred D. Miller Jr. is Professor of Philosophy and Executive Director of the Social Philosophy and Policy Center at Bowling Green State University. He is the author of *Nature, Justice, and Rights in Aristotle's Politics* (1995) and coeditor of numerous collections, including *A Companion to Aristotle's Politics* (1991), *Freedom, Reason, and the Polis: Essays in Ancient Greek Political Philosophy* (2007).

GERARD NADDAF is Associate Professor of Philosophy at York University in Toronto and Past President of the Canadian Philosophical Association. He is author of *The Greek Concept of Nature* (2005), coauthor of *Anaximander in Context* (2003), and translator and editor of *Plato the Mythmaker* (1998). His current projects include a book on Plato and the idea of nature and another on the influence of allegory on the origins of early Greek philosophy.

RAMONA NADDAFF is author of *Exiling the Poets: The Production of Censorship in Plato's Republic* (2003). Associate Professor of Rhetoric at the University of California, Berkeley, she is also codirector and editor of Zone Books.

C. D. C. REEVE is Delta Kappa Epsilon Distinguished Professor of Philosophy at the University of North Carolina at Chapel Hill. His books include *Philosopher-Kings* (1988, reissued 2006), *Socrates in the Apology* (1989), *Practices of Reason* (1995), *Aristotle: Politics* (1998), *Plato: Cratylus* (1998), *The Trials of Socrates* (2002), *Substantial Knowledge* (2003), *Plato: Republic* (2005), *Love's Confusions* (2005), and *Plato on Love* (2006).

P. CHRISTOPHER SMITH is Emeritus Professor of Philosophy at the University of Massachusetts Lowell. His books include *Hermeneutics and Human Finitude, The Hermeneutics of Original Argument*, and three commented translations of the work of H.-G. Gadamer. He has published more than forty articles on Hegel, Nietzsche, Heidegger, and Gadamer, and in general, on the German reception of Ancient Greek philosophy.

WILLIAM WIANS is Professor of Philosophy at Merrimack College in North Andover, Massachusetts. His research concentrates on Aristotle, particularly on issues revolving around the theory and practice of Aristotelian science. He is editor of *Aristotle's Philosophical Development: Problems and Prospects* and is former director of the Boston Area Colloquium in Ancient Philosophy and coeditor of its *Proceedings*. He is writing a book about the problem of human knowledge in Greek thought.

PAUL WOODRUFF is Darrell K. Royal Professor of Ethics and American Society and a member of the Department of Philosophy at the University of Texas at Austin. He has translated or cotranslated four plays of Sophocles' and one of Euripides', as well as a number of dialogues of Plato's. He is the author of *Reverence: Renewing a Forgotten Virtue* and *First Democracy: The Challenge of an Ancient Idea*.

Index of Names

Numbers in **bold** indicate a main discussion of a major literary figure (e.g., Homer, Sophocles).